TAPESTRY THE MIRROR OF CIVILIZATION

TAPESTRY
THE MIRROR OF
CIVILIZATION

by

Phyllis Ackerman

AMS PRESS

NEW YORK

Reprinted from the edition of 1933, New York
First AMS EDITION published 1970
Manufactured in the United States of America

Library of Congress Catalogue Card Number: 74-108123
SBN: 404-00279-X

AMS PRESS, INC.
NEW YORK, N. Y. 10003

PREFACE

TAPESTRY has been especially closely bound up with the life of every time, for, on the one hand, it has been part of household furniture, and, on the other, one of the luxurious adornments enhancing the prestige of the great personalities that have determined or epitomized history. Yet though they have been thus closely a part of life, tapestries are today even less approachable than most of the pictorial or decorative arts, for they have ceased to have any essential function in our own life. They are wholly of the past, isolated in the institutional blankness of museums or in the museum houses of the rich. If these valued but only passively accepted relics are to become again real and vital, and even in museums there is little excuse for anything that is inert, they must be made once more what they originally were, personal.

This book is an attempt to make tapestries living objects of aesthetic perception by revealing them as part of life: images of active beliefs or surviving echoes of almost forgotten cults; counters of the commerce that has swept streams of ideas back and forth across the world; records of the habits, amusements, follies and illuminations of the human spirit; reflections of marked individuals, in their greatness, their failures and their absurdities; weather vanes of economic, social and ethical currents. Only when understood in these intimate relations will the tapestries have their full meaning, and hence, in so far as they are beautiful, their full beauty.

The book also is intended to serve as an introduction to a detailed and comprehensive study, to appear in the coming year, of the tapestry of France and Flanders between about 1350 and 1520, the so-called " Gothic " period.

Sir Joseph Duveen, and Mr. Milton Samuels of P. W. French and Company rendered special assistance in assembling some of the illustrations. Margaret Lewisohn and Eleanor Sachs read most of the book in typescript and made valuable suggestions. Special recognition for many kinds of help is due Arthur Upham Pope.

CONTENTS

[vii]

LIST OF PLATES

[ix]

[x]

LIST OF PLATES

[xi]

CHAPTER I

THE ANCIENT EAST AND
THE EGYPTIAN TAPESTRIES

IT was not until Adam and Eve were expelled from the Garden of Eden that Adam began to delve and Eve to spin. As long as man was content to eat the beasts that he could catch and the wild plants that he could gather, he led an unsettled, disorganized life; but it involved a real economy. The animals that he ate provided hides and furs to wear. When he settled down, comparatively speaking, and began himself to raise the animals and plants that he needed for food, in flocks and fields for tillage, his wife began to weave.

Weaving was devised so far back in the history of humanity that almost every people has attributed its invention to a goddess who remained the utmost mistress and patron of the art, but its earliest history can be only glimpsed at long intervals, darkly. In the first two matured civilizations that have been revealed, in the Sumerian cities on the Chaldean plain, three thousand or more years before Christ, and at Mohenjodaro, perhaps even earlier, weaving had certainly already become more than a craft, an art. In the one, wool and linen both were wrought into cloths of varied qualities, and there were dyes to stain the fabric, notably, for gala costumes, bright red; in the other, cotton was dressed, spun and woven. But this we know only from records. No single scrap of these fabrics has survived, so that we can scarcely even surmise what they may have been, what weaves were used, what patterns wrought, or how. Bits of linen have been found at low levels in the Susa excavations, but they are only plain cloth so that they provide no evidence on the possibility or extent of ornamented textiles. Similarly the Egyptian mummy wrappings, which are fairly numerous even from quite early dynasties, are all plain cloth.

No decorated weaves are known until about 2900 B.C. Then tapestry appears, not, to be sure, the actual stuff, but a record so accurate that there is no doubting the fact. In the mastaba of one, Hesy, at Saqqara, there are painted on the walls a number of textiles, and one of them is unmistakably tapestry. The fabric is used for a tent, or rather a tabernacle, a pavilion made with timber uprights and cross beams but with the wall filled in with woven material lashed to the wooden frame. The tapestry panels carry a pattern of concentric lozenges, yellow, light blue, and red in varying succession, with black outlines between. In such a design, as tapestry is normally woven, every color margin would be punctured with a succession of perforations, a grave weakness in a textile that was to meet the strains and wear of a tent wall. But, as the painting painstakingly indicates, this has been obviated by dovetailing the lines of juxtaposition, carrying the wefts of one color into the adjacent color area in groups, probably of about three, and vice-versa, alternately, to make a serrated margin that minimizes the weakness of the weave. It is a device that shows, not only complete control of the technique, but experience of its defect and experiment in overcoming it. The patterns of all of these tabernacle textiles are strikingly un-Egyptian. Clearly they were made somewhere in Western Asia and the affiliation of some of the designs with the ornament of the beautiful painted pottery of Susa I strongly suggests Elam.

A craft so well developed certainly not only persisted but advanced to further accomplishment, yet no new records give any insight into its course for another thousand years or more. Then in the paintings of Minoan Crete appear garments that were quite probably executed in tapestry and, if so, show a marked progress, for they are decorated with representative themes, a bucranium with many-branched, tree-like horns flanked by confronted guardian sphinxes couchant, crouching griffons, and swallows in flight (Third Middle Minoan Period, c. 1700–1580).

So tapestry as a technique of the loom is assured of ancient lineage, but tapestry in its full connotation is much more than this. It is the application of this technique to free pictorial designs, its use in translating illustration on a mural scale, and whether or not any of the ancient Eastern Mediterranean civilizations had such tapestry it is impossible to say. Perhaps they felt no need of woven wall coverings, for other types of decoration were early developed, especially in Mesopotamia where building was with brick, making a surface so rough that in any structure of pretensions it had to be faced. Coatings of stucco were applied from the first and this suggested painting. Metal reliefs and mosaics also were used. Later many rich materials were employed, panels of cedar or handsome quarried stones, and when the utmost lavishness was desired, segments of gold and ivory were inlaid or bits of lapis lazuli were inset. In great palaces there were revetments of enamelled bricks making huge, bright-colored, high-glazed pictures. With these gleaming polychrome surfaces, textiles may have been superfluous.

Yet if the ancient Orientals did not create mural tapestries, a great potential aesthetic value was neglected, for through these two millenniums, in all the varying cultures, certain artistic qualities were consistently maintained which would have been most sympathetic to this medium. The races differed greatly in their innate aesthetic endowment, artistic insight fluctuated through every degree, from genius to the trite and perfunctory, and skill varied from finesse and virtuosity to stupid clumsiness; but in spite of all these inequalities and through all the multiple divergences and modifications of styles, a certain basic character persisted, such that, had these peoples produced tapestry they would have realised the essential and significant capacities of the art.

For, in the first place, the arts of all the ancient East are symbolic rather than realistic. The pictorial themes are illustrative, but in most instances the aim is balanced between record and magic, so that the forms have been more or less standardized by a tradition that partakes of the nature of ritual and hence tends to the abstract. It is just such conventionalized illustration that can be most appropriately presented in tapestry.

Yet, on the other hand, the conventions were not, save in

[3]

occasional degenerate exceptions, standardized as mere inert formulae, for the whole early Oriental world was tumultuous with force, and intense in emotion, so that the representative arts of the Ancient East are imbued with a vitality that is a mean between the two extremes which meet therein, mere symbol and violence, again exactly the balanced compromise that tapestry requires.

This vivid but formalized vivacity was, moreover, invested with sumptuous ostentation, for the East accepted without question the beauty of richness and the fitness of display, once more an assumption favorable to tapestry which is never an art of modesty but needs embellishment and the exploitation of material luxury. And finally the Orient clothes its life in color, intense tones, and multiple polychromy, the vibrant deep hues that are essential to pictorial woolen hangings.

The dominance of these aesthetic ideals through so many centuries over such an extended territory was no accident, but the direct reflection of the basic conditions of living. The populations that had founded the fundamental ideas common to all these civilizations were very near the margin of subsistence. Life was a struggle of which they were necessarily acutely aware. They were straining every effort to wrest sustenance from inimical nature, competing with invisible, mysterious forces that might at any moment wipe out the crops which were their only shield against starvation. In the rudimentary forms of their religions this awareness of struggle is made overt in the mythology, but even in the most developed forms the idea is still of primary importance. The Judaic God is the victor in the struggle, an absolute monarch who holds a crushed humanity in an arbitrary and usually irrationally cruel dominion. Zoroastrianism and later Manichæism introduced the struggle into the very cosmogony. Throughout these early Eastern creeds, and so throughout the arts, the struggle motive, in one symbolism or another, is constantly recurrent.

Equally important as a reaction to the ever looming menace of starvation was the vivid awareness of the concept of fertility. Seeds and the yield of seeds, the fecundity of cattle, the flow of the mother animals' milk, these tipped the trembling balance

[4]

between death and life. From the very beginning, therefore, the cult was focussed on the idea of fertility which merged into the more inclusive idea of Life. Thus a Tree of Life was sanctified. This usually grew on a mountain and was often conventionalized in forms determined by mystic numbers, three and seven. Later the tree sometimes became a pillar. There was also a Plant of Life, likewise tripartite. In close connection was the Water of Life. The principle was, moreover, embodied in a Deity, occasionally a god, more often hermaphrodite, later almost always a goddess. The god was early connected with the sky and was therefore assigned astral symbols, especially those of solar connotation. Associated with all these phases of the idea were animal attributes, notably the horned animals, so that the god wore in some personifications a horned head-dress. Birds also, practically always Raptores, entered into the complex. The fertility goddesses were commonly attended by some of the great cats. Different centres and different ages varied this pantheon and its appurtenances, but for centuries the dominating idea through this region continued to be the notion of fertility.

The arts of these races were symbolic because, in the unequal contest which was the obsessing fact of their life, magic control had to be exercised through every resource. They were infused with emotional tensity because the struggle involved relentless strain and the desperateness of the situation justified them in ready violence. Nor had they any counterbalancing motives to restraint, for they prized exaggeration of emotion as an earnest of vitality, an intensification of the awareness of living which was the personal equivalent of the fertility that they venerated, a manifest of life abundant. Their love of richness and likewise of brilliance of color were other facets of this same impulse to conscious vitality, and ostentation, moreover, was justified as a demonstration of victory, which was the moral aim in a life of struggle.

Power, richness and multiplicity, sumptuous materials displayed in profusion, a great deal of everything in every dimension of quantity, huge buildings, enormous columns, a crowding of decoration, unlimited repetition of figures, contrasting

[5]

colors, lavishness, and complexity defined the canons of taste; but these peoples were controlled in life by an innate profundity of religious feeling, and in art by the corresponding spirit of the cult and the hieratic forms of its conventions, guided from the beginning, it would seem, by a powerful and certain native instinct for decorative relations. Surely artists animated by these principles would have created tapestries near the summit of the art.

The Cretans, especially, have left specific proof of the genius of their decorators for cartoon design. What better model could a tapestry weaver ask than some of the paintings of Knossos, where the artists had developed a style of mural that maintained a perfect compromise between realism and convention, illustration and decoration, silhouette and details, with clearly contrasted colors distributed in varied areas to make a carrying but never monotonous or intrusive block design? Thus there is the painting, found in one corner of the Palace of Knossos (Second Middle Minoan Period, c. 2000–1700 B.C.), of a slim, naked youth, the body silhouetted in an arbitrary greenish blue against a reddish brown ground, as he leans over to pluck yellow and white crocuses and arrange them in two flat green bowls. Again, the painter who depicted the court ladies, chattering together on the grand stand (Third Middle Minoan Period, c. 1700–1580 B.C.), would have been an ideal cartoon painter of genre scenes, for he had mastered the tricks of arrested pantomime which make pictures self-explanatory and are the key to the more intimate forms of decorative illustration. A lady in blue turns and lays her hand on the next lady's knee to say something sweetly spiteful. Two ladies in blue are exchanging intimate confidences. The one on the right certainly has a lover. The next lady has had an exciting adventure, and the next is laying down the law. And so it goes. Every phase of female gossip, the emphasis on trivialities, the excitement about nothing, the clatter of tongues in endless words said just to be talking, are conveyed by the movement of hands, the twist of bodies, the tilt of heads. Here are the fixed moving pictures that are the ideal of tapestry design.

The Eastern civilization when it spread into Greece was

[6]

already old and showing its fatigue. The discovery of the Mycenaean art some fifty years ago aroused excited admiration, but this was a reaction of surprise. The subsequent uncovering of the parent civilization in Crete has shown that the mainland branch, relatively late, was not only provincial but vitiated with decadence. Its life was proportionately brief. In a few hundred years, before 1000 B.C., it stops abruptly. There is then a blank gap in the history of the country, bridged only by remains of pottery. In these, the skill and the basic technical ideas of the original Mycenaeans are carried on, but the decoration, the determining conception and taste, have been drastically changed. In place of a degenerate naturalistic ornament that tended to be abundant but random, there is a new scheme of geometric design, free yet controlled, clear, definite, and systematically organized.

Another culture had filtered into the eastern Mediterranean world. Tribes of a different group were shifting down from the north, seeking more propitious lands. Racially they were perhaps ultimately akin to some, at least, of the builders of the Oriental states. Possibly all of these stocks had come from the central Asiatic steppes, splitting apart in some remote moment of their southward and westward drift, so that this section eventually reached the plains of Thessaly. But however that may have been, whether it was thanks to some native dissimilarity or to a different experience of the tribes since their lives diverged, the new inhabitants of Greece had, certainly, a contrasted mentality.

They were not obsessed by the consciousness of struggle. They took account of the fact. It is represented in Greek mythology by various episodes, notably the war between the Titans and the Gods. But they never permitted it to be ultimate. To them the normal seemed, not a sudden and extreme oscillation of competing forces, but a distributed equilibrium. Life, and by deduction reality, were not a violent and absolute alternative in which success for one meant defeat for the other. It was a multiplicity of facts and possibilities all of which could be, should be, maintained, if the balance could be found; and this meant organization, rational planning, and control.

[7]

Being thus intellectuals, the Greeks eschewed magic symbolism and sought and achieved in their arts objective representation. At the supreme period this reached its highest form, the translation of the particular into the idea by generalizing intellect. By the same token they aimed, not at intensity of emotion, but at the restraint and moderation that promote effective intelligence. Similarly, not ostentation and abundance were the motives, but self-command and its concomitants of dignity, order and that equilibrium which for them was the basis of life.

Greece produced fine fabrics of different sorts, but again there is no evidence whether or no there were pictorial wall tapestries. From the classical period (*c*. 400 B.C.) we have only two bits of stuff, two fragments, found in South Russia in the Kuban, one with floral ornament and the other with ducks and stag heads. These seem to be tapestry woven, but they are only small-scale, garment materials.

Literature, however, bears witness to the existence of larger and more complex illustrative textiles, and it has usually been assumed that these must have been tapestries; but Homer's Helen executed an equally elaborate scene, and the text seems to indicate that she wove, not tapestry, but a kind of compound cloth, with the figures in one color, probably white, on a purple ground, the white weft carried clear across the loom, doubled on top of the underlying purple thread, to make the pattern, rendering the illustrations in silhouette rather than in the flexible polychromy of the tapestry bobbin. Certainly the art of silhouette illustration was carried in Greece to its maximum fulfilment, both as representation and as decoration. Accepting the limitation of black masses with only reserved inner details to refine the expression and intensify the vitality, the vase painters broached and conquered every type of realistic illustrative problem, the presentation of speed and force of action, the drama of incident, the feeling of varied episodes, the significance of typical moments. If these modulations of representation could be conveyed on the pottery in black on terra cotta or red on white with such skill, beauty and conviction, they could and quite probably would have been similarly depicted in just one tone on another on woven fabrics. And perhaps that is why the Egyptians of the first Christian centuries when they used patterns of classical style, though weaving now in tapestry capable of unlimited color change, almost always presented them in only two colors, black and white, or red and white, or green and white, in silhouette. Indeed there is one type of Egyptian silhouette tapestry that points very convincingly to such an origin and may give a very faithful replica of the prototype. For in this style most of the ground areas are, not in either the purple or the white, but in the two streaked together, a weft of the one alternating with a weft of the other (Pl. 3, a). Just so might the extra pattern weft of a compound cloth such as Helen seems to have made, been fitted into the ground where it was not needed in solid masses to create the silhouette design. But however Pallas and Arachne and the other great weavers of Greece did fashion their webs, we can well believe that within their categories they were supreme, embodying the rationality yet sensibility of the Greek spirit, the naturalism that yet transcended specific fact in universal forms, the gracious rhythms of Greek physical and emotional poise.

The Oriental world tore itself to pieces through the fatality inherent in its sense of struggle. The Greek world slowly died by the creeping paralysis implicit in the intellectualism which had made possible its brilliant achievements. A mentality that faced fact with a cold eye and an unswerving reason had many advantages as long as facts were a means in the building of life, necessary for the achievement of a state and for the ideas to guide these immediately absorbing processes. When that work was done, however, and there was nothing left to do with life but live it, there was no living left.

The world was a set of facts for what they were worth, and life consisted in making what one could of them. Given an intellect, one could make a self-respecting pattern of living and get what values there were in the life of the mind. Lacking that resource, one could always amuse oneself, elegantly if one were sophisticated, excitingly if one were emotional, childishly or violently if one were of the mob. And so the rationality of the Greeks sapped their strength, beyond power of resistance

[9]

when a new invasion came from their own provinces in the north. The invasion that came this time was not the migration of a foreign people seeking larger and surer crops, but the challenge of a royal house of ambitious, expansive aims; and so expansive was that ambition that in the second generation, in the youthful person of Alexander, the power of the family had swept across most of the then known world. But because it was an individual conquest and not a racial movement which created this empire, it neither destroyed nor recreated the civilizations through which it passed. It added to them, but that which it added, the Hellenistic culture, was already senescent.

Seventy cities owed their being to Alexander's might, but one typified the character of his accomplishment. Alexandria was an old settlement when he went to Egypt, but he gave it not only a new name, but a new status as capital of the Egyptian domain (332 B.C.), and thereby he endowed it with a still greater importance as commercial link between the East and the West. Thanks to this trade, it was for nine hundred years a rich and brilliant metropolis, fluctuating in prosperity, but maintaining an active and characteristic city life.

Created in decadence, battening on profits that represented, not primarily real production, but only exchange, Alexandria was the epitome of luxurious urban degeneracy. The factual frankness that had inoculated classical Greece with death, eventuated here in its reduction to futility, naïve materialism. It was a materialism not formulated as a philosophical theory, but assumed as the unconsidered presupposition of life. The intellectual reaction from the desperate scepticism that was its concomitant, was a series of dogmatic philosophies, almost hysterically welcomed by virtue of the absolute revelation they claimed, their gnosticism. Ingenious rather than profound, the tendency reached its most elaborate and famous development in the work of Philo the Jew, who interpreted the Old Testament as a complex allegorical exposition of classical Greek philosophical ideas.

For the rest, Alexandria sought the same refuge from life's futility that had already depleted Greece itself, fled inescapable

[10]

vacuity by the only possible means, its frank acceptance, and amused itself. But in addition to this Hellenistic heritage, there was also a strong intermixture of Oriental elements. Beneath the Greek veneer there was a large Egyptian population, and two of the five city wards were predominantly Jewish. Moreover, there was exorbitant wealth. Consequently, Greek moderation ceded to unchecked extremes. Everything was exaggerated to an explosive inflation.

A large and elaborate academic institution provided the equipment for the intellectual entertainment known as professional scholarship, and it was productive and insignificant in proportion as the mechanical organization was admirable. The literature of Alexandria was encyclopaedic in quality as well as quantity. In its lighter aspect, when it pandered to the easier pleasures of the merely literate, the erotic motive was the major absorption, treated now, for the first time, romantically, with gradations from romance to pornography. Sex and clothes, food and drink, talk and a luxurious décor in which to set them were all exploited to give contents to time.

Alexandria's arts were the mirror of her shallow soul and the summation of her two constitutive elements, the Greek and the Oriental. In the earlier centuries the Greek influence dominated. Representative designs were realistic, abstract patterns and geometrical forms were complex but clear and rationally organized. There was a basic control and reserve, with ample spacing, plan, and balance, and sober, limited colors. The Oriental influence, however, increasingly modified and finally obliterated these merits, substituting for realism conventions that, in the end, were illegibly irrational, exaggerating silhouettes, crowding design, compounding the most irrelevant motives and rendering these compact and confused fantasies in vivid and varied colors, made as polychromatic in effect as possible by extreme fragmentation without relation to any representative function. The Eastern aesthetics of power and fertility, with its ideals of multiplicity and richness, triumphed over intellectual design that had maintained intelligibility, clarity, and order.

The resultant style, varying from century to century accord-

[11]

ing to the proportion of one heritage or the other, was rendered in different media by the dexterous fingers of the native Egyptians, and so successful was it in its ingenuity, however superficial, that it made, after some centuries had passed, a constitutive contribution first to Rome and then to Byzantium, an addition to the grammar of decoration which, through the Roman descent, was to have some twenty centuries of posterity.

Tapestry was an ancient craft in Egypt. Three fragments exist that date from about 1500 B.C. Two are of little interest in design as they have only hieroglyphics, though one has documentary value, bearing the name of Thoutmes III (*c*. 1503–1449). The third is more interesting. In a powdered pattern of lotus and papyrus flowers is a tablet upheld by two uraei, bearing the name and titles of Amenothes II (*c*. 1449–1423 B.C.). On either side is a narrow border, one with lotus flowers and buds, the other with a disk design. The ground is white, the pattern is in blue, red, brown, yellow, and green, outlined with black. All are entirely of linen. Though the ground is cloth, the pattern is in true tapestry weave, but the warps and wefts are not perfectly straight, not consistently at right angles to each other. Both curve at places in deference to the design, and some details are drawn in with a free bobbin. Yet it is skilful weaving in that it is finished on both sides and so is reversible.

Egypt at this date had learned much from the Orient. Thousands of skilled craftsmen from Syria had been brought in as a result of the Egyptian conquests in the East, and they had introduced into the rigid hieratic style of the Nile Valley a lightness and grace, a quality of charm, quite alien to the fixed immobility of the native invention, vivifying and alleviating it. Had they brought, too, this technique of tapestry weaving? Impossible to say. The actual motives are Egyptian and the Egyptians had long been skilful weavers; but the only textile fragments prior to this dynasty that have been found, though in some instances they are remarkably fine and evenly wrought, are never more than simple cloths.

Probably this use of the tapestry technique to render colored designs on a plain cloth ground continued in Egypt, for two millenniums later essentially the same type of fabric was being made. At this time, however, the design is usually rendered in wools. The graves of Egypt of this period, from about the fourth to the eighth century A.D., have yielded vast quantities of woven stuffs, most of them examples of this combined technique, wool tapestry-woven repeats or bands, panels or rondels inserted in a linen cloth, the insertion in most instances having been made directly on the loom. Several of the cloth warps are used together as a single warp for the tapestry, the cloth wefts are stopped at that point and the wool tapestry wefts are introduced. Such decoration was employed, not only in garments, but also in curtains and cushion covers. In addition, however, to this composite weaving, there are true tapestries also, entire panels of wool, though the warps are usually of linen. Some of these were certainly wall tapestries in the full, modern European sense.

The commonest patterns for the garment inserts were geometrical motives taken immediately from Greece, rendered in some shade of purple, brown or black and white. As formal designs many of these entrelacs, often quite complex, are able and inventive, and technically they are interesting, for all of the inner outlines, the delineation of the design, are done with a fine white linen thread passed through the solid tapestry ground with a free bobbin.

But garment trimmings were by no means limited to these abstract devices. The repertoire was extended, not only with floral ornament, but more especially with figural scenes of endless variety, and in these the essential character of the Alexandrian school is preserved. True, Alexandria herself, when even the earliest of these tapestries was on the loom (4th or 5th century A.D.), had already begun to descend the long steep slope of her decadence. Moreover, most of them were made, probably, not in the city itself, but in outlying districts conscious of continuity with the pre-Hellenistic Egyptian world, by Copts whose veins perhaps held no drop of Hellenic blood. Yet in spite of all this, the Alexandrian mentality is there. For when a city has been as large, as rich and as brilliant as Alexandria was, even after her communal death, unless barbarians, earth-

[13]

quake or fire obliterate institutions and monuments, there are many centuries of vitality left in her traditions. And when a capital has been so striking and gay, she is bound to have left a widespread imprint on the provinces even though they deplored her immoralities, for in proportion as respectability is dowdy, it secretly yearns to look wanton. So these tapestries, made after the eclipse of the capital, in country centres that had never countenanced her doings, preserve her spirit to the best of their feeling and skill.

The world capital of scepticism, Alexandria was intelligently materialist. Things, at least, were real, and since the sole certainty in life was the present reality, one savoured things. Hence her painters created studies in still life, making more accessible the interest, visual and tactile, of things. Later, in the fifth century, Egyptian weavers worked to the same end. In the Museum of Fine Arts of Moscow are two small tapestry panels, rose, violet, and green, each with a little pile of exquisitely ripe fruit on a leaf. A bloom covers the firm but juicy pulp, the globes of peach and plum round out in full maturity, the leaf is cool and smooth. Renoir never conveyed more lusciously the seen and felt anticipation of sweet acidity, cool, sun-warmed flesh, velvety skin over firm cheeks. Yet in these Egyptian pieces there is no taint of imitation of another medium. They are woven wool, taut and regular. But not only is there no contradiction in the qualities of subject and material; one is employed actually to enhance its opposite.

Appealing to the same interest and comparable in quality, is a panel with bright fish floating in their light-streaked, cool, green world, in the Musée des Tissus of Lyons. The beauty of marine life was first fully exploited in the Minoan civilization of Crete, a maritime power. There the designers not only invented endless patterns of sea weed and shells, but they painted whole frescoes of the under-water world. In the Alexandrian school, fish were widely used for decoration, especially in mosaics. Here in this tapestry the weaver has preserved the fresh translucency of their liquid universe and the cold slipperiness of their bodies, as well as the brilliant patterning of their varied hues and the grace of the sliding movement.

[14]

The materialistic interest embraces decorative animal portraiture, too. Thus in the Kaiser Friedrich Museum there is a peacock, not in the obvious ostentation of full display, but trailing his purple, green, and yellow glory behind him, his hauteur maintained by the lifted sway of the neck as he steps his deliberate pavane. All of these tapestries are essentially Greek in their naturalism, their grace, and a fine quality of aristocratic intelligence.

But the enjoyment that still life and the related subjects offer, the expansion of pleasure by the intenser realization of the quality of common objects, would be too subtle for a numerous clientele. Hence these themes are rare in Egyptian tapestry, especially pure still life. The usual motives are contrived for the amusement of more obvious minds. The random juxtaposition of incongruities is a ready source of entertainment. It is the key to most popular jokes. Far more subtly and sensitively developed in relation to pathos, it is the program of Charlie Chaplin's screen personality. Crudely applied and pandering to primitive instincts, it provides also slapstick comedy. It gave rise in Alexandria to a peculiar style of design.

Controlled by the symmetrical and justly spaced rigidity of a formal scheme, satyrs and baskets of fruit, goddesses and garlands, pavilions, masks, goats, ribbons, cupids, scrolls and any other element that could be made picturesque were set forth, each item with the utmost realism, the whole an aimless phantasmagoria. Here is the ultimate pictorial cynicism. Nothing is valued in itself. Everything is a means to an end, of equal weight because of no weight at all. And the end is futility. In this typically Alexandrian invention the Greek and the Eastern elements of her heritage are suspended in equilibrium; for most of the specific motives are Hellenistic and, at least in the earlier periods, they are rendered in a Hellenistic style. The conception of their combination, however, in this abundant incongruity, is Oriental, though, on the other hand, the control of the complexity by open spacing and symmetry is again Greek. Because such designs were first revealed to the modern world in underground Roman chambers, " grottoes," they were called "grotesques," and fantastic irrelevance was thus formulated in a new adjective.

No Egyptian tapestry exists with a fully developed grotesque, but many of the finest small panels from garments show a compressed version of the idea. Some of these are in silhouette, black or purple on white or, rarely, the reverse; some are more realistically treated in full polychrome. In these condensed grotesques, cupids, bulls, birds, goats, flowers, baskets of fruit, fish, acanthus leaves, hares, pomegranates, lions, vases and the vine are formally organized in endlessly varied combinations.

In the same spirit as the grotesque but less complex are fantastic representations suggesting allegory but not troubling to have any meaning at all. The hybrid quality of the Greco-Oriental amalgamation is especially noteworthy in this type. One very beautiful panel in the Kelekian collection, unique in quality and condition, shows two sea princesses mounted on unreal creatures of the deep (Pl. 1). Each lady carries a fluttering scarf, blue for the blond one who holds a mirror, enamelled and jewelled, yellow for the black haired one who rides a magnificent, fish-tailed, winged bull. The ground is solid red, the border saffron with half palmettes, dark blue, green, and red, forming an ogival lattice. It is a brilliant decoration, full of vitality.

One of the grotesque elements played an especially large role in Alexandrian art and its derivatives, the cupids. These naked male infants, usually formless with fat, winged or not, are presented in many types of pseudo-occupation. A decadent society would almost inevitably cultivate every device of sex exploitation. Excitement is the easiest and one of the most general temporary escapes from life, and its readiest and most universal means is sex. Naked boys were not only the symbol, but also the direct suggestion thereof, and for both men and women, since pederasty was very extensive in the Oriental and late Classical worlds. That they should so often be simulating tasks is, however, less obvious and more interesting, gathering grapes, picking fruit, catching ducks. The caricature of work is the ultimate symptom of disgust with life.

In the invention of the grotesque and the elaboration of

[16]

PLATE I

SIRENS.   Egypt, probably 5th or 6th century

erotes Alexandria produced decorative resources that would thereafter be ready to hand for every period of bitter frivolity. The Renaissance revived the grotesque with a hodge-podge of imitated classicism (cf. p. 163), and the eighteenth century evolved an effeminate and even more derivative version (cf. p. 278). Similarly, the putti recur in the Renaissance, so that puffy, naked loves busy themselves, frittering away time with fruit and flowers, in the very court of the Virtues (cf. p. 125), and in the eighteenth century they strangle their geese in the Stanislas Place of Nancy or, over thousands of mantels and doors, loll, pink and soft, on whipped cream clouds, in a sweet, obscene vacuity.

Naturally the pleasure mad, sex mad, desperate world of Alexandria loved the dance. It had, moreover, inherited a wide repertoire from three civilizations where the art had played a great role and been highly developed; ancient Egypt, Greece, and the East. The dances that are shown in the tapestries, however, seem to correspond most closely with the Hellenistic styles.

The Dorians danced in worship and because theirs was a military society they perfected the war dance. The classical Greeks continued the war dance and gave it further significance, making it not only a preparation for the practice of arms and a homage to Mars, but also a part of general bodily training for beauty and skill. To the same end they created, too, purely gymnastic dances which were related, but more varied in movement and executed without arms. Both of these types were active, even violent. The soldier, nude, with spear and shield, mimicked combat, attack and defence, retreat, sudden assault and sudden ruse. Often he pitted himself against a ghostly foe, but sometimes the rhythmic pantomime was performed by a couple, a simulated duel. The gymnastic dances gave opportunity for every kind of leaping, bending, twisting, and stretching agility.

Contrasted with these were the ritualistic dances, stately marches with patterned steps and sacerdotal mien. Or in gayer festivals the chorus might run and glide and whirl. Such dances pass gradually into the purely expressive inventions, either conveying an emotion or depicting by gesture a whole episode.

These took a special form in theatrical dancing, executed by the chorus in connection with the drama and mirroring its character, tragic, comic or even satirical. An extreme form of the expressive dancing, which also had ritualistic associations, developed in the Bacchanalian orgies. And finally, there was purely personal dancing, in private festivities, for individual enjoyment or gaiety. Altogether there were, according to contemporary lists, more than two hundred distinguishable dances, and in executing these every step, movement, posture, and gesture that is known to the modern dance was employed, save the true toe dancing of the French ballet technique.

To the classical Greek each of these dances had its high significance wherein the ethical portent was of equal weight with the aesthetic effect; but by Hellenistic times amusement had superseded meaning, and even the famous Pyrrhic dance, the greatest and most respected of the war dances, was executed by young girls as a spectacle. This degeneration accelerated rapidly in the atmosphere of decadence of Alexandria, so that the dances recorded in the Egyptian tapestries, while technically they were still doubtless on a high level, had as social expressions lost any deep reality.

By far the finest Egyptian tapestry of the dance that has been found is a series of fragments in the Kaiser Friedrich Museum in Berlin. The chorus, as far as it remains, consists of a nude youth with a purple scarf, a nude white woman with a blue scarf, a negro woman in a draped green and red tunic that reveals rather than conceals her body, and a woman fully dressed in a green gown. They are executing a dance that is vivacious, suggestive perhaps. The very appearance together of the nude, the half clothed and the fully clothed subtly enhances the excitement. But it is not an orgiastic dance. The pattern of the movements, however active, is still formal. The youth poses, the left foot over the right, knee flexed, toe touching, the scarf caught between the thighs making a dark background to throw into relief the modelling of the leg. The woman in the green gown, on the other hand, advances the right foot, pointing the left to one side, the left hand flung over her head clacking castanets, the right arm swung out behind. The nude woman

[18]

PLATE II

repeats essentially the pose of the youth, while the half dressed negress, also with castanets, reverses the movement of the woman in green. The rhythmic pattern is carefully composed.

Dances are represented in uncountable silhouette dress trimmings in endless variety. Indeed, a systematic and inclusive analysis of this material would provide a very interesting and probably almost complete history of the dance of this period. In the military dances, the soldiers, nude save for a fluttering scarf and carrying their shields, advance, recoil, leap, parry, drop to one knee, swing to one side, usually matching their supple rapidity against an imaginary foe (Pl. 2, a). The dignity of the religious dances is far less common. The worship of the gods was dead save for festivals hung on the excuse of doing honor to the lesser patrons of revelry, and the orgiastic Astarte devotions. The dances that these inspired, the wild flung head, the rushing steps, the whirling, sweeping, twisting bodies in self hypnotic intensity, are often seen. But commonest of all in the tapestries are the exhibition dances, graceful, pictorial but non-representative, presented, that is, for the beauty of the forms and the pleasure of the rhythms, but without pantomimic intent, though usually they are flavored with eroticism (Pl. 2, b).

As in every society dominated by the motive of escape, hunting was a pastime for the well to do and unintellectual. Consequently this theme, too, took its place in the tapestries. No wholly pictorial representation of the hunt has come to light, but there is a number of similar hangings with silhouette figures in black or purple or sometimes in a fine indigo, on a linen ground, cavaliers and their prey, lions, hares, and wild horses. These varied motives are usually evenly spaced to form a powdered pattern, the " landscape " being represented by detached, semi-conventional plants, alternating with the riders and the fleeing beasts. These hunting scenes are more Eastern than Hellenistic, recalling in some of the conventions certain of the early Oriental rock reliefs, though the open spacing is more Greek in quality.

But perhaps the most important theme in the Egyptian tapestries is portraiture. The personal counterpart of materialism is individualism, the ethical counterpart of scepticism is egoism, and the instinct for survival is not diminished one whit by the acceptance of its impossibility. There may be no gardens of the blest, where the soul will wander, perpetually cool and regaled, but this world is going on, at least for a time. Rulers can build monuments, savants and artists leave works, but almost any individual can arrange to perpetuate his face. There are many ordinary portraits woven in wool. At the best they are attractive designs, at the worst a child's scrawl daubed with gaudy crayons. There are, too, ideal figures in a portrait style, notably Apollo, and an elderly bearded man representing the Nile in the Moscow Museum, in the finest quality of a delayed Hellenistic style. And there is a very colorful Ceres in the Textile Museum of the District of Columbia. She is a charming, golden haired girl, her curls bound with a green fillet, her cheeks daintily pink. A green cloak with yellow lights reveals a pink gown under it, and her necklace is set with emeralds. In one hand she has a basket of ripe fruit, in the other a green, rose, and yellow thyrsus. This pure polychromy is enhanced by the background, striated in yellow and two tones of blue. Here the drawing retains a definite Greek feeling, but the richly varied polychromy verges toward the Eastern taste.

Heads of a portrait character were used, too, as an element in formal designs, only the head itself, as a rule, without even the neck. This motive, the more eccentric since the rendering of the face is often wholly naturalistic, was developed in Roman ornament, notably in pavement mosaics. Relief heads so treated serve as an architectural ornament, applied directly to the flat wall without any frame or mediation, at Hatra. In the Egyptian tapestries they are used in two outstanding examples, as well as many crude fragments: a panel in the Textile Museum of the District of Columbia and a fragment in the Kelekian Collection. In both cases the motive is used in a lattice, the alternate motives being birds and baskets of fruit.

But far and above all the other known tapestry portraits from Egypt is a large panel in the collection of Mr. and Mrs. Robert Woods Bliss. Here is the fashionable lady of Alexandria of perhaps the sixth century A.D.; for surely she must have lived

PLATE III

PORTRAIT OF A LADY. Egypt, probably 6th or 7th century
Collection of Mr. and Mrs. Robert Woods Bliss. See p. 21

in Alexandria or some gay city, this rich lady of the great world, even though her tapestry was found in Upper Egypt at Achmîn. Her large dark eyes are skilfully enhanced with kohl, her thick black curling hair is arranged in an evenly undulated coiffure. Her green gown is simple, but she is weighted with jewels. A crown of red enamelled flowers graces her head, a wide necklace of gold and colored stones lies on her breast, and long pendants dangle from her ears (Pl. 3). Nor is this a simple portrait. It is one of those adulatory representations that constituted both an acclaim and a portent of good luck. She is attended by two maids and half a dozen putti, each bringing a contribution to her success in life. She is proclaimed the All Blessed, but to her that hath, more is being given.

Alexandria, anguished by its own unbelief, sought, with ever recurrent and anxious hope, alleviation in the new religions. Every revival in a fresh form of the Oriental cults went through a period of notoriety, and devotees flung themselves into the dogmas of special schools. So Christianity received an ardent welcome, in its turn, and the city became a stronghold of faith, a hotbed of heresies. The tapestries reflect this aspect, too, but usually in rather a makeshift, incidental way. A cross is introduced into an old design, or current figures are adjusted to the Christian saints. Of the conventional Christian motives, by far the finest is a series of eagles, the bird of Christ, in red silhouette, holding a cross in his beak. An especially large and beautiful example is in the Vatican. Of more than average interest, too, are some bands and panels that depict the dragon conflict of Saint George, the most popular religious hero among the Copts.

But above and apart from all these incidental Christian bits are two fragments so dignified and so fine that they have almost automatically been classed as Byzantine, the scholars forgetting that it was not Alexandria that had to borrow from the political capital, but the imperial parvenue that had to garner where she could find. If these tapestries look Byzantine, it is because they perpetuate the style that Alexandria lent to Constantinople.

One, in the collection of Mrs. John D. Rockefeller, Jr., impressive in its hieratic reserve, shows the head of a male saint who has been one of a spaced row of saints. One of them, probably his immediate companion, was Saint Theodore, so the name has become attached to the one that remains. It serves as well. All that is left is the head fully affronted, with disjointed bits from the costume. The large blue eyes stare at an ultramundane focus. They are a little sunken into the brown and rose shadows of the upper lid and the blue bistre below. The thin cheeks, slightly flushed, are partly covered with the soft brown beard. The carmine lips hint of sensuality. He wore, originally, a simple brown cloak over a plain white, blue-shadowed gown, and his halo is a plain white oval against solid red. It is a high-keyed, somewhat neurotic personality for whom religion is an emotional excitement, asceticism an inverse self indulgence.

The other piece, which is more complete and may have been part, originally, of the same panel or, if not, was from a closely related design, shows a fluttering angel filling the spandrel of an arch. To a dark people the denizens of Paradise are blond. The angel has golden curls and light blue eyes. The wings sweep up with graceful strength to fill the rectangular corner of the irregular space. Her body floats gracefully, defined by the clinging folds of a simple white robe, also rendered with blue shadows. Three red and white stars are bright against the dark blue ground. Probably the complete panel showed saints in the straight, affronted row familiar in Byzantine design, under a richly jewelled arch, a section of which remains on this piece, with an angel in each spandrel, the whole enclosed in a white border, sections of which are attached to both fragments, carrying a garland of red and white flowers. Both pieces were found at Achmîn.

Meanwhile, Persian fashions, especially in costumes and textiles, were sweeping across the Byzantine world and the Egyptian weavers followed the mode, copying in their tapestry wools the shuttle woven Persian silks. The patterns are usually fantastic animals or birds, or less often cavaliers, some with a plant that may be anything from the minimum indication of a line and two leaves to an elaborate tracery that develops into a covering for the field. In the most characteristic Persian designs each major repeat is enclosed in a circle, but the Egyptians often omitted this element. The Sasanian designers had also a trick of spotting contrasting colors in "jewels" over a surface, with no realistic intent, merely to enliven the effect, and this the Egyptian weavers did imitate.

With the passage of the centuries the Greek realistic forms decayed gradually into conventions in the Oriental style which became increasingly obscure and ambiguous. Usually degeneration takes the form of simplification and the substitution of geometrical units for the representative fact. This is, to a certain extent, true in the later Egyptian weaves (7th to 8th century). There is a style of silhouetted human figures in blocks. But far more common and conspicuously typical is the degeneration into complexity, resulting in composites that sometimes defy analysis and often are quite illegible, especially in those designs where a grotesque has disintegrated and fallen together in an inextricable mélange of putti, fish, birds, flowers, and detached lines, without beginning or end or focus. There are none of the principles here of elimination, fragmentation or substitution such as can be traced in most decadent design, no reason or plan to the devolution. The Egyptian mind, one of the less intellectual versions of the Oriental spirit, simply melted in confusion.

In one special form of this aesthetic senility the pattern is rendered in long, thin, quavering lines. This style attains an effect of comparative clarity simply through attenuation, but really there is the same mental confusion here as in the compacted style. The outlines trail vaguely to no purpose and no destination, and one element wanders into another in a series of aimless accidents. Realism has passed into abstract ornament, not as a process of decorative selection and interpretation, but as a result of the failure of comprehension.

CHAPTER II

THE EMPIRES OF ROME

PROBABLY one of the best customers for the Egyptian tapestry shops was Rome, for Rome had little organized industry of her own. True, there was extensive weaving there, but it was largely a domestic work, a responsibility of the Roman housewife, and such looms, even in the rich households where slaves toiled in a kind of private factory, could hardly have produced the more pretentious stuffs, at least not in any great quantity. Silks Rome obtained from the Orient. Fine embroideries she imported from the East, too. Probably she bought her tapestries from the Nile.

This dependence on distant centres for her merchandise is typical of Rome, her rise and fall. Whether it was tapestries, philosophy or wheat, Rome bought rather than created; but there comes a time when you can no longer buy if you do not create. Rome fell.

The Roman mind was Greek intelligence debased to the level of common sense. The Romans had the Greek awareness of fact, together with their instinct for order, but these were drained of creative energy and, by the same token, without the intellectual force to command the illumination of abstract ideas. Had the Romans not come into a world of exhausted wreckage, it is doubtful whether, given their limitations, they would have had a career. But the Orient had lashed itself out in its own extremities, and Greece had stopped short in the embarrassment of cynicism. Rome, like the average person of all the ages, could salvage the useful remnants, clean them up a bit, fit them together nicely, and make quite a good appearance.

Such an unintellectual race should have been stodgy and

thrifty, but instead, it suffered from the chaotic emotions of southerners, not the passionate intensity of the East, but a volatile instability, both frivolous and cruel. As a result, the Romans of the Empire were not content to be safe, reasonably well off, and regular. They wanted idleness, luxury, excitement, and change.

All of these things, however, cost money, and none of them produce it. Moreover, Italy did not provide a sub-structure of great natural resources. And finally, to make matters worse, the kind of life this temperament ultimately created, full of entertainment, display, nervous stimulants, and variety, attracted those of like disposition from all over the world so that they concentrated in the Capital, there to consume that which they neither could nor would produce.

Rome could earn a living to meet the constantly mounting demands of her citizenry, only by capitalizing her one talent, skill of organization. She could and did regiment the world into a system in which she herself was the centre of exchange. Then, seated at the wicket through which the commodities of the world were passed, including most probably the tapestries of Egypt, she proceeded to take toll.

Had she used these revenues of the middleman to recapitalize her sources of supply, acted as a banker and taken only a reasonable interest, she might still have kept the system running. But idleness, thrills, and change are all waste. Faster and faster she ate up the riches that passed through her hands. Circuses come high and bread to feed a population only to watch those circuses higher still.

The most rapid and corrosive solvent of institutions is unsound economy. Rome was internally disintegrating from a disbalance between production and consumption, wealth and poverty, when the first Barbarians were vague rumors somewhere in the North. Then the deluge came. The Germanic Barbarians, tall, blond, powerful, and ruthless, swaggered through the Roman colonies, crushing the feeble governments under their broad, trampling feet. Generations passed. Tribes shifted, destroyed each other, amalgamated and settled down. Their conquests were solidified. They were established in their domains.

During this long period of struggle all of the finer arts must have fallen into general disuse; yet there was no time when traffic with the Orient wholly ceased. Monks came to guide the rules of their orders in new foundations, and brought relics and church gifts, and there were even professional merchants importing and offering the Eastern wares. Textiles, surely, were carried in some of the holds that unloaded in the ports of Italy and Southern France, and quite possibly tapestries from Egypt were sometimes in the lot. So Sidonius Apollinarus (430–488 A.D.) saw "brilliant cushions and stuffs on which, produced by a miracle of art, we behold the fierce Parthian with his head turned back, on a prancing steed, now escaping, now returning to hurl his spear, by turns fleeing from, and putting to flight the wild animals which he pursues." This sounds very like the Egyptian hunting tapestries (cf. p. 19). And Fortunatus, the lyrical monk of Poitiers of the sixth century, admires, in one verse, the green parrot on a wall hanging, again a pattern which occurs on many Egyptian tapestries; but perhaps this was only embroidery, wool on linen or on wool.

The solid, dogged North had prevailed, yet the memory of the pride and pageant that had been Rome still dazzled the northern mind, tempting a German militaristic politician to play the Emperor. Charles, later to be called Charlemagne (c. 742–814), was a business man with just that sort of mind. He managed his farms with a complete accounting system, an eye to every detail and an expectation of progressive profits, and he built up his empire with the same point of view, steadily impelled forward by the kind of ambition that works hard and mounts in measure with its own success. When most of the hard work was behind him and security, comparatively speaking, and wealth were at hand, he undertook, both for himself and his kingdom, to live better, to have better clothes, better buildings, more education, a little music, in short, all of the nice things of life. But over and above this sound German determination blazed the star of the awed Barbarian vision, the shining majesty that had been Rome. And so Charles had himself made Holy Roman Emperor. Being Emperor involved the maintenance of an elaborate court with all the luxuries: gold-woven

[26]

silks, jewel-encrusted ornaments, gargantuan feasts of rare viands, fine wines, and pompous display.

All this was borrowed, in basic idea, from the other Emperor of Roman Heritage, the Byzantine Basileus. Luxury and elegance to the ninth, tenth, and eleventh centuries could mean only Byzantine extravagance. Nor was it merely by contrast with their poverty that Byzantium seemed so glorious to the Western Emperors. The Eastern capital really was a city of dazzling and lavish splendor, the supreme realization of the ancient Oriental taste for rich display. Her palaces were walled with vari-colored marbles and curiously veined stones, or lined with polished metals. Above these jewel-like dadoes were still more jewel-like mosaics, or paintings glorifying the prowess of the family, or pointing some sympathetic moral in a graceful allegory. Doors were hung with bright hued silks, unstintedly interwoven with gold, or embroidered with further histories. And through these gleaming rooms walked men and women garmented in metal-encrusted brocades, with broad gold pectorals close set with masses of vari-colored stones, and girdles heavy with rubies, emeralds, and sapphires. Everywhere were vivid colors, burnished surfaces, the play of light on glistening fabrics, its reflection in glowing depths.

That Charlemagne had any tapestries is quite improbable. The very brilliance of Byzantium would have discouraged tapestry, for wool can never look as rich or shine as glossily as silk, and there is a sobriety in its weight that rebukes effeminate ostentation. The shimmering lavishness that Byzantium required was wrought on the hundreds of imperial looms by the quick and steady passing of shuttles laden with silk and metal threads, and such silks, we know, Charlemagne did own. The solider and less pretentious art of woollen mural hangings was very probably still largely or wholly in abeyance.

Charlemagne's power was personal. It could have survived only had he had an equal son. The Piety of Louis, his successor, was not enough. The second " Roman " Empire fell apart, and a Barbarian did not again try to make believe he was Emperor until a hundred years later, when Otto I of the Saxon House (936–973) had himself proclaimed Holy Roman Emperor.

Otto's court and those of his successors were far more luxurious and glamorous than Charlemagne's had ever been, with richer luxuries, more costly displays, and, a notable advance, court artists to make sumptuous, impressive portraits of their Imperial Majesties. But probably here, too, tapestry played only a minor role. Yet one Ottonian tapestry does exist. It is, however, a tapestry only in weave, not in spirit or style. As light and thin as possible, it follows in pattern a Byzantine silk that followed, in turn, one of the even more famous Sasanian silks. Indeed, this tapestry is so Oriental that it is a question whether it was woven in Germany or perhaps imported there from the Eastern capital. Only a certain awkwardness in the drawing of some details and perhaps, too, a dullness of color suggest that it is Western. In a rondel is a griffon, the foreparts eagle, the hindquarters lion, seizing a human faced bull. Perched on the eagle's rump is a hawk. The rondel is decorated with a conventional wreath of heart-shaped flowers, common in Byzantine textiles, and at the tangent points are smaller rondels with lion masks, while the interstitial ornament is a quatrefoil composed of two lion masks and two fleurons. The border has a simple foliate entrelac carrying bull masks (Pl. 4).

The central motive, the composite eagle-lion beast, seizing a human faced bull, is older than history. It is already an established convention in the earliest Sumerian art (c. 3500 B.C.), though there the animal has an eagle head and lion body, while here it has an eagle body and lion head. Both this beast and the bull were attributes of the fertility god, and the combination originated doubtless as one expression of the basic Eastern struggle motive (cf. p. 4). It has been suggested that the human face on the bull was derived from the bison which has a strikingly human looking head and which was indigenous to those districts in the neolithic period.

The style of the tapestry, while far less ancient, is of respectable antiquity, too, for a griffon essentially the same, not only in structure but even in details, appears on an Hellenistic marble bas-relief in the Louvre that was almost certainly copied from an Oriental textile. In both, the eagle has a small head on a long neck, banded with a wide collar. The wing sweeps

PLATE IV

So-called Tapestry of Saint Geron. Probably Germany, 10th or 11th century

Schlossmuseum, Berlin. See p. 28

up with the tip curved over and is decorated at the base with a leaf, while the tail has a foliate tip.

The arrogant pride of the Saxon Emperors which fostered the imitation Byzantine display burned equally in their daughters and sisters, but where, in the man's world of the Middle Ages, could a woman find for it an outlet? Perhaps, to a certain extent, as a Prince's wife, but even a Prince's wife was, after all, only a wife. There was, however, one domain in which a woman of intelligence and force of character could find scope for her qualities. As Abbess of one of the great foundations she would owe allegiance only to the King, directly; she would control vast properties; would command her own armed knights, and even possibly be represented in the National Diet. Here was a Princess's opportunity, and one after another they profited by it in rich abbeys set up by the royal family just to offer such a career to its women.

Foremost among these royal establishments was the Abbey of Quedlinburg. Quedlinburg was founded by a queen of the Ottonian line, Mathilde (968), wife of Heinrich the Fowler, the grandson of the first head of the house; and the whole series of Abbesses were from the royal family, daughters of Kings, named sometimes to the office from birth, as in the case of Mathilde, daughter of Otto I. All of these royal Abbesses wielded great power and many of them interfered effectively in the Government, notably that same Mathilde who practically ruled the Empire during the minority of her nephew, Otto II, and again in 997 when he went to Italy. Moreover, these Abbesses were not merely administrators and politicians. True to their family traditions they were art patrons, too, so that many of the finest illuminations were painted in the convents, and skilled needle women were trained there to embroider wonderful vestments.

Outstanding among the artistic Abbesses was Agnes who assumed the direction of Quedlinburg in 1186. She was herself a miniature painter, but she was even more interested in weaving, so she gathered about her skilful women and trained and supervised them, making Quedlinburg famous for its tapestries.

In the Church of Halberstadt, not far from Quedlinburg, there remain three tapestries that are almost certainly from

[29]

Agnes's convent atelier. The first shows the History of Abraham. Abraham, a white locked, square bearded patriarch, is erect in the door of his house. God leans out of his Heaven, proclaiming: " I am eternal," and the three angels stand before the Prophet, two of them with wings drooping, the one in the centre with wings upstretched, only just alighted.

In the next scene Sarah emerges from the door, bringing supper for the three angels who are already at table. She wears the simple dress of the time, straight, with deep hanging sleeves and a head veil that fits in pleats like a cap and is caught around her neck as a scarf. It is a graceful gown, but here it is drawn with the rigid, stubby outlines of an anxious child, so that it has none of the lissom rhythm that it presupposes.

In the third scene the old man, sword and torch in hand, leads the procession to the sacrifice, relentlessly. Isaac bears on his shoulder the faggots, forecasting the weary pilgrimage of Christ carrying his own cross, and a serving man follows, leading a saddled ass. The crudity of the drawing and the directness of the statement give this scene a fitting monumental inevitability.

In the actual sacrifice, Abraham holds Isaac, crouching on the ground, by the hair, but the angel leans down from Heaven, making the arresting sign of blessing. The space beneath the angel is filled with a clear, wiry acanthus tree borrowed from a Byzantine textile that had, in turn, taken its model from a Sasanian silk, and below this is a charming colt, a natural, appealing little beast, startlingly real and human in this hieratic world.

Finally, quite unrelated to the major theme, comes Michael, a commanding figure, his violet cloak fluttering in a rigid arc, his blue gown in symmetrical fan folds, stepped in a right angled zig-zag, his white under robe looped in deep ovals in the opposite direction and the whole emphatic linear contrast cross-cut with the diagonal of his long white spear. The dragon rises up straight beside him, balancing on its gracefully twisted head, wings sweeping doubly up, body coiling twice on itself, then springing out in a three-fold floriation.

The Eighteenth Chapter of Genesis explaining the story of Abraham is printed on bands above and between the scenes, and

PLATE V

CHARLEMAGNE AND THE FOUR PHILOSOPHERS. Germany, 12th century
Halberstadt Cathedral. See p. 31

below and at the end are wide borders of the Greek meander, seen in perspective and rendered in three colors, a favorite motive of the time.

The second tapestry shows the Redeemer and his Apostles. In the centre is Christ the Lord in a red cloak and green robe, enthroned in a mandorla, holding in one hand the open book, with the other blessing. The abstract fixity of the figure conveys relentless authority. The mandorla is supported on either side by Michael and Gabriel, each immobile in the midst of a step that he will never complete. The frozen symmetry of the group makes it perpetual. On either side are the Apostles in an even spaced row like the regular beats of a tolling bell, their vertical rigidity emphasized by stiff, upright name scrolls. This is eternity.

These two tapestries, especially the latter, have an impressive directness, finality reduced to the minimum terms. But it is largely accidental, an immediacy that is the result, not of transcending the medium after a complete exploration, but of accepting the restrictions of inexperience.

The third piece at Halberstadt is quite different in style, as it is in theme and conception. The central figure is Charlemagne (Pl. 5). Later, at the close of the Middle Ages, Charlemagne became one of the romantic heroes (cf. p. 88); but that was a legendary Charlemagne, the great Christian Knight. To the Ottonians he was a hero as an historical fact, for he was their one Western link with the Rome which was their ideal, a fulfilment in their own world of the family hopes. So Charlemagne is shown, enthroned in a central lozenge, distinctly reminiscent of Christ enthroned in a mandorla, and instead of the four symbols of the Evangelists in the corners, there are four classical philosophers. Above are the Greeks, Socrates and Plato,[1] below, the Latins, Seneca and Cato. Each has a message conveyed on a banderolle. Charlemagne says: " Life is brief, and honor, power and beauty are all fleeting in this world. Seek rather, then, to give happiness." Socrates says: " I count nothing certain." Plato again says: " No one is long endowed with beauty or strength." Cato and Seneca take a different turn, the one

[1] Probably. The heads and names are missing.

[31]

recommending that " He who tarries with a gift reduces his bequest "; and Cato that " He who gives quickly gives double." And finally on the outer border is inscribed: " Man may long seek a rational explanation, but he will scarcely find it, much less prove it."

Thus Charlemagne is made a profane deity, exponent of a worldly realism. At the crest of the Age of Faith an unqualified scepticism and factual pessimism are flatly stated. Life is short, its values transitory, reason helpless. Given such hopeless futility, the major virtues are those that offer mitigation, kindness and generosity.

Was, then, faith, even in that age of its triumph quenched by the cool directness of some minds? Perhaps, at least to the extent that the point of view found sufficient sympathy to be embodied in a convent-woven tapestry and preserved in a church treasury. Doubtless the devout, looking at this panel, added in their own minds the usual reassurance of the period, that suffering here would be recompensed by felicity hereafter; but the tapestry does not take this view. It offers suggestions as to how to make the best of it on this earth by means of friendly regard for others and liberality, a kind of humanism a good two centuries before the Renaissance.

Both the idea and the style of this piece are derived immediately from Byzantium. Constantinople at this time, in reaction from the fervors of the Iconoclasts, had turned with enthusiasm to the Greek and Latin philosophers and in art to the Hellenistic style of the Alexandrian School. The Charlemagne tapestry, though almost certainly woven by Agnes in the convent of Quedlinburg, shows the Byzantine fashion of the moment not only in its Roman materialism and common sense, but also in the essentially Hellenistic figures, draped in formal, classical gowns, that are at once realistic and conventional.

Even more Byzantine is Agnes's masterpiece, which has remained at Quedlinburg. This is not a tapestry, but a knotted pile fabric. It is woven, not like a Persian or Turkish carpet, but rather like the Egyptian carpets of which bits have been found, suggesting that Europe may have learned the technique from that source. A single strand of wool is passed around only one warp once, crossed on top and cut off. Only the compactness of the surface, compressed with a comb, holds the strand crossed. One such "knot" is looped around every other warp in one row, and around the other alternates in the next row, and between is a single weft woven in and out to hold the warps together. Originally the fabric was very shaggy, with a pile three-quarters of an inch deep, but about a century ago it was shaved down to show the brighter colors underneath so that now it is only about a third of an inch deep.

The subject seems, at first, rather random. Originally it was a big carpet, twenty-six feet long and twenty wide, with the field divided into five horizontal bands. In the top row is the marriage of Pietas, the son of Sacerdotum, with Justitia, the daughter of Imperium. The young man, in a violet cloak, patterned in red and white crosses, and a yellow gown, embraces the maiden who is in a green dress, her hair flowing about her shoulders. Sacerdotum, in a red cope over a green dalmatic, wearing a mitre and holding a crozier, is enthroned on the right; Imperium in a red cloak and blue gown, on the left. He holds a scroll inscribed *Juste judica,* judge justly. Three Virtues attend: Fortitudo, a young man in a red cloak and yellow gown, holding a sword; Prudentia, a young woman with flowing hair, in a green cloak and violet gown, holding a snake, and Temperencia, a woman in a yellow dress pouring water out of a jug. The right end of the strip is missing. Probably the other two Virtues, Hope and Charity, stood there.

The next two bands show the Marriage of Mercury and Philologia. The allegory, taken from Martian, the North African writer of the beginning of the fifth century, was popular in the Middle Ages, serving often as a text book. Mercury, who is here the personification of Reason, a young man, nude save for a draped mantle, wishes to marry, and considers Manteca (Divination), Psyche (the soul), and Sophia (Wisdom). The three young princesses stand before him, the first in blue, the second in green and the third in lavender. But with all he is unsuccessful. He meets, however, Philologia, a young girl, who masters all learning, and Hymen presides at the meeting, a priest with the triple tiara.

[33]

The actual wedding takes place in the row below. Mercury, in a brown gown, is enthroned. Philologia, likewise in brown, is led up by her mother, Phronesis (Good Sense), who wears a massive gold collar and pectoral. Genus serves as scribe to write the marriage contract, and finally Chaste Love points to the marriage bed, while Labor leans down from the sky to assure Philologia that she will ever be divine.

The marriage bed is a charming piece of furniture and gives a welcome glimpse into the domesticity of a time that we are too prone to think of as a century of cathedral building, forgetting that to the people of every age life is primarily an affair of housekeeping, having nice furniture and the right clothes and making good marriages. It is the kind of bed, of excellent simple design and sturdy construction, that persisted in country furniture, especially in that other Saxon country, England, until machines destroyed tradition and character. And Phronesis, and Agnes, were good housewives, for the bed has a nice purple cover and a blue pillow with white corners, put on with a neat bit of fancy work.

These two strips follow Martian quite exactly and the authorship is emphasized by a portrait of Martian himself, seated holding a scroll at the beginning of the tale. It is the first of a series of " author's " portraits in tapestry (cf. p. 214).

The next band is altogether lacking. Perhaps it showed the Arts and Sciences who followed in Philologia's train, a device adopted by Martian to include a condensed encyclopaedia which made his book one of the most popular texts in mediaeval schools. The bottom band, however, is two-thirds complete and introduces still a third subject. Cyprus, the ancient fecundity earth goddess, in a green dress, rises from the earth between two plants, a palm and a vine (Pl. 6). She holds a wheel which is supported by a lad, also in green, who kneels before her, Love. On the left are the Laughing Heavens, Autumn, and Spring, three young women, the last blowing a horn; on the right, is a naiad pouring water from a jar. The rest is missing.

What prompted the choice of these subjects when Agnes directed the nuns before the great loom? The Marriage of Mercury and Philologia was a favorite theme throughout these cen-

PLATE VI

DETAIL OF A KNOTTED CARPET. Germany, 12th century

Quedlinburg Cathedral. See p. 34

turies. Two hundred years earlier, Hedwig, Duchess of Swabia, had given to the monks of Saint Gall some vestments that she had embroidered herself, including a white stole worked in gold with scenes from the same allegory.

The goddess Cyprus in the bottom band might also be sympathetic to the nuns. She has a far more ancient history. Three thousand years before Christ the Sumerians, focussing on the principle of fertility, formulated the idea of such a goddess (cf. p. 5). Thereafter she appeared in the succeeding civilizations under many names: Nina, Nana, Ishkana, Ninharsag, Isis, Astarte, Cybele, Demeter, and, in one special aspect, Venus. She had, as her male associate, sometimes a brother, more often a son. She is variously represented, but in many forms she wears a long robe and a crown. She was a dominant figure in the Pantheon which the Germanic tribes brought with them into Europe. She is the Freya of the Scandinavians (cf. p. 53).

She lingered on so persistently in the German mind that the Christian church had to accept her in the guise of local saints. Sometimes she is merged with the Virgin herself so that, in districts where the old fertility goddess had been primarily a tree goddess, there is a cult of Our Lady of the Oak or of the Linden. Indeed, the original Virgin is in essence this same principle, the Mother of God linked mystically to her son so that they become joint objects of the worship of life eternal, for fertility in the ancient concept was life, the force of life. Thus when these local tree goddesses were fused with Mary the mother of Jesus, it only meant that Nana or Ishtar, or whatever name one chooses for the earlier embodiment of the principle, was coming unto herself through two divergent but parallel lines of development, one through the Central European tribes, the other through the Near East.

But in addition to such concealed survivals as phases of the Virgin or as local women saints, the fertility goddess was also carried on in Christian times in her original form. She appears as the Earth on Carolingian ivories. During the close connection between Germany and Italy under the Ottonians, German themes were carried into distant Italian monasteries. Hence Mother Earth in much the same form, which is practically the form she had had in Mesopotamia four thousand years earlier, appears in manuscripts of southern Italy of the eleventh and twelfth centuries.

Here, then, is the Mother Goddess of all ages, attended by one of her handmaidens, a naiad, and by the Seasons. The Abbess might, without conscious reasoning, have found the subject to her taste for she was herself profiting, in her independence and power, so contrary to the spirit of her age, by a lingering respect for women of the priestess class which she owed to the latent memory of the Great Goddess. But what about the third subject in the tapestry, the marriage of the children of the Church and the State, and why this combination of themes?

The records tell us that this tapestry was intended as a present to the Pope but that it was never given to him. Frederick of the Red Beard, that handsome blond giant, amiable and violent, astute and full of phantasies, the perfect knight, dreaming of being a greater Charlemagne, true to the contradictions of his character and his times, in his ardent desire to unify the Western Christian empire as a solid whole, had waged a protracted war with the surrogate of Western Christianity, the Popes. Supporting first one and then another anti-Pope in order to hold Italian cities which the recognized Pope was determined to get, Frederick was persistently unsuccessful until at last he was driven to compromise. And, with the accession of the new Pope, Gregory VIII, this compromise became a genuine accord.

This new amity Henry VI inherited when his father died in 1190. Henry, meanwhile, had expanded the family claims on Italy, but without detriment to the Papacy, by marrying Constance, the widowed Queen of Sicily. Now Henry had inherited not only his father's domains and titles but also his large ambitions and unrestrained imagination. When his wife's son, King of Sicily, died, he went in person, in 1194, to take possession of the kingdom, for there was no other male heir; and he found in the Palace of Palermo as part of his booty, the lovely young widowed queen. Instantly his constructive political fancy began building a whole scheme on this charming young person.

She was Irene Angel, daughter of the Basileus of Byzantium. If Henry could bring her within his family he might have a chance of realising his greatest dream of all, of laying hands on the Eastern Empire and thus once more uniting Christendom under one Emperor, one Church. So Irene Angel, a beautiful intelligent girl of sixteen, the child of the most luxurious cultivation the world has yet seen, was married as a political hostage to Henry's younger brother, Duke Philip of Swabia.

Only ambition dictated the marriage, but love was its fruition. Philip, too, was but sixteen, a youth of modest build but with a fair face, blond and fresh, with grace of body and manner and with a delightful wit. The boy and girl were enraptured with each other and, become man and woman, even through bitter troubles they maintained a passionate devotion.

Is not this, then, the theme of this tapestry? For it must be remembered that, by tradition, the Abbess of Quedlinburg had a finger in politics. With this carpet the Pope would be reminded first, that the marriage, the unity, of the Church and State, ever precarious, alone assured all the Christian Virtues to the world, and, second, it would be brought to his attention that when the youth, Mercury (or Philip), a blond boy of medium height, marries a young girl, Philologia (or Irene), a rational order is assured to the world and all blessings flow therefrom. Hence the World, the Earth, for the two Empires were the terrestrial universe to the mind of the time, gives her blessing to both unions, that of the Church and State, and that of the Western and the Eastern Empires.

Perhaps, too, there was an incidental reference to the fact that the wedding of Philip and Irene was in May. For the representation of the Earth goddess was associated in South Italy with the Spring Festival which, to give it Christian sanction, had been translated into the blessing of the Easter candle, accompanied by a curious ritual of pagan flavor which extolled the bees and the spring. This ritual was inscribed on long scrolls, commonly called *Exultet* scrolls from the opening word of the text, and the Earth figure was one of the standard illustrations. Again, the presence of the Earth goddess may have expressed the characteristic marriage blessing, the hope of fecundity, fertility for the union as well as prosperity for the world at large as a result of the political consequences that were expected to

[37]

result from it. It is in its wealth of complex references that allegory realizes its potentialities and falls into its weakness.

In the border of the tapestry were represented various Virtues of which only two now remain: Modesty (Pudicitia) and Kindness (Dulcedo) . These were perhaps attributes of the charming Irene whom a contemporary chronicler described as a rose without thorns, a dove without claws.

The minor figures in the cartoon are inferior in quality, but in the major episodes the style is almost wholly Byzantine, showing the romantic realism of the Alexandrian tradition, so much in favor in Byzance at the time. The drawing does not, however, meet the standards of a first rate artist of Byzantium but seems rather the work of some lesser man or of some artist out of touch with the capital inspiration. Was it, perhaps, adapted from some manuscript painted by a Greek, the work of one of the transplanted Greek illuminators responsible for much of the manuscript decoration of southern Italy for two centuries or more?

This carpet, so pregnant with propaganda, was never given to the Pope. No, for Gregory VIII died and Innocent III succeeded him, and Innocent III was quite another stamp of man, with plans for power of his own. Henry, also, had died in the interval (1197) and Philip was the candidate favored for succession by most of the German princes. Philip had already begun to stretch the web woven by his father over the Eastern domains. Irene's emperor father, Isaac, had been dethroned in a popular revolution. Philip supported her brother for a brief restoration of the house, but the brother was killed, leaving Irene the only heir to the family rights, and this claim Philip was prepared to press on his own behalf. Did Innocent III want to see the imperial power so overshadow his own? Certainly not. Innocent was an Italian noble, proud and authoritative. The Papacy was just at its height. He supported the rival, less dangerous imperial candidate, Otto of Brunswick, and though Philip and Irene were duly crowned King and Queen of the Romans, the papal support was in the end decisive. Thus inevitably the ambition of the brilliant but undisciplined Frederick Barbarossa collapsed of its own excessive inflation, leaving behind the ragged fragments of this curious carpet.

[38]

CHAPTER III

THE NORSEMEN AND
THEIR DESCENDANTS

MEANWHILE another branch of the Teutonic invaders who had settled in the North and had there maintained a point of view and manners of their own had been creating grievous embarrassments for Charlemagne's successors in the West. Immediately after Charlemagne's death, his Empire had fallen apart. Louis the Pious, unable to control, hence anxious to placate, had frittered away his inherited responsibilities and power to his family, to bishops and barons, and to the Pope. Released by his feeble generosity, Germany had affirmed its separate existence and Italy also had gone its own way, so that when Louis was succeeded by his youngest son, Charles the Bald, he controlled less than modern France together with Flanders.

This was, however, but the beginning of the dislocation. Charlemagne had unified his kingdom by force of personal will. It was a coherence externally imposed, not a cohesion. Before France could fuse into a true unity by virtue of its inner sympathies, it had to undergo utmost distraction and distress. The intrusion of these new invaders from the North contrib uted to the disintegration. Not until they were absorbed would France be reintegrated to a strengthened and more balanced national personality.

The Norsemen had come out of the vague hinterland that now is Russia some time in the centuries preceding the Christian era. They had drifted up by slow degrees from the region just above the Black Sea. They were Barbarians, but native to their Iranian racial tradition was a powerful inventive art, intent on the decorative delineation of the fleet strength of animals, a genius that bourgeoned in the magnificent gold and

bronze reliefs of their brothers, the Scythians and the Sarma-
thians. Nor had their innate aesthetic impulse been isolated. A
thousand years before Christ the Phoenicians, trading on the
shores of the Black Sea, had carried into this district the mis-
cellaneous culture of a commercial eclecticism, garnered alike
from Mesopotamia, Asia Minor, the Mediterranean islands, and
the Nile. Later, the Greeks had planted their unemployed in
vacant territory in this vicinity, to serve as outposts of their
rapidly maturing civilization and customers for their wares.
Thus these Teutons, large, blond, heavy of foot, dogged but violent in emotion, bore in their turgid minds shadows of a varied
past.

Like all the Germanic peoples, the Norsemen were fundamentally agriculturists but they had become also valiant sailors,
and it was into their audacious and enterprising seafaring life
that they infused the ruthless militarism of the race. In frail
and shallow craft they conquered the ocean by dint of sheer
courage and skill, appearing without warning on the coasts of
France, pillaging and marauding with lusty cruelty. Then sail-
ing up the rivers, they penetrated the country, eyeing covetously
wider and more permanent riches, the land itself. Pursuant of
this more serious ambition, they became soldiers by land, as
well as sea, then colonists, then diplomats, until by the agree-
ment of Saint Clair sur Epte about 911 they were legal posses-
sors of large territories in north France, in Normandy and the
Cotentin, including such goodly cities as Rouen, Lisieux, and
Bayeux.

The Norsemen had, in their own Scandinavian land, had
tapestry. Bits with figures and trees, of the first half of the ninth
century, were found at Oseberg in a Norse ship that had been
used for the burial of a chief. But the first complete piece, from
a church at Baldishol, dates from the end of the twelfth century.
It represents two of the Months, a favorite theme since the
classical period, which was developed in every medium in the
Middle Ages, the same figures being repeated endlessly, with
only slight changes, though there were also, from time to time,
wholly unorthodox inventions. The tapestry shows April and
May. April is a sad looking gentleman with a pointed beard, in

a gown that is very tight but flares at the cuffs and feet and is slit up the front. In most illustrations of April at this period the personage holds a flower in one or both hands, or even a tree, but here he simply points to heaven and earth and the trees stand on either side of him, thin wavy trunks with trefoil foliage on which perch, precariously, three birds, stiffly at right angles to the ground. May, more interesting, defies the traditions entirely. He should be a falconer, ahorse. He is, instead, a knight in a high pointed bacinet with a long straight nasel, the chain camail continuous with the close clinging coat of mail that protects him to the wrists and to the calves. He holds his reins jauntily in his left hand, while he carries in his right an ogival shield, quartered decoratively, and a spear. His wooden, piebald horse is set to buck, with a wicked look in his eye. Each figure is framed in an arch that is labelled with the title. Above, there is a narrow running reciprocal border, below a wide border with a five fingered palmette on an undulating stem.

The tapestry is crude, grotesque, amusing, but the interesting feature is the treatment of these illustrative themes as textile decoration. In April, the tree breaks up into a complicated geometrical reciprocal and the figure, and especially the birds, so merge with this that the whole constitutes a unified block pattern out of which an interpretation can be analysed rapidly, but which counts primarily as a woven design. Similarly in May the knight rides against a spotted ground which envelops his equally spotted horse and shield, and fuses with the imbricate of his coat of mail so that, whereas April is an invention in angles, May is a composition in dots.

But embroidery was perhaps even more important to the Norsemen than tapestry. The Viking graves have yielded many fragments, usually wool on wool, most often plants and birds in conventional symmetry, but occasionally, too, figures from more ambitious designs; and the Sagas tell of large and elaborate illustrations made in this technique. Thus Gudrun when she "stayed in Denmark for seven seasons (three years and a half) . . . made embroidery, and worked thereon many great deeds and fine games, which were customary at that time, swords and coats of mail and all the outfit of a King, and King Sigismund's

[41]

ships gliding along the shore. They also embroidered how Sigar and Siggeir fought on Fyen. This was their enjoyment." But it was Brynhild who "surpassed in handiwork all other women. She made embroidery with gold, and sewed thereon the great deeds of Sigurd, the slaying of the serpent, the taking of the treasure and Regin's death."

The greatest remaining monument of this art of the Norsemen was found in their new French domains, the so-called " tapestry" of Bayeux. It is a long strip of heavy, coarse linen, embroidered in eight colors of worsted in couching and stem stitches, with the history of the Conquest of England in 1066 by William, Duke of Normandy. First given publicity in the eighteenth century, it caught the attention of Napoleon who used it in 1803 as part of the propaganda preparing for his conquest of England. Since 1729 when Dom Bernard de Montfaucon first drew and published it, it has been the subject of countless discussions, scholarly, pseudo-scholarly, frankly sentimental, and in the guide book style, which mingles random gleanings from all sources.

By 1066 the Norsemen had assumed a place of great importance in France. Six Dukes in direct succession had established peace, definitely repulsed French attempts to retake the territory, extended their domains and built up prosperity and cultivation. Meanwhile England had undergone the same experience as France. The Norsemen had appeared there, too, raiding and destroying, at the end of the eighth century. Later their invasions took on a more serious character, with plans for permanent conquest, and this they effected so completely at the opening of the eleventh century (victory of Swein, King of Denmark, 1013) that thereafter the King himself was a Norseman, Cnut, hero of legend (1016–1035).

When William came to power in Normandy there was on the English throne Edward the Confessor, son of the Saxon king Ethelred, who had preceded Cnut, but with a Norse mother, Emma, daughter of the second Duke of Normandy. Edward, moreover, had long been an exile in Normandy so that he had strong Norman sympathies. He was without heir so that his successor was problematic. The choice lay between

Harold, son of the leader of the Saxon nobles, candidate of the anti-Norman party, and William, whose claim was based only on the assertion that Edward had promised to leave him the crown.

In the many publications on this embroidery the problems most bitterly disputed have been, as is the way with art historians being learned, date and provenance. Odo, Bishop of Bayeux and half brother of William the Conqueror, plays an honorable part in the story as depicted. But Odo, ambitious and unscrupulous, fell from William's good grace in 1082. So it is deduced that the embroidery must have been made before then, even hazarded that it was prepared for the dedication of the Cathedral of Bayeux in 1077. But Robert, whose character was even more unsavoury than that of his uncle Odo, restored Odo to favor after William's death in 1087, so that the embroidery might equally well have been made then. Other scholars have labored to show that it must antedate 1095, for short tunics, such as appear on William's men, were out of fashion by then. But actually the dated monuments which we have from this time are too few to establish any assurance that all good men at arms lengthened their tunics after a given year.

The provenance has been contested with equal dogma and futility. Was it made in England? Quite possibly, for the English women were already famous for needlework. But Agnes of Blois had a hanging showing the history of William from the death of Edward the Confessor, with legends explaining each episode. Probably, then, it is " French." No, indeed, " English," for the Ð is drawn in an " Anglo-Saxon " style and Bayeux is called Bagias as in " Anglo-Saxon " records.

But really the Channel was of no importance at all in this case, and whether the needle was plied on one side or the other of those few miles of water is insignificant. For the thing itself is essentially Norse. A number of closely related embroideries of the same period are known and all are Scandinavian. Some of these pieces are cruder in execution, notably a series from Skag which are of about the twelfth century, but others are quite up to the standard of the Bayeux work and very similar in general effect, especially a twelfth-century example from

[43]

Höylandet in Norway, showing the Adoration of the Magi. The Bayeux piece was certainly not executed in Norway. Probably it was worked right there in Normandy. But it was the creation of a mentality which, however many generations the stock had been away from the Fatherland, was still essentially Norse. It is Norse in general character, in specific features of the illustration, in details of the style, and, most important of all, in idea.

For the true theme of the embroidery of Bayeux is the central motive of the Norse code, the sanctity of the oath. The embroidery shows William conquering England, but it illustrates this moral. William may be the hero, but Harold as the villain is of exactly equal importance, and the real protagonist is Perjury. Thus while the embroidery depicts facts, the subject is not history but fable, true episodes but fitted to the demonstration of an idea. Hence it seems improbable that the piece was made very soon after the event. Before the story could have taken such a form it had to become a tale that was told. This consideration, as well as the relation with the Scandinavian work in both tapestry and embroidery, makes an attribution to the twelfth century seem reasonable.

The Norse law revolved about the dependability of the oath and the oath was incorporated into the religion so that it had the deeper emotional hold of sanctity. Not only did the solidarity of the Norse state depend on the inviolability of the oath, but the whole system of justice devolved on sworn testimony. Norse literature constantly returns to the theme of the sacred oath and the loathsome oath breaker. There was no absolution from this delinquency, no temptation, however overwhelming, that might be pled in extenuation, and the higher born the man, the more inflexible the obligation. The Bayeux embroidery is the warning story of a broken oath and the penalty that was paid.

The story starts with Harold talking to Edward the Confessor and it has been assumed that Edward is dispatching him to tell William that he will be the next King of England, though there is no title to specify this. Harold and his companions set off ahorse but come to a church which they enter to worship. Harold's perfidy will be the more vivid if it is made clear that

[44]

he observes all the external pieties. They banquet on the shore and then embark in their boats, but by mischance land in the domains of Guy de Ponthieu who exercises his customary right, and holds them for ransom. This was merely the eleventh-century version of detention at the port of entry for lacking a proper visa. William is informed and sends emissaries to negotiate Harold's release, one of them Turold, probably the Constable of Bayeux. By a queer error three episodes have been reversed here so that the messengers arrive before they have started. Turold from this point on takes, apparently, the role of prudent and faithful counsellor, providing both anticipatory warning of the catastrophe and a foil to Harold.

Guy de Ponthieu delivers Harold to William who leads him to his castle. Thus Harold, in accepting rescue and hospitality, seals for the first time the bond of loyalty to William. William then holds council, a scene usually described as a ceremonial audience for Harold. The visitors from England stand on the right and beside William's seat is Turold, gesturing to point, it would seem, a warning. The council evidently has to do with the betrothal of Harold to William's daughter Edwiga, for in the next scene she appears, learning the news from a clerk. In this betrothal, Harold, by becoming potentially a part of his family, for the second time commits himself to William, for in the Norse social system the ties of family loyalty were especially sacred.

Among the Norsemen a guest was expected to fight for his host like one of the host's own retainers, so when William starts on an expedition against Brittany, an independent Duchy with which Normandy was constantly at swords' points, Harold accompanies him. Harold shows himself a worthy man at arms, indeed a hero, for he rescues some of the Normans from treacherous quicksands. The moral will have greater force if some of Harold's good qualities are brought out. Moreover this and the success of the expeditions at Dole, Rennes, and Dinant (all three battles are illustrated) give the occasion for the climax of this episode when William knights Harold in the field. Here is the third obligation of good faith binding Harold to William.

The army returns to Bayeux, and now comes the turning point of the drama. Harold swears the oath of allegiance. The

[45]

scene has the solemn formality that always accompanied great oaths in the Norse world. William sits in official state on his high seat, wrapped in his cloak of nobility, holding his naked sword. He is attended by two of his men, one of them evidently Turold who is again making a decisive gesture, marking the significance of the event. Harold stands between two small altars filled with relics, hands outstretched above them, giving his sacred word.

Harold then goes home to England and makes his report to King Edward who immediately thereafter dies. The second turning point of the story follows at once. Three men representing the Anglo Saxon nobles come to offer Harold the kingly power, symbolised by three emblems: a staff, a crown, and a battle axe. Will he succumb to temptation or maintain his word and honor? In the next scene Harold is crowned by Archbishop Stigant, and his subjects, raising their naked swords above their heads, swear fealty. The populace outside acclaims enthusiastically. But there is a moment of strain, hesitation, warning. Whoever composed this story understood the professional tricks of the drama. He introduces suspense, which is also anticipation, by showing the same crowd that had been gaping and cheering at the coronation, swung around to watch, startled and arrested, Halley's comet, blazing a fiery trail across the sky. The pause is continued. Harold can still save his honor and himself. A messenger rushes to tell him of the alarming portent. But Harold, rising from his throne, with violent emphasis reasserts his position (Pl. 7). The die is cast and the action now builds up to the catastrophe.

Messengers cross the channel to tell William what has happened, and he at once gives orders that a fleet be built. Trees are hewn, keels laid, the ships are launched, arms and supplies are loaded, and the Norman army sets sail. On the coast of England, under the direction of Wadard the equerry, provisions are commandeered from the frightened peasants and a great banquet is prepared and served. Throughout Norse literature a banquet precedes every great emprise. Then William takes solemn counsel with his brothers Odo and Robert while his soldiers build a camp. One of his men who has been sent to

PLATE VII

Bayeux Museum. See p. 46

DETAIL OF THE BAYEUX EMBROIDERY. Norman, probably 12th century

reconnoitre comes to report, and the first open act of war is committed. Two of the Normans burn down a house. Incendiarism was a formally recognized gesture of revenge among the Norsemen, and true to the code, a woman and child are here escaping, for the innocent were never allowed to perish.

The rest of the embroidery is given over to the Battle of Hastings (October 1066). The knights ride forward. A herald, Vital, communicates between the two enemies, giving formal announcement of the impending contest, challenge and reply, a Norse custom. The combat is engaged and proceeds in mounting fury. Two of Harold's brothers are killed. The catastrophe is moving to a climax. But again the action hesitates for suspense. The Norman troops falter, Odo must urge them on. William raises his visor to disprove the rumor that he has come to grief and the attack is launched again with renewed élan. Calamity comes rapidly to the English. Turold is seen in the thick of the fight, cutting down the men around him, re-echoing his theme, warning and fidelity. The climax is here. Harold is killed and his men escape in panic flight.

On either side of the strip is a border, with varied designs that serve, in part, as a chorus, underlining and expanding the main theme. Thus from the moment of Harold's departure from England the prophetic note is sounded in a half dozen scenes from Aesop's fables illustrating shrewd cunning, treachery, ingratitude, disastrous ambition, greed: the fox and the crow; the wolf and the lamb; the wolf and the crane; the hawk and the tortoise; the lion, the heifer, the goat and the sheep hunting the stag.

Two episodes a little further on mark the time of the year. It is the month of May when William rescues Harold, for peasants are plowing and sowing, while gentlemen are flying their hawks. Then Harold's perfidy is explained as a phase of original sin. Adam sins with Eve and, a bit further on, Cain kills Abel. These two groups of figures have been wordily and aimlessly discussed, and usually, a revealing comment on the modern mind, their naïve directness has been called, not merely lewd, but even pornographic.

The note of shrewd cunning is sounded again, with a repetition of the fox and the crow, when William and Harold leave for the Brittany campaign. Then the choral commentary lapses until just before the catastrophe when it reopens with a repetition of the Adam and Eve, Cain and Abel scenes, slightly modified, like the recurrence in inversion of a musical theme. And then the fables begin again: the lion and the ass twice, the fox and the goat again, and then twice, just as the battle is being engaged, a cat stealing a fowl. This, as will be seen, is especially pointed.

Most of these episodes have been in the lower border. In the upper border there is another specific reference. Just as William sends for Harold there are two cocks, one golden, the other dark red. To the Norsemen, cocks were heralds of doom. A cock with a golden crest and a deep red cock from the netherworld would crow together to announce the end of the world. Peter's cock crowed thrice.

From time to time the main scenes overrun the margins. Thus all through the Battle of Hastings the lower border is used to show the advance of foot soldiers, the dead and the plundering of bodies. But aside from these spaces and from the fable and other illustrations, the rest of the border design consists of animals, almost always symmetrically confronted in pairs, usually flanking a tree.

This design, of animals, birds or fantastic beasts, flanking in balanced reversal a plant which is usually on a hill or mound, has had the longest and widest continuous history of any motive in the whole world of art. It was already well established when the Sumerians lived at Ur. Scandinavian peasants were still carving it in wood at the end of the nineteenth century, may, indeed, be doing it even today. In the five or six thousand year interval it has been used throughout the ancient East, in Greece, the Far East, India, through a sequence of civilizations in Russia and variously in all the countries of western Europe; it has served as symbol in the primitive Eastern religions and been adapted by both Buddhism and Christianity, and it has recurred in almost every medium of the decorative arts just as a convenient and effective pattern.

The two hundred examples of this motive in varying forms

on the Bayeux embroidery have always been considered merely decorative, but a closer consideration of many of the animals shown seems to indicate that they were, for the most part, not chosen at random. Hawks and leopards predominate in almost equal balance; there are many geese, some lions and a scattering of other beasts.

Now the Norse believed that every man had his *fylgja* or guardian spirit which took the form of an animal indicative of his character. Certain animals were especially associated with chieftains, notably the Raptores. Harold leaves England carrying his hawk, proudly wearing its grillets. He may be only taking with him his equipment for the hunt, for he is accompanied by a pack of hounds also; but, on the other hand, when Guy de Ponthieu comes to seize him, Guy has no hawk, yet when he leads Harold off, prisoner, he carries a hawk belled, while Harold's hawk, now bereft of its grillets, rides on his hand, turned backward. Are these not symbols of conquest and defeat? It seems quite probable, for when Harold is again a free man, ransomed by William and riding to his castle, his hawk, once more with its grillets, is returned to its proper position on his fist. Furthermore, when Harold lands in his own domain there are hawkheads carved on the ends of the roof beam of the castle and a large hawk head over the portico. And his throne in his own palace, after the coronation, has hawk heads carved on the back, while during his oath taking, a pair of hawks roost under his feet, and again during his momentous decision to hold to the crown, another pair of hawks rest on his palace roof.

William's thrones, on the other hand, are carved with leopard heads, as is the door of his house where his daughter stands to hear of her betrothal and also the stern of the ship in which he sends Harold home, as well as some of the vessels in his expedition of revenge, though not all, for many chieftains contributed to that fleet. Therefore if Harold is the hawk and William the leopard, when, in the border just at the beginning of the Battle of Hastings, a cat seizes a bird, William's conquest of Harold is predicted.

The goose seems to belong to Turold, the faithful and warn-

[49]

ing counsellor, for it is emblazoned on his shield.[1] The goose on account of its warning cry is associated with portents by the northern peoples. Finally, the lion, which is far less frequent and is most conspicuous at the beginning, evidently belongs to Edward the Confessor, for both of his thrones are carved with lion heads and they ornament the prow of two of the ships in which he sends Harold to Normandy, the stern carving of one being, apparently, Edward's own portrait head. Guy de Ponthieu's emblem, judging from the carving on his high seat, is a levrier, but this does not appear in the border, a fitting omission since he plays so small a part.

Actual chairs of about this period, carved with animal heads, are preserved in the Copenhagen Museum. It is a type of decoration that goes back to the Ancient Eastern predecessors of the Norsemen's culture in their original home, for animal head finials appear on a seat in one of the bas-reliefs of Nineveh. Moreover the use of animal emblems, which antedates true heraldry, also goes back to early Eastern sources. From Sumerian times on, every god had his animal attributes, and these were usually represented with him as a mark of identification or even substituted for him, when the iconography had to be compact, as on a seal. Since the King was a surrogate of God he, too, assumed such emblems, and so the custom developed in the course of time, though the exact history would be difficult to trace.

A few of the exceptional animals in the borders are interesting, just because they are ambiguous. Thus when William holds council, after he has accepted Harold as his guest, two peacocks perch on the roof. The peacock has a long history as a bird of ill omen. It appears nowhere else in the embroidery. Is it not another note of warning? Far more curious is the bull-man, the torso of a man on the hindquarters of a bull. He appears twice in immediate succession, his arms flung wide, just as William is sending for Harold, immediately before the two cocks of doom. The bull-man in this and many other forms is Gilgames-Enkidu of the Ancient East. The Norsemen knew the theme, for he appears in one of his most characteristic attitudes, with a lion on either side, on a gold pendant of the fourth century

[1] Less clearly in one instance where it has become fantastic and ambiguous.

from the Bangstrup find. In the ancient mythology he, too, was a figure of fatality, reminder of inescapable death. Had he kept any such meaning among the Norse? Again, there are the griffons, sufficiently frequent (there are fifteen pairs of them) to suggest that they were the *fylgja* of some minor character. This phantasy creature also goes back to Sumerian times, but it played an especially important part among the Scyths as a guardian. One animal episode in the border is obviously pure comedy, a setter barking valiantly at a spitting cat.

The embroidery gives many other interesting glimpses of Norse traditions. The famous Viking ships are particularly well depicted, a shallow hull with high curving prow and stern carved with animal heads, with one mast terminating in a cup-shaped crow's nest. They are an almost exact copy of the boats which the Phoenicians used two millenniums before and which were still in use in India about the Christian era. The Sanchi tope shows a ship which might almost be a Viking craft, with an upswinging prow composed of a griffon with lion head and paws, eagle beak and wings, and a high stern in the form of a fish tail, hung with a garland. The Norsemen painted their boats in many colors, as the embroidery shows, and they had one great square sail, " the tapestry of the mast," made of wool, also bright colored, often striped, as in the embroidery, some-times even trimmed with fur.

William's ship is particularly fine. It was the Mora, given by his queen Mathilde. On the tall prow, curved with a most gallant swing, is a lion head, perhaps her emblem; on the stern is the figure of a boy, blowing a horn. At the mast head is a lantern to guide the other ships at night, and above that a cross to announce the Pope's sanction of William's mission.

The Norsemen's horses are particularly striking. William's own mount, evidently bred of Oriental stock, had been brought to him from Spain, and apparently this was the equine ideal of the Norsemen, for all their animals are of the same general conformation, with a small domed head on a very long neck. Most of them, moreover, are, like the horse of the knight representing May in the Norwegian tapestry (cf. p. 41), fantastically piebald. Multicolored destriers with conspicuous mark-

[51]

ings were so much admired in the twelfth century that the
heroes of the romances of the time are commonly described as
mounted on animals of this type. It has even been suggested
that the horses must have been painted. The fashion certainly
came from the East where it had prevailed at least as early as
the Sasanian period (222–650 A.D.), for silks of that origin show
splashed and spotted polychrome horses. The horses in the
Bayeux embroidery might almost have been copied from Persian models, so true to type are they in their pied contrasts of
color.

The palaces shown in the embroidery are exceedingly interesting, with their vaulted halls or arcaded galleries, the
roofs domed and turreted, the walls patterned in polychrome
stones, and the columns richly colored. These Norsemen, too,
had looked to Byzantium to learn how a king should build his
home (cf. p. 27).

When Edward is being buried the cortège is accompanied by
two boys, ringing bells. This custom can still be seen in the
funerals of some of the more remote villages of Normandy. At
the church where the burial service is to be held a boy is climb-
ing on the roof to set up a golden cock, bird of fate and finality.

In the Battle of Hastings neither side carries the emblem of
the leader but each has a special flag. William's is the one sent
by the Pope in token of his support, emblazoned with the cross.
Most of the English soldiers, on the other hand, have on their
shields another form of cross, as they did when they appeared
at William's court. But Harold has the Wessex battle banner in
the form of a serpent or " dragon," made to inflate with the
wind as it blows out from the end of a spear as if the real beast
itself were keeping watch. Dragon banners had been in use in
the Ancient East and among the Scythians, and the custom was
imitated by the Romans. Whether the Norse brought the idea
with them from their former home near the Scythians, or
whether they copied it, rather, from the Romans, is not clear,
but realistically shaped banners that expanded in the wind were
one of their traditions, and they took various forms. So Sigurd's
mother made him a banner when he went to war. " It was in
the shape of a raven, and when the wind blew on it it seemed

[52]

as if it spread its wings." Both the dragon and the raven were attributes of Odin, God of War.

The peasants of all the Scandinavian countries have been tapestry weavers and tapestry has held, also, an honored place among the home industries of the Germans and the German-Swiss. The Scandinavians and Germans have been, moreover, the only peasants of Europe to develop this weave to a major place among the domestic crafts. Did it occupy this important place in these countries where the population had remained closest to the traditions of the Teutonic invaders because it was one of the arts that they had brought with them from their original country? They had carried many ideas and memories into Europe from their land north of the Black Sea with its eastern heritages. Thus the Mesopotamian fertility god who had a sister sharing his functions (cf. pp. 5, 35) is parallelled by the Norse deities Frey and Freya, a brother and sister, and the latter assumed, in addition to her fertility significance, the patronage of romantic love, like the later versions of Astarte. Thor was the Thunderer, and the Great God of the ancient East had been in some versions the God of Thunder. Thor's hammer was an object of veneration and a protective amulet. The Minoans worshiped as symbol of a god, an axe. And so on in many details. Was tapestry weaving also carried by them from the East into Europe in their cultural kit?

If so, whence had it come into that distant region vaguely called Scythia? The Scythic culture was an extension of that of the Iranian plateau and the earliest tapestries known, far antedating the Teutonic migrations, seem to have been woven in the Iranian centre, Elam (cf. p. 2). But such remote origins can be considered only speculatively.

The Norwegian trick, already noted in the panel of the Months (cf. p. 41), of converting an illustration into a semi-conventional decorative design out of which the realistic elements emerge, continues in the later peasant work. Persons materialize out of compositions of blocks, angles, and dots so that a close geometrical structure proves, for example, to be a king and his court.

There are four such designs, all of which date back at least

[53]

to the seventeenth century, which were repeated times innumerable over a period of two hundred years. One, of which one rendition is dated 1625, has an interlocking design of irregular color areas, terra cotta, gray blue, light green, yellow, white and tan, from which the Magi take shape, trotting up on arched necked rocking horses and kneeling before Mary and her child enthroned on a carved chair, while a procession from Noah's ark, including a donkey-unicorn, frames them in an oval (Pl. 8). In the second, depicting the Marriage at Cana, all the spaces are filled with a close mesh of textile designs, stripes, checks, lozenges, chevrons, and meanders, with the figures in block form fitted into this. An early weaving of this cartoon from Drangedal is dated 1653. The third represents Salome dancing before Herod, and here the figures are mingled by carrying across their clothes similar and continuous designs of dots, diapers or reciprocals. Toro Rasmusdalen of Upper Glimsdal, Böverdalen, wove and signed one of these in 1613. And finally, the especially favored theme of the Wise and Foolish Virgins is illustrated by wooden cut-out figures arranged formally in two horizontal rows like a conventional repeating design, with, however, varying internal details. One rendition of this is dated 1646 but many versions are known, most of them from the eighteenth century, the later examples increasingly geometrical.

Here is an abstract art, uncalculated but perfectly apt because automatically developed from the movement of the bobbins and the weaver's habits of surface decoration. This treatment prevails throughout the native Norwegian work, determining even the more pretentious panels for which the conventional Flemish Renaissance cartoons served as models. Always there is a continuous, interlocking pattern in which the figures are embedded, without fracturing the close textile surface.

With the advent of the Arts and Crafts Movement in the last quarter of the nineteenth century an organized effort was made to revive hand loom tapestry in Norway. The outstanding contemporary school of painting was sympathetic to the medium and the craft tradition had never been wholly obliterated, so that the undertaking had as much success as could be expected

[54]

PLATE VIII

THE ADORATION OF THE MAGI. Norway, 17th century

See p. 54

for such an artificial enterprise. Competent weaving translated conscientiously the paper-doll picture-book style of illustration popular in all the Scandinavian countries at the time, giving pleasant, unimportant decorations of an easy but thin charm. In more recent years modernist movements in painting and decoration, emanating from Paris, have pointed the way to a revival of the principle of the old Norwegian work, with continuous surface patterns into which semi-conventional figures are fitted as a coherent element. Thus a cartoon of a unicorn by Märta Måås-Fjetterström constitutes a textile intarsia strong enough for the solid weave and sufficiently varied in detail to have an intimate interest. But this and all its kin suffer inevitably from the vacancy of unreality, the blankness of a composition theoretically thought out, not created.

In Sweden, although weaving in various shuttle techniques was highly developed from an earlier period, there is no evidence of true tapestry production before the sixteenth century when King Gustave, toward the middle of the century, employed some Flemings. The products of these royal looms are just Flemish tapestries woven away from home. But even the wholly native peasant work, the cushion covers and long narrow pieces for the backs of benches, made by good housewives during the endless winter days to make the farm living room brighter and impress the neighbors, usually show this derivation from a foreign tradition. They are simply Flemish tapestries made primitive because peasant fingers are thick.

The commonest design is a mass of crudely vivid flowers, especially red and yellow streaked tulips, in a large scale, crowded mosaic, with animals and birds fitted in, on a black ground. They are a coarsened and disorganized version of the large scale floral verdure of the early Renaissance, effective because of the direct energy and unselfconscious vitality which makes peasant art attractive in a strained and complicated world. Most of these pieces date from the eighteenth century, though the tradition is obviously older and some examples may be from the century before. A dispersed version of essentially the same design shows the elements separated and presented as a powdered pattern. In certain parts of Sweden these designs are rendered in finger weaving, the most primitive tapestry technique, in which the threads are both inserted and pressed into place directly with the fingers.

There is, also, a large group of eighteenth-century cushion covers with a stiff wreath surrounding a scene, usually an Annunciation, with flat, wooden figures. This style suffers from tonal poverty, for the dyes are almost always limited to dirty brown and inert greens, outlined with lustreless black: In still another style, figures in block silhouette are fitted into a rigid geometrical framework, a type of pattern doubtless imitated from the Near East. This is a legitimate kind of textile design, directly determined by the medium; but as treated by the Swedish weavers it is emasculated to a fixed blankness. Both this style and the cushion covers of the Annunciation type are apt to have a dry disparateness which would be more appropriate to carved wood. Wall tapestries with figures are comparatively rare in Sweden, but they show always a degeneration of the Flemish style.

Tapestry was woven all over Germany and Switzerland and there is a basic similarity in all the work; but it can be divided with reasonable distinctness into four main districts — Switzerland, the Upper Rhine including Alsace, the Middle Rhine, and Nuremberg and the vicinity.

The Swiss tapestries are for the most part strikingly decorative. In one outstanding type large fabulous beasts introduced from heraldry into a fairy tale world, are shown in charge of dainty little doll people, against a close ground of leaves and flowers, predominantly in a strong contrast of almost complementary red and green. The warders of this elaborate menagerie are frequently wild people, covered with a curly haired hide. Often there are long swinging scrolls, conveying, in letters of black and red, the story of the piece. In another style men and women in heavy brocades stand on either side of a fountain or tree, like wood-cut fashion plates, while in still another group larger saints, like carved wood sculptures, are placed against huge patterned damask, often under architectural canopies.

One favorite theme recurs frequently in Switzerland and also in Germany, the Hunt of the Unicorn. This elusive animal,

PLATE IX

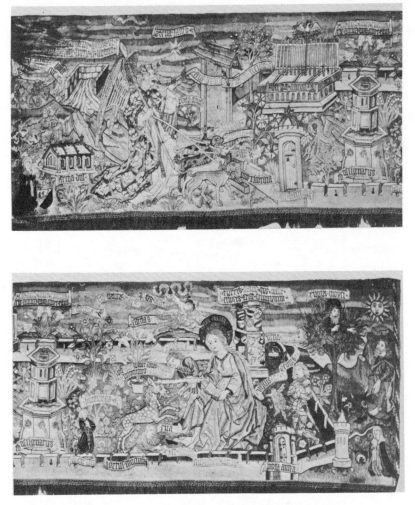

THE HUNT OF THE UNICORN. Switzerland, late 15th century
Historisches Museum, Zürich. See p. 57

whose mythical status was disputed until a few years ago, was never questioned in the Middle Ages. He lived in some remote country, usually in that same ambiguous region where dwelt the equally mysterious Prester John. His horn was a general panacea but was most important as an antidote for poison or even detector of its lurking dangers. The horn was, however, as hard to come by as it was greatly to be desired, for no ordinary hunter, whatever his prowess, could bag this prey. The unicorn could be trapped only with one lure, a perfect virgin. To her he would yield himself willingly, laying his head with its long horn in her lap. Then, were the virgin ready to betray him, he could be seized.

This Ancient Eastern legend, which had many ramifications and variations dating back to at least the second millennium before Christ, was assimilated, in the early centuries of the Church, to a Christian significance that exploited the erotic implication, sublimating it. The virgin was the Virgin Mary, the pure milk white unicorn was Christ, his submission the Incarnation and Annunciation, with the Immaculate Conception shadowed in the background. Around this focus were assembled all the attributes of the Virgin, the emblems of the litanies from the Song of Songs and the Old Testament parallels, a gradual accretion of symbol and allegory.

The subject in its most complete and complex form appears in a tapestry in the Zurich Museum (Pl. 9). The Virgin, a jointed doll with long, crimped flax hair and red disk cheeks, sits in the Garden Enclosed, which is shut in with a circular wall built of blocks, with a tiny Golden Gate made of fancy blocks. In the background are two little houses built of square plain blocks, of equal size, though one is the altar whereon Aaron's Rod bursts into leaf and the other is the Tower of David. Between them is an iris for Charity, the Rose without Thorns of Humility and the lily of Chastity. In the centre of the garden is the Fountain of Life flowing out in three streams, and beside it nests the Pelican feeding her three young. In a far corner is the Cup of Gold. In the sky on one side is the Star of the Sea and on the other Aurora, the sun. Behind the Virgin kneels Gideon with his Fleece; outside is Moses with the Burn-

[57]

ing Bush. On the left, outside, is the Lioness licking her three cubs and the Ark of the Covenant with the Four Rivers of Paradise flowing below. Within the garden on that side is Gabriel, the hunter, sounding his horn, with his four hounds in leash: Truth, Justice, Peace, and Compassion. He has driven the unicorn straight to the Virgin who has seized his horn, while the dove of the Holy Ghost descends toward her, closely followed by the miniature Christ child carrying his cross. Meanwhile, however, Adam has speared the unicorn in the side and Eve is catching the sacred blood in a chalice, recalling Mary Magdalen.

Here, in these delightful nursery figures that might be illustrating any fairy tale, are compacted the whole theory and ethics of the Christian Church: the Fall and Redemption; the Church (the Pelican and the Lioness) and Communion (the blood caught in the chalice); the Messianic expectation, implied by the anticipation of the Old Testament figures; the Trinity (there are three flowers of Virtue, three streams from the Fountain of Life, three young feeding at the Pelican's breast and three lion cubs); the seven Virtues, though they are not the traditional ones; the Resurrection, for Gabriel winds his horn.

The tapestry is dated 1480 but another weaving of exactly the same cartoon, but without the donors who appear on the Zurich piece, and lacking minor episodes on the left, passed through the auction market in Paris twenty-five years ago; and this was dated 1563. The cartoon remained in use eighty-three years.

In the Upper Rhine work the subjects are often illustrations of elaborate romances. Here wild people are especially active. They hold court, wage war and make love in adventurous plots that more than ever demand the banderolles to clarify the complications. But in spite of these fantastic subjects, there is, in general, more effort in this district toward realism. The tendency is away from decoration in the direction of illustration as a more literal record, until in some later and more pretentious pieces the designer goes beyond realism to caricature, a development that appears also in German panel painting of this period.

[58]

A piece from this part of Germany in the Colmar Museum gives an amusing and typical before-during-and-after Fountain of Youth scene. The Fountain of Youth was a popular obsession for forty-five hundred years, from the Sumerian period through the Renaissance. The tapestry shows first, both above and below, the aged and infirm arriving. Some are still strong enough to come on horseback, but one is hobbling on crutches; another is borne on a litter, praying hopefully; still another poor old thing is pushed in a wheelbarrow, while one bearded patriarch, himself venerable, carries his little old wife in a basket on his back.

They all enter a turreted gate on the left that leads into a circular paved court with the Fountain in the centre. They peel off their clothes, climb over the high curb into the water, and so stimulating is the magic bath, that their hair grows instantly into thick curls, they chatter and gesticulate excitedly and immediately after they hasten to the banquet table to satisfy their rekindled appetites. The rest of the tapestry is missing.

In the Middle Rhine district the ground patterns of foliage, flowers and vines becomes heavier, more curling and more scalloped so that in some of these pieces the slim little paper dolls are about to be crushed in the ornament. There is, too, a conspicuous use of heraldry, so important to the Germans with their Teutonic consciousness of the family organization and their pride of race.

But the really fine tapestry of the native German style was woven in and around Nuremberg. The earliest pieces that can be attributed to this district go back well into the fourteenth century. The earliest known piece, in the City Museum of Freiburg, has a conventional repeating pattern, interlocked scalloped lozenges, carrying, alternately, addossed regardant parakeets flanking a flower, and a humorous, bestiary creature, that varies a little in the different repeats, but is always both appealing and genuinely funny. The pattern is derived from the East but has been largely recast in the European taste. This conventional design is skilled in drawing and refined in decorative effect, but the earliest figure pieces from this district are rather uncertain, sometimes downright crude. Yet the Prophets on a long band in the Saint Lawrence Church of Nuremberg, however awkward, have biblical dignity, and their full, thin mantles flow and swing in rhythmic waves and folds.

By the first quarter of the fifteenth century, the Nuremberg tapestries, though still naïve, have real feeling, sometimes a fine spiritual elevation and impressive sincerity. The Nuremberg weavers never attempted sophistication and never achieved elegance, but their work, widely varying in quality but with a certain common character nevertheless, was always stamped with genuineness. The childish and primitive style continued throughout the Germanic countries without any fundamental modifications into the eighteenth century. Then by degrees the growing uniformity of fashion discouraged the craft, and none of the efforts at revival have met success.

CHAPTER IV

THE FOURTEENTH CENTURY

A CHILD, tasting the bitter sting of unjust punishment, helpless in the face of adult power, his pathetic trust shattered, takes refuge from deception and defeat in dreams of vindication and reward. When he grows up — and the compensatory visions become more real than the aching present and his hurt.

The Jews, impressionable and emotionally unstable in a difficult world, put their trust in God. They were the chosen people. Jehovah would take care of his own. But political defeat and suffering and, above all, the persecutions of the Maccabaean Age (second century B.C.) drove them, bruised and shaken, into a spiritual corner. And so they began to dream. Seers, of whom the most notable was Daniel, voiced revelations of justice for Israel, punishment for the enemy, the recognition from Jehovah that the Jews really were the elect.

It is easier for a child to dream than an adult. To him, time is still long enough to provide a future sufficiently remote to have the insubstantial shimmer in which dreams take shape. Indeed, the adult can dream whole heartedly only if he is still in part a child, if some overstrained and unappeased emotion has held a portion of his mind in immaturity. And even then he is inhibited, for to the adult the future is nothing but another, not very distant present, an embarrassment which he can solve only by putting his dreams outside of time, in another dimension. All of the Jewish revelations show hopes fulfilled in a moment of eternity, beyond this acrid present, in a universe above terrestrial despair.

Driven by fear and hope combined, the dream takes shape, clothed in oblique images and masking symbolism, and the utterance comes forth, lulling reason with rhythm, in measured, sonorous phrase. Strangeness, mystery and rich cadences quiet any disturbing criticism from common sense, and the dreamer assures himself, his people, the generations, of the ultimate solace of his raw and bleeding pride. In proportion as the wound is subtle, the healing phantasies will be evanescent, complex, perhaps even extravagant. The child that has been beaten may gloat simply on his own future brutality, but the child whose secret inner sensibility has been exposed and scarred weaves a more devious vengeance and indirect ultimate success.

John the Presbyter, a Jew, nerves vibrant and close to the surface of a thin, pale skin, sat on the Island of Patmos and saw the faith of his fathers, the one glory of Israel, falling into perversion, abasing itself in vile association with creeds without the Law, sinking in disrepute. Paul had boasted that he had penetrated the " deep things of God," rekindling the ever-glowing mystic urge to Gnostic speculation in the Jewish breast. For half a millennium the Jews had bound themselves into secret societies to plumb Reality, envisioning the ultimate, God and his nature, his creations and emanations, and making magic with their cosmogonic insights, manipulating especially the potent numbers of Chaldean fame. Such magic, borrowed from the practices of Babylon and Persia, led the adepts to loiter perilously near infidelity to the high, ascetic monotheism of their race. Now in the first century, A.D., in a world grown tired equally with struggle and satiety, Paul had breathed his inspiration on the embers, so that Gnostic practices were running riot through the churches of Asia. To be sure, Judaism had never condemned speculative mysticism; but this was a degenerate age which needed but small excuse to turn from the abstractions that bordered on Babylon to her base, fleshly heritage, the perverted religion of Astarte that could enflame jaded or distraught minds. So John sat on Patmos and sent his epistles, combating Paul's, to the seven churches of Asia, denouncing Nicolaites (II, 6,15) who had seduced the people to idolatry and fornication, and fulminating against Jezebel (II, 20).

It was not Gnosticism that John abjured. He was himself of

gnostic temperament and steeped in the numerical lore of the Chaldeans. It was the use of Gnosticism to voluptuous ends that bitterly offended him, a perversion that revolted him the more pasionately just because he did attach his faith with childish seriousness to the glamorous and violent figures of this involved symbolism. So, when he dreamed his dream of solace, it was the sinners' own idols of multiple-headed beasts that, urged by the fervor of John's outraged belief, castigated the profaners with their scorpion tails. And thus in excoriating his contemporaries for their breach of monotheistic rigors, he created for later generations a pageantry of fascinating horrors. And because of his passion, and because of the rich, traditional furnishing of his Oriental mind, John made of his dream an extraordinary design; multiple, turgid, unrestrained, with the teeming abundance of the East, but with the merits, too, of these Oriental defects, so that it is vivid, insistent and enduring in its own peculiar distinctness.

Nor was John content merely to solace himself in these vengeful hallucinations, counteracting his spiritual pain in an aesthetic of horror. Seer, devotee, emotionalist that he was, he was also a Hebrew, and as such, true to the ethical evangelism of his race. Jew to the core, he constrains his raging, morbid emotions to a Puritan end and shapes his nightmare pattern to vindicate the moral law.

Later, others took up the dream and recast it to their personal bias, until finally a Christian compiler made of it one more document for the propaganda and proselytism of the Church, substituting the Lamb of Christ for the Lion of the older revelation. And in this form it has come down the Christian centuries so that as it stands in the New Testament today it has this triple character: an Oriental design, dwelt on as a balm to wounded pride by a visionary who is half a child; an exhortation to the impious, and an apologetic for an authoritative creed.

The thirteenth century loved the Apocalypse. Countless illuminators carefully drew the dragons and angels, the bearded Elders, the flames and streams and crashing cities, the lamb, the eagle, and death. But they loved it neither as a rebuke nor as an exegesis. They loved it as an aesthetic revel and an affirmation, drew the lion with seven heads swaying heavily on a long neck and the bat-winged hound of hell for the same reason that they copied griffons from Eastern silks into the stone carvings of their cathedrals. The universe was an unmapped wonderland and man was childishly avid for the marvellous. So he twisted strange serpents on his capitals and enjoyed the Apocalyptic fiery warriors who would obliterate a third of humanity, crashing across the world on lion-headed horses with dragon-headed tails. These men used the Apocalypse in the same spirit as the negro evangelist, exhorting his brethren in deep velvet tones to remember the lamb that is bathed in blood.

But it was in the fourteenth century that the Apocalypse really came into its own. Six hundred years had brought Christianity in Western Europe and especially in France to the same uncertain moment in which Judaism was shaking when John sent out his letters to the seven churches of Asia. France had passed through the glory of supremacy, of dominance, high purpose and supreme creation. After the dissipation under the Carolingians, when the whole social order fell apart because it had not yet been riveted by an inner necessity, there followed the gradual but close interlocking of the kingdom during the twelfth and thirteenth centuries, fashioning the soul of France. And this new born national spirit realized itself externally in the cathedrals, in brilliant universities, the lustre of Abelard, advanced cities and Louis IX, who brought both ability and justice to his rule, exaltation and high ethics to his life, one of the few figures in history who merits equally as king and saint.

But nations spending creative force in great accomplishment tire, even as individuals do. The two Philips, who followed Saint Louis, son and grandson, sustain the appearance of power through the rest of the century. But the moment of supreme expansion and display, when Philip the Fair and his Queen rode through the streets of Bruges to survey the prosperous province of Flanders, newly added to the realm, was the turning point to disaster. Two years later (1302) the chivalry of France lay slaughtered in a heap of costly armor in the canal of Courtrai, and the burghers of Flanders, going back to their

[64]

wool and looms, carried four thousand pairs of gilded spurs to deck their chapel walls as votive memorials.

The fourteenth century proceeded in disaster and increasing despair. War laid waste France, sundered families, slaughtered the population with famine and Black Death; a debased coinage would not buy even the minimum decencies of life; hunger sapped courage, consumed morals; insanity sat on the throne; the great of the kingdom pursued their private ambitions with greed and treachery. The travail of giving birth to France as a nation and a culture had spent her people's ethical force. Chaos resumed and life was unbearable.

Because life was so unbearable and the individual was so helpless in his anguish, good men turned away from it and learned from mystics of the German race, which always melts readily to sentiment, to expend themselves in private religiosity. As when John beat his breast on Patmos for the sins of overtired Israel, so again in exhausted France eyes were straining through the blinding light for an immediate vision of God. Once more the exalted sought beyond doctrine for insight. Again, having won their certitude, they were using cosmogony for magic, a more refined magic, to be sure, a spiritualized superstition, but aimed to the same end of security. For the minute, daily details in the lives of the convinced mystical devotees were regulated by the symbols of their visions, usually, as in the Gnostic practices, controlled by numbers. Thus Suso quaffs his water in five draughts for the five wounds of Christ, but quaffs the last a second time, because both water and wine flowed from Christ's side. Such a sanctification of life assured both renewed communion and ultimate salvation.

Now, too, however, there was only a narrow, unclear boundary between the gestures of illumined piety and gross blasphemy. The spirit can be infused into the commonplace only by the truly spiritual. To merge them in the mind of the ordinary man is to clog the soul with earth until in the end it turns wholly to unclean clay. When fleshly love can be elevated by phrasing it in the idioms of the love of God it is but a short step to using God to license lust. While preachers discussed, sometimes in genuine devoutness, the exact intimacy of Mary and Joseph, prostitutes solicited openly in the church, sacred processions were drunken, indecent roisterings, and the long watches of holy nights were shortened with unrestrained orgies. John's message from Patmos was needed again.

So those of missionary spirit blazed the Apocalypse before the misery- and sin-besotted public, from books, from windows, from walls. The monsters of their bestiality were set to walk before the depraved in loathsome actualness. The spirit of the Middle Ages was not yet dead. The immaturity of the public mind could still be shaken by nightmare threats. John's crowded Eastern phantasmagoria was such a perfect instrument of re-straining terror for the fourteenth century intelligence, that the artists could limn its extravagance with personal conviction and simple force.

The most impressive illustration of the Apocalypse dates from this period of desperation, mysticism, infantile fear and superstitious faith, and it is set forth in tapestry. The remnants, incomplete, pathetically pieced together, patched and rewoven, constitute the greatest monument in the history of European textile art. Indeed, these panels are the only European tapes-tries that remain to us which entitle us to claim tapestry as a medium of supreme aesthetic invention.

This is the famous set of the Cathedral of Angers. It was ordered in 1377 by Louis I, Duc d'Anjou (1339–1384), son of King John the Good and brother of Charles V, Jean, Duc de Berri and Philip the Bold of Burgundy (cf. pp. 318 ff.). Louis borrowed a book from the library of Charles V to serve as a general model for the iconography and had the cartoons made by a Bruges artist, Jean de Bondol, who did all kinds of paint-ing, pictures, miniatures, and ordinary decorative jobs. The weaving was done in Paris, under the direction of Nicolas Bataille, the outstanding man in the business at the time. He had his own shops but also was a general merchant, buying and selling other men's wares. His clientele included many of the most notable men of the time, the King, Amedée VI, husband of Bonne de Bourbon, and the Duc d'Orléans.

The first pieces of the Apocalypse have the initials L and M for Louis and his wife, Marie de Bretagne. Louis died in 1384 and was succeeded by his son, Louis II, who in 1400 married Yolande d'Aragon, and the last pieces bear her initial, Y. Since they have only Y and no L for her husband, it seems probable that they were woven after his death in 1414. The seventh piece of the set was at one time in the possession of Anne de Beaujeu, daughter of Louis XI.

The composition of the set is based on the number seven, which has a very ancient history as a mystic number and plays an important part in John's visions. In Christianity its significance was commonly attributed to the fact that it was composed of three for the Trinity and four, which was the number of the human soul, since into it entered the Four Elements.

At the beginning of each piece is a huge figure (the panels were eighteen feet high), a solemn, bearded man seated in a white marble portico, attended by angels. Each represents the Bishop of one of the Churches of Asia and the marble dais is the Church itself. The ground is violet. Four whole figures remain with the set at Angers, there are fragments of a fifth, and a sixth is in a private collection in Paris. The seventh has disappeared.

The rest of each piece is divided into two equal horizontal bands, each of which is subdivided into seven panels that are alternately on red and blue grounds, so that the general effect is of a vast red and blue checked design (each piece was nearly eighty feet long) with a narrow strip of sombre purple at regular intervals; for with the pieces hung continuously, as they were doubtless meant to be, the figure that is the full height at the beginning of each piece would recur like a tense pause in the steady beat of the composition, a hesitation in the rhythm that is also both a resolution and another deep, thundering opening chord.

Against this even, momentous pulsing of the base, the designs are rendered in lighter colors, the swaying melodies of draperies and sweeping wings, the climactic chords of crashing cities, the arpeggios of scrolling banderolles, the light, almost breathless tones of the sky and the tremulous trills of thin, spiral vines moving through the pattern in a treble echo of the surrounding themes. And across the top of every piece was a band of sheer, scalloped clouds, with delicate angels, the thin, clear, aching tones of the woodwinds, the suffering of the pure.

Every scene is felt with a penetrating realization of the nuances of the spiritual drama. So when the seven-headed beast of blasphemy, horned and diademed, lion-throated, emerges from the sea and takes the symbol of power from the ancient serpent of evil, equally seven-headed and horned and diademed, the lion moves with heavy, grim contempt, the dragon twines his tortuous necks and sneers sardonically, the turgid waters swirl in marble patterns and John looks on, a frail old man with the eyes of a hurt child (Rev. XIII, 1, 2) (Pl. 10).

Each of the fourteen panels of every piece has its own composition, complete within itself; but it is always related to that of the surrounding panels, by contrast, parallelism or as a varied echo, so that the movement flows, stops in a rigid, emphatic counterpoint, resumes its sway in the same measure, to be arrested again in the chord of a geometrical design. The conception and development are symphonic.

Thus the first piece begins, after the opening announcement of the majestic patriarch in his temple, gleaming against the violet shadowed ground, with a slow and simple statement, John standing quite still, listening to the voices from the seven churches, spaced and immobile. The tension increases with a mystic, elevated figure of God, the sword blade naked in his mouth, John prostrate before him. Meanwhile, below there is a long, shuddering arpeggio of a white scroll held by the angel who shows John the Conqueror, an aged man on a white horse, the tone all pallid and disembodied. Above, the movement of the theme stops in the formal harmony of a geometrical design, Christ in a pointed oval, framed in the symmetry of the signs of the Evangelists, set free in a quiet space, and on either side in regular squares above and below, the Kings, Prophets and Apostles, evenly balanced in compact groups. The whole scheme of composition is thus summarized in this poised moment, a figure in isolation the full height, horizontal bands on either side. Then the composition swings on, with slashing wings, sinuous scrolls, draperies flowing like glacial waters, a little heavy with their semi-opaque silt, rippling on themselves in a

PLATE X

Angers Museum. See p. 68.

DETAIL OF THE APOCALYPSE. Paris, 14th century

strong current. The angel is unfurling the summons to the un-
worthy, while John weeps and an aged man tries to lead him
away. The movement has not attained its full momentum when
it is halted again, but less decisively this time, in a tense, swoop-
ing but massive line, the strings all in concert; the Elders are
laying their crowns at the feet of Christ who sits, isolated and
emphatic in his narrow ovoid, intensified with sharp stars, conveying soundlessly the dignified poignancy of the brasses. And
the scene below underscores this climax eerily, with the long,
hard block of the altar, unreal in space, and the vertical beat
of the seven rigid bodies of the elect reaching up to the angel
that streaks down from a mass of insubstantial cloud which
obliterates the corner, all white with the impalpable intensity
of a dream. And so it goes its Beethoven way, never quite real,
yet playing directly on the nerves with a physical immediacy.
How did an artist of Bruges, the factual, sentimental city of
polished prosperity, ever create a thing at once so evanescent
and yet so fleshly in its emotionalism? The earlier manuscript
that he consulted lent him some motives and the general forms,
but not the vividness of realization or the grandeur of musical
development. This is the Apocalypse itself, chanted to an un-
heard orchestra, taking its own form in space and color.

A century and a half later the Apocalypse was again rendered
in tapestry; but this is neither the vision of a tense Jewish mind
nor the emotional refuge of a quivering soul. It is the busy
propaganda of a well organized institution, with the bustling
intrusiveness of the complacent proselytizer. The Church had
need of propaganda. Calvin and Luther had shaken the souls
of the conscientious. Humanism and the frivolity for which it
gave excuse had sanctioned the indifference of the light-minded.
Every device of evangelism was summoned to save the power of
Rome.

This set, in the Spanish State Collection, consisting of eight
pieces, was bought by Philip II (1527–1598) from William
Pannemaker (cf. p. 165) in 1561. But while it was thus acquired
at the height of the Renaissance, the cartoons must have been
drawn at least three decades earlier, for they are in the style of
the earlier Van Orley School, showing similarities to work of

[69]

Philip Van Orley (cf. p. 155). In character they are still essentially Flemish, with but little imitation of the Roman fashion so current at this time (cf. pp. 158 ff.). Indeed, they even have some flavor of the fifteenth century.

There is no grand formality to this composition, no subtle modulations held within a clear, fixed structure as in the Angers set; but the designer has felt the monumentality of the text sufficiently to prevent his scenes from wandering in the crowded formlessness characteristic of much of the work of the school (cf. p. 132). So every panel is fixed on a definite architectural frame. This frame is the same for all except the first of the set: an oval or rondel at the centre top, with the other episodes arranged in a wide, shallow segment of a circle beneath this, swinging up on either side. It is neither an ingenious nor an altogether happy arrangement, this bursting egg in a nest, repeated in every piece, and there is only a rudimentary rhythm in its development, but it does prevent confusion, and in general the set is well above the average of the time and type. The introductory piece is less successful, the composition being divided into four uneven blocks, two cubes of unmatched size above, awkwardly unbalanced, and below two implied and insufficiently organized rectangles.

In this first piece John, who in this instance is a young man and quite characterless, is seen sitting on Patmos, listening to the seven churches, plump young Flemish women with wings, while another angel shows him the vision of himself, prostrated before God, who holds the book and has the two-edged sword coming from his mouth, seven stars in his hand and seven candlesticks around him (Rev. I, 9–20). Here there is a curious detail. In the fourteenth century the personage who spoke from the Heavens was God the Father. Here it is Moses. The purely Jewish character of the original Apocalypse is made clear. The parallel vision on this same panel is the twenty-four Elders prostrating themselves, and here the All Powerful is Jesus, with the lamb with seven horns and seven eyes resting his forepaws on Jesus' knees (Rev. IV, V, 1–8). Even so stood the ram of the Great God of the Ancient East.

In the second piece the Four Horsemen rush out of the sky,

[70]

PLATE XI

Spanish State Collection.   See p. 71

THE APOCALYPSE.   Brussels, 16th century

followed by the symbols of the Evangelists. Below, Death, a fleshless lunatic on a lean nag, rides recklessly through a quarter of the earth, attacking the inhabitants, who fall before him in theatrical attitudes, while above, the angels are giving white robes to those immolated for the word of God (Pl. 11). Above on the right is the angel, carrying the cross, crying to the four angels who were to wreak the vengeance of the lamb on earth, warning them to do no harm until the servitors of God have been marked on the forehead; and below is the angel marking the hundred and forty-four thousand (Rev. VI, VII 1–8), twelve times twelve, and twelve is again three, the Trinity, times four, the soul of man.

In the third piece the oval above shows the lamb surrounded by the four symbols of the Evangelists and before the throne the great crowd of all nations with palms in their hands (cf. p. 126). They are obtaining from the lamb the water of life (Rev. VII), a stream of his blood from the wound in his side which is received in the communion cup by a Bishop. Every opportunity is taken to insist on the doctrine of the Transubstantiation, so grievously and dangerously challenged by the Protestants, the faith that the actual blood and body of Christ are present in the wine and the wafer.

On the left is God, God the Father himself this time, giving trumpets to seven angels, while another angel swings a censer of many perfumes (Rev. VIII, 1–5), and below are all the dreadful results of the sounding of the first five trumpets. Hail, mingled with blood, falls; volcanoes burst; the sea turns to blood; the great star Absinthe drops, darkness descends and another star falls on the well of the abyss whence emerge three of the mystic locusts (Rev. VIII, 6–12, IX), horses with dragon tails, men's faces, women's hair and sharp wings, who look, in spite of the fearsome words, absurdly innocuous. On the other side is the sounding of the sixth trumpet with the voices coming from the four corners of God's altar in Heaven, while below is the myriad army of destruction on lion-headed horses, and below that the four avenging angels annihilating a third of humanity (Rev. IX, 13–21).

In the fourth piece the angel, in the centre, lifts up his right hand to heaven (Rev. X, 1–6), but he addresses, not John, but the two Witnesses. Then in the upper left corner, in the far distance, an angel gives John the reed to measure the Temple of God (Rev. XI, 1), and the two Witnesses prophesy to the people, fire coming out of their mouths (Rev. XI, 3–5). The beast from the abyss, a leopard with seven lion heads on writhing necks, kills them, while the men look on and, rejoicing, give each other gifts (Rev. XI, 7–10). The seventh trumpet then sounds, and in the cloud framed circle above, the twenty-four Elders prostrate themselves before Jesus (Rev. XI, 16), the ark of the covenant appears (Rev. XI, 19), and below is the Virgin of the Apocalypse, enveloped in the sun, the moon beneath her feet and a crown of twelve stars on her head, while below again is the dragon with seven crowned heads and ten horns, watching her (Rev. XII, 1–4).

In the fifth piece Michael and his angels battle with the hosts of Satan in a thunderous chaos of rolling clouds and twisting serpents (Rev. XII, 7–9). Meanwhile the dragon, spewing forth a river, pursues the Virgin, but an angel gives the Virgin wings that she may escape (Rev. XII, 14). There follow all the curses of blasphemy. The leopard is seen on the edge of the sea in the far distance, receiving the sceptre from the dragon (Rev. XIII, 1, 2). The episode is here recorded as a simple fact, quite lacking the visionary intensity of realization of the corresponding Angers piece. In another group the people have elevated the dragon on a column to adore him (Rev. XIII, 4). Then in another tumult, balancing Michael's battle, the Beast triumphs over the Saints (Rev. XIII, 7), valiant warriors who fall before him, helpless. Above comes still another creature from the serpent's foul world of sin, a lion-lamb, and he is worshipped; but beyond all this, in a remote world irradiated by a transterrestrial light, is the lamb on Sion surrounded by a hundred and forty four thousand people (Rev. XIV, 1).

In the sixth piece the angel with the Evangel floats in the sky, making his announcement to the Tribes through a priest, whose robe is embroidered with the repeated word, Credo, Credo. A second angel follows, pointing to Babylon, the fallen (Rev. XIV,

[72]

6–8) . Above is God on his throne, holding a sickle, surrounded by angels, the lamb in glory below him. Angels call on him to punish the sinners. One of these angels wears a rich cope of cut and voided velvet, with a lion couchant in rays of glory, eagles above about to take flight, and doves. Christ is the lion and Christ is the eagle and the dove is the Holy Ghost (cf. p. 178) .

Finally God himself comes down with his sickle and cuts the harvest of wheat, while an angel presses the grapes in a great vat so that the red wine flows out in a river as deep as a horse is high (Rev. XIV, 14–20) . And here again is the emphatic reassertion of the ultimate and unshakable reality of the Eucharist. Meanwhile, in the Heavens, the Lion of Saint Mark gives a flask to each of the seven angels, the seven churches. This is the official warning pronunciamento against the Lutheran heretics. Return, return to the true Evangel and take the wine that is the real blood direct from God. For if ye do not, lo, wrath will descend upon you. Faith is not passive. Faith demands vengeance on the infidel. The wine in the flasks turns to searing poisons and four of the angels pour it on the earth in a rain of horror, disease and drought (Rev. XVI, 1–10) .

The fifth angel appears in the next tapestry spilling his vitriol directly on the throne of the beast of blasphemy, while his worshippers stand about in dismay; the sixth pours his out into the Euphrates while the three beasts standing on the bank vomit up filthy spirits, and the last splashes his wine into the air and makes a crashing hail (Rev. XVI, 10–21) . The Great Prostitute, Babylon, then appears, mounted on her scarlet animal, holding up her cup of gold (Rev. XVII, 3–4) . But disaster comes to Babylon, so that her people grovel in anguish at her feet while she sits enthroned, until at last she herself falls into the sea in a mass of flames (Rev. XVIII, 7, 8) . This episode, John's attack on the hated, rich Rome that persecuted his people and dominated the world, was a great embarrassment to later commentators. John's very specific picture of the luxury and thriving commerce of the Empire and his shrewd prediction of the economic ruin that would, and did, fall on the world when her markets ceased to consume the expensive products of all the tributary countries, had little relevance thirteen centuries afterwards to Christian propaganda. The chapter could only be interpreted rather feebly as a polemic against licentiousness in general.

At this complete destruction of the city of indulgence the Elders, in the ring of cloud above, fall on their faces before God (Rev. XIX, 4), and below is celebrated the wedding of the Lamb (Rev. XIX, 7, 8). A half dozen richly dressed men and women are gathered about a table, scattered with roses and cherries, with the Queen of Heaven enthroned among them, fondling the Lamb. This is certainly the most awkward and ludicrous religious image ever devised. Then the heavens open above and the white horse appears, bearing the Faithful and True, the Word of God, followed by his army. And then God again presses the grapes in the vat (Rev. XIX, 11–15), always the defence of the communion.

The eighth and last piece is given over to the battle between the Kings of the earth and the beasts of blasphemy, a violent contest in which two of the beasts are killed (Rev. XIX, 19–21) and the third is seized by an angel who descends, carrying a chain (Rev. XX, 1, 2). Above in the sky Jesus sits in judgment with the Book of Life open before him (Rev. XX, 11, 12), six of his Apostles about him, Peter, Paul and John, James and two others; while through another rift in the clouds appears the Holy City (Rev. XXI, 2). And finally John of Patmos is shown again with the angel pointing out the wonders to him.

The designer has followed, for most of his ideas and even for some of his specific figures, the engravings of Dürer which set the model, directly or indirectly, for almost all of the many illustrations of the Apocalypse at this time. But he has not merely copied. He has adapted and arranged, attended carefully to detail, been minutely accurate, worked not only industriously but also conscientiously. He has, moreover, infused his own personality into the work, which is unfortunate, given the subject, for he was obviously a correct man, consciously well bred, hardly the qualities needed to interpret the mind of a somewhat morbid Jew. But, on the other hand, the unconscious palliation incident to filtering the text through a commonplace mind doubtless made the Apocalypse more palatable to his audience, so that, all elements added together, he did succeed in creating a notable document of religious instruction. It has nothing to do with religion.

CHAPTER V

THE FIFTEENTH CENTURY

WHILE Europe was still in the making, with Norsemen to be combated at one end of the continent, Saracens at the other, infidels and barbarians constantly threatening on the east, and pirates of various origins raiding suddenly all the coasts, fighting was the main business of a large proportion of the male population and it kept them almost steadily employed. But in the fifteenth century the bases of European society were beginning to shift from a military to a political and commercial foundation. Feudalism had almost given way to trade.

In this new régime, the professional soldiers, in spite of numerous skirmishes here and there, found themselves, a good deal of the time, without a job. For the common soldier this meant the loss of a livelihood, and he tried to compensate by becoming a mercenary, hiring himself out wherever there was a chance, or, when employment failed entirely, turning bandit. For the titled military leaders it meant loss of occupation. The really busy people at this time were the merchants.

By the same token the women of the titled class, too, found a great deal of time hanging idle on their hands. When their lords had been off at the wars for months and years, leading an expedition at the other end of Europe or even in remote Palestine or Egypt, the responsibilities of the family properties, whether an estate or a whole province, had devolved largely on them. Moreover, industry being then only rudimentary, they had had to be, not only governors and sometimes judges over their people, but also overseers of the various workshops that supplied the needs of their huge households, the spinning and weaving rooms, the woodworking shop, the tannery, the forges;

[76]

and when their managerial duties were done, they often themselves helped with the spinning or weaving, or set a good example to their maids with the embroidery needle.

By the fifteenth century, however, governments were too well
organized to need intervention from the lord's lady, save when
she had a special taste or talent for the refinements of politics,
like Isabelle of Burgundy, wife of the second Duke, who surpassed her husband as a diplomat, negotiating some of the most
delicate of his treaties. Similarly, industry was too highly developed to require the maintenance of such extensive domestic
workshops. Thus at every court there were numerous idle ladies.
The aristocracy had become, by the necessity of changed conditions, a leisure class.

Idleness is ever haunted by the looming menace of ennui for
which the only antidote that the average man can understand is
entertainment. But entertainment was one of the industries not
yet organized. The commercial theatre did not exist, much less
all the other forms of ready-made pleasure now to be had for the
price of a ticket. Anyone who wished to enjoy himself had to
create, somehow, his own enjoyment. The titled classes of Europe knew only one kind of life, that of the régime that had
already passed. Feudalism, moreover, had given them their
power and glory. They sought their amusement, therefore, in
the occupations of feudalism, thus unconsciously evading the
fact that their best moment had gone forever, even as today the
leisure class carries on a fictitious continuation of the life of
the aristocracy which has ceased, as an active force, to exist. So
chivalry from being the structure of society became the game
of the vacant rich.

Since fighting had been the reason for existence of the
feudal order, the upper classes turned to imitation and ceremonial fighting as the most important of their amusements, and
every great occasion was marked by sumptuous tournaments,
or, if there were no occasion, a mock need was imagined as an
excuse. A nobleman, wishing to entertain, invented a tale of a
suffering lady to be succored, and published himself abroad as
her champion, ready to meet all comers at a given time and
place. Knights would arrive, even from far countries, to find,

[77]

at the appointed rendezvous, an elaborate stage set. Thus Jacquet de Lalaing, darling of the Burgundian court and epitome of the gallantry of the time, continued his fairy tale game for a whole year in defence of an unnamed Lady of Tears, obviously the Virgin. A lady, representing the heroine, was presented in a magnificent silk tent. Jacques and his attendants had an endless wardrobe of costumes and horse trappings to grace the scene, brocades and embroideries, jewels, gold fringes, and plumes. Every challenging knight was royally welcomed and costly mementoes and prizes were lavishly dispensed.

At the same time, the aristocracy perpetuated the great battles of history and romance in their tapestries. Thus four large tapestries of this period (*c.* 1450) in the Historical Museum of Berne, originally probably in the possession of the Duke of Burgundy, illustrate Julius Caesar's conquest of Gaul. Caesar is accounted one of the feudal knights, so his Gallic wars are depicted, not in terms of Roman legions, but as battles of this very date, an anachronism that bothered no one, since the historical sense had not yet been cultivated.

The set begins with the election of the three Consuls. They are seated together in a pavilion, surrounded by nobles who come and go on their horses, discussing the affair. Caesar then goes forth to the Gallic Campaign, his doublet emblazoned with the two headed eagle of Rome, citizens kneeling in homage, and soldiers, all well mounted and armed, following. In the second piece, the din of battle fills a crowded composition. Ariovistus is conquered, but his army attempts to escape in boats. The masts and rigging are highly decorative. The text is charming in its naïve effort to make sure that Caesar's victory is no humiliation for the French: " Thus Caesar won the domination of the French without force or suffering, and found them loyal and to his liking." In the third piece comes the famous passage of the Rubicon, relieved of Latin complexities, and made entertainingly romantic by a lovely lady with flowing hair, the spirit of Rome, who rises from the stream and calls on Caesar's help. He serves her well, on the second half of this panel, by giving violent battle to Brutus, Cato, Pompey and several others, as the text explains. Finally, we see him tri-

PLATE XII

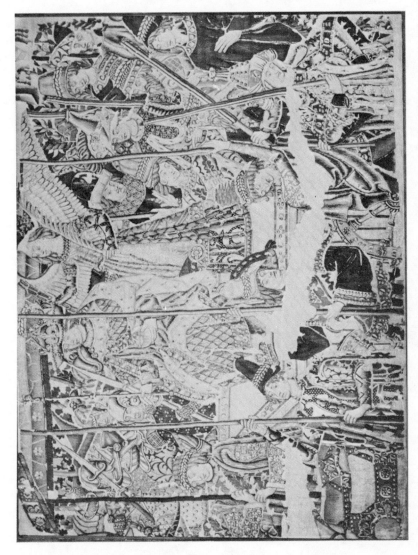

THE TRIUMPH OF CHARLEMAGNE. Probably TOURNAY 15th century

umphant, in a canopied car borne on the shoulders of devoted youths, preceded by trumpeters, followed by his soldiers, and welcomed by fashionable ladies. He is crowned in state, and the text reminds us that he became one of the Nine Great Heroes (cf. p. 88).

Clovis (*c.* 466–511) is the next outstanding figure in the history of France whose military exploits are commemorated in existing tapestries of this time. Two panels that now belong to the Cathedral of Rheims were very probably, like the Caesar, in the collection of the Dukes of Burgundy, for a History of Clovis decorated the banquet hall at the wedding of Charles the Bold and Margaret of York. The first piece begins with the Coronation of Clovis, with the throne under a brocade canopy, courtiers gathered about, and knights kneeling to do homage. Then Clovis rides out to the battle of Soissons, one of the last struggles between the invading Franks and the old, Gallo-Roman civilization. Clovis, the Frank, won, and we see him, his banners unfurled and his soldiers' spears silhouetted against the sky, finally taking the city. In the second piece, Clovis and his queen Clotilde establish the church of St. Peter and St. Paul, standing, with their court, in the midst of the building, while the masons construct the walls around them. But war comes again, this time against Gondebaud of Burgundy, Clotilde's wicked uncle who had murdered both her parents in order to seize that kingdom. Once more there is a compact mêlée of soldiers ahorse and afoot, with pole arms and banners, dominated by Clovis's silken flag quaintly emblazoned with three frogs. Thereafter he attacks Alaric, a Visigoth who had his realm in the south of France. Here he would have come to disaster at a stream in flood, had not a miraculous deer, who bounds away at the edge of the tapestry, shown him the ford. The other four pieces of the set are lost.

Charlemagne's deeds, as recorded by some of the popular romances, were the subject of a number of series at this time, but unfortunately none of them have been found except a tattered fragment that belongs to Saint Mark's in Venice, representing the Triumph of Charlemagne (Pl. 12). The Emperor rides on the triumphal car, holding the symbols of his power, the sceptre and the crystal globe, his fleur de lys crown encircling a wide, jewelled hat, with the imperial ermine over a gold and pearl embroidered robe. Behind him stands an angel, bearing the palm of victory and ready to crown him with the laurel wreath. Five young men in damask doublets, their high hats also encircled with laurel wreaths, carry over him a canopy. He is accompanied by a mass of foot soldiers in nail studded hauberks, and helmets or chapeaux de fer, and followed by richly robed dignitaries, many of them also wearing the triumphal crown and some carrying long torches.

Naturally Roland, the favorite epic figure of France, was extolled in tapestry, too, and fortunately one piece remains, representing the moment of his great sacrifice. The hero appears five times in successive moments of the Battle of Roncevaux, though the scene is treated as if it were a single composition. First he kills Marsillus with Durendal. Again, he is laying about him lustily with his good sword. In the third incident he sounds his oliphant. The fourth is his attempt to break Durendal on a rock. Finally he lies down under a tree to die. Roland is an awkward figure, long-legged, ill-jointed, and many of the details are childish — blood that flows in too conspicuous drops, a mild and stupid horse that stares into space, toy trees; but the clash and confusion of exhausted fighting is there, carrying a real conviction of desperation, violence and heroic death.

William the Conqueror (1027/8–1087) also inspired romances and hence tapestries, doubtless replete with battle scenes to feed the aristocracy's interest in the technique and drama of their ancient trade; but these have all been the victims of time. The Dukes of Burgundy owned a William the Conqueror set at the beginning of the fifteenth century, but not a trace remains save the item in their inventories. The Dukes had, likewise, some of their own battles commemorated in tapestry, notably the great victory of Roosebecque. But here again the centuries have taken their toll.

But though so many of the historical battle tapestries have been destroyed, a number of others remain, celebrating the prowess of purely romantic heroes. The most numerous and familiar are those devoted to the Trojan war, for it was a very large set and frequently woven, so that more than a dozen different pieces still exist, some in several renditions. It was founded on a compilation of Trojan romances made for the Duke of Burgundy which was translated into English and printed by Caxton, protégé of Margaret of York, and thus became the first English printed book. Here the passion for fighting is indulged without stint and almost without alleviation as battle after battle is unrolled, with only slight variations in the confusion and brutalities, ending finally in the episode of the wooden horse, a huge beast covered with silk damask. This, or a similar set, was given to Charles the Bold in 1472 and served him on a number of historical occasions.

Thus in the mock fighting of tournaments and the woven fighting of tapestries the knights of the fifteenth century tried to convince themselves that they were still the knights of old. But tournaments could fill only the daylight hours. There was still the evening to make gay for the pleasure hungry, restless guests gathered for the fêtes. Conversation served but for the intellectual few. Story telling was hardly brilliant enough, a bourgeois amusement that gave the host no chance for competitive display. The natural recourse was, then as now, first eating and drinking mightily, and second, the dance. Banquets and balls were arranged, the most ambitious of the latter being costume balls.

Whether or not these occasions were often put in tapestry is rather doubtful. The fifteenth century had not yet become quite as self conscious as we are today so that ordinary life was, in general, recorded only incidentally. But the banquets do appear as episodes in other histories. The story of Esther and Ahasuerus gave an especially good opportunity to show the ceremonial meal. The finest of the existing Esther sets, in the collection of the Cathedral of Saragossa, has an excellent banquet scene.

A great dinner in the fifteenth century, in the house of an important lord, was a very stately and sumptuous affair. The table was set with a richness and beauty that makes even the finest modern service seem meagre and dull. There was, first, the *nef*. This was a great container, usually in the form of a ship, hence the name, in which napkins and lesser utensils were enclosed, probably because they were not deemed decorative enough. Hardly second in importance were the salt cellars, large vessels conceived in fantastic forms. Some of Cellini's most amazing virtuosity was lavished on these fantasies. They, also, might represent ships, but the designer's imagination was given free scope in many far fetched conceits. Thus the Duke of Burgundy had one in the form of a dragon, stretched out on a terrace, surrounded by fruit trees bearing pearls, and the cover was encrusted with pearls and set with a serpent's tongue, a sure protection against poison, the ever present menace of the time. The ewers were equally rich, with curious figures, enamelled and jewelled. One that belonged to the Duke of Burgundy took the form of a lady, emerging from an enamelled flower, holding a bow and the branch of a tree, all set with diamonds, rubies and pearls. Then there were the flagons for the wines, engraved, embossed, enamelled, jewelled, and the tall cups, high footed goblets and ample drinking bowls.

When the dinner began each course was carried in on a great silver-gilt or golden platter, and the fish or entrée or roast was often arranged in a set, decorative form like the *pièces montées* that are still the pride of the chefs and pastry cooks of Europe for showy occasions. The game, especially, appeared in effective presentations, a peacock or a swan complete in its own plumes. Finally, to perfect the beauty of the table, there were sometimes flowers, not formal bouquets making a barrier between the guests, but separate blossoms scattered charmingly on the board.

The service was conducted with ritual dignity by a series of retainers of graded status. The chief of these was himself a man of rank. It was his duty to oversee the meal, so that every dish was presented to his inspection, and he personally carved the meats, using a handsome set of knives each specified to a purpose, a huge one for the great roasts, with a blade so wide and long that he could pass the slice of meat on it to his lord; smaller ones for game, and very small ones for the bread. He and the other more important officers of the household were richly apparelled, and the lesser servants, varlets, and pages, were liveried in their master's colors, embroidered with his tokens and device.

[82]

PLATE XIII

THE BANQUET OF ESTHER AND AHASUERUS. Flanders, 15th century
Saragossa Cathedral. See p. 83

PLATE XIV

THE MONTH OF JANUARY. Flanders, late 15th or early 16th century *Duveen Bros.* See p. 83

All this is beautifully shown in the Saragossa Esther set (Pl. 13). The table is covered with a simple white damask, the better to set off the gold and colors. There are two *nefs* with high poop decks, mounted on wheels in order that they might be easily moved, and in between is a peacock in his full natural glory, set on a platter decorated with the monograms of the host. The peacock was an especially highly valued bird. Emblem of both pride and immortality, it was often used to swear by when knights pledged some oath in common, each partaking then of a bit of the meat to bind their word. The salt cellar is a tall cylinder with lion feet and a domed cover. A silver shield bearing his initial lies before Ahasuerus, who presides in a high backed chair, designating with his sceptre the courtiers who may address him. The major domo, distinguished by a baton, leads in a procession of servitors, each carrying a platter ceremonially. Pages present other dishes for approval and pour the wine. On a high sideboard in the background more gold and silver is displayed, plates, bowls, bottles and jugs all of different design; and as the banquet proceeds, trumpeters sound their horns.

A simpler family entertainment illustrates the month of January, the chill days when it is good to stay at home by the roaring fire and eat heartily (Pl. 14). Here there is neither *nef* nor ceremonial salt-cellar but at each place there is a wide, low wine bowl and a flat rectangle of silver to serve as a plate. Rectangular plates were fashionable in the Roman Empire. A platter of game is on the table and a tall jug. Master and mistress sit side by side on a bench, with two other women and a man on the other sides of the table, and the old father, in a furred and brocaded robe, warms his hands at the hearth. A varlet and two pages wait, and a maid servant cooks pancakes over the fire, the bowl of batter on a stool beside her. The parrot is in a cage overhead; the family cat, looking unpleasantly stuffed, is in the chimney corner, and an Italian grayhound trots briskly about. There is no great ceremony here, but there is warmth and savoury food and solid enjoyment.

Balls are even less frequently seen in the tapestry of this time. Indeed there is only one presentation and that may not

be intended for a ball, though it gives the effect of a costume
fête. It is in the collection of the church dedicated to the Virgin
at Saumur and shows wildmen mingling with people in elegant
clothes. Wildmen were a favorite subject for the costume parties
of the time, a predilection which nearly cost France a king, for
at a gay gathering in Paris, Charles VI and some of his boon
friends came gambolling into the dance in tights, covered with
tow to represent a hairy hide, and in the excitement, the highly
inflammable tow caught fire at one of the torches. All were instantly enveloped in flame, but a lady, recognizing the monarch, with great presence of mind threw him into a tub of water
that stood in the adjacent pantry. Most of his companions were
burned to death and the shock was one of the factors in finally
unbalancing Charles's always unstable mind.

In the Saumur tapestry ladies and gentlemen in court costume mingle with sauvages covered with this same kind of hairy
hide but wearing fashionable hats and cloaks. Two monkeys
chatter and scamper on an artificial looking grotto, and in the
balcony are musicians playing trumpets and rams' horns, a
noisy orchestra.

As the aristocrats of the fifteenth century found their chief
pastime in an imitation of the serious work of the preceding
generations, war, so their predecessors, the great feudal lords,
had depended for recreation principally on a fictitious revival
of the central business of their ancestors, hunting; for hunting
had been the major source of sustenance of the barbarians who
were at the foundation of feudal Europe. This amusement was
carried on into the fifteenth century. All kinds of hunting, with
hawk and hound, with spear and bow, ahorse and afoot, were
pursued with avidity by men and women alike, and the burghers
and their wives and even the peasants took a turn at it on a
fresh autumn day, so that hunting rights were jealously guarded.
Even hard working Louis XI, who from his youth had scorned
the frivolities of fêtes, was addicted to hunting to such a point
that he undertook to reserve all hunting rights in his personal
domain for himself, and a sure way to his favor, or as sure as
any, for he was a crafty soul not apt to inconvenient loyalties,
was the gift of a well trained falcon or a good dog.

[84]

Naturally such keen hunters were glad to have reminders of their pleasures for inclement days when field and forest were impossible, so hunting tapestries were produced in quantities, and many of these remain. The most interesting set, because the earliest that we have, save for tattered bits, and because, too, it seems to illustrate the hunts of a particular person rather than just the theme in general, are four in the possession of the Duke of Devonshire. These tapestries were found nailed on the walls of Hardwick Hall, cut and torn and faded, but now, cleaned and restored, they have resumed much of their original charm. In one, boar and bear are the quarry. The former are hunted afoot with hounds and short spears, jobbing spears they are called, a sport still popular among English residents in India. The bears are brought down by the hounds and run through with a sword. This was certainly a dangerous game for dog and man alike, and sometimes the man lost, as a later piece of this set shows. In the second tapestry, deer are being pursued afoot with spears, and the hounds are allowed to eat the entrails out of the still warm carcase, an unattractive bit of realism. At the opposite end of this panel the ladies and gentlemen are letting fly their falcons, to bring down wild geese. In the third piece they are again hawking, many on horseback. In the fourth, the otter is pursued into his hole by trained hounds and speared by the huntsman, while the ladies and gentlemen watch; children are catching swans, with sticks and their bare hands, no easy task, for an angry swan is an unpleasant foe; and on the further side of the tapestry two Orientals arrive on a camel, while two others rout a bear from his cave. It is here that a bear has a hunter down and is mauling him mercilessly, to the great excitement of a crowd of onlookers. All of these ladies and gentlemen wear patterned robes trimmed with furs and gold appliqués, and fashionable headdresses that are equally complex for the men and the women, for the hunting costume of the time differed in no whit from ball or banqueting array, and all three demanded the utmost elaboration. Thanks, indeed, to the splendor of the Burgundian court, Flanders at this moment set the fashions for the smart world of all Europe, so that even in the rich and culturally more advanced Italy gentlemen wore the slashed and intricately draped turbans of Flanders and ladies carried on their heads top-heavy horned hennins, both fashions originally taken, probably, from the Orient.

It has been assumed that these tapestries must celebrate the hunts of some particular lady because the initial M recurs in the harness decorations and many of the costumes are trimmed with marguerites, pointing, it would seem, to some special Marguerite. Moreover, one of the ladies has a dress embroidered with a device, *Mont le desire,* presumably a personal motto. It has been suggested that the lady in question might have been Margaret of Anjou who married Henry VI, an attribution that would, perhaps, account for the presence of the tapestries in England. But there were many Marguerites, Marguerite of Scotland, for example, the pathetic child who was the first wife of Louis XI, who so detested and scorned her in his callousness that she died, too discouraged to fight death, murmuring, "Fie on the life of this world."

Every important occupation assumes religious significance in an age of faith, and so in an earlier period, before hunting had become only an amusement and when Christian devotion still flamed intensely, a mystic hunt had been conceived, signifying an essential and venerated doctrine of the church (Cf. p. 57). With waning piety symbolism becomes literature, hence in the fifteenth century, though this mystic hunt was continued and was illustrated in tapestry, the religious figures and emblems were converted into a realistic episode. A famous series devoted to this subject, formerly in the Château de Verneuil and now in the possession of Mr. and Mrs. John D. Rockefeller, Jr., shows, first, the hunters starting out through a wood. In the second panel the party of a dozen men sights the quarry, a milk white unicorn which kneels beside a stream at the base of a fountain, dipping its horn in the water, while a company of other animals watch, a lion and lioness, a panther, a weasel, a stag, and a snarling, cadaverous mongrel dog. In the third panel the chase has begun, with the fleeing beast menaced by a ring of spears and set on by the hounds. In the next piece the unicorn makes its desperate last stand against men and dogs who close in upon it, the odds hopelessly against it. And in the last

PLATE XV

THE HUNT OF THE UNICORN. Flanders, early 16th century
Collection of Mr. John D. Rockefeller, Jr. See p. 87

panel its end comes in two episodes; above, the dogs pull it down and the men drive their spears home, and, below, the body is borne home, slung across a horse, and offered to the lady of the castle who comes out, dressed in rich but heavy mourning, to receive the sacrifice (Pl. 15).

So regarded, this is merely a hunt of the period, spirited and colorful, unusual only in the mythical prey, though to the mind of the fifteenth century a unicorn was quite as real as a giraffe. But shadowed through this hunting party is an ancient allegory of the cult, for the unicorn is Christ, the hunt is the Incarnation and Annunciation, and here at the same time, with the persecution and suffering and the final wound in the side, it is the Passion, so that the lady who receives the lifeless body in the end, solemn in her black brocades, is Mary, Mater Dolorosa.

A delightful feature of the fifteenth-century hunting tapestries is the hounds, drawn with enthusiastic appreciation of their grace, lithe strength, and speed. No matter what the quarry, most of the dogs are always of the greyhound type, and in conformation and points the breed is, at the best, very close to the bench requirements of today. The small, so-called Italian greyhound also appears, sometimes in the hunting pack, more often as a personal pet. For the stag hunts the St. Hubert hound is usually introduced, evidently the ancestor of the modern bloodhound. Toy dogs had their recognition, too, primarily ragged little Maltese, while in the early sixteenth century, spaniels, of the cocker type, and French poodles are fairly common. Shepherds are often accompanied by large, strong, heavy footed animals, the forefathers of the useful if racially ambiguous dogs still favored by the peasants of France.

Fighting had been the chief business of the feudal lords and hunting their chief amusement, but the real foundation of their life was one major principle, which, however dimmed in practise and sadly forgotten over long periods, was nevertheless central to the theory of their social order. This was the concept of service. A knight, of whatever degree, swore to serve his overlord, to serve the church and to serve woman, to protect her, to rescue her. It was by fighting that he fulfilled, largely, all three of these loyalties, but each had its ideal obligations, too, and

[87]

these persisted when the need for the more practical assistance was largely or wholly gone.

The loyalty to the overlord was reflected and continued in a hero worship that became as formal and conventional as the tournaments, with their trappery and etiquette. Even the heroes to be worshipped were standardized in a neatly symmetrical system: three from the ancient Hebraic world, Joshua, David, and Judas Maccabæus; three from classical tradition, Hector, Alexander, and Caesar; and three Christians, Charlemagne, Arthur, and Godfrey de Bouillon, hero of the first Crusade. Three was a mystic number and three times three triply potent. Each of these heroes had his coat of arms and each his outstanding exploits which were commemorated in doggerel rhymes. If possible, a proud lord would manage to construe the hero that he chose as his own ancestor, following, in this, the same impulse that made the Homeric leaders claim descendance from the Gods or, even earlier, made the royal houses of Mesopotamia, three thousand years before Christ, trace their lineage to the deities. The Dukes of Burgundy, with a typical grand gesture, selected, not one of the regular heroes, but Hercules the Indomitable, saw to it that he was accounted the founder of their house, and had his fame celebrated in books, tapestries and dramatic presentations, notably on the occasion of the wedding of Charles the Bold and Margaret of York when the Twelve Labors were enacted, transposed into Christian moralities.

Louis XI, on the other hand, took as his model Charlemagne, but while, in so doing, he was following the fashion, a rather unusual concession for such a hard bitten, practical man, the selection was probably based on a considered judgment, too; for Louis, working to transmute his feud-torn, distracted domain into a unified, prosperous, well governed France, must have seen the similarity of his task to that of his great forebear on the throne. And so he must have focussed his admiration less on Charlemagne the warrior and Emperor than on Charlemagne the administrator who actually accomplished all that he, Louis, hoped to do, tied together divergent, fighting provinces, forced obedience in a world that had almost forgotten law, and ran his vast farms with minute attention to detail, to make a handsome profit.

The Heroes, either singly or in the complete set of nine, made an excellent subject for tapestry. A number of hero tapestries of the sixteenth century remain, a continuation of the fifteenth-century style, but they are degenerate in every way, coarse in weave, crude in drawing, dull in color, interesting only as a distorted reflection of the earlier pieces that are lost, for very few earlier examples are known. There is, however, one splendid panel from the fourteenth century that hangs in the hall of Harbor Hill, the country residence of Mr. Clarence Mackay. Arthur, crowned in his majesty, holding his blue banner embossed with three golden crowns, *azure, three crowns or,* as the heralds had it, sits on a great throne under a ribbed vault painted red. He wears a red cloak lined with unspotted ermine over a blue doublet also emblazoned with the three crowns or, and blue armor. On either side in lesser scale, as befits their lesser significance, are members of his court, each under his own painted vault, a chamberlain, four bishops, and a dwarf.

Aside from such tapestries, which thus presented portraits of the heroes, there are whole sets devoted to their histories. Alexander was particularly favored in this way, perhaps owing to the dramatic interest of the romances wrought in his name. Two pieces of an Alexander set in the Palazzo Doria in Rome probably, like the Caesar and Clovis, belonged once to the Dukes of Burgundy. The first begins with Alexander's boyhood adventure. His father, Philip of Macedonia, receives a challenging letter from Nicolas of Caesarea. He entrusts the campaign to the youthful Alexander who bids goodby to his parents, regally crowned and ermine cloaked, and rides off on his horned horse, Bucephalus. His battle, however violent, is victorious but he comes home to find his father on his death bed. The King kills with his own hand the treacherous Pausanias and crowns his son. On the second piece Alexander again wages war, under his personal banner which bears a lion enthroned, holding a battle axe. His army uses small cannon that shoot, with a fiery blast of raw powder, solid stone balls. After this he undertakes to visit heaven. This trip of Alexander to heaven had been in-

[89]

troduced into his history in the Orient and thence brought into
the mediaeval romances. The Orientals were early fascinated
by the idea of going up into the sky, a primitive religious notion
of aeronautics. Thus more than twenty-five hundred years before Christ the Sumerians told the story of Ectana, who did a
service to the eagle in return for which the eagle agreed to carry
him aloft. But Ectana had no success. He got dizzy and the eagle
got tired and so he fell to earth, just as did his successor in the
Greek myth, Icarus, when he tried putting wings on his shoulders. Alexander had better results, perhaps because he designed
more carefully his aeroplane. It is shown here consisting of an
iron car to which are attached four griffons. The griffons are
urged to an upward flight by legs of mutton stuck on poles just
above their reach — the donkey and the straw theory. Later,
Alexander goes under the sea in a glass bell, and finally he
struggles with misshapen, hairy monsters who are abetted by
crocodiles.

The feudal devotion to a patron was equally practised by the
towns, for each had its patron saint to whom the Cathedral or
finest church was usually dedicated, and just as a knight would
trace his descent to his hero, so a city often attributed, if not its
foundation, at least important moments in its early history to
its saint. The lives of these saints were rendered into tapestry
to decorate the church, usually on long, horizontal bands to
hang around the choir.

The earliest remaining example is in the Cathedral of Tournay. The fragments, torn and faded by years of misuse as a floor
covering in the servants' quarters of the Bishopric, are only a
memory and an indication of what the set must have been,
attractively naïve, with its doll-like figures and toy town buildings. We see the two saints, Piat and Eleuthère, convert the
heathen who are about to make a burnt offering of sheep;
preach; destroy the idols; build the church with the help of
the converts and baptize them, a whole family sitting up together in the font while water is poured over them, and others
squatting in wooden tubs brought in to accommodate the crowd.
Up to this point Piat has been the hero. The career of his pupil
and successor, Eleuthère, now begins. He goes to Rome, riding

off on a rather underfed horse, and the Pope names him Bishop. He resurrects a girl, to the apparent delight of a chained monkey, and baptizes her. Much of the set has been lost, but doubtless the rest of it represented the usual succession of miracles which did not make, truth to tell, very exciting illustrative material.

Another important Saint's life, from the middle of the century (1460), the Life of Saint Peter, is also in the church for which it was made, the Cathedral of Beauvais. Fortunately this has suffered less violence than the Tournay set, though some pieces are lost and others have been scattered. Peter goes through many vicissitudes, beginning with his imprisonment. He sees visions, performs miracles and is finally martyred. Each of the numerous episodes is shown in a very compact scene, with, at the most, a half dozen participants. Many robes are brocaded or jewelled, the architecture is carved and studded, and there are innumerable small banderolles carrying the single word *paix* in honor of the peace recently regained in long suffering France.

The feudal service to the lady, that fair damsel in distress who was the excuse for so many entertaining jousts both in the romantic poems and in real life, could be continued only in shadow and convention in the more settled world of this period. Dragons no longer roamed the earth, seizing maidens, fairy enchantresses on white horses did not appear now in the woods; the good old days were gone. The world had become prosaic. All the more important, then, to keep and foster the poetry; so in the courts of the nobles of this time another element of elaborate make believe was practised, the ideal devotion to a patroness. The knight wore her emblem. Adorer and adored exchanged tokens; poems passed back and forth, highly formalized doggerel, most of it, that any one of rudimentary education might successfully manufacture; and the devoted and the beloved vaunted their attachment, to the vanity of both. This ceremonial fiction had been instituted two centuries before, especially in the romantic courts of Southern France, but in the fifteenth century it became all the rage, and many an otherwise bored hour was filled with the play of this adulation. If in some instances the relation became more serious, it was evidently in most cases trivial enough.

Numerous tapestries of this time show the scenes of courtly devotion as they were daily enacted by the aristocracy. The lady and her knight sit beneath a tree in gallant converse; he offers her a gift or reads her a poem or touches his harp as accompaniment to his praise. Sometimes she is content to listen, sometimes she weaves a chaplet or sews a fine seam, or sometimes even tells her beads.

The idea found a direct echo in the invention of the Heroines to parallel the series of the Nine Heroes. The Heroines were not so conclusively identified as were the Heroes, but among the favorites were Helen, Penthesilea, Semiramis, Penelope, Lucretia, Judith, and Esther. So Penthesilea appears in her armor, partly covered by an embroidered skirt, on a tapestry in the Paris Musée des Arts Decoratifs, and the Boston Museum has a charming fragment showing Penelope at her loom, though this was not part of a Heroine set, in the strict sense (Pl. 16).

The greatest lady of them all, however, in this sentimental exaltation of womankind, was the Virgin Mary, whose cult was especially favored during this century. Many tapestries were devoted to her in all of her aspects, some where she appears as the feudal lady in courtly elegance to fulfil the expectations of the aristocracy, others, objects of a humbler and more fundamental faith, where she is shown, however glorified in patterned robes, as the holy woman of simple humility.

Mary the great lady appears in an Annunciation that belongs to the Musée Gobelins in Paris, an interesting tapestry in that it gives an excellent glimpse into the private chamber of such a lady at that time. Her bed, curtained and covered in silk, fills the centre of the room between two latticed windows. On one side is an oak bench, with an iron candle holder fitted to its hooded top, provided with a few cushions. Beside the bed, on the other side, is a narrow wooden armchair, and beyond that one of those small oak chests that the French call a *bahut*, with a few silver dishes displayed on it. In front, is the Virgin's reading desk, with books, a glass carafe and a jar on the shelves, and beside it a low, plain bench. The floor is tiled and on the walls

Plate XVI

PENELOPE AT HER LOOM. Flanders, early 16th century
Boston Museum of Fine Arts. See p. 92

PLATE XVII

The Annunciation from the Bayeux Life of the Virgin. Flanders, 1499
Bacri Frères. See p. 93

is a small, framed, illuminated prayer. It is a well and beautifully furnished room.

The Virgin's bedchamber in another Annunciation from a series of the Life of the Virgin given by Léon Conseil to Bayeux Cathedral in 1499, is less pretentious but even more interesting because unusual (Pl. 17). The walls are covered with violet cloth, there is a plain plank door, a wood cove faced with planks bound with simple mouldings, lattice paned casements and a tiled floor. It is meagrely furnished with only a wooden bench to serve as *prie-dieu* and the bed; but this bed is most unexpected, for it is a couch-bed, consisting of conventional oak bannister ends with acanthus leaf finials on the posts, but with the mattress hinged in the middle so that in the day it could be raised to make a kind of sofa, a most modern looking invention. It is covered with a light green tapestry with a pattern of leafy branches, a type of which not even a fragment exists.

A truly chivalric celebration of the Virgin constitutes the theme of one of the most famous sets of tapestry, the Lady and the Unicorn of the Musée Cluny which has been repeatedly reinterpreted in the last hundred years and always misunderstood. There are six panels, in each of which the Lady appears in a different rich costume, all of them, however, in some combination of the Virgin's colors, blue and red. In two, she cherishes the unicorn, the symbol of Christ. In one of these she grasps his horn with one hand, while with the other she holds the banner of her virginity, *gules on a bend azure, three crescents argent,* a red flag with a diagonal blue band, embroidered with three silver crescent moons. This scene, by an elaborate but well established symbolism, represents the Immaculate Conception (cf. p. 86). In the second piece she is seated and the milk white beast crouches, his forepaws in her lap, the noble head reflected in an oval, golden glass, which she holds. This is an established allegory for the Incarnation, based on a symbolism of very ancient origin, for the Hittite goddess of fertility, two thousand years before Christ, carried a mirror as her emblem.

In the other four pieces the Lady is attended by a little maid and various of her attributes are emphasized. Thus in one she is the Virgin of the Rose Garden, in another, where she stands under a blue pavilion embroidered with tears, she is the Lady of Sorrows. Clearly the set was made for someone who had vowed himself in chivalrous style to the Virgin, even as did Jacques de Lalaing of the court of Burgundy, for on this tent is inscribed: *Mon seul desire*.

The simpler Mary lives her life through four long panels in the collegiate church of Beaune. She is born in the well furnished but unpretentious setting of a sound middle class family. She is presented in the Temple, affianced, married, and the infant Jesus is born. And then occurs an interpolated, delightful homely scene. Mary is having a quiet day in her carpenter husband's home, seated before the big fire holding her baby. Joseph comes in to join her, but is stopped by an angel who tells him the mystery of Jesus.

Such intimate domestic episodes were not rare, for the people at large felt very close to Mary who, mystic woman that she was, nevertheless was but a woman whose life had been just a miraculous epitome of their own. So in the Bayeux series, long since scattered and largely lost, Mary and Joseph are shown affectionately together in the porch of their home, just after she has met Elisabeth.

This desire to have a more intimate association with the human, domestic Mary had produced, during the Middle Ages, a quaint legend of the Family of the Virgin according to which Anne was thrice married, first to Joachim, then to Cleophas, and then to Salomas. By each husband she had one child, a daughter, and each time she named her Mary. Mary Cleophas married Alpheus and had four children — James the lesser, Simon, Jude, and Joseph the First. Mary Salome married Zebedeus and had two sons, James the Greater and John the Evangelist. Especially in Germany, but also sometimes in Flanders, the three Marys with their husbands and children are shown, all together, but Mary the Virgin just with her two sisters, quietly chatting and working, is the unusual theme of a very fine early sixteenth-century panel, formerly in the Stieglitz collection and now in a commercial collection in New York. The Virgin sits in a canopied chair in the centre, holding her child

[94]

PLATE XVIII

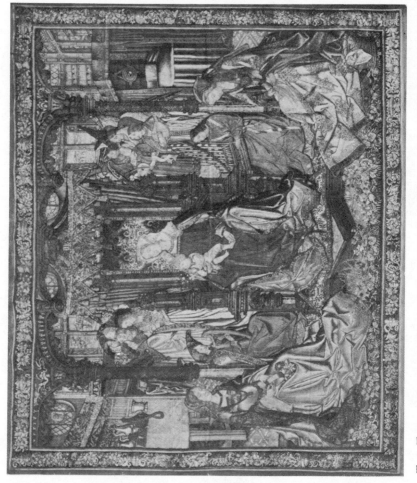

THE THREE MARYS AT HOME. Flandern, early 16th century.

who plays with a rose. The one sister plaits a chaplet of roses, while the other sews. Behind, on either side, is a choir of angels. A dresser holding a modest array of plate fills one corner of the room, a curtained bed, the other, and in the background is Joseph, just coming home (Pl. 18).

Naturally other phases of the Christian faith were perpetuated also, for almost every church in northern Europe of any importance had its tapestries. If they did not depict the life of Mary, they represented usually the life of Christ, or even more often his Passion. The latter was often compressed into one composition, the several episodes crowding the scene with a mass of personages, but centred always on the Cross itself.

Such simple Christian devotion was not disturbed in the North by the dawning literary and philosophical fashions of the Renaissance, even among the most sophisticated classes. Humanism did not mean there, as it did with so many of the Italian intellectuals, scepticism or even cynicism. Yet the elegant accomplishments were much in vogue, and even became a theme for tapestry, though with true northern conservatism the mediaeval convention of scholarship lingered on, so that the subject usually took the form of the Seven Arts. A piece in the Rochester Museum, of the middle of the fifteenth century, follows the older formula, with Astronomy and Arithmetic, each a damask clad lady, enthroned side by side and at their feet the most famous exemplars, Galileo and Boethius. The influence of the Renaissance, on the other hand, is more evident in three pieces, each of which represents one of the Arts. Arithmetic, which is in the Musée Cluny, shows a woman and a half dozen men calculating. The other two are more interesting, for Music, in the Boston Museum of Fine Arts, presents a symposium of composers, singers, and players of various instruments, while Rhetoric, in the Paris Musée des Arts Décoratifs, illustrates a meeting of a Chamber of Rhetoric, a characteristic and influential type of society of the time.

The music guilds were only informally organized, but every town had its group of professional musicians and many fashionable ladies and gentlemen also played with considerable skill.

Thus Duke Philip the Good was an able harpist. The Netherlands was, indeed, the musical centre of the day, both in the study and expansion of the polyphonic forms which were leading to modern harmony, and in the development of the orchestra. The societies of professional musicians constituted orchestras and were called on to participate in every great public event, solemn or gala, and also to furnish gay melody for many private parties.

The Chambers of Rhetoric, which flourished throughout the Netherlands with a membership drawn from the substantial bourgeoisie, including the upper artisan class, were the product of the deliberate intellectualism of the dawning Germanic Renaissance, though in many instances they evolved from older societies of simpler social character. The brethren met to discuss ideas and appreciate each others' literary efforts, and every so often an inter-city contest would be arranged at which representatives from all the towns would compete, either at writing a poem on a given theme or finding the answer to a kind of pseudo-philosophical or theological riddle. The question at one such competition, for instance, was: What is the greatest mystery that God has revealed to man? and the prize winning answer was not brilliantly original: The Transubstantiation. All this was in keeping with the heavy and effortful scholarship that was just coming into vogue in Flanders. But this was only one facet of the Rhetorical societies. Teutonic sentimentality, not to be quenched by any imported fashion, decreed that these portentous bodies be named after flowers, and imposed on every group a motto. Thus the three great organizations supported by the Antwerp burghers were the Violets, the Marigolds, and the Olive Branch, and typical slogans asserted: "My work is divine"; "The spirit blows where it lists"; "All for the best." Similarly, no classicism however correct could suppress native joviality, so that at the contests the great banquet was quite as important as the dissertations, while some of the cities required every participating body to provide a float for a procession. The Violets of Antwerp, for example, being associated with the painters' guild of Saint Luke, arranged, for the Malines competition of 1493, a *tableau vivant* of Saint Luke Painting the

Virgin. In short the Rhetoricians managed the characteristic German combination of a genuine if self-righteous striving for ideas, with a rollicking good time.

Processions were one of the favorite celebrations in Europe at this time, almost any occasion providing for a parade. The great holy days were always marked by such demonstrations, executed usually with the solemnity of a mass; they were an essential feature of the reception of every distinguished visitor, and guild or even private fêtes often included a more or less formal march of the participants through the streets. The theme became popular in the arts, for it fitted well into any long horizontal space that had to be filled and was readily organized in a decorative composition. Thus many of the Italian painted marriage chests had a cortège of one kind or another on the front panel, and there are a number of tapestries with similar representations. One, in the home of Mr. William G. Mather of Cleveland, is especially interesting because it shows a float set with one of the allegorical tableaux which were outstanding features of the lay processions. Peace and Love, two charming girls in handsome brocade dresses, are seated in a carved chariot escorted by a half-dozen men and women afoot, each playing a role in the pageant, Fidelity, Loyalty, Gaiety (*Liesse*), and Felicity, all attractive young ladies in their loveliest clothes, and Marriage (Hymeneus) and Procreation (Geneus), dignified old gentlemen in rich, sacerdotal looking robes with an Oriental flavor. More women, Fame, Delight, Sweetness, and Peace, two blowing horns, lead the group. Allegories were devised specifically for such affairs, often more complex than profound in their conception, but they were accounted a great success if they provided a pretty display and gave the members of the group a chance to wear effective costumes.

With too much pleasure and too much play came, inevitably, ennui and a resulting search for new and more refreshing or stimulating diversions. These took two characteristic forms that have recurred at intervals throughout the history of Western civilization: first, a return to the simple life, an idealization of the peasant and his lot; and second, a romantic Orientalism. The Roman composed sentimental pastorals; the bored courtiers of eighteenth-century France posed as guardians of combed and beribboned flocks. The fifteenth-century aristocrat, from the same motives, visited his peasantry, played at their tasks and games and represented them in his tapestries. Pastoral tapestries must have been produced at this time by the hundreds for they appear in practically every inventory and scores of them are left.

A romantic interest in the Orient likewise has served at intervals in Europe's history to stir jaded taste. Late Rome was addicted to Oriental religions with elaborate secret initiations and symbolism, and France in the eighteenth century eked out the rather tiresome decorative style of the time with pseudo-Oriental elements (cf. p. 277). The Orientalism of the fifteenth century dates back to the post-Crusade romances in which the hero was often sent to wander in Palestine, Egypt or some less definitely designated Oriental world of misadventure and miracle. It was fed by the trade in Oriental luxuries, precious stones, enamels, and the most beautiful gold woven silks the world has ever seen, from the looms of Byzantium, Asia Minor, and even the more remote but artistically superior cities of far Persia. It took various forms, for instance a passion for foreign beasts, so that every prince, even the thrifty Louis XI, had his private menagerie. René of Anjou rather outstripped his rivals by adding a tiger, an almost unknown animal up to then, to the usual collection of lions and elephants, and the subject fascinated him so that he had the walls of one of his palaces decorated with "Alexandrian" animals. He also collected Oriental costumes and had a penchant for Turkish rings, engraved with Arabic letters.

Finally the mode was reflected in tapestry. The immediate occasion for the most famous of these sets was the trips of Vasco da Gama to the Indies (1497–1499 and 1502–1503). Manuel, the King of Portugal, conceived the idea of having the adventure woven on the Flemish looms, to the lasting glory of his kingdom and his house. Whether or not his project was carried out according to the original program, we do not know. It was an ambitious scheme, calling for twenty-six large panels. But it seems probable that King Manuel's idea was the origin of a set that ap-

PLATE XIX

THE CAMP OF THE GYPSIES. Tournay, early 16th century
Collection of M. Germain Seligmann. See p. 99

peared about this time, known as the Portuguese in India, with a series of fantastic processions featuring elephants and giraffes and half naked, turbanned savages, and one or two pieces devoted to a perilous and bloody lion hunt.

The pastoral and the Oriental fashions met in the interest in gypsies, presumed to be the descendants of exiled Egyptians, whence the name. One popular set was known as the Caravan or the Egyptians, and showed a dozen scenes of their camp life, their hunting, their cooking, their card playing, the lords and ladies from the castle visiting them, and their fortune telling and begging (Pl. 19). It provides an interesting record of the persistence of the gypsy types and habits, unchanged in essentials down to the present day.

The aristocracy's passionate pursuit of entertainment excited, meanwhile, the usual admonitory reactions, sermons warning them to think less of the pleasures of this world and more of their Christian duties and the life to come. These sermons, rendered in allegorical form, became also the subject of tapestries. One set, of which the finest example is in the possession of Mr. and Mrs. Arthur Lehman of New York, was known as the Hunt of the Mortal Deer, the deer being an ancient symbol for the human soul. The fleeing beast is here pursued in turn by Nature, Ignorance and Vanity, Necessity, Old Age with eight hounds, and Illness and Death. Finally the Author, seated in his study, sounds his gruesome warning:

> Man whose life is quickly past
> Is hunted even to the last
> Like the badgered deer.
> Think, then, of your life and deeds,
> What rewards you have to fear,
> When Youth is no longer here,
> And Old Age and Death draw near.
> What defences can you say
> When your soul escapes its mesh
> And the worms feed on your flesh,
> And you face the Judgment Day?

So the pageant of fifteenth-century life is displayed on these hangings of multi-colored woven wool: the King and Queen in such guise as the parents of Alexander or the triumphant Charlemagne; the Church in the lives of Saints, with the Bishops and clergy assembled at their offices or performing their miracles; the knights, in their battles and in their state, and finally the people, working, playing, loving, and fighting. It is the chess set of the Middle Ages, complete and in an ever changing game.

In addition, moreover, to all these various types of figure tapestries, quantities of simpler pieces were woven for various practical uses, for wall hangings in less important rooms where it was necessary to have some thick cloth to keep out cold and damp; to spread on beds and couches, or to mitigate a little the rigor of the straight, hard, wooden benches; even, it would seem, to put on the floor as rugs, to make the walls of tents, and as coverings for the sumpter mules in the travelling trains of the great. These were usually decorated with semi-conventional patterns adapted from the heraldic bearings of the owner or his devices or initials, or they were verdures.

The verdure, which was used as a setting for figures, as well as plain, was of respectable antiquity in the history of tapestry. In the early fifteenth century the pattern consisted usually of branches of trees and small bushes, realistically drawn, scattered over a dark ground. Probably the idea was immediately derived from a cheap and easy type of decoration popularly used at public fêtes of the time, consisting of great sheets of cloth with branches and flowers pinned on them, but behind this was a long tradition that went back to the Egyptian cloths with powdered floral patterns in tapestry weave (cf. p. 13), and then again beyond that two thousand years to the early Egyptian linens with flower repeats in tapestry (cf. p. 12). As the fifteenth century advanced, the verdure conventions were modified, both branches and bushes ceding largely to smaller flowering plants, more closely set. The ground is usually dark blue, though in a few handsome examples light red is substituted. Green ground verdures also appear in the inventories but no examples are known (cf. p. 93). Later, a light tan also is introduced. Toward the end of the century the drawing of the plants tends to deteriorate, and in the sixteenth century they are commonly reduced to semi-geometrical spots of color, crowded close together into a mosaic predominantly of triangular units, a lifeless degeneration of the theme originally so poetic and redolent with charm. The verdures at their best remind us that one of the diversions of the time, even for the most sophisticated court ladies and gentlemen, was to wander at dawn into the dew-sparkling spring fields to gather wild flowers and frolic in the fresh sweet air. They are the epitome of the quality which is one of the chief sources of delight in the tapestry of the time, a still untarnished naïveté of soul.

CHAPTER VI

THE FIFTEENTH CENTURY
WEAVERS AND DESIGNERS

THE wealthy nobles, spending at random the taxes wrested, often at the cost of grave sacrifice, from their towns and wide plantations, selected the subjects of the tapestries that were to adorn their walls and, through their patronage and their example, influenced also the spirit in which these themes should be interpreted. But the actual work was done by humbler folk who lived in some of those very towns that were so heavily taxed, two classes of craftsmen being of almost equal importance in the finished work of art, the painter who prepared the design, the cartoon or *portrait* as it was sometimes called, and the weaver who, with his bobbins, rendered it in the wool.

What margin of precedence there might be between the two should certainly go to the painter; for it was he who determined the artistic quality of the tapestry, fixing not only the general composition but even, usually, the minute details. If it was a complex or exceptional subject he might be guided in the selection and sequence of his episodes by a literary man, usually of the church, who would prepare a kind of scenario. Occasionally, as in the case of the Apocalypse of Angers (cf. p. 66), he might even follow the illustrations of a manuscript, though there is no reason to think that that was often the case. Probably, in other instances, he took as his model an older set of tapestries on the same theme, but in more familiar scenes, like the hunts, he must often have been left to his own observation and invention.

There were painters who specialized in tapestry cartoons and trained apprentices who, in their turn, made from this their chief livelihood. Perhaps these men designed cartoons for other craftsmen than the weaver, too; for the wood carvers who made the huge altar pieces of the Crucifixion, with multiple, very real looking figures cut out in the full round; for the glass painters whose windows sometimes so resemble tapestries, or for the embroiderers whose needle-wrought panels are even closer to the woven scenes. Certainly some of them made real paintings when they had the opportunity, but others were not trained at all in the complex technique of painting on wood, but only in the simpler work of the cartoons, rendered in tempera on a flexible linen ground. *Portraitists,* this class of artists was called, in quite a different sense, therefore, from the modern use of the term. And all these painters, whatever their grade of competence or prestige, were always glad, in the intervals between their more important orders, to freshen up the colors on a statue, brighten the city clock with a bit of gilt and red, produce a dozen banners and shields to decorate the town hall for a special event, or even paint the coat of arms of a visiting notable on the cask of wine that the City Fathers would present.

The commission for a cartoon would usually come from the head of a weaving shop, the master weaver being moved to add to his stock of designs either in response to a specific order, or merely to keep up with the styles and have something new to show at the next fair. But, on the other hand, the painter might enjoy the prestige of getting the work direct from the client himself, lord or churchman, through his secretary or man of affairs. Later he might also know the humiliation of having his noble client reject his effort, but perhaps his pride would be somewhat salved by the certainty that he could collect his fee, even though the luckless design was never put on the loom.

The order received, he set about first to make a sketch, a pencil drawing, sometimes with the colors lightly washed in. It is hardly surprising that practically none of these preliminary essays from this period exist. Then, great sheets of linen having been sewn together to the full size of the projected tapestry, the sketch was enlarged to the proper scale and laid in, first in outline and then in color. Even the patterns to be shown on the garments were rendered in full detail. Doubtless in this the apprentices helped and other workers of less than master status.

The finished cartoons when fresh and new were almost as handsome as the tapestry — so handsome that the patrons often arranged to own them when they had served the weavers' need, and churches, especially, had a thrifty habit of hanging these painted replicas throughout the year, keeping the valuable tapestries for the great fête days. Indeed, such painted linens, known as *toiles peintes,* were also made solely as substitutes for tapestry, with no intention of their ever being woven. In Bruges the trade in these far cheaper but very effective painted hangings was so large that there was a special class of painters who did only this work, and *toiles peintes* were often called *toiles de Bruges.* When the cartoon was ordered through the weaver it became part of the capital assets of his business, a considerable piece of property to be accounted for in his will; for if the tapestries were a success, the cartoon would not only be worth its original cost, but would have, in addition, the value of known salability. Because they were so much less durable than the tapestries, very few of these *toiles peintes,* also, have survived, but the Cathedral of Rheims has a notable collection of them, some made as early as the second quarter of the fifteenth century.

From time to time popular cartoons had to be refurbished or brought up to date in the details, especially of the costumes. Such changes were a ready source of dispute between the painters, jealous of their professional rights, and the weavers. For the weaver really had to be a competent draftsman himself. Unless he had both skill of hand and sense of form he would not be adequate to the niceties of his difficult craft. How easy for him, therefore, to take a brush and save his sous when he needed a little change or addition in a cartoon! But to the painter that meant the loss of a job, infringement of rights, and perhaps the danger that ultimately unlicensed men might take his very living away. And so the two crafts had to chaffer and consult and formulate strict laws (p. 315).

The designers of the cartoons have remained, until recently, almost wholly anonymous. Occasionally a name is recorded in contracts or accounts, but only two or three of these have been related to known tapestries. The painters of Flanders were workmen, soundly trained but often illiterate, industrious but poor, with no more self conscious pretensions as artists than their fellow craftsmen in the wood or leather trades. Now and then one of outstanding brains and talent like Jean Van Eyck might rise to an exceptional position in the confidence of a great lord, but most of them were simple artisans, intent on doing their job, without any idea of expressing or exploiting themselves. The apparent anonymity of the Flemish tapestries and paintings of this time, the lack of signatures in the accepted modern sense, has always been attributed to this artisan point of view. But though they were unselfconscious workmen, they were also tradesmen, earning their living by their wares against active competition. They could be sure of profiting by their own abilities only if their work was identified. They had, too, no medium of advertising save their own designs. Moreover, it was to the advantage of all the craft to have the work of each man indicated, so that every one would bear the brunt of his own deficiencies and be liable for any failure to meet the requirements in the quality of the materials or the technique. Thus every book illustrator in Bruges was early required to have a registered mark and insert it into every order executed.

It was fashionable at this time to embroider initials or even whole phrases on garments and horse trappings, a fashion that is revived from time to time in the form of monograms. The alphabet was recognized as decorative, so much so that sometimes it was even used without apparent sequence or sense. There were, too, many stuffs patterned with Arabic letters, imported silks from the East or clever copies made on Italian looms. The cartoon painters took advantage of these designs of letters to introduce into many of their *portraits* decorative inscriptions that served as their own trade marks. Sometimes a painter would even write his name straight across a cloak or saddle cloth, interrupting the illustration like a sign, but in general such a " signature " would be inserted less conspicuously, fitted into a series of letters that do not spell anything, or reversed to make it less obvious, or traced in imitation of an

Eastern script. To the clients of their own day, already acquainted, probably, with at least the better known artists, these half concealed names were not necessarily mysterious. But today, with only the vaguest clues to guide us, their deciphering and identification take patience and ingenuity. Often, moreover, they have been distorted by the weavers or changed by old and scarcely traceable repairs. It is really no wonder that the tapestries have long been accounted anonymous and the authors robbed of their just fame. By degrees, however, some of the schools are beginning to emerge, so that at last, after five hundred years, families, whose names have survived only as a series of entries in the archives, are taking form as generations of talented, inventive men.

Similarly the weavers, too, sometimes had their names woven into decorative inscriptions, though less often, it would seem, than the designers. The records however are more adequate for the history of the weaving shops, so that quite a number of tapestries of this period can be attributed to specific weavers on documentary evidence. After 1527 the law required that a registered city and shop mark be woven into the selvage of every tapestry (p. 316).

The first great centre of tapestry production in Europe was Paris, in the thirteenth and fourteenth centuries. The guild there early attained recognition and status, and one member at the end of the fourteenth century was sufficiently a man of property to stand as one of the gauges for the ransom of King John, captured by the English in the Battle of Poitiers (1356). This weaver, Nicolas Bataille, had the most notable clients in Europe at the time, the King of France, his brothers the Dukes of Anjou and Burgundy, the next Duc d'Anjou and the King's son, the Duc d'Orléans (cf. p. 321). Indeed, he sold so many important tapestries in such a short time, it seems probable that they were not all woven in his own shop but that he functioned also as a dealer, placing orders with other weavers and selling their output.

Only one set of tapestries woven in Paris at this time remains, the Apocalypse of Angers (cf. p. 66); and it is his work. The cartoons, however, were not Paris made, but were done by a Bruges painter, Jean Bondol, who was attached to the King's service. Two other panels, a King Arthur belonging to Mr. Clarence Mackay (cf. p. 89) and a Presentation of Jesus in the Temple in the Cinquantenaire Museum, and one fragment with a page, also in Mr. Mackay's collection, complete the inventory of our remnants from this school. Of the Paris painters who must have often collaborated with the weavers we know nothing.

Arras was almost as old a tapestry centre as Paris and of equal or perhaps even greater importance. The city was so closely associated with this art that its name became the common term for tapestry in both England and Italy. But here again time has been grudging, so that there remains but one set definitely attributable to the city, the life of Saints Piat and Eleuthère in Tournay Cathedral (cf. p. 90), dated 1402 and bearing the weaver's name, Jean Feré. A few other scattered fragments are also almost certainly from Arras, but they are not documented. The painter of the cartoons for the Piat and Eleuthère set was a Tournay man, so that in Arras again we know nothing of the local painters who co-operated in the industry.

Arras was destroyed by the English in 1435, and the industry was wiped out. But meanwhile, a neighboring city had been growing in importance, Tournay. Tournay was an ancient textile center. It had been a depot for supplies for the Roman army, and plain wool weaving certainly began there very early. Tapestry weaving, however, does not appear to any extent until the fifteenth century. Thanks to the abundance of records, the number of tapestries left, and the close association of the industry there with the Dukes of Burgundy, greatest of all tapestry collectors, Tournay is the most interesting of the early tapestry towns.

Among the weavers the first outstanding personality is Robert Dary who wove a resplendent set of tapestries for Philip the Good's Order of the Golden Fleece, illustrating the story of the Fleece and of Gideon. But it was the Grenier and the Poissonier families who were the center of the Tournay industry. The first and greatest Grenier was Anthony. He displayed his work at the Bruges fairs, selling to merchants even from the far corners of France, but his most important work was done for the Duke of Burgundy. In 1459 he sold him an Alexander that may be the one now in the Palazzo Doria (cf. p. 89). Later he sold the Dukes innumerable pastorals, an Esther set, and an illustration of the Knight of the Swan romance, two fragments of which still exist, one in Cracow and the other in Vienna, in the Museum für Kunst und Industrie. He dealt in wine also, and was active in the affairs of the town. Two sons carried on his business into the next century.

The Poissoniers, who were also known under the Flemish form of their name, Viscre, both meaning Fisher, appear in the records just at the moment when the prestige of the Grenier shop was waning, at the beginning of the sixteenth century. In this instance, also, the founder, Arnold, was the most important of the line. It was he who produced both the Gypsy set (cf. p. 99), and the Vasco da Gama series (cf. p. 98), and when he died in 1522 he left a very large stock of valuable hangings that were sold to members of the English court, in Germany, and in various cities in France and Flanders. Three others of the name, whose relation to Arnold is not clear, continued in the trade for several decades.

Among the painters, three families stand out, dynasties of cartoon designers. First there are the Kiens or Chiens, a troublesome lot, for the first of them to appear on the roll of the Painters' Guild, Henri, stirred up the people against the city government and had, in expiation, to make a pilgrimage to Rocamadour in the Dordogne, no small journey when it had to be done ahorse or, if he could not afford the mount, even afoot; and his son Jean, or perhaps it was his grandson, who was also Jean, gilded sheets of pewter and sold them as real gold, a misdemeanor for which he, too, had to make a pilgrimage, and pay a heavy fine to boot. Four generations of Kiens worked at the craft and other masters whom they had trained carried on for another two generations, so that it was a continuous school from 1423 to about 1525.

The second family, the Le Bacres (c. 1451–1514), were less distinctive as individuals, but this was only because they were law abiding and so failed to get into the city court registers. As designers they were on the whole even more talented. Three generations of this name appear, with a number of apprentices one of whom also trained pupils, his own two daughters, the only women cartoon painters of the time that have so far appeared, Marion and Helaine Regnault (apprenticed 1502). The third family, the Le Feires, lasted for only two generations (*c.* 1423–1540), but their pupils continued through three more, and produced many cartoons. Little or nothing is known of their private lives.

Meanwhile Bruges, which had been the most important commercial center in northern Europe, was doing some tapestry weaving; but the documents are too scanty to indicate whether it was of primary importance. Her school of painters was, however, preeminent and there were also numerous lesser practitioners of the art, some, as has been said, trained only to make the *toiles peintes*. Some of these lesser painters and some, too, of the panel painters, made tapestry cartoons. These, however, were not necessarily woven in Bruges; for these Flemish towns, while jealous of each other and in keen competition, were also in a close intercourse which meant a constant interchange, so that it is dangerous if not impossible to identify dogmatically any painting or tapestry as the work of one city or the other solely on the basis of its style. Thus one of the outstanding Bruges cartoon painters, designer of the Beaune Life of the Virgin (cf. p. 94), moved to Tournay, and his family and pupils carried on there the style of his atelier for two succeeding generations.

Each of these four centres, Paris, Arras, Tournay, and Bruges, produced, at its moment of supremacy, a distinctive style. The tapestries of Paris are large in scale, the figures monumental; the drawing is broad, the draperies sweep in ample folds, the compositions are openly spaced, the details sparingly used though elegantly drawn, the whole conception is rarefied in spirit and interpretation and they are rendered in clear, rather high keyed tones of a corresponding quality. The tapestries of Arras are at the opposite pole, small in scale, the figures tiny and fragile, the draperies insignificant, the pattern composed of a mosaic of detail in which foliation weighs almost equally with the personages, the color dark and opaque. While all of the Arras tapestries known are distinctly inferior as works of art, they do reconcile more completely than any other Lowland weaves the necessities of illustration with the requirements of textile design. Intermediate in all respects between these extremes are the tapestries of Tournay, the figures approximately life size and with a convincing factuality equally remote from the heroic isolation of the Paris types, on the one hand, and from the doll-like unsubstantiality of the Arras cartoons, on the other. Similarly, the draperies are representative rather than expressive, but they do have a definite decorative function that is lacking in the pieces assignable to Arras. The details and accessories, notably the architecture, are full and ornamentally developed but never override the people, and the colors are bright and quite varied, though solid and somewhat opaque. There is no attempt at beauty but there is strength and energy, a tonic ugliness. Finally the Bruges cartoons, which have only recently been distinguished from those of the Tournay school, are definitely different, with a markedly linear, calligraphic style that is always on the verge of being scratchy, figures that are less than life size though actually almost as tall because so elongated, the body slim and swaying, the head proportionately small, giving an opportunity for flowing lines; and both the detail and the colors are dictated by a desire for richness, the whole effect being far less vigorous but more sumptuous than in the Tournay productions.

Thus each of these four cities made its distinctive contribution, but though the styles are so specifically characterized one cannot therefore confidently attribute a tapestry to any one of them merely on the basis of the style. For designers moved from town to town, met and mingled and modified their habits in so doing, cartoons were shipped from place to place, and mannerisms were adjusted to meet changing demands. The origin of some pieces remains ambiguous and the work of some painters does not coincide with the qualities associated with the cities of their residence.

Thus there is Baudouin Bailleul whose work looks like a more elegant and refined product of the Tournay school, but who was never registered in the Painters' Guild there. He has been especially famous as a tapestry designer, owing to one record of payment for the cartoons of an important but long vanished set, woven at Tournay, and to a couplet in an almost contemporary poem. The tapestries were those illustrating the History of Gideon and of the Fleece woven by Robert Dary for Philip the Bold's Order of the Golden Fleece which he founded to honor his marriage with Isabelle of Portugal and to perpetuate the glories of the vanishing chivalry (cf. p. 336). The couplet occurs in some very bad verses by Jean Lemaire who was the official literary attaché at the court of Marguerite of Austria. In her honor he wrote the Crown of Marguerites which includes a survey of the famous painters of her realm, and there Baudouin appears:

And he whom one finds busy morning, night and noon
Baudouin Bailleuil, ever painting a cartoon.

No trace of the Golden Fleece set has been found so that Bailleul's work has never been known, leaving a tantalizing gap in the history of the art, but now the deciphering of decorative inscriptions has identified some of his tapestries, most of which have hitherto been attributed to Tournay.

Similarly the early work of Brussels, of the middle of the fifteenth century, seems to be very closely akin to that of Tournay. Unfortunately, however, it will probably never be possible to identify the Brussels school of that period with absolute certainty, for all of the records of the industry and also of the Painters' Guild were destroyed by a fire in the town hall, so that both weavers and designers are known only through odd, scattered documents, entries in accounts or records of the guilds of other cities, especially Antwerp, where a number of Brussels artists established themselves in the early years of the sixteenth century. The most notable weaver was Peter van Aelst. In 1497 he sold some pastorals to the house of Burgundy and in 1502 he was given an official post by Phillip the Fair to whom he also made some important sales. After the death of Phillip, he was involved in trouble with the Queen for having carried off some tapestries without due authorization, and was imprisoned; but evidently the matter was righted, for a few years later he was granted a court appointment with Charles of Luxembourg and did a great deal of work for Marguerite of Austria. His most famous order, however, came from the Pope, Leo X, who in 1515 commissioned him to weave a set of twelve panels showing the Acts of the Apostles after cartoons by Raphael (cf. p. 156). He sold tapestries, later, to Leo's successor, Clement VI, and to Charles V. In the last ten years of his activity his business was so extensive he had some difficulty in financing it so that he had to borrow money from German banks, pledging tapestries for the loans. He seems to have been a dealer as well as a weaver, for in 1522 he sold Maximilian an Indian set with elephants and giraffes, which seems almost certainly to have been the set already associated with Arnold Poissonier (cf. p. 108).

Owing to the loss of the guild registers it is practically impossible to identify conclusively any fifteenth-century Brussels cartoon painters, but an early sixteenth-century designer has become very well known, thanks partly to the number of mistakes that have been made about him by historians of art. His name is Jean van Roome. The first trouble in tracing his history came from the fact that, in the one document which associates a tapestry with his name, a record of payment for the cartoons of a panel illustrating the Judgment of Herkinbald now in the Cinquantenaire Museum in Brussels, van Roome had a collaborator named Philippe. It has taken three quarters of a century to decide how much of the credit for this cartoon should go to Philippe and how much to Jean. The second trouble came from the fact, long overlooked, that there were two Jean van Roomes, both tapestry designers but of successive generations and practising quite different styles, the one in Tournay, a pupil of the school of Kien (cf. p. 108), the other in Brussels. At last, however, by the study of inscriptions and much stylistic comparison, both Jean van Roomes are beginning to be clear.

Lesser cities in the Low Countries also produced tapestry in the fifteenth century, but not in important quantities and probably for the most part in inferior qualities. It is these four centres, in an overlapping succession, Paris, Arras, Tournay, and

Brussels, which must be credited with the production of the greatest tapestries at the time when tapestry was at its highest level as an art.

In all these cities, and in most of the lesser towns as well, both the painters and the weavers belonged to guilds and it was in these organizations that their life was centred; for they not only determined all the conditions of the trade, but they provided also the artisan's only means of functioning in the rights and responsibilities of the community, and supplied at the same time his social pleasures and prestige. In every craft the regulations varied somewhat from place to place and time to time, but the main outline of the organization was constant. There were three grades of members, Masters, Associates (*compagnons*), and Apprentices. A boy entered into apprenticeship, sometimes in childhood, sometimes in his early teens. His parents or guardians paid a certain fee, and as a rule the Master took him into his house and cared for him. In many guilds only one apprentice at a time was permitted. Beginning with humble tasks, grinding paints or cleaning palettes in a painter's shop, for example, he was taught by degrees all the technique of the craft. The length of apprenticeship varied according to the difficulty of the trade, the rules that had been set and the age at which the boy began, but the minimum was usually three to four years and the term seems generally to have ended in the late teens or beginning of the twenties (cf. Ap. II).

Then came one of the great moments in the artisan's life. He prepared his masterpiece, an example of work prescribed to exhibit his skill, submitted it to the guild committee, paid an entrance fee and gave a grand dinner at the inn for the committee or sometimes for all the Masters. There were quantities of heavy food, noisy toasts in Flemish beer, enough dignity to impress the young man with the seriousness of his new position, enough buffoonery and laughter to relieve the solemnity.

The entrant into the guild might, in most trades, qualify for either one of two rankings, Associate or full-fledged Master, the difference being, it would seem, primarily a question of the dues paid. As Associate he would be entitled only to work for wages for a Master. As Master he would open his own shop,

[113]

could have an apprentice, and might in time become one of the officers of the guild. These were usually elected every year, they represented the craft in the city administration, and when the guild was powerful often became determining factors in the government. But whether Associate or Master, whether he remained an obscure nonentity or became the Dean himself, the craftsman would be assured by the guild of a certain status and it would provide him, every year for the rest of his life, with a series of notable festivities, the background of his social self-respect, an opportunity to share in the brilliance and color of life.

The guilds were not Utopia. There were cruel masters and underfed and overworked apprentices; the wage earners were chronically underpaid; guild laws, invented for the protection of the members and the maintenance of standards of quality, were distorted and exploited by the rich and shrewd heads of the craft to their own advantage; ethically indefensible and economically unsound discriminations were perpetuated. In short, an unanswerable indictment against them can be specified at great length. But all these evils were fundamental to the basic economic system, and they can with equal or greater justice be charged against practically every other social order the world has yet known. The guilds were a notable contribution to the advance of civilization in two senses, in maintaining a standard of workmanship and in alleviating the meanness and misery of the life of the common man, mediating somewhat the bitter disparity between his toil and poverty and the gay, spendthrift display of the upper classes.

The nobility had their Joyous Entries when they rode through the streets in gold-shot silks, a-glitter with jewels, but the humble weaver or dyer had his chance to parade, too, especially on the great saints' days and above all on *Fête-Dieu* when, with his guild, he could make almost as brave a showing as royalty itself. First came two torch bearers in colorful cloaks of office, each carrying an elaborately carved and gilded chandelier on the end of a long pole, with a huge wax candle alight. Then came the banner of rich stuff, painted or embroidered with the figure of the patron saint and the emblems of the craft, heavy with gold fringes, the staff likewise painted and gilded and the bearer in his special ceremonial costume. Probably a carved and painted wood figure of the patron saint would be carried under an ornate canopy next, and perhaps a sculptural group showing a master at work at the trade. Then followed the members, all in their very best clothes, and at the end were the officers in silk and velvet robes embroidered with the guild arms. At intervals were corps of musicians with silver trumpets, flutes, and drums. After the corporations of artisans came the societies of archers and arquebus shooters, mounted or afoot, and the monastic orders and ranks of notable citizens sumptuously dressed. In an Antwerp procession of the early sixteenth century one conspicuous group consisted of widows, all dressed in white from head to foot. The ecclesiastics were in their richest gold-embroidered vestments, escorting a statue of the Virgin under a splendid canopy. At the end were chariots and floats carrying *tableaux vivants,* showing the Annunciation, the Adoration of the Magi and other sacred episodes, while at the very end Saint Marguerite led a dragon, followed by Saint George and other cavaliers. Any man, whatever the drudgery of his days, in such a company must have felt his spirit lift.

After the procession every guild marcher was given a little medal or *méreau* by the officers and this entitled him to share in the guild banquet afterwards. To be sure, these guild entertainments often became an embarrassing financial burden and many were the plaints formulated against them and the restrictions put upon them, but when the members sat down in their bravest array to a big dinner, with plenty of wine and the massive silver vessels, that were the guild's pride, set the length of the long board, they must have felt that after all this was not so very different from the banquet that the lords were having up in the castle.

Moreover, just as the aristocracy had their tournaments with all the glamorous pride of mimic war, so too the guildsmen had their archery and arquebus competitions; for almost every artisan, in addition to his trade corporation, belonged to the local society of Saint George, devoted to shooting the arquebus, or the Brotherhood of Saint Sebastian, composed of bow and arrow companies, and in addition to their local meetings these had not only inter-city, but also international contests, as brilliant and gay in their way as the fêtes of arms of the nobility. Even royalty graced them sometimes with their presence, adding to their lustre. Thus when Tournay was at her height as a tapestry centre (1455), she held an arquebus shoot to which many foreigners came. The town hall was painted green for the occasion, and that and the market place were hung with green draperies, but the uniform of the Tournay guild was red, with embroidered insignia. The first prize of two silver ewers went to the company from Lille, which came under the leadership of Anthoine, Bastard of Burgundy.

All these occasions of public rejoicing were important in sustaining the self-respect of the ordinary worker and so in giving him both the confidence and the integrity of standards which were the sustaining conditions of the fine craftsmanship essential to the decorative arts. The guilds were a compromise and a palliative in an unjust world, but they did make possible the stained glass, the wood carving, the metal work, even the painting and the tapestries, of the fifteenth century.

CHAPTER VII

THE TAPESTRY OF THE REIGN
OF MARGUERITE OF AUSTRIA

JUST at the turn of the fifteenth century a kind of tapestry begins to appear, in increasing numbers, which is the reflection in every respect of a substantial middle class society. The individuals depicted are of a sound stock but not pedigreed. One of the favorite themes is moral allegories which enjoin conservative conventions, and the general style bespeaks the universal qualities of the type — solidity, standardization, and lack of grace or pungency. John the Baptist preaches in the wilderness to Flemish merchants with well invested fortunes. When Jupiter comes in a golden rain to the rape of Danae, he finds a plump young woman whose respectability it is hard to doubt. Saint Helen discovering the true cross, Andromeda waiting for Perseus to rescue her, Justice and Compassion struggling before the throne of the Lord for the soul of errant man, even Mary and the Elizabeth whom she meets, are all sensible women in their early thirties, well but unostentatiously dressed, without much taste, wholesome in body and mind, undisturbed by fancy or aspiration, destined to be good wives and mothers for a manufacturing, trading, banking race. In the allegories these thoroughly normal people recommend the well tried virtues, taking for granted that life is a problem of achieving security; and all these cartoons are drawn in steady, heavy lines, with the figures in compact groups that build up into stable if repetitious structures, clothed in thick masses of drapery. The colors are strong but often somewhat opaque, so that the effect is never brilliant though it may be rich. This is the triumph of the bourgeoisie. The busy merchant who had accrued unto himself, directly or indirectly, so much of the most fundamentally significant activity of the fifteenth century, has already prevailed sufficiently to impress his character and preferences on some conspicuous aspects of the art of his time.

Flanders was the most appropriate country to launch a style perpetuating and extolling the quality of the trading class, for this area of the Lowlands had been industrial since Roman times, with a town civilization, a stubborn and politically effective artisan class, and a long predominance of successful manufacturers and merchants, which had shaped the national character, both physical and mental. Nor had the attributes of aristocracy noticeably diluted this mercantile quality of the Flemings, for the upper nobility of the district were largely alien, often in blood and almost always in spirit, speaking French and leading a life apart from the rest of the nation, patterned on that of the peers of France.

Up to this period, however, the influence of this detached nobility had assured to Flemish art, whatever its Teutonic brusqueness and downright ugliness, a dignity of high breeding; but at this moment the middle class could undeflected stamp itself upon the national taste, because royalty itself shared, indeed epitomized, their character. Marguerite of Austria (1480–1530) was Regent of the Netherlands. She was neither Flemish nor middle class, yet she typified both.

Marguerite was the daughter of the Emperor Maximilian of the house of Hapsburg and of Marie, daughter of Charles the Bold of Burgundy by his second wife Isabelle de Bourbon, who was also of the Burgundian house. When she was three, she was taken to France to become the Dauphine, and she lived there until she was thirteen, so that French was always her most natural tongue. Changes in the political situation annulled this marriage, and then at seventeen she married Don Juan, the Infante of Spain. But this was only an interval, for in two years she returned, a widow, to remarry, in another scant two years, and go back to France as the Duchess of Savoy. Thus when at twenty-seven, again widowed, she came to the Low Countries as Governor, she had spent scarcely a third of her life there and none of the most significant years. Yet she came home, spiritually, to her own people.

In character, she was the epitome of the good wife of the merchant class. In each of her marriages, all of political convenience, she promptly, with a good deal of sentiment displayed for public approval, fell in love, and was ready to assimilate her husband's language, nationality, customs, amusements, and point of view, recutting her personality to the matrimonial cloth. She had, that is to say, a thoroughly female mind, with no notion of self-respect in the man's sense of maintaining the integrity of her individuality. But there is a reverse side to these thoroughly female minds. Their apparent passivity in submitting to their husbands is only a device of domination. The good wife has strong maternal instincts, and the mother business is to run things. Marguerite was decidedly the managing woman. Doubtless this type of female mind occurs in every class, but in modern Europe it has been especially typical of the well-to-do bourgeoisie. The lower class woman has had her own hard work in the business of living, her job to do, exactly as the man has his, and this puts them on a parity in which she has no need to function through him. The aristocratic woman, on the other hand, is a luxury object, a piece of fine china in a well polished vitrine. She has nothing to do with any work and in the most highly evolved moments of civilization, which means the semi-decadent epochs, maternity is made a minor feature of her life. She is, in effect, a legitimate courtesan. She has her own social absorptions, her own personality and her own standards as a decoration. The rich middle class woman, however, remains, like all things intermediate, in an ambiguous compromise. She may imitate the aristocratic social ornament, but her scope there is limited. She is above working. But she can be a good wife and keep herself busy running her husband. Hence the thoroughly female mind like Marguerite's, to whom this is the normal satisfaction, has, from the fifteenth century down to recent decades, found the most perfect conditions of development in this class.

Marguerite, moreover, looked Flemish and middle class. She was a well set up woman in the Germanic taste, big, strong, and healthy, with a perfectly round skull and round face, the solid nose firmly clamped in at the nostrils, full soft lips, a round hard chin, round hard bright pink cheeks, and long yellow crimped hair, an old fashioned bisque doll head. Indeed, she was such an average specimen of this type that hundreds of the women in this style of tapestry might, whatever their tapestry names, be portraits from life of Marguerite.

A set of nine tapestries in the Spanish State collection, though probably it did not actually belong to Marguerite, illustrates not only the most elegant development of the style associated with her régime, but also the essential qualities of her mind. Marguerite, like all her type, was a conventional, conservative woman, devout in a sensible way. She was one of the first to take steps to suppress Protestantism. The tapestries in this set present the standardized ethics of a practical woman, well adapted to managing children, husbands or subjects, and they convey the maxims in an elaborately evolved allegory which seems intellectual but does not upset the mind with any ideas.

The set illustrates a common theme, the Triumph of Fame, which had been presented in its most popular version by Petrarch in his series of Triumphs. But in Petrarch Fame was only one of the earthly values, triumphant, to be sure, over Death, and far superior to love as an aim in life, but nevertheless not the final solution, for that lay in Eternity alone. To the moralist of this tapestry set, however, Fame is the ultimate compensation for life, and all the virtues are means to that end.

Fame, moreover, is here interpreted, not in any great sense, as glory, but just as good reputation, necessitating no heroic deeds or noteworthy achievements, but only conformity with the decencies of nice people, and the audience is encouraged to be moral with the promise of esteem and an admiring epitaph. Such homely didactics would hardly seem sufficient to inspire nine very large tapestries, but the author was a well trained preacher. He dresses up his common sense and his not very enlightening remarks in all the allusions of the learning fashionable at the time.

The series begins by presenting the brutal facts of life with frank pessimism. "Fortune amuses herself by scattering both roses and stones at random, and rules everything according to her caprice. All benefits, no matter how hard earned, are obtained only by the favor of fate, and each and every individual

escapes ever present death only by her grace. To those to whom
Fortune is unkind nothing but sorrow falls, and to every man
comes, in the end, black, depressing death." Fortune tears
through the heavens on a rearing steer, scattering roses and
stones, and shows her utter irresponsibility by entrusting the
destinies of man to a young woman, who stands on a rock in
front of Fortune's castle, in the midst of a seething flood, and
carelessly whirls around the Wheel of Life. Rome had good
luck. She sits atop the palace of Fortune, holding a banner emblazoned with seven moons, one for each of her hills; and so,
equally, did some of the Emperors, — Julius Caesar, for example, who sits on the opposite side, in full panoply of war,
holding the same banner, while Curius leans out of a balcony,
and below, Servius Tullius lies in his cradle attended by his
nurse. But they are the rare exceptions. The rest of the panel
is given up to the sufferings and horrors of all kinds of people:
Melantho, daughter of Proteus; Romulus and Remus, suckled
by a wolf; Perseus and Andromeda; Metellus (which one is
not indicated), and a number of ordinary, unnamed men, a
merchant, a king, a monk, a shepherd. All these barely cling to
the coast of the sea of life, or keep afloat with difficulty in its
dashing waves. Arion, playing a harp, rides on a seahorse, a
kind of porpoise, an amusing combination of two Arions, one
the lyric poet of Methymnes, the other the horse that Neptune
materialized which, in the original myth, was a real horse, but
here, out of association with Neptune, has become a finny creature. Europa rides beside him on her bull, a really handsome
animal. One poor wretch is being burned alive. Polycrates, the
tyrant of Samos, cowers in fear. Danae is afloat with her child
in a boat, and Hero, beside her in the water, pleads to be taken
aboard, while Leander swims away in the other direction.

All these conglomerate episodes take place on the left side
of the castle, but the other side is equally agitated. A young
nobleman leaps off a balcony to his death, crashing a column
as he goes. His world has been thrown upside down and he pro-
tests, as he leaps (the message inscribed on a panel that he holds
in one hand), "God overturns all our affairs with a sudden,
spasmodic impetuosity." The man is unnamed. Is it Pierre de

Bourbon, the adopted son and son-in-law of Anne de Beaujeu? He was robbed of his rights and properties by the vengeance of Louise de Savoie who loved him madly. She pursued him, half from the wrath of a woman scorned, half from the cupidity which was the reverse of her silly extravagance, and to effect his destruction she inflamed against him and his rich house the envy of François I, who always had need of more money than he could command for his luxurious frivolities, and who could not bear to be outshone. Driven by their machinations to treachery to France, Pierre died, in desperate, rash fighting as a soldier of fortune.

Below is Priam in his death agony; Cleopatra is fainting; Appius Claudius is just lapsing into unconsciousness, and Poverty, a ragged old hag, is railing and ranting beside him. The curses of the poor, to whom Appius Claudius denied all consideration and relief, pursue him even beyond the grave. Prixius keeps afloat on a ram. Is he still guarding the Golden Fleece? Hecuba nearly drowns. Seleucus is transfixed by an arrow. The Empress Eudoxie, no longer imperial but only a banished woman of letters, simply dressed, quails before her approaching end. And numerous nameless individuals are thrown from their horses, fall in sudden death, or supplicate God in vain, while a ship in the distance founders, all hands on board.

Meanwhile Vulcan in the heavens, aided by many spirits blowing his fire, forges more bolts for the relentless Jove, and it is all the more horrible, all this anguish, because it is Spring. Phoebus, enthroned on a lion and a levrier, is attended by Zephyr and Primavera, carrying a flowery branch. Only one person in the whole hideous tempest of the universe is undisturbed. He stands on the balcony behind Curius regarding it all with singular detachment. He is the author.

Life is horrible and death is sure. Given these inescapable facts, what can we do about it? Death cannot be evaded but, according to the second tapestry of the set, there is one sense in which it can be overridden and this way, and this alone, will also provide compensation for the precarious misery which is existence. "Fame breaks open even the tomb to call up the dead, and in every direction extols the great with her trumpets of praise." Fame is the greatest good and conversely, calumny is the greatest evil. "Calumny horrifies all men of every rank and brings terrifying ills."

Fame is shown in the traditional personification, a lady riding on an elephant, blowing two trumpets. She is escorted by the great: Holofernes representing the Bible; Pompey from the Classical world, and Roland from Mediaeval romance, and on the other side are women, including Hippolytus. The group stands in the middle of Fame's castle and on either side are two-storied galleries. In these are ranged Thales, Statius, Horace, Theodosius, Boccaccio, Pliny, Petrarch, Tullius, Claudius, Orpheus, Ovid, Homer, Aristotle, Terence, Plutarch, Bede, Quintilian, Socrates, Troyus, Plato, Catullus, Virgil, and Sallust. It is the Renaissance five-foot bookshelf, plus a few rare items.

The martial heroes in front of the palace correspond in character. Achilles crouches down. Is this because he has already been wounded in the heel? Ulysses and Theseus are his immediate companions, and beside them is Alexander, his horse about to run away. On the opposite side, on an equally fractious mount, is Julius Caesar. The author inserts Socrates again, doubtless to signalize his dual personality as a soldier as well as a philosopher. He is flanked by Themistocles and, amusing irrelevance, Samson. The others are just what might be expected: Menelaus, Hector and, on the other side, Hannibal, David and a great many unnamed warriors. The women, whom the designer has scattered rather thinly through the crowd, have been more of a problem to the author, but he has managed to assemble Penelope and Camilla, the latter an unusually learned reference (she was Queen of the Volsques and came to the help of Turnus against Aeneas); Deiphil, an old standby, daughter of Adrastus and wife of Tydeus; Lucretia and Judith; but the rest of the women he has had to leave unidentified. Arion, evidently a favorite, comes in again in the background, and another favorite, Prometheus, gallops on Pegasus across the sky with a rubric calling attention to the swift animation of his steed. Glaucus and Proteus rise from a distant sea.

Yes, Fame is a kind of everlasting life beyond the grave. But these are all the heroes of history, great minds, great leaders, brilliant, brave beyond any threat of peril and often, besides, profiting by exceptional opportunities. What have the compensations of these rare ones to teach us of every day? But the third tapestry is reassuring. " Kindly Nature summons with her trumpet all who really covet assiduously the attainment of the heights of honor." And no talent, no riches, no especial attributes are needed. Only goodness and sincerity. Be good, sweet child, and let who will be clever. " Whom fair Virtue sends, Honor receives on the heights with praise; whom Ambition brings, for that very reason she shuns." And, what is more, every man can be sure that his merits will be recognized. " The learned writings command zealously that those decorated by Honor be forthwith fittingly venerated."

Honor in this presentation is Christ himself, enthroned as King of the Virtues with Victus and Victoria, two floating genii, holding a chaplet above his head. The court is like a meeting of the Order of the Golden Fleece, with women, however, admitted to full rank. Eight heroes of history sit in the stalls, with their valets above, holding their shields of arms. Six are the regular Heroes (cf. p. 88) : Charlemagne, Godfrey de Bouillon, and Arthur, David, and Alexander, and Julius Caesar, with four random additions: Saint Louis, Henri, Constantine, and Octavian. And at their feet are the heroines, a richer selection of women here: Florence of Rome, Marguerite, Elizabeth, Lucretia, Thamiris, Helena, Esther, Deborah, and Sarah.

Stairs on either side lead up to this court for the reception of new candidates, with Triumph presiding on one side and Worth (Dignitas) on the other. And outside wait those who fain would enter: Caius Caligula, Niobe, Medusa, Anthony, Joab, Julian the Apostate, Jezebel, Nero, Holofernes (headless) , Tullia, Danae, Clytemnestra, and Pasiphae, the mother of the Minotaur. Nature and Scripture float in the sky, trumpeting to the souls to present themselves. It is, in short, the Last Judgment in terms of Humanism, with all the usual features, the elect, those to be weighed in the balance, the rejected, and the archangels sounding the last call.

[124]

But what distinguishes the saved from the damned, by what rights and merits do some enter, by what lack are others kept out of Fame's eternity? The next five tapestries answer this. A man wins the esteem which is the crown of life and the victory over death, through prudence, moral enlightenment, piety, justice. These qualities make the good man and he will have the recognition and rewards. The only wisdom he needs, moreover, is innate. Thus, according to the fourth tapestry: " The natural powers of wisdom in man lead many to the holiest heights of virtue. Virtue welcomes those whom Astrea has deigned to lead and, friendly to them, bestows upon them gifts of palms." Astrea is the Goddess of Justice, but also, a double reference that the author doubtless considered neatly subtle, it is the Zodiacal sign of the Virgin. Prudence is of special importance in this pictorial disquisition, for it is expounded in three panels. The first of these, the fourth piece of the set, shows a castle with a tripartite portico. On the left stands Prudence, holding a mirror, her foot resting on a skull. Before her is the company of her devotees, led by Scipio Africanus, in full armor, with Charlemagne kneeling beside him, and behind are Evander, who civilized Latium, Adrian and Trojan, Virginia and Susan, and a host of unnamed. The central section is occupied by Faith enthroned, a torch and the tablets of the law in one hand, a church in the other, and under her feet Muhammad, an impressive prophet who looks more contemplative than crushed. This is the court of all the Virtues, for Prudence must be interpreted in the broadest sense, really Virtue as such. The other two ecclesiastical Virtues are on either side, Hope with her ship and spade, Judas under her feet; and Charity with a star and heart, a king under her feet. Below, grouped about the throne, are two of the remaining secular Virtues, on one side Temperance with a clock and pair of spectacles, crushing an imperial tyrant, on the other, Justice with sword and scales, crushing Nero; and down in front are two unusual interpolations, Observation and Religion, each with a book.

In the third compartment is the fourth secular virtue, Fortitude holding a castle, and before her are the great exemplars, with Thamiris at their head. The honored ascend a staircase on the right, each bearing a palm, Cassandra and Claudia in their number. The palm of honor appears on a Sumerian bas-relief of the middle of the third millennium B.C., in the Louvre, carried in the same way by Goudea, the princely Governor of Lagash. As Governor, his chief business was to guard the agricultural lands of his community from the next city, or wrest further fertile areas, which usually meant date palm plantations, from neighboring groups. Also as Governor he was the local representative of the Divine Power which, in its primary aspect, was an embodiment of the fertility principle, with the palm as a major emblem. Thus it was rational for Goudea to carry the palm branch over his shoulder as a mark of victory and authority. But by the time this tapestry was designed the symbol had long since become merely an arbitrary convention, so taken for granted that no one asked its origin or import.

Similarly the pose of the Virtues, each crushing an enemy under her foot, is borrowed from the ancient civilizations of the East. The Assyrian monarchs, vaunting their prowess in imperishable monuments carved in the living rock, are shown thus, partly as a boast, more as a charm, for the attitude had magic potency, assuring the permanence of the conquest. A millennium later the Sasanians, again perpetuating their achievements, chose the same pose, this time with Rome grovelling under their heel. Neither Assyrians nor Sasanians meant much to the Renaissance mind, but the Renaissance designers revived this magic gesture, without knowing its origins, for the Christian virtues.

In the next piece a chariot is built to take Prudence on a trip to the heavens. For though wisdom is innate, it must be served by all the faculties. " The followers of Aonis (the son of Neptune) build a superb chariot at the behest of the God Horeus, with the guidance of the seeress Phronesis (Good Sense) ." The builders of the chariot are the Seven Liberal Arts. The chariot is for the " Five great leaping horses led down by fair Physis as a gift to Prudence from the great Jove." They are the five senses. " The horses are harnessed by Concord, and Reason takes the reins." Thus native wisdom is developed by the use of all the senses, a good education, mental balance and rationality.

The Seven Arts build the chariot under the direction of Intellect, who is attended by Intelligence, working a bellows; Caution, with a mirror; Circumspection, with a compass; Insight, with the armillary spheres; Docility, with a bundle of reeds; and Memory, holding an anchor with a dolphin twisted about it. Prudence herself watches from a throne on a high platform, her pet snakes wrapped about her hand, attended by Faith, an old woman this time, and Reason with a triple mirror. A guard of honor is posed on a pedestal at either side, Deborah, her banner emblazoned with a fawn's head, and Judas Maccabeus, his banner bearing an anchor with a dolphin entwined.

Meanwhile, on the left, Prudence appears again, accepting the gift of the five horses, which are also seen above in a prior stage of their journey, descending from the throne of Jove. And on the right Prudence is presented a third time, commanding Concord to her service, while Jacob adores from afar. In a fourth appearance she instructs Reason to take the reins, and finally she renders homage to Wisdom who is the Virgin, Queen of Heaven, crowned and carrying a sceptre.

In the next tapestry Prudence makes her ascent. Education has awakened insight. "The chariot bearing Prudence shines in the heavens, and there she contemplates the profound intentions of God." At the same time it must not be forgotten that knowledge alone is not enough. Knowledge must be virtuous knowledge. "Knowledge is the severe Virtue who punishes vice." Thus fortified she can even control fate. Reason lashes the horses to an ever greater speed through the thunderous clouds toward the throne of the Virgin, Divine Wisdom, while Prometheus rushes on from the other side, borne through the air under the patronage of Pallas Athena. Below, Truth and Virtue conquer, beating a satyr, Vice, and holding imprisoned Fortune, under the guard of Fortitude and Temperance. From two high towers Seneca, Solomon, Horace, and Plautus watch. The galleries below are crowded with the lesser virtues, rejoicing in the triumph: Constancy, Firmness, Patience, Restraint, Moderation, Charity, Tolerance. And in a row below are still other virtues, gossiping animatedly: Sensibility, Fidelity, Kindness, Mercy, Virginity, and Chastity (who have a lot to say to each other), Modesty and Abstinence who are both very old. On the far right Discretion, attended by Generosity, receives heroes and heroines, among whom Thamyris is again conspicuous. None of these comfortable, contented people pay any attention to the miracle above their heads — Prudence in her chariot, sweeping through space.

It would seem that the revelation of Divine truth should be the culmination of the author's message and the end of the tapestry series. But no. He has the preacher's prolixity. Piety must now have specific adulation. "By natural piety man attains to an illustrious position among the great and heroic. If the veneration of God is your supreme concern, in his nobility he will bless you eternally. The pious mind is vaunted in epitaph, is ever honored, and always carries with it a fair repute for worthy deeds." Samuel anoints a shepherd from a ram's horn, in the company of Abraham, Moses, Esther, and Helen. Trajan holds court, with a glittering attendance, under the patronage of Phoebus and Natural Nobility. He was a good man in spite of the fact that he had not the advantage of Christianity. On the other side a Christian knight receives his accolade, while Civic Nobility escorts the chariot of a king, Good Government. And above all, supreme, the Virgin kneels in glory for her eternal coronation by the Trinity.

The moralist takes another deep breath and goes into the next tapestry which is concerned with Justice. Justice is inculcated primarily by warning examples. "Jupiter took just vengeance on the audacious boldness of Phaeton when he cast him down into the shining waters." Justice, in short, presupposes modesty and moderation, and appreciation of the significance of one's station and its duties. "The severe punishments of Sisyphus, Ixion, Titus, and Danae were merited, for their crimes were serious."

Justice sits enthroned, again with sword and balance, Herod her prisoner, Fortitude and Temperance her companions. Thamyris and Scipio are her honor guard, their banners emblazoned with bees. Thamyris, the Scythian Queen of bloody repute, must have been the author's favorite heroine, for she appears four times in the set. Below, Grace receives the homage of David and Samuel, Reverence welcomes Isaac and Rebecca, Worth receives two queens. Seated on either side are more of the excellent company: Truth, Observation, and Concord, Discretion, Fidelity, and Compassion. Again the noble of legend and history cluster on either side: Sarah and Abraham, Camilla, Antoninus Pius, Anne, all ages and all types. And meanwhile in the sky, presumptuous Phaeton's chariot is overturned by the righteous wrath of Jove, and the King and Queen of the gods cast the wicked to torment eternal.

The author is falling into the hopeless dilemma of good and evil. Frankly facing at the outset the irrationality of brute chance and emphasizing the arbitrariness of suffering, he now takes partial refuge in the theory of the vengeful but just God. He is getting mentally tired, for he repeats again, verbatim, the injunction to piety that he has already used.

Then comes the peroration, recapitulating the advice. But suddenly the author deserts the whole problem that he had set out to solve. He had begun, bravely, to try to justify and guide life in a world of accident, and he had counselled a homely morality. Then, almost surreptitiously, he had suggested a direct mystic apprehension of God. Now he gives up the problem and without sequence or justification simply makes a sweeping promise of satisfaction for all.

"If you wish to enjoy eternal consideration, let Fame and Nobility glow in you. That Fortune's wheel or Malice, with its dishonoring spite, may cause you no evil, follow all the teachings of a just order. Act so that Reason dominates the senses and think, like a wise man, of death where God gives protection, however severe, effacing evil habits, leading you away from evil acts. Then Astrea, more brilliant than the evening star, surrounded by the other virtues, her sisters, will enhance your courage and render you worthy of all consideration and give you what you want. Adieu."

This flatly anticlimactic moral is pointed with a wealth of warning examples. Cain kills Abel. In the midst of a troop of roistering satyrs and vices having a riotous orgy, including

Cupidity and Licence, Jezebel is crushed under the hooves of the horse of Depravity. Zoroaster and Malice are of this company (Pl. 20). On the other side Death, with a group of ruthless knights, is driving relentlessly through the ranks. Tullus and Julian the Apostate fall. Sardanapalus throws himself from a turret. Men and women, crowded into two galleries, watch this Roman circus. Incontinence and Irrationality sweep through the heavens. And calmly isolated from this Apocalyptic tumult, the author sits in his study down in the corner, a bird swinging in its cage, lilies in a jug on his desk, his books higgledy-piggledy on the shelves, in a disarray that parallels the quality of his mind. And he surveys with complaisance his great opus.

Despite the welter of figures, the multiplicity of incident, the violence of action, these tapestries present, after all, only the typical, fashionable, moderate sermon, addressed to the intelligent faithful who are trying to be both rational and believing, just the sort of thing Marguerite of Austria would like to hear. The ethics are conservative and well tried. Keep your eyes open, learn all you can, be reasonable, don't let anything disturb your beliefs — don't, that is, upset the established order — and even if life is pretty dreadful, nevertheless you will come out somehow all right. Of course the thinking straddles at every point, but that is inevitable. Had the author fully faced facts he could not have made either his sermon or the set of tapestries. It has been suggested that the author was Marguerite's favorite rhetorician, Jean Lemaire. The assumption is at least plausible.

Each one of these panels really represents a scene on a stage, an elaborate *tableau vivant,* or a moment of pantomime. Such presentations, known at the time as *entremets,* had been popular for some two centuries. For every Royal Entry into a city, at every great banquet, every marriage or triumph or other pretentious fête, platforms were erected to hold groups depicting allegories, deemed appropriate to the occasion. These might be very simple indeed, a ship rigged up to hold a half dozen musicians, or merely a pretty girl dressed to represent one of the virtues of the guest of honor. But they might, on the other hand, be quite complex; developed, really, into a brief drama.

[130]

PLATE XX

DETAIL OF A MORALITY. Brussels, 16th century *Spanish State Collection.* See p. 130

So Duke Philip the Good of Burgundy, when he gave the Feast of the Pheasant, to pledge his never-to-be-fulfilled vow to lead a crusade (February, 1454), at the climax of his banquet appraised his guests of his devout intention with such a performance. A Saracen giant, robed in sacred Muhammadan green, entered, leading an elephant equipped with a castle wherein sat a nun, who made an appeal for rescue. A Knight of the Golden Fleece then entered with attendants, and recited verses which ended in the ceremony of the oaths.

The nine scenes òf the Triumph of Good Repute are *entremets* expanded to the most ambitious scale and staged in the newest style, inaugurated in the theatres of the French Renaissance. The mediaeval stage that had been developed for the Mystery Plays had consisted of a series of little boxes or "mansions," each denoting a different place, but all exposed simultaneously so that the action could leap from scene to scene without delay or hindrance. The secular moralities and farces, on the other hand, had been presented on almost bare boards, open on three sides, with only a curtain across the back through which the actors emerged or vanished as circumstances required. The French Renaissance scenic designers tried to maintain a mean between these two extremes by subdividing their stage into several loci convenient to the plot, but at the same time unifying these four or five sets by building them into an architectural scheme. To make more plausible the concurrent presentation of such diverse places as a painter's studio, a graveyard, and a bedchamber, the Renaissance enthusiasm for exaggerated perspective was exploited.

So in the first panel of this tapestry series, multiple incongruous episodes are shown by the device of a castle with four different chambers or balconies open to view, a sea sweeping about this building to a distant perspective on one side, two rocks amidst the waves, and, on the other side, a subordinate platform. This, and every one of the sets of the subsequent panels, are so designed that they could be practically constructed for stage use. Even the various aerial phenomena like Phoebus seated on high, or the chariot of Prudence rushing through space to the throne of the Virgin, were not incongruous with a stage presentation, for spectacular effects had been an almost necessary element of any dramatic production during the preceding centuries, and the most ingenious mechanical devices for apparitions, flights, and descents into limbo had been contrived.

In some respects these tapestries, and all the others of the style, are Gothic still. The composition is always arranged to cover the maximum area. A cloth is being decorated without leaving unpleasant blanks. It is, moreover, a mural design, flat, without conspicuous holes. The figures are still drawn with some regard, at least, to silhouette, and the blues and greens, reds and occasional violets are rich substantial dyes, appropriate to the thick wool. All these are merits of the fifteenth century.

Yet the style is not in any respect pure. The surface is covered, but not with the delicate and varying detail of textile enrichment, only with large areas of plain color, rarely broken by linear design. Similarly, the floriation is sparse, and not enough advantage is taken of the minor properties. Nor is the design, though it is not yet really three dimensional, wholly integral to the surface. There is little distance and no atmosphere, but the figures have become substantial and real. Folds of the garments exist, not for variety of line, but for modelling. Indeed, the composition of a group of people is almost always conceived as a mass not really of bodies, but of silks so substantial that they stand alone in heavy folds, one above the other, with faces and hands inset in the pile of stuffs. Thus though there is not yet space, there is solidity. Again, in constructing these lustrous textile heaps, while the figures do have silhouette, this no longer has either the continuous unity or the expressive force of an earlier age. It is interrupted by the broken folds of clothes, lost, too, in the compact juxtapositions. All these features show an infiltration from the Renaissance. One style is breaking down. The other has not yet evolved.

This ambiguous character of the tapestries of Marguerite of Austria is largely the reflection of the transitional quality of her decades. It was a moment of divided loyalties in Belgium, for though with stolid northern slowness, Belgium itself was still holding to the exhausted Gothic taste, in France, which was always partly home to Marguerite, the classic style was in full dominance, while in Italy, where Flemish artists went to spend their *wanderjahr,* the Renaissance was already old, becoming almost decadent. The uncertainty that inevitably resulted from these conflicting influences produced also such indecisive buildings as the Tribunal of Malines, originally Marguerite's own palace, constructed in 1517 under the direction of Rombout Keldermans, who was wholly late Gothic in habits, but from plans made by Guy de Beauregard, a French enthusiast for the Renaissance.

The two artists who were long supposed to have been entirely responsible for the hundreds of tapestries of this type — Jean van Roome and Maître Philippe — were certainly among the foremost practitioners of the style (cf. p. 112). Jean van Roome takes first rank officially, Maître Philippe surpasses him in merit. Jean van Roome was one of the court artists of Marguerite and he produced *patrons* prolifically, not only for tapestry, but also for glass and especially for sculpture and ornament. Equally important with his tapestries are the statues of the Church of Brou, which Marguerite built as a memorial to her last husband, and which Matthew Arnold celebrated in poetry as banal as the church itself. The sculptures were done from Jean van Roome's sketches, and in every respect they preserve the same quality as the tapestries. Pleasant young women of good, but far from noble, breed, gather their heavy skirts about them in broken folds. They vary their attitudes, register the appropriate emotion, but they do not live as individuals and they never feel.

It is very probable that Jean van Roome made the designs for the Triumph of Fame. There is so little individuality in the work of most of the men who turned out this style of cartoon that attribution is precarious save where, as is often the case, there is a signatory inscription. If this set is his work, that tends to confirm the identification of Lemaire as librettist, for Lemaire and van Roome worked together on the Church of Brou. But whether Jean or another one of the score or more other adepts of the style made the drawings, this set, in idea, in development,

in delineation, in quality, the explication of the obvious with
a multiplicity of repetitive details, represents Marguerite and
thereby typifies the early Flemish Renaissance, the fashionable
but always conservative culture of a nation of thrifty merchants,
graceless, serious, obtuse, northerners to the core.

CHAPTER VIII

THE FONTAINEBLEAU LOOMS

THE sixteenth century was well under way and the European aristocracy was enjoying an unprecedented wealth and luxury. From the Americas came masses of gold, the accumulated treasures of an ancient, mysterious civilization (cf. Chapter XIV), while from the East, purchased with these riches, came the extravagances of a long established sophistication, deep pile velvets and lustrous satins enriched with gold, heavy carpets in glowing colors, pearls and precious stones, spices and perfumes, the sensuous refinements of the age-old cultivation of the Orient. Europe, after centuries of bestiality, struggle, heroism, and constructive effort, was achieving elegance.

On the stage thus sumptuously set, three marked political personalities confronted each other, each equipped by character and place to profit by the expanded opportunities, but each approaching his rich chances with a different personal quality. All three, Charles V (1500–1558), François I (1494–1547), and Henry VIII (1491–1547) were cousins. Charles V was the Renaissance version of his forebears of the house of Burgundy. For two hundred years his maternal family had been trying to hack out of Europe a new state, in stubborn disregard of the boundaries that were already defining nationalities. Charles V married this ambition for an autonomous domain to the old fiction of the Holy Roman Empire, summarizing the politics of a period of which he was definitely the end. Yet though his ambition was so romantic and obsolescent, his intellect was modern, so that he counted greatly on political manipulation and the cold astuteness of an opportunist diplomacy to make prevail his mediaeval aims.

François I was six years older than Charles V but he was far more completely the expression of his age. Man of fashion, and deliberately man of the world, he was the royal culmination of that leisure class which had taken form in the preceding century, the actor of himself as conscious sophisticate. With him began in France the social order that terminated in the Revolutionary guillotine, the conception of the court as a group, primarily concerned to amuse themselves and to be displayed as superior beings to the dazzled populace, enhancing thus the separateness of their class and giving added lustre to the ultimate of their class, the King. Whatever work the ruler and his ministers might do, at law, diplomacy, and arms, they must never appear to be working or too responsible. All must be effortless. They must be glittering players, exempt from the sobriety of mediocrity, concentrated on the trivial in order to emphasize the unimportance of the serious.

From the very beginning women were an essential adornment of this world, and they very soon became a major factor therein. There had been influential women before this, chamber plotters like Isabeau de Bavière who further embroiled the unhappy France of her husband's insane years. There had been conspicuous mistresses, flaunting their favoritism, Agnes Sorel of the daring décolletages. And there had been strong women like Isabelle, Duchess of Burgundy, skilled in the anxious intricacies of their states. But for the first time women as such were given a primary social place, pretty women, coquettish women, women whose profession it was to be feminine. Which means that it was their business to be lovely and not too scrupulous about being beloved. The royal eye was a roving one. François in his teens was already an experienced gallant. The royal hand was a fondling one. Beauty was complacent even to fleeting favors royal or, lacking the attention of the most high, conquests among lords and lordlings piqued the senses and gave content to the endless vacant time.

Charles and François represent the common blood come to a diametric contrast, the one embodying the French clear intelligence, the capacity for calculating objectivity, the other the Gallic talent for frivolity, for sophisticated elegance, two aspects of the same relentless realism, the one facing fact cynically, the other dismissing the realization of the inevitable with cynical fictions.

The third cousin, Henry VIII, had nothing of his French great-grandmother left in him, but he had a good deal of his Welsh great-grandfather, Owen Tudor. For Henry was a tradesman in his soul. He merchandized his balance of power between Charles V and François I, selling to the higher bidder, always at a good profit, and at the same time shrewdly keeping free, both from personal hazard in the military episodes, and from really entangling commitments, with a crafty, insular policy. The court that Henry VIII established was self consciously of the Renaissance, but Henry VIII, for all that he imported Erasmus, never really knew anything about the Renaissance. He was merely keeping up with the neighbors in a regal way, watching his colleagues from the tail of his eye, so intently anxious lest he make himself ridiculous that he could not look at his own pretences straight enough to carry them through convincingly. The scion of beer drinking stock cannot become a connoisseur of wines.

Thus there was a royal figurehead for each of the three dominant phases of society that were at the moment in unstable equilibrium. Moribund feudalism was epitomized in Charles V. The newly evolved class whose occupation was to flaunt its lack of occupation was gracefully symbolized in François I. The ambitious merchants saw their type succeed in Henry VIII. But each of these three monarchs, conscious of the world importance of his role, gave his personality the same regal setting, gorgeous clothes, encrustations of jewels, magnificent armor, great castles, massive plate, famous painters, and, essential element of halls of state, series of tapestries.

Tapestries were wholly lacking from the tradition of Henry VIII. England raised the finest wool, but she had neither the designers nor the weavers to convert it into storied hangings. From time to time royalty and nobility had patronized the Flemish craftsmen, who were their best wool customers, but even these purchases were relatively few, and there was no sign of a native industry. Indeed, London at the time of Henry VIII had to look entirely to aliens for things of beauty and fine workmanship, so that there were large groups of foreigners settled there to provide the luxuries, a big Flemish colony dealing in the finer woolens, numerous French of various crafts, and Italians for silks and armor; and English cooking was already famously bad.

But though Henry had no tradition of tapestry, he was consciously living up to his position, and so he had to have a collection. A good deal of this he seized wherever he could lay his hands on it. At one time he took from Richmond Abbey alone thirty-five pieces with hawking and hunting scenes. When Wolsey succumbed in 1530, a victim of the seductive and venomous Anne Boleyn, the whole of his collection was absorbed into the royal storerooms. Wolsey was the son of a butcher, eaten by an ambition that was not balanced by nice scruples or the finer discriminations. He had the vulgarity necessary for an effective politician, and he did his buying wholesale. In 1522 he got at one swoop for Hampton Court one hundred and twenty tapestries. Lesser victims also yielded their quotas from time to time to Henry VIII, and for the rest, he bought his tapestries in the open market ready made, and in general he bought them cheap.

The resulting accumulation was quite what one would expect. It was very large. At his death there were 2560 pieces. It was random and inclusive. There were two hundred and fifty pieces illustrating the Old Testament, two hundred and seventy-seven showing classical themes, and some subjects were repeated over and over. There were sixty-three pieces showing the history of David, fifty-three devoted to Jacob and forty-five to the Prodigal. There was, apparently, not one famous, outstanding set, and most of the lot was obviously of poor quality. Henry had got his largest consignment and probably his best bargains in Tournay when he controlled it between 1513 and 1518. There were six hundred verdures, most of them, judging from the descriptions, clearly of Tournay origin, and hundreds certainly of the coarsest grade.

To Charles V, as scion of the House of Burgundy, tapestries were an essential and intimate part of life. For six generations his ancestors had been masters of Flanders, the home of the supreme looms, and from generation to generation they had amassed a family treasure in the art. Charles V carried this tradition on in the same spirit and with the same discrimination as his forebears, though his accessions were naturally in the new style of his time. The Dukes of Burgundy had immortalized their most important victories in tapestry, the Battle of Roosebecq, and the Battle of Liège. Charles V followed suit, choosing Vermeyen (c. 1500–1559), the foremost cartoon painter of the day, to render in triumphal array the episodes of his expedition to Tunis.

The expedition of Charles to Tunis (1535) was a flank aggressive defence against François I, for François, violating all of the traditions of Christianity, had made an alliance with the infidel, Suleiman the Magnificent of Turkey, sending him as token of alliance his ring. It was a decisive act, the public acknowledgment that the cause of the Crusades was dead, that Christianity was no longer a united force against the abhorrent followers of Muhammad. Only a humanist like François, sceptical and cynical, could blatantly have taken such a position. In return, Charles V seized the obvious advantage of becoming the defender of the faith, and so he proclaims himself on the tapestry: " Caesar, wishing to contest with the impious armies of the Turk and the forces that take their orders from Suleiman, and that wage on all sides relentless war against the Spanish kingdom, Charles V, with the blessings of heaven, assembled his troops and his fleets and attacked the African troops."

The panel, the first of a set of ten now in the Spanish State Collection, shows a pictorial relief map on a tilted perspective so that the distant coast of Africa is as visible as the near coast of Spain, with Barcelona, the Emperor's point of departure, in the foreground, and on the right stands the painter, Vermeyen, leaning against a column, his compass in his hand. He is a tall, rather spare man, very tired, with sagging eyes, drawn cheeks, and relaxed mouth and the long, crinkly, parted beard that made the Spaniards call him El Barbalunga.

The second panel shows His Imperial Majesty reviewing his troops in the smiling countryside of Catalan. He wears fur hip boots over his shining armor, a heavy panache of plumes sweeps down his back, and above him is unfurled the forked pennon of the Virgin of the Apocalypse. He is a goodly Christian knight, going forth to do battle for his lady, Mary, the Sun and the Moon. His army prances by in review, the aristocracy of Spain, Portugal, Germany and his Italian possessions, men of race all, arrogantly armored, on highbred nervous horses, and in the middle is the little prince, proud on his rearing pony, grasping a spear three times his own height, with a cluster of plumes set high to add to his childish stature, and one long ostrich feather curling regally down over the horse's croup. The armies pass and wheel and assemble in companies, and a secretary is seated under a tree to note it all down.

The third piece shows a long stretch of the African coast with the ruins of Carthage in the distance and in the foreground the fleet, busy with disembarking, boats overloaded with soldiers, with their horses crammed in with them, bare backed sailors struggling with a bellying sail, men giving orders, noise, confusion, flags, drums, oars, arms.

The next four panels show the battle and victory at Goleta. The first is the attack, with groups of armed men in furious fighting in the foreground and the troops spaced in squadrons on the plain that stretches away without limit. Here the Orientals appear for the first time, carefully observed types, picturesque but not obtrusively theatrical. In these cartoons Vermeyen has profited by the Renaissance science of composition. He has tied together the scattered activity of the battle both by geometrical organization and by the interplay of movement. There is a fulcrum in the centre front defined by a bearded man on horseback, and emphasized, though without violation of the naturalness, by crossed spears above his head. A cavalier and a bowman afoot on the left balance two men afoot and a dead body on the right, a somewhat lighter group, but made sufficiently heavy by the greater distance from the centre, the longer beam of the balance. Both these groups are held to the fulcrum by the long crossed spears. Then, at the outer end of the balance, on the right, are two horsemen, equalled in the opposite corner by a single sharpshooter kneeling, re-enforced in the immediate background by a whole squadron. Meanwhile this line of people makes a triple scroll, initiated on the left by an oval swing, swaying up slightly in the centre and coming to a full stop on the right with the emphasis of a shield. At the same time, in this scroll, there are three triangles of movement and interest. The background is also organized, with less complexity but with equal care.

The fifth piece is a naval battle at Goleta with a very decorative effect obtained by the repeated parallels of oars in groups of three. The sixth piece is a sortie of the enemy with a great, sweeping oval that rushes around through the dashing movement of cavalry. A group, in the lower right corner, of women bringing the soldiers wine, is carefully studied, a striking statement of fact. The seventh piece is again ships, the Taking of Goleta, a pattern this time of masts and their rigging, fascinating and beautiful as boats always are.

There are then two pieces given over to the Taking of Tunis. It required ingenuity to get any variety into so many similar scenes but Vermeyen was quite adequate to the needed invention. This time the main episode is a hand to hand conflict with spears which gives an opportunity for varied diagonals, differently tilted. This he cuts across boldly with another spear precisely horizontal, even more boldly balanced on the left by still another, absolutely vertical. The Sack of Tunis in the ninth piece gives the best opportunity of all for depicting the Orientals, squatty women with the excess fat of the harem, and rugged, statuesque men.

The tenth and last piece is the re-embarkation of the army. Here Vermeyen launches into a daring perspective, with undulating sandhills in long, almost parallel ridges, going directly away from the eye, and a double row of galleys running in a straight line right into the third dimension.

Though Vermeyen was a man of his time he was not as completely victimized as most of his contemporaries by the standardized Renaissance cartoon style (cf. p. 156). True, his sailors are emphatically anatomical and many of his Orientals smoothly Italian, but at the same time his direct northern respect for fact survives the classical formulae and the studio tricks. The breadth of panorama, the atmosphere, the careful presentation of sun and winds are Renaissance — weaknesses, certainly, from a pure tapestry point of view, but merits in historical painting. The polished armor, on the other hand, the sweeping plumes, the sleek horses of the army on parade, the minor episodes in the crowded rowboats, the details of Tunisian dress are all values derived from the Flemish habit of accurate record. In the combination of the two influences, Vermeyen achieves a personal and convincing representation, so that Charles V, though he created no atelier but simply made use of the resources he had politically inherited, has nevertheless left an individual contribution to the history of tapestry.

Vermeyen designed two other sets of tapestry which were destined to have a far wider currency and more general renown, but neither of them has redounded to his personal credit; for the one, illustrating the story of Vertumnus and Pomona, remained anonymous until recent years, while from the other, a series of the Months, his name was still more completely effaced, for it has been known for generations as the Months of Lucas. The Vertumnus and Pomona series, which consists of a half-dozen panels that have been rewoven many times, introduces an original though typically Renaissance compromise between decoration and illustration which is very successful. Every scene is set in a pergola, each of different design, with elaborate sculptural supports and complex detail. The emphasis is balanced with nice precision between this ornamental architecture and the figures, and the vista beyond is devised with the same formality, representing in each instance the limited view of a severely patterned garden.

The Months, on the other hand, are purely pictorial. The obviously impossible attribution of this series to Lucas van Leyden (Lucas Jacobsz, 1494–1533) has long since been abandoned, yet the recognition of Vermeyen's authorship has been curiously tardy, though the stylistic evidence, once it has been examined, is more than ordinarily conclusive. January is a banquet with two-faced Janus presiding at the table, and three couples dancing the Torch Dance which was part of the traditional New Year's festivities in Germanic countries. In February

The Autumn from the Months of "Lucas." Brussels, 16th century. See p

a dozen men and women are gathered around a blazing fire, some playing backgammon, others cards, while a cat sits complacently in the middle of the floor, and Bacchus, Pan, and a group of satyrs disport themselves outside. In March the garden is planted under the lady's supervision, while some of the men and boys fish in the nearby stream. In April lords and ladies picnic beside a lake with the music of a lute and zither, and the peasants gather greens and guard the sheep. In May there is an archery contest, in June sheep shearing, and in July falconry. August is the Harvest and we see the harvesters being paid off while the hay is stored in the barns (Pl. 21). September is stag hunting, with the quarry swimming a stream, the hounds in pursuit. October is the vintage with a lord and lady sampling the new wine. In November the next year's crop is sown, and December shows a gay skating party. The easy naturalness of these illustrations is a tribute alike to Vermeyen's skill as an historical painter and to the soundness of the Flemish genre tradition.

The popularity of Vermeyen's Months is reflected in another set closely similar in style, the original cartoons of which date from about the same time, though the only known weaving, eight panels in the Austrian State Collection, must have been made a century later. Here the Torch Dance for January is being rendered by only one couple, the gentleman with the torch and the lady carrying an arrow, to the music of a flute and a drum, with a jester accompanying the musicians. The dinner takes place in February, a single couple warming their hands before a fire while a maid serves the meal, and a cat and dog fight under the table. March is again gardening, April picnicking, May is a riding party, June sheep shearing, in August the additional farm hands that have been taken on for the harvest are paid off, in September the lords and ladies hunt, and in December they skate. It is interesting to see in both this and the Vermeyen set that seasonal labor for the harvest was already established.

In the background of François I, tapestry was almost as insignificant as in that of Henry VIII; but François, as man of fashion, was inevitably patron of the arts. It would not suffice him, therefore, to buy what he might find, ready prepared, or even to place orders with known designers and established shops. He must make a more intimately creative provision for his tapestry needs, must found his own royal atelier and support his special painters to supply cartoons. A dozen weavers were established in the Château of Fontainebleau, some Flemish and some Parisians, about 1535. The painter responsible for most of the cartoons was Claude Badouyn who was assistant to Rosso, the master designer for the whole Château, and later (1535–1550) assistant to the greater Primaticcio.

Only one Fontainebleau set from the time of François I remains, an incomplete series of mythological and allegorical episodes now in the Austrian State Collection. These repeat the wall paintings of the great gallery of François I in the Château, copying, indeed, not merely the paintings themselves, but also all the stucco and carved framework, including, at the top, the beams of the ceiling seen in perspective. Even the nineteenth century would sponsor no perversion of the art as specious as this.

The first panel shows Danae; the second the Death of Adonis; the third the Battle of the Centaurs and the Lapiths; the fourth Kleopus and Bito, sons of Kydippus, priest of Hera, leading the way to the Temple of the Gods; the fifth Hermes at a fire altar; and the sixth François I himself as a Roman Emperor. Poor François had tried, at terrific expense of bribery, to become Roman Emperor, but had lost to Charles V. Perhaps he found some consolation in seeing himself dressed to the part.

Under Henri II (1519–1559) the Fontainebleau atelier continued, producing, inevitably, tributes to Diana. Powerful in body but feeble in spirit, this neurasthenic sportsman was the reduction to absurdity of his brilliant but weak father, the type of the society man which his father had established, evolved in one generation to a regal but none the less ridiculous extreme. Thus, whereas François encouraged the ladies to set the tone of his court, found promiscuity a necessary stimulant, and granted his mistresses not only important private, but also conspicuous public places, Henri burlesqued gallantry in the elaborate ostentation of his devotion to Diane de Poitiers, vaunted his mistress persistently, and made her not only dictator of the court, but virtually ruler of the kingdom. François was an ardent hunter. With Henri the pastime was almost a mania. François was fond of active games. Henri worked at them on a fixed schedule. To François elegance was a necessity. Henri cultivated conspicuous waste. François made brilliant entertainments a notable feature of court life. Court life during Henri's time was a succession of receptions, balls, concerts, pageantry in which the actors were their own self-aware and satisfied spectators. All the trivial, extravagant, shallow aspects of François's disposition constituted the focus of Henri's personality.

This was due, perhaps, to Henri's unconscious attempt to reestablish his unsteady self confidence. For Henri was a neurotic, made so, first, by the lonely miseries of a Spanish prison in his most impressionable boyhood years, second, by his father's open distaste for him, and third, by the physical defect that for ten years made it impossible for him to provide an heir, and so struck at the very foundation of his self-respect. Slow witted, illiterate, untutored in government, he could not aspire to emulate the more significant phases of the popular father who scorned him, but he could assume the more obvious characteristics. Yet the very frivolity of the qualities he was adopting was contrary to his own essential character. Morose to the point of sullenness, shut into himself and rigid, by attempting to imitate his father he increased the conflict in his own inner life, still further truncating his limited capacities. He maintained his psychological equilibrium by two devices, instinctively chosen and in the circumstances sound: first, restraint and mechanical regularity in his daily life, and second, refuge from direct action and responsibility, so that he functioned in practically all his major duties through others.

Two stronger characters delegated for him, and it is significant that both were of the preceding generation, for the uncertain youth had never known the sympathy of his father and had scarcely known his mother at all. The Constable de Montmorency, fifty-three when Henri succeeded at twenty-nine, was substitute king, checked only by two lesser members of the Council. Diane de Poitiers, exalted mistress, seventeen years older than her royal lover, was an equal power, finding nothing either too large or too unimportant for her determined interference. Small wonder that Henri clung to her throughout his life, in spite of her graying hairs and dimming eyes. When he was a neglected adolescent, rendered morbid by both external and internal suffering and unexpectedly faced with the anxieties of monarchy, he got from her his first taste of triumph in the illusion that he had won her love, a thrilling conquest for the stupid boy, for she was one of the most beautiful and powerful women in his father's dazzling and frightening court. Thereafter she not only functioned as his surrogate mother, but substituted also for his mind, his will, even his physical passion, which was naturally deficient. With her mature experience she supplemented his inadequacies in every way, and he could live through her when he had not the psychical energy to live for himself.

Nowhere is this more evident than in the realm of the arts. Henri, uneducated until too old to form the habit of education, and perhaps not capable of it anyway, had no taste and no interest in any form of beauty. Yet it was part of the role of a king to be a great builder and patron of the arts. Above all was it necessary for his father's son, striving not to be too much eclipsed. Here, as in so much of his life, he could function through Diane. Vast treasures, some even from the public funds, were poured into her hands, to build, adorn, elaborate.

Thus the rule of Henri II is in most respects, but above all in the arts, the rule of Diane de Poitiers, so that it is fitting that the only set of Fontainebleau tapestries left from this time honors Diane, illustrating the legends of her patron goddess. Four of the pieces hang in Diane's Château d'Anet. The first shows Latona turning the peasants into frogs; the second Diana and Iphigenia; the third Diana and Orion, and the fourth the death of Meleager. A fifth piece in Rouen shows Diana fleeing from Jupiter to save her chastity, a useful bit of propaganda in the campaign that Diane never ceased to wage to protect her reputation. A sixth piece, a fragment of which passed through the art market in New York, shows the Triumph of

Plate XXII

The Triumph of Diana. Fontainebleau, 16th century. *Wildenstein & Co.* See p. 147

Diana, with the goddess mounted on a chariot attended by maidens (Pl. 22).

Diane was of François's generation so that the tapestries of the two reigns, François I and Henri II, are in style one and the same, with François's the determining taste and personality. Through and through the courtier, the art that he fostered was purely of the court. It had no French precedents and no contacts outside of that small, royal, unreal world. Founded and largely carried on by artists imported from the fashionable courts of the Italian Renaissance, who manipulated with unexceptionable skill the standard repertory of that already wearied style, the school of Fontainebleau made but negligible concessions to the fact that Fontainebleau was in France.

Yet the Fontainebleau tapestries are the forebears of the eighteenth-century French tapestries, just as François was the first of the modern kings of France, predecessor of the Louis' of the eighteenth century. Fontainebleau represents the beginning of the skill, the elegance, the artificiality, the emptiness, and the perversion of the medium that came to a culmination two hundred and fifty years afterwards (cf. pp. 270 ff.) in the finished and futile *tours de force* of the Gobelins and Beauvais shops. The subject may be the death of Adonis, but it is a picture of lucent flesh, the sheen of silk, fluffy clouds, sleek wings, and chubby cupids. Boucher's Loves of the Gods were but an echo two centuries late (cf. p. 277).

There are, too, a few grotesques left from the Fontainebleau atelier, and in these the sophisticated frivolity of this court art is most inventive. Luscious fruits and martial panoplies, contorted birds and aimless valances, cupids, fire altars, standards of forgotten symbolism, cauldrons, masks and sculptures, with infinite details of insects, fringes and scallops, are all crisply drawn and openly spaced, in an airy but never exiguous silhouette. And they frame, with casual incongruity, the death of Joab. Here again the devices of the eighteenth century are already exhausted. Behagle and Berain were but a delayed derivative.

Impudently accomplished, the painters of Fontainebleau exploited all the merits of their intentional limitations, so that they created exquisite bits and even an occasional lovely whole. Their long-legged, high-bosomed, relaxed women are aristocratically seductive. Leda with her swan, or Venus half reclining in the grass are timeless voluptuousness, but with no fleck of the tarnish of vulgarity, and a lithe Diana amidst her carefree maidens, soft-skinned but taut-muscled, is the exciting apotheosis of ripe young maturity.

The Gods are ever young in Fontainebleau, young in sportive love, and beautiful. Even Neptune is in his pristine manhood, lolling, careless of his rearing sea steeds, while a mermaid fondles a centaur just beyond. The colors, too, for the most part, have kept the tones of youth, clear and high keyed, the gamut of exquisite fatuity. Sensuous, sometimes lascivious, the style is the more cynical because so impeccable in taste.

In short, the artists of Fontainebleau had precisely the qualities that the King required. They were finished, elegant, unconcerned with common clay. Their emotions were of the theatre, well produced. They never made the error of earnestness. Their pseudo-classical ladies were full of lure, but poised; their heroes, well bred even in their lust. The langour of their decadence was sympathetic to the disillusionment that values above all lightness of touch. It is not a wholly trivial art because it is the art of intelligence deliberately being trivial.

CHAPTER IX

THE FLEMISH RENAISSANCE

AS the sixteenth century advanced, the native Flemish style in tapestries ceded progressively to the prestige of the Italian Renaissance, and in proportion as the natural taste and predilections of the northern painters succumbed to the international style, the cartoons were increasingly deficient in character.

The work of Bernard van Orley (c. 1493–c. 1542) represents a hesitant compromise between his innate tradition and his Roman instruction in the new mode. Bernard van Orley's parentage is uncertain, though presumably he was the son of Valentine, a painter, and it is generally supposed that he was originally trained by his father. In the first decade of the sixteenth century he went to Italy and became acquainted with Raphael. He was Master in Brussels by 1515, and shortly thereafter became court painter to Marguerite of Austria.

His outstanding work in tapestry is a series of hunting scenes. The attribution is based on the testimony of Karel van Mander, and it is somewhat verified by the initial B on the collar of a dog in the December Boar Hunt, evidently a continuation of the fifteenth-century trick of using half-concealed, decorative signatures (cf. Chapter VI). Bernard signed his paintings quite frankly in many instances, but in a few cases there, also, he records his authorship in a decorative arrangement. The landscapes, which are an important feature of the designs, are said to have been made by William Tons who specialized in landscape painting. The cartoons have been woven many times but by far the finest set is in the Louvre.

The series is always called the Hunts of Maximilian, again on van Mander's identification, but Maximilian died in 1519 and the people in the tapestries wear the costumes of about 1535. That they were royal hunts, is, however, unmistakable, for the double-headed eagle decorates the collar of one of the hounds in the December Boar Hunt. The Governor of the Low Countries at the time that they must have been designed was Marie of Hungary (1531–1555), sister of Charles V, and she was greatly given to the hunt. Moreover, van Orley was her court painter. Probably, then, the tapestries should be called the Hunts of Marie of Hungary.

Each panel represents a month. In December and January boar are hunted in a leafless, icy landscape. In February the King and Queen receive the hunters at their court. March and April are for hawking, while in May the lords and ladies picnic, with amorous sportiveness, in the woods. By June stag hunting has begun, with the heavy-eared hounds, and it continues through July, August, and September. Both October and November find the hunters gathered for repasts in the forest.

In organizing his compositions Bernard has made use of a system that he must have learned in the studio of Raphael. Every design is built on a basic geometrical form. Bernard's schemes, however, are monotonously limited. Thus seven of the cartoons are experiments with the oval. January is a plain horizontal ellipse. October is the same ellipse but smaller, and counterbalanced with a pair of figures in the immediate foreground on the right, a somewhat less obvious arrangement. June and November, which differ in design only in being the reverse of each other, show the same balance of an oval against a double vertical, but the oval is now itself vertical. In June an overconscientious respect for accurate perspective has weakened the ovoid, so that the weight of that side is frittered away, but the effect is partially saved by the independent equilibrium of the landscape, in which a group of vertical trees on the left is balanced on the right by the flattened plane of a level field that is kept intact by a well defined further boundary. In April and December horizontal half ovals or crescents are used, in the one the ends upturned, in the other the reverse. The effect of April is compromised by lack of emphasis on the right horn. February is a compound of the two crescents, a shallow

S lying on its side, with a small horizontal oval of buildings in
the background fitted into the right half. It is unfortunate to
have seven out of twelve compositions, which are already embarrassed by a monotony of subject, all done on one geometrical
figure or its sections. No wonder the set seems repetitious.

Two others have still less interest of design. March is an in-
coherent scatter, May a simple triadic symmetry and the figure
on the right is not strong enough to hold the balance. The remaining three are by far the most interesting. July shows a
compact group of seven men held together, not by spatial or
lineal relations, but by the interplay of movements, another
Italian trick which Bernard probably learned also from the
Raphael school. August is again a composition of movement,
the streak of a swift stag pursued across the heavy, repeated
uprights of the trees. September is an arrangement into the
third dimension, with a group of riders standing in the lower
right corner, played off against a castle on the far side of a lake
in the upper left distance.

But it was not only these tricks of design that Bernard had
acquired in Italy. He had also absorbed some of the Roman
conception of realism. The Flemings had always been realists,
but they had focussed their skill, amazing within its limits, on
the accurate representation of surfaces. The Italian Renaissance
introduced into the painting of Europe an interest in the
factual representation, first of volumes and then of the structure
of those volumes. Some of these devices, too, Bernard had
learned. A group of people is no longer a solid mass of textiles
and their folds, with incidental faces and hands, as it had been
for Jean van Roome (cf. p. 132). Under the thick satins and
stiff brocades there is palpable human flesh.

Finally, the Italians had developed a wider significance in
the painting of light which Bernard adopted. The Flemings
had long been interested in light on surfaces. It was part of
their preoccupation with textures. But the Italians worked on
light in space, creating air. This was the obverse of their interest
in volumes, the complementary aspect of their concern with
the third dimension. Because he followed them in this also,
Bernard, collaborating with Tons, who also had profited evi-

dently by some Italian instruction, lets atmosphere for the first time into tapestry. The woven world is suddenly filled with sharp icy chill, or with the sun-warmed smell of Spring, or light puffy breezes. And the heavy horses and lithe lévriers chase the fleeing quarry, not through a pattern of leaves, but through a living countryside.

But though Bernard made full use of all that he had gained in his Italian experience, he was by no means wholly Italianate. Basically he remained a Lowlander, adequate, conscientious, industrious, continuing the tradition of his native school by portraying wholesome men and women, elaborately dressed in the very best quality stuffs, with good jewelry, well kept horses and healthy dogs. He respects the people that he draws, but he respects equally their worldly goods. The thick velvets, the ample collars of fur, the heavy jewels are granted their unstinted due, and richness is of greater worth than grace.

The Hunts of Marie of Hungary suffer from the limitation of the subject. Any chef would be embarrassed to find twelve different ways to serve roast beef. They suffer still more from the dual authorship; for in every case except February, which is largely an indoor scene, the composition has the effect of two designs put together, the landscape and the figures, and in most cases they are simply fitted into each other, not really fused. Almost always the figures constitute one self-enclosed system in the front, while the landscape is an almost independent conception beyond. But they suffer most of all from Bernard's own ambiguity of aesthetic aim, his attempt to assimilate his new Italian acquisitions to his Flemish heritage. When a great man insists on trying to maintain all of the values of conflicting purposes, whether it be in politics, or life, or art, he will either destroy himself in the attempt or, rarely, when his greatness really does touch genius, he will achieve a superhuman grandeur. When mediocrity undertakes to reconcile disparate values, one quality in the end is almost certain to annul the other. Old wives' wisdom holds. No one can have his cake and eat it too. One falls between two stools. The product is not fish, flesh, fowl, nor good red herring.

And so it is in the tapestries of Bernard van Orley and his

kind. Neither Flemish nor Italian, neither fifteenth-century
nor Renaissance, neither illustration nor decoration, neither a
convention nor complete realism, they are handsome, but compared with their predecessors they are amorphous, flat. The
Hunts of Marie of Hungary are well wrought, opulent, correct,
and a bore. They show nice people in pleasant places, and
everyone is too polite to have a really good time.

Bernard is by far the best known tapestry designer of his
time; but fame is not necessarily a measure of relative worth.
A nameless man has met the same transition problem with
more simplicity in a series of eight tapestries of unequal size,
comprising twelve scenes, illustrating the Legend of Notre
Dame du Sablon. The set, which was formerly in the Spitzer
Collection, was made for Francis de Taxis, Master of the Posts,
and finished in 1518.

The Legend of Notre Dame du Sablon recounts the story of
Beatrice Stroetkins, an old woman of Antwerp. It is the year
1348, but, following the conventions of the time, the scenes are
represented as taking place when the tapestry was made. Beatrice lies in her bed, dreaming of the Virgin who appears to her
in glory and bids her search out, in the Cathedral, an ancient
and neglected statue of herself. In the next piece Beatrice goes
and gets the statue of Mary, and we see her lifting it out of its
niche, while in the foreground she pleads with the wardens of
the church, four substantial burghers, to allow her to take it
away. The altar in the background is decorated with the images
that have supplanted the neglected statue, a panel with the
Virgin Enthroned and a painting of the Annunciation.

In the next piece, now in the Kaiser Friedrich Museum,
Beatrice takes the statue to a painter to be restored, and we
have an excellent illustration of a painter's studio of the
period. And in the same panel she returns the figure, all fresh
in new colors and gilt, to the church. But Beatrice's pious task
is not yet done. The Virgin appears to her again as she lies in
her bed, bidding her this time to take the statue to Brussels. So
she goes to the church and begs the wardens for permission to
fulfil the miraculous command. In the background of this
scene is an interesting bit of genre, showing the informal feel-

ing about churches at that time. Two ordinary citizens sit gossiping in a chapel at either side of the altar, as if they were at a tavern table, and one even drinks wine out of the chalice.

The wardens refuse Beatrice's request, but she is not allowed to accept her defeat, for she is again haunted by dreams in which the Virgin appears to reiterate her instructions more insistently. In short, Beatrice is the perfect type of the officious nuisance, making herself a job by finding excuses for good deeds. All of these three scenes are on one panel (Pl. 23).

Desperately determined, Beatrice takes the image away. With it she goes down to the harbor, gets into an empty boat, and it glides miraculously through the water, divinely guided to Brussels. In the background Beatrice and an old man do homage to the statue, enthroned at the foot of the mast, while little amorini angels hover protectingly above. In the foreground the elders of Brussels, gathered on the quay, decide that their city has been divinely ordained as custodian of the statue, and send word to Antwerp that they are assuming the responsibility.

In the last piece, which is in the Cinquantenaire Museum in Brussels, there are again three scenes. Beatrice lands on the quay where she is received by Charles V and Francis de Taxis, who had commissioned the set. In the centre the statue is borne with full honors to the Cathedral. Charles V and his younger brother Ferdinand carry the litter over which amorini hold the canopy. The Chapter, in full canonicals, precedes, and a crowd of worshippers gathers around, including Francis de Taxis, who kneels in the foreground. Finally, the rest of the royal family come to worship, Marguerite of Austria in a green and yellow cloak lined with ermine, over a red damask dress, and Ferdinand and his four sisters, all with the long Hapsburg jaw. Francis de Taxis is repeated, almost identically, and above is Beatrice again, devoting her life to the adoration of her spiritual child and queen.

The style of the Notre Dame du Sablon set is very close to that of Bernard at some points, but it could not be the work of Bernard himself, for it is more sensitive, more reserved. Another, more refined personality, which is also closer to the

PLATE XXIII

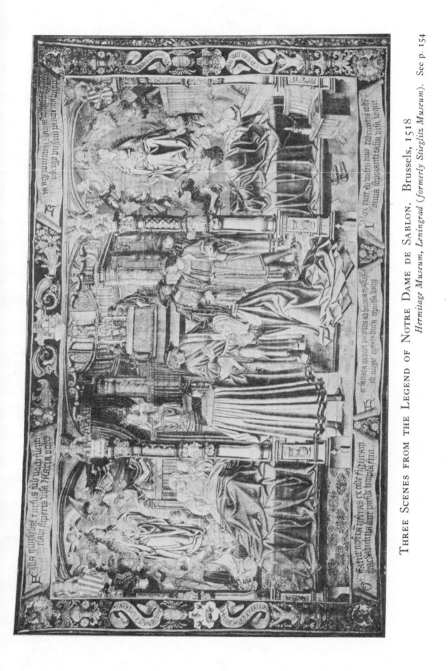

THREE SCENES FROM THE LEGEND OF NOTRE DAME DE SABLON. Brussels, 1518
Hermitage Museum, Leningrad (formerly Stieglitz Museum). See p. 154

fifteenth century, is reflected here. The attribution of the Hunts of Marie of Hungary to Bernard, based on the assertion of van Mander, is verified by the initial B inserted decoratively on the collar of a dog (cf. p. 149). Similarly in this set, on the purse of a man in the group of burghers who arrange to receive the statue, is the initial P. Bernard had an older brother Philip, of whom nothing is known save that he was a painter. If Bernard signed his cartoon on a dog collar with a B, was it not his brother Philip who signed his on a purse with the initial P?

Moreover, in the simple but conspicuous scrolls dependent from the P can, without any undue strain of imagination, be read the name Orle, in the kind of compound, compressed rendition commonly used a few years later in the signatures of Brussels weavers. The man who wears the purse is a young man, though no longer a boy, for the first sagging under the chin has begun. He is about the age that Philip van Orley would probably have been in 1516 when the cartoons must have been drawn.

For the most part this designer seems to have specialized in miniature tapestries, the rich small panels with religious sub-jects made for private chapels. So a square Adoration of the Magi, formerly in the Somzée Collection, is evidently by this man. The Virgin sits enthroned in the middle and the three kings and their attendants crowd around, all the figures in vignette in a compact mass, with the elaborately wrought ves-sels that are offered to the child set on a table which frames the composition across the bottom. Or again, there is in the Cin-quantenaire Museum a piece, equally small and also square, with Anne and Mary enthroned side by side, playing with the infant Jesus who squeezes a bunch of grapes into a chalice, in symbolism of the Eucharist, while on either side an angel is in attendance, the one singing, the other accompanying on the harp. These finished and elegant small tapestries are very close to paintings in style, suggesting that the designer probably was more accustomed to using his talents in this other medium. Throughout he maintains his northern directness and is quite unaffected. Yet he does not cling to any stubborn archaism but makes his peace with the new mode by using rounder

[155]

forms, freer groupings, and a more open treatment of the three dimensions.

The qualities inherited from fifteenth-century Flemish tapestry, which enriched the work of both van Orleys, and to a lesser degree of Vermeyen also, lingered on in spite of the fact that the cartoons that were to initiate a complete change in style had already arrived in Brussels. In 1514 Leo X (1476–1521) had ordered from Raphael (1483–1520) a set of designs illustrating the Acts of the Apostles, to complete the decorations of the Sistine Chapel. The Pope was a humanist, by innate temperament an urbane epicurean, by conviction a common sense rationalist, and by education a classical scholar. Raphael's cartoons corresponded to his predilections. They are suavely finished products of the impersonal realism automatically produced by an accomplished classicist of the time, but they have little relevance to their Christian theme and still less to tapestry. In each cartoon a group of large, highly modelled figures fills the foreground, set against a distant landscape or before an architectural screen heavily embellished with standard classical elements. The compositions are simple and too transparent. The figures are conventional and characterless, their gestures theatrical and obvious. The demonstrative poses, however dramatic, never ruffle the Olympian calm; no emotion vitalizes them, no conviction gives substance to either the forms or the expressions. The resultant effect is empty and commonplace, yet these tapestries caused such a stir that, once the style had been assimilated, they revolutionized cartoon design. Moreover, they have maintained their fame down to the present day. Their success was doubtless due partly to the prestige of Raphael's name, partly to their novelty, but principally to the circumstance that they embodied the reaction from fifteenth-century romantic realism to the Renaissance pseudo-classical romanticism, and they had just that combination of the grandiose and the sentimental that the taste of the next three centuries admired.

Six renditions of the cartoons were in use for more than three centuries, and seven factories, at one time or another, wove the set or parts of it, some of them repeating it a dozen times, so that it is not surprising that nearly sixty series or parts of series are in existence today, as well as three sets, at least, of the cartoons, more or less complete. The original paintings from Raphael's studio are in the Victoria and Albert Museum. They are on paper and in very bad condition, having been cut in strips for the convenience of horizontal loom weavers, so that they are even weaker than the tapestries. Though Vasari claims that Raphael colored them with his own hand, he also gives credit to Raphael's pupil, Gianfrancesco Penni (*c*. 1488–1528), for important work on them. Other pupils who are supposed to have collaborated are Giovanni da Udine (1487–1564) and Caravaggio (*c*. 1492–1543). Raphael was paid a hundred ducats apiece.

The woven versions vary greatly in elegance of drawing and quality of color. The original weaving was entrusted to Pieter van Aelst of Brussels, who found the high keyed fresco tones, hatched to simulate the smooth strokes of a brush, the light-washed, vanishing distances, and the paucity of decorative detail so contradictory to his habits that he deepened the color, defined and hardened the landscapes, and embroidered one or two of the garments. He also enriched them liberally with silk and gold, in accordance with Leo X's preference for the lavish and sumptuous, the cost of weaving amounting to 1500 ducats apiece. The set was delivered in 1519, but it was destined to hang in the Sistine Chapel only eight years, for when Charles V plundered Rome it was stolen and scattered. Three years later Clement VII retrieved some of the pieces, which had come up for sale in Lyons, and several others drifted back to the original ownership in the next few years, there to remain until the end of the eighteenth century when they again came on the market. One of them was burnt at this time to extract the gold, but that proved unprofitable, so the remaining panels were sold to a Genoese from whom the Pope (Pius VII) again bought them back in 1808, since when they have belonged to Saint Peter's.

The original cartoons were presumably left in Brussels where van Aelst continued to weave them, producing seven sets. The paintings came to Rubens's attention, and he persuaded Charles I to buy them for the Mortlake factory in 1630, where they were woven twelve times. In 1649 they were sold with the effects of Charles I, but Cromwell bought them for £300 for the government. Sir Christopher Wren designed a gallery at Hampton Court expressly for them, but they did not remain there long, wandering from one royal residence to another, until late in the last century when they were installed in the Victoria and Albert Museum.

The innovations in the conception of tapestry implicit in these cartoons were so profound that it took nearly two decades for them to be assimilated. But once they had been adopted by the Flemish designers, they practically obliterated the preceding styles. They were the vogue, and an art that is producing for the market must respect demand. The change affected almost every external aspect of the draftsmanship, methods of composition, scale, modelling, perspective, light, and the treatment of detail. It completely revised, too, the color. The introduction of sun-lit landscapes and aerial perspective and, to a lesser degree, the fallacious idea, derived from white marble sculpture, that the classical world had been colorless, led to a paler and thinner palette, quite irrelevant to the thick texture of the fabric.

But the most fundamental revolution was in the point of view. The Flemish artists of the fifteenth century thought in terms of illustration. They were concerned with statement. It was a period of unreflective creative energy, of men who wished the arts to record with their own directness their life and manners, their achievements, passions, diversions, and aspirations. The Renaissance, on the other hand, was devoted to style. Wealth and security left a surplus of energy that recoiled on itself in a selfconscious, manufactured culture and, in the arts, in an expensive, fabricated elaboration. Even in Italy, the land of its origin, the essential unsoundness of such deliberate and theoretical intellectual and artistic mannerisms soon led to a decadence that resulted either, on the one hand, in over-sweet affectations or, on the other, in frigid and vacant conventions. In Flanders, where the style was learned by rote, without the illumination of innate sympathy, it became an inflated and distorted formula. In both the graphic and decora-

[158]

tive arts and somewhat, too, in literature, classicism remained
for the Northerners, a set of rules, carefully learned and conscientiously and systematically applied with native thorough-
ness, but never sensed or appreciated, until the genius of
Rubens fused this externally acquired culture with the racial
character (cf. Chapter XI).

The court chroniclers of the fifteenth century had been kept
busy setting down facts. The great Rhetoricians and their followers in the sixteenth century labored over allusive, flattering
inventions. The architecture of the fifteenth century had been
richly wrought, but the tracery and foliations, however intricately scrolling, were the development and embroidery of
the structural elements. In the sixteenth century in Flanders,
decoration was the product, not of the mason, cutting directly
in his building stone, but of a pencil and paper designer like
Hans Vriedeman de Vries, and it was applied to the already
conceived buildings like the galloons, buttons, puffs, ruchings,
tassels, braids, and stitchery of the clothes. The fifteenth-century
painters limned, impartially, ugly men and women and their
well kept goods. Their sixteenth-century successors gave their
sitters prettiness, attitudes, and a stage set, the Antwerp man-
nerists using the grim Christian episodes to show simpering
little ladies in their silks, and gallants in their rakish hats amid
enormous, unsubstantial ruins and canvas scenery, while still
later Flemish painters converted any scene into a display of
modelled muscles.

Pieter Coeck van Aelst (1502–1550) and Michael Coxcie represent the best quality of the new style of work. Coeck was a
much traveled man, for in addition to the trip to Rome, an essential part of his artistic education, he probably accompanied
Vermeyen on the expedition of Charles V to Tunis (cf. p. 139)
and later, in 1533, went to Constantinople to learn about
Oriental weaving and undertake some negotiations concerning
tapestries with the Turkish Sultan, Suleiman the Magnificent.
But though he made sketches and notes on the Turks which
were published posthumously as *Les Moers et Fachons de Faire
Turcq,* his cartoons do not profit by any of the novel types,
picturesque costumes or varied landscape that he had a chance

to see. He automatically followed the fashion, and drew the usual semi-animated Roman sculpture. His sets, the most noted illustrating the life of Saint Paul, enjoyed great fame, but his cartoons are only perfunctory mutations on a limited repertory of tricks. The style reappeared with slight individual differences and varying degrees of skill in countless other series produced by his confreres in the next hundred years, for example, the popular and often repeated deeds of Scipio Africanus. There is no more feeling in any of these designs than in an art school set of plaster casts.

Coeck's figures are excessively long legged, a distortion which he adopted, apparently, to facilitate exaggerated postures, devised partly to incorporate bas-relief conventions and partly to intensify the dramatic gestures. Thus he commonly arranges his personages with the torso twisted to give the maximum surface, while the legs are in profile, spaced and flexed wherever possible, and the head likewise is in profile. The theory is sound, as the pose permits the most vivid definition of silhouette. Again he throws his principal figures, whenever he can, into an oblique motion and this theory, too, is sound, as the disbalance of this slanting line does give an impression of precipitancy and urgency. But though Coeck had thus learned his theoretical lessons accurately, he brought to their application too little innate feeling ever to achieve a design of genuine artistic significance.

Coxcie (1499–1592) was the first Fleming to develop the Roman grand style. In 1531 he painted a fresco with life size figures in the Chapel of Santa Barbara in Santa Maria dell' Anima, to the order of the Flemish cardinal. He worked on this three years, and spent seven or eight years altogether in Italy. His most important tapestry series, illustrating the History of Cadmus, and a second showing the Exploits of Charles V, made to the order of Philip II to whom he was court painter, are not known, and probably were never woven, but one large and popular set, of which many renditions exist, is attributed to him very credibly. It shows various episodes of the Old Testament. The finest and most complete version is in the Wavel Castle in Cracow, the property originally of Sigismund Augus-

Plate XXIV

Cartoon from the Creation of Man by Michael Coxcie.
Brussels, 16th century   *Stuttgart Museum.* See p. 161

tus (1548–1572), while another excellent set in Florence belonged to Cosimo I de' Medici, who bought it in 1553. Another piece in the Florentine Collection with the Carrying of the Cross, which must be by Coxcie also, shows his docile assimilation and facile practice of the Italian theatricalism of the period. His style is far more refined than that of Coeck, his talent, however second rate, more sensitive. Suave figures, nearly life size, with smooth, well rounded flesh, move gracefully in decorative settings. If the attempted combination of grandeur and elegance has hardly risen above pretence and sweetness, that is less the fault of Coxcie than of the Italian taste of the time (Pl. 24).

A host of lesser men produced innumerable inferior imitations of the work of these leaders, for tapestry was now an increasingly profitable industry and quantity production, tentative at the end of the fifteenth century, was the central aim. Flanders could manufacture decoration for Spain, Italy, France, Germany, England, and herself because, thanks to the standardization of the Renaissance, the fashion in all these countries was the same. The result was a multiplication of mediocrity unalleviated by any fresh invention. Moreover, at the end of the century, when the market demand was at its height and the weavers were rushing their products off the looms, a very poor quality of red dye was introduced which has, in the course of time, either been quite effaced, leaving the entire hanging blue and yellow, or remains only as a muddy reddish tinge. A few years ago these dull, musty pieces were considered more antique looking and artistic, but fortunately the adulation of poor condition and dirt has now practically disappeared. The more intelligent demand for color, however, has produced the evil of " refreshed " or re-painted tones. But even this is preferable to the burnt out, dingy rags that were at one time admired, for the restoration, however specious, at least brings the tapestry nearer to the artist's original intent.

The change of fashion affected not only the figure tapestries, but also the purely decorative designs. In the opening years of the sixteenth century strange conventional plants were introduced, covering the whole surface with heavily serrated leaves, remote descendants of the acanthus crossed with the common thistle, and huge polychrome flowers with exaggerated pistils and stamens. Now, at the height of the Renaissance, trees and plants were set, not as a flat pattern, but in perspective, making thick forests, a theme that continued in varying interpretations for the next four hundred years. Or else, a conventional garden in the new classical style is portrayed, with geometrical beds, fountains, pergolas, sculptures, and pavilions. The color of these is usually very dull, flat green, at the best relieved only by a little opaque blue. Tiny figures fill a minor part, either classical dolls in flowing robes, or more convincing men and women of the time. In the forests they hunt various prey or play games, in the gardens they wander, flirt, and pretend to work.

The most interesting set of this type illustrates the lives and love of a shepherd and shepherdess, Gombaut and Macé, continuing the fifteenth-century pastorals, motivated by sentimental yearning for escape from life's fatuities into rural simplicity, but freighted with the inescapable consciousness of death (cf. p. 99). Though the earliest known weaving of this series dates from the middle of the sixteenth century, the cartoons must have been painted some twenty-five years before (Pl. 25). Its popularity persisted even into the seventeenth century, when it enters into a hard deal that Molière's Miser tries to negotiate. There are seven panels, each showing the peasants in rather small scale in a conventional leafy landscape, with explanations in French doggerel on banderolles. In the first, the hero and heroine are ten years old and chasing butterflies; in the second, fifteen, playing croquet and already making love; in the third they are twenty and dancing; in the fourth, twenty-five and having a picnic; they are then affianced; in the sixth they are married, with the Gallic witticisms considered appropriate to the occasion; and in the seventh they meet old age and finally death.

> So will the end come to us all
> Our pleasures suddenly will pall,
> Illness and age descend;
> But if in Heaven at last we end,
> Conquered, resigned we'll take death's call.

PLATE XXV

SCENE FROM THE LIFE OF GOMBAUT AND MACÉ. Brussels, 16th century

Germain Seligmann Co. See p. 162

Man will gain naught in fruitless flight,
There is no shelter from Death's might.
We all must pass into his hands,
The great and small of all the lands.
God is our refuge in this plight.

Raphael, accustomed to treating wall decorations as an architectural whole, had his cartoons supplied with wide borders,
those at the top and bottom with bas-relief scenes from the life
of the Apostle Paul or episodes from the career of Leo X when
he was the Cardinal Giovanni de' Medici, the others elaborately
ornamented with the grotesques characteristic of Raphael's
atelier, fruit and flower swags, pergolas, and allegorical figures,
in an irrational but well constructed sequence. Borders, to be
sure, were no novelty. They had always been an essential part of
tapestry, even in the early Egyptian work (cf. p. 12), though
for a time during the fifteenth century many tapestries seem
to have had only a band of inscriptions across the top and of
flowers in natural arrangement across the bottom. But all the
borders up to this time, Hellenistic (cf. pp. 16, 22), Roman-
esque (cf. p. 38), and Gothic, had been distinctly subordinated
to the general scheme. Now they assumed a life of their
own.

In the increasing commercialization of tapestry, however, the
borders, especially, suffered from standardization. The side
borders from the Raphael set, which had probably been composed by Guilio Romano (1492–1546), were used over and over
again with varying permutations and rearrangements, and certain other cartoons were also repeated endlessly, notably one
illustrating the earth, the waters under the earth, and the heavens above. Up either side are storied hills where roam the beasts
of creation. Across the bottom is the foamy deep inhabited by
sea horses and various finny monsters. At the top is the sky, thick
with birds. Other stock borders were created by recombining
standard figures of pseudo-classical ladies with assorted allegorical labels, set in bowers between bunches of flowers, resulting,
sometimes, in quaint juxtapositions. Thus Poetry, Labor and
Law, Diligence, Experience, repeated twice, once sitting and

[163]

once standing, Architecture and Mother Love are all brought together to keep solemn watch around a bear hunt.

The designers of the lesser tapestries of this period are anonymous, for the inscription of names in decorative semiconcealment on garments, banners, and tents had been almost wholly abandoned, but the records indicate a practical monopoly of cartoon painting in Antwerp. A settlement at Antwerp is mentioned as early as the fourth century and in the eleventh century it had the honor of having as Marquis, in title if not in fact, the shining knight, Godfrey de Bouillon; but it attained importance only after the closing of the harbor of Bruges, as a business city, a commercial character that is reflected in the school of painting there, for the Antwerp painters developed a large output on a kind of factory system, adapting purchased models, printed book illustrations, with a minimum of inventive effort. True, Bruges, when she was mistress of Flemish art, had likewise been well fed by her ships and fairs, but Bruges had had also a regal role, housing some of the finest extravagance of the Dukes of Burgundy. Antwerp, living wholly by barter and profit, could not rise above that quality, and so it is fitting that she should have been the centre of tapestry designing when the art was controlled by quantity production.

But though most of the designers are anonymous, the weavers, on the other hand, now signed their products in accordance with a law (1528) that every tapestry have on the margin the registered city and shop marks. The latter are usually in the form of complex monograms, sometimes a whole name spelled in an interwoven compound of letters. Many of these have not yet been deciphered, but others, in spite of their ambiguity, have been identified, with the help of the numerous documents that give the names of all the greater and many of the lesser weavers. These constituted veritable dynasties, a family often controlling an important shop through several generations.

Brussels almost monopolized the industry, with legions of weavers, dominated, however, by a few outstanding names. At the beginning of the century Pieter van Aelst (c. 1532) was the foremost master. He had an official status granted by Philip the Fair. He wove at least one set of cartoons of Jean van

Roome's designing, the Passion, of which a full series is in the Cathedral of Trent and a single panel in the Spanish State Collection, both decoratively inscribed with his name; and through his hands passed also the series that initiated the Roman style, the Acts of the Apostles by Raphael.

Even more famous and influential was Willem von Pannemaker (1578) who supplied tapestries to Maximilian, Marguerite of Austria, Marie of Hungary, Charles V, the Duke of Alba, and Philip II. It was he who supervised the translation on the looms of the Vermeyen cartoons of the Conquest of Tunis (cf. p. 139), and his mark appears on the fêtes of Henri III (cf. p. 176).

In Pannemaker's later years a family that was to be prominent through several generations came to the fore — the Geubels, the founder of the dynasty being Franz, who was already sufficiently famous in 1544 to be given some work on the Tunis series. Toward the end of the century, about 1585, Jakob succeeded as head of the business. He died in twenty years, but his widow continued his work for another decade. The shop produced a vast quantity of merchandise of different grades, all in the standard, readily marketed style. But weavers' names are of little significance in the history of tapestry as an art. If they were incompetent they might defeat the artist's purpose, but any Master in the Brussels guild at this time was sufficiently skilled to be accurate and for that very reason to contribute little or nothing, positively, to the finished effect.

CHAPTER X

CATHERINE DE' MEDICI
AND HENRI III

WHEN a style has become set in a rigid formula, especially in an industrialized art, only the influence of a striking individual produces innovations or even variants. In the personal arts like music and literature (for they, too, can be " industrialized " in the theatre or journalism), the revivifying force of individuality will come from the artist himself. But in the decorative arts like tapestry, the personality of the patron is decisive. So in the sixteenth century, out of the undifferentiated mass production of tapestries with classical figures or with semi-realistic landscapes, only those few series emerge as distinctive which were the response to some marked character. François I created a style by his patronage (cf. p. 147); Charles V put his stamp on one set (cf. p. 142), and in the second half of the century Catherine de' Medici (1519–1589) and Henri III (1551–1589) both left their imprint, each according to his own self.

Catherine owed her very origin to the struggle to control Europe between François I and Charles V. François I needed the support of the Pope, Leo X. The Pope, on his side, was watchful for a brilliant marriage for his nephew Lorenzo. If it was a French marriage it would have the added advantage of getting an ally, for the Medici, too, were looking for international support. So between them King and Pope arranged the betrothal of Lorenzo and Madeleine de la Tour d'Auvergne who was of royal blood, and François I gave them a regal wedding at court (1518), with a ballet of seventy-two ladies, followed by a day of elaborate tournaments.

But in one year and three days after these glittering festivities, Madeleine was dead, leaving a two weeks old daughter who had cost her her life, and Lorenzo, who had been suffering from an uncured wound and a ravaging disease when he married, died six days after. Catherine Marie was an orphan. Sole legitimate heir of the Medici claims in Florence, she was from that time on the shuttlecock between the battledores of Papal policy and Florentine republicanism. By the time she was six she was set up as the future Princess of Florence. From these high hopes, within two years, the poor child, buffeted from one extreme to the other in constant uncertainty, found herself an incidental victim of Charles V's sack of Rome. In the end, however, the Mediceans won, and Catherine went back to her family, which consisted of a bastard brother and a bastard cousin. They were only boys of seventeen and eighteen, but they were already young men of the world, with a passion for pleasure and elaborate entertaining. With them she lived in the Medici palaces in Rome and Florence, in the midst of gay fêtes and pompous public displays. Thus from prison the child of eleven suddenly rebounded to luxury and dissipation.

But for the third time Catherine's fate was to be determined by the Franco-Spanish contest for supremacy. François needed again the help of the Pope, now the other Medici, Clement VIII (Pope 1523–1534). A royal alliance would be a tempting bait. He offered his second son, Henri, as husband for Catherine Marie. After much negotiating and many changes of plan, the bargain was finally sealed, and Catherine was decked out with gorgeous clothes and a dazzling suite of over a thousand persons, to escort her to France. It was only when she arrived there that the child of fourteen was told what was happening to her. The marriage was not only celebrated but also consummated at once (1533), and the celebration lasted thirty-four days.

When the gaieties were ended Catherine found herself in the worst plight of her whole harassed life. Her husband, a sullenly introverted little boy only twenty days older than herself, wanted to have as little as possible to do with her. The court despised her as a parvenue. And she was producing no heir. Then at the end of three years came a flash of hope. The older prince died. Henri became the Dauphin, she the Dau-

phine. It was a position of importance that demanded consideration. But there followed immediately even sharper bitterness.
Diane de Poitiers, a widow seventeen years his senior, sophisticated, intelligent, calculating, took Henri in hand, and he remained forever thereafter her property, body and mind (cf.
Chapter VIII). Catherine, consumed with jealousy and hatred,
scorned and helpless, had to steel herself to dignity in order to
conceal her shame.

Catherine had, moreover, no compensations to pit against the
disgrace. She was an outsider and, in the eyes of the French
nobility, in spite of the royal blood of poor little dead Madeleine de la Tour d'Auvergne, a plebeian. The commercial stain
on the Medici escutcheon made her socially unacceptable.
Moreover, she was conspicuously ugly. Her face was coarse and
fat, her features heavy and ill formed, stiff black hair, thick
black brows, protuberant black eyes, big nose, large pendulous
lips; and as she got older she got enormously fat. Her only
beauties were her hands and legs. She made the most of them
but they were not enough. Moreover, she was not stupid. She
had the intelligence to know just how badly off she was.

After ten years of sterile marriage between the Dauphin and
the Dauphine, the court physicians really put their minds on
the problem of getting an heir and, turning their attention
finally to Henri, succeeded in rectifying the defect, so that in
the next thirteen years poor Catherine had to bear ten infants.
She was almost incessantly pregnant while her husband publicly devoted himself to Diane.

Thus in the first forty-two years of her life Catherine de'
Medici was subject to almost every type of psychical injury
which experience can bring: childhood uncertainty, violent
reactions of fortune from one extreme to the other, sudden
freedom from control in an undisciplined society in adolescence, disappointment, neglect, humiliation, intense sex jealousy, and constant and almost unmitigated shame.

Then she found herself a widow, not only master of her own
life but also Regent of the country, and so important was that
widowhood to her that she made it the motive of the set of
tapestries which is her contribution to the history of the art.

Catherine's enthusiastic embracing of widowhood reflected a complexity of motives, of which she was probably largely unaware herself, but the basic impulse was certainly to compensate for her long endured humiliation. She who had had to suffer Diane to rule the country was now official Regent. She who had never been a wife but only, first, a political counter, and then a breeding consort, could, by being a widow, demonstrate that after all she had been the real wife; and if she were a widow conspicuously enough perhaps her world might forget in time how little she had been a wife. And finally, it is quite possible that her imagination was haunted by the example of her rival, for Diane had always staged conspicuously her widow's role. The very insistence of her suffering at Diane's hands would tend to make Diane a secret obsession, impressing Catherine's suggestibilty. And then, too, now that at long last she, Catherine, had come into her own, her patiently but bitterly awaited triumph would be made the more obvious by the parallelism of their widow's weeds.

The set of tapestries exalting Catherine's widowhood consisted, in the original designs, of seventy-four pieces, forty-six of which are given over entirely to the business of being a widow. Moreover, all the borders display the emblems of bereavement: a rain of tears that does not extinguish a burning brazier, for sorrow, no matter how intense, will never quench the flame of her memory; funeral palms, cypresses, torches upside down, broken mirrors, and Death's scythe.

The set was founded on a very bad poem by Nicolas Houel, a pharmacist attached to Catherine's train and busily devoted to her. It is an allegory (the sixteenth century could hardly bear to be direct), based on the history of the two Artemisias, Queens of Halicarnassus. The second Artemisia (355 B.C.) was also a professional widow and built a tomb for her husband, Mausolus, which was one of the wonders of the world and added a word to the vocabulary of burial. Artemisia had had, too, a young son to educate. The parallel was perfect. And then it was so nice that she was named Artemisia, hinting gently that after all Catherine really was the favorite, even of her rival's own patron goddess, Diana (Artemis). But even all this happy coincidence was not enough for Nicolas. His patroness must be made a more triumphant heroine. There had been a first Artemisia who accompanied Xerxes and distinguished herself at Salamis. Catherine had combated the Protestants. Of that, the less said the better, but the courtly Nicolas was undaunted by facts, so, fitting together the two classical prototypes, he contrived a parallel between the first Artemisia's campaign against the Rhodians and Catherine's affair of the Protestants.

While comparatively few of these tapestries exist, and a number were apparently never woven, a complete summary of the series is possible, for most of the drawings have been preserved, scattered in various collections, some of the cartoons remain, and the lacunae can be filled in from Nicolas's manuscript. The first piece shows the Queen, surrounded by the Seven Arts and four Virtues, Faith, Hope, Charity and Justice. The second gives the title with arms and emblems. The third is a kind of frontispiece, with Catherine and Artemisia together, surrounded by statues of victories. Then the theme really begins. The King dies. In the next piece he lies in state, protected by a stag, a bull and two lions. How persistent these animal emblems are. They were the main attributes of the Great God from Sumerian times on, and hence guardians of his representative on earth, the King.

The next twenty-two pieces compose the funeral procession. The set was designed under the direction of Antoine Caron, an inferior product of the Fontainebleau school, much cherished by Catherine, and director of her court fêtes. He converted the King's cortège into a triumphal entry, with free borrowings from Mantegna's Triumph of Julius Caesar and from standard illustrations of Petrarch's Triumphs. The whole procession in full display would, beginning at the beginning and going back, show: first, nobles and pages carrying armor and swords; then a golden chariot carrying Immortality, a woman with a globe and palm: three philosophers walking together; a chariot drawn by a unicorn, bearing Apollo playing a lyre; the chariot of Time drawn by the Four Seasons; a chariot drawn by rhinoceros; a chariot drawn by elephants, imitated from a Triumph of Fame; a chariot drawn by lions; a group of caparisoned horses; a number of children on horseback; various animals bearing chandeliers; three white bulls; a group of men carrying crowns; soldiers carrying towers mounted on staves and the model of a castle; more soldiers carrying huge urns and vases; still more soldiers carrying urns, three tapestries altogether being given to these groups; soldiers with trophies, with again two tapestries for the theme; a mounted captain; a group of trumpeters; and, at the end, children and priests.

After this astonishing array has filed by, there comes the funeral itself in nine pieces. First there is a provisional burial, then sacrifices, then the funeral banquet and then Artemisia makes offering of a golden lion, installing it on a pedestal. In the next panels priests gather around the temple, offerings are made, funeral chants are sung, a funeral oration is delivered, and finally the Queen gives the orator a gift of a golden casket.

Here ends the first book. The second, which is devoted to the Education of the Prince, is announced with its own title showing a statue of the Queen flanked by statues of Wisdom and Justice. She has now become Regent, and the first piece represents a group of heralds announcing to the people an edict inviting them to present their grievances. As a matter of fact Catherine's subjects when she took over the power in 1560 had grievances enough. The Guises were in power and the Protestants, under their harsh and arrogant rule that annoyed even ardent Catholics, had very little chance for liberty or justice. The next piece shows the people presenting their causes to a judge, and then the Queen herself receives the delegates of the people at her palace, after which there is an Assembly of the States General. It was at this assembly that the Guises planned to inaugurate what would have amounted to an Inquisition, but the death of Catherine's oldest son, the sickly François II, put a sudden check to their power.

This is followed by another scene of sacrifice to the gods, preceding the coronation of the King, the child Charles IX (1560–1574). After the coronation, he banquets with his mother in a garden, and the architects come to submit samples of stone for the King's tomb.

At this point begins the training of the Prince, in thirteen panels. Savants give him the book of knowledge and soldiers the sword, forecasting the two main branches in which he is to be educated. The book learning comes first: philosophy; mathematics and astronomy; the arts. His intellect is now complete, and the really serious business of kingship, war, must be undertaken in mimic anticipation. He learns to ride; to fence; to take a fort; to marshal an army; to manoeuvre a fleet. He practises, too, all the supplementary physical exercises, swimming, wrestling, stag hunting, and boar hunting.

Then the Queen resumes her business of widowhood and the King's tomb is begun and carried through in eight pieces. She consults with sculptors and architects; they submit to her the model; the excavations are begun; the Queen places the first stone; the walls are built up, and finally the tomb itself is shown. It is a circular domed chamber with a classical portico at one side. Inside are statues of the Virtues set in niches, and outside, of the Arts. The sarcophagus itself has bas-reliefs, and mounted on it is a semi-recumbent figure of the King. The dome is crowned by a triumphal quadriga.

Building a tomb was the chief occupation of widows. Marguerite of Austria had a whole church constructed for her husband and herself at Brou (cf. p. 133), and Diane installed a gorgeous tomb for her elderly husband, Louis de Brézé, in the Cathedral of Rouen. It is of alabaster and black marble, relieved with gold, a figure of the dead on top, a figure of Louis as living at one side, and on the other Diane herself kneeling in prayer. It bears the inscription: "Here to thee, Louis Brézé, this tomb is raised by Diane, thy wife, stricken by thy death. One with thee in life in utmost fidelity, she will be one with thee in the tomb."

Catherine de' Medici's tapestry set terminates with the Siege of Rhodes in nine more pieces, beginning with the council of war, the Queen appearing as an Amazon in a helmet. At the actual fighting before Rhodes she is again in the forefront. Then she embarks in a ship to approach the city, hoping that the Rhodians will take it for one of their own boats. The trick succeeds so well that the enemy admit her within the walls. In view of Catherine's double faced policy with the Protestants, any emphasis on this kind of ruse would hardly seem tactful, but when deceit and diplomacy are so similar, the diplomat, if successful, can take equal pride in either one.

The Queen is next seen distributing the booty; then she erects in the public square a statue of herself and the City standing together, the latter being marked on the forehead, an Apocalyptic reference (cf. p. 71). She and her son then visit the monuments of Rhodes, and after that they look at the Menagerie. Finally, she sets sail for home, and at the end is the Triumph, with Pallas in attendance on the Queen's chariot.

Conspicuous in a number of the designs are handsome châteaux and beautiful gardens belonging to the Queen, and here again was salve for a long sore wound. Catherine had spent a good deal of time at Chenonceau when the Château belonged to François I, and had looked forward to having it as her own when François died. But no sooner had Henri inherited it, than he gave it to Diane. Catherine was so furious that for once she did not conceal her vindictive loathing of Diane. Though Henri gave her the Comté of Clermont and the Barony of the Tour en Auvergne to appease her, she only bided her time, and as soon as possible after Henri's death took Chenonceau away from the enemy. But she could not get the Château d'Anet into which Henri had poured wealth for his mature mistress, for it was built on a property that Diane had inherited from her husband. How bitterly she resented the magnificence and fame of this exquisite house and its lovely gardens where Henri had often dallied in happy retirement is manifest in these tapestries. One of them shows Catherine in possession of a house that is almost its counterpart, even to an exact copy of the famous Diana fountain in the court, and another imitates the gardens, where formality and nature were blended with sure French taste.

Small wonder that Henri III, the child of these two psychically injured people, Henri II and Catherine de' Medici, should have been a nervous deficient. Henri was, moreover, not only the victim of his immediate heritage, but also the issue of a history of degeneracy through several generations. Ironically enough, two lines which, through their mental instability, brought tragedy to France, sprang from Charles V, *le Sage,* one of the soundest, wisest, most reflective kings that France has ever had. From this stable, normal, intelligent father was born the insane Charles VI, whose madness nearly occasioned the disruption of the country, and Henri III, who was almost as disastrous a ruler, participated doubly in the strain, through the other line, the house of Orléans.

In the Orléans branch the heritage took a milder form. There was no insanity. Mediocrity of intelligence was combined with a forceless amiability that was, at first, only a weakness, with no marks of actual defect; but almost all of the men of this family countered the strain of life with the readiest of evasions, pleasure, took refuge from responsibility by making amusement a business. With fine clothes, random extravagances, flirtations, games, entertainments, pretty poetry, a tasteful promiscuity, they kept themselves busy playing at life so that they would not have to live. Was it not the unconscious device of unstable personalities to avoid the facts and efforts to which they were not adequate?

Louis, Duc d'Orléans, was a political factor in the distracted affairs of his mad brother Charles VI, but he won his power and exercised it largely as a successful ladies' man, the plotting gallant of Charles's ambitious and treacherous wife, Isabeau de Bavière, and he had always a dancing foot and an eye for a new flirtation. His son, Charles d'Orléans (1391–1465), man of fashion and fashionable versifier, was the victim of his sensibilities, so suggestible that he readily betrayed his family's cause by alliance with his father's murderers, the house of Burgundy. He sampled illicit delights more gingerly, but maundered in verbal sentimentalities. His son was Louis XII (1462–1515), an extravagant and silly man, with his gilt hat, and his wild schemes, fluctuating violently between impractical plots and expensive fêtes; and his grandson, through his daughter Claude, was Henri II, and so we come to Henri III. Or, again, we reach the same descent through the other son of Louis d'Orléans, Jean d'Angoulême, a man whose personality was paralysed by a long imprisonment in England. His son, Charles d'Angoulême, however, was true to the family character, trivial and self indulgent, an incessant philanderer. François I, his son, initiated a court that was a perpetual entertainment. For all of them pleasure was a passion. Probably it was a necessity.

The underlying instability marked, in this branch of the family, by this protective pleasure pursuit, did not come to the surface until Henri II. Childhood sufferings as a prisoner in Spain left psychical scars that were inflamed by his father's antipathy; but his mental balance was supported by his reliance on two stronger personalities, Montmorency and Diane (cf. p. 145). In Henri III, on the other hand, the deficiency was compounded by his maternal inheritance from Catherine de' Medici, and consequently in him the implicit defect of the stock was made fully manifest, so that the family weakness for pleasure became almost a mania.

The biologic flaw was evident in Catherine's other sons. The eldest boy, a weak and pimply youth, died young. The next brother, Charles IX, charming but frail, was not able to rally from the nervous shock of the massacre of the Protestants on Saint Bartholomew's Day, and so succumbed to tuberculosis. Henri III himself was a cyclothymic neurotic, with such typical symptoms as vegatonia, and with the instability that is the characteristic feature of that kind of abnormal personality. Physically the deficiency resulted in migraine, digestive disorders, and a recurrent skin eruption. Mentally it made him unable to keep his attention long on any purpose; caused him to be the victim of disorganizing fears; gave him a marked tendency to react violently in sudden unpremeditated decisions; made him anxious for the reassurance of personal popularity, though, owing to his neurotic self-absorption, he was socially obtuse; made him, too, the victim in all respects of an erratic emotionality, not the deep formative emotions of the strong, but the quick, extreme, visible excitability without control of the nervously defective; and, finally, it arrested his psychical development so that he was a permanent adolescent. Moreover, the eroticism that had colored the life of most of his forebears suffered a proportionate exaggeration, taking, as so often happens with men of this type, perverted forms.

Such a psychopathic constitution might, in another age, have produced another personality. Religious fanaticism is easy to this type. They have a taste for martyrdom and, indeed, Henri III sampled that in passing, making pilgrimages afoot, muttering Paternosters, and taking part in processions with the Blue Penitents, tied up in a sack, fingering a chaplet of skulls. The stage with its opportunities for self display and vicarious erotic satisfaction attracts them, too, and Henri did enjoy masquerade and mummery. But for the basic resolution of his life, true both to his family and his time, he turned to pleasure.

The sixteenth century was an age of pleasure. Men's energies were temporarily released from the hard work of living. States were quite well defined, governments and commerce reasonably well organized, the needs of life were, comparatively speaking, automatically met. So faith was waning fast, for faith is the emotional correlative of an absorbing active purpose. With faith went both its inhibitions and its hopes. Life was what it was, and quite probably no more. Get what you can out of the present, have a good time, and have it as consumingly and intoxicatingly as possible, so that you can evade anticipating the end. This was the ethics of the typical sixteenth-century man, and it was the ethics of Henri III, intelligent within his limitations, sceptical, scoffing at life, and getting away from it in a series of excitements at any cost.

And all this is summarized in a set of tapestries, now in the Uffizzi Palace in Florence, illustrating in eight panels the Fêtes given for the Polish Ambassadors at the time that Henri, then Duc d'Anjou, was elected to fill the vacant throne of Poland (1573). A year later, when the death of his brother Charles IX left Henri heir to the throne of France, he secretly escaped from his Slavic kingdom, which he detested as an isolated, barbaric place of exile, literally running away ahorse between dark and dawn.

The first piece shows the Court leaving one of the Châteaux to journey to Paris for the reception, and here again the property is made to resemble the Château d'Anet (cf. p. 173). Catherine is borne in a litter.

The great banquet for the Ambassadors was given at the Tuileries and Catherine appeared there as Pallas Gallica, wear-

ing a morion and carrying a halberd and a shield decorated with
the Gorgon's head, while Henri, also wearing a helmet and
carrying a sceptre and scales, was Jupiter, and entered mounted
on an eagle with a dragon under his feet. But this is not represented in the tapestries. They show only the outdoor entertainments, with Catherine in her sober widow's garments and Henri
either in court costume or, when the games require it, in armor.
The statues, however, of Pallas and Jupiter in quite this same
style preside at one of the festivities, where there is jousting on
foot. Henri himself is in the foreground here, with various
members of his court, attended by two little pages, while Catherine sits in a classical pavilion at the back, surrounded by her
court.

Pallas appears again, at a second fête, mounted on a chariot
drawn by four horses abreast, driven by a charioteer and escorted by her maidens. But here the parallel deity is, not Jupiter, but Venus on a similar chariot, with Love mounted behind.
The chief entertainment is a great mock cavalry battle, and
Catherine watches from a platform in front, on the left, accompanied by Henri of Navarre, later Henri IV, Louise de Vaudemont whom Henri III had married in 1575, and a dwarf, while
other ladies of the court stand opposite. An array of beauties is
on display in a pavilion in the background, waited on by a
group of naked little boy pages from Cupid's train. An orchestra
of eight girls in classical gowns play lutes, viols, and lyres.
Two corps of trumpeters sound a fanfare and the lesser spectators ahorse and afoot, are massed by hundreds outside the
barriers.

Henri de Navarre and Louise de Vaudemont are again present, with the Duc de Guise,[1] in a fourth panel where there are
water games, groups of men on rafts attacking with spears a
fabulous dolphin that spouts a fountain. On a distant raft a
half-dozen mermaids and mermen are blowing trumpets and
horns, while the rest of the orchestra, with bass viols, are hidden
in the bushes on shore nearby. A triton and a nereid astride
dolphins, and other mermaids and mermen disport in the waves.
Catherine holds her court on an elaborately carved and deco-

[1] The identification is not absolutely sure.

rated boat, and on the bank other guests dance ring dances or picnic in the woods.

Another water scene shows an assault of five ships on a little wooded island in the centre of a large square pool. Henri and his wife stand in the right corner, she looking rigid and antagonistic, he evidently trying to persuade her attention to the mock battle. The island is guarded by a detachment of foot soldiers. On the far side is a castle, and all about the edges are rows of spectators.

The sixth panel illustrates the game of quintaine, with mounted men and women tilting with spears at a dragon set on a column. Henri is in the foreground, in armor, about to get to horse to take his turn. The seventh panel represents another kind of mimic battle, an attack on a great figure of an elephant that stands on a platform, supporting a small fortress. In the foreground are Henri, his unstable and discontented brother the Duc d'Alençon, whom Catherine tried to marry to Queen Elizabeth, and Louise de Vaudemont.

In the last piece a ball is in progress in a garden (Pl. 26). Really the court had only two kinds of entertainments, the games of war that appear on the other pieces, and balls. Pageantry was often combined with one or the other. In this panel Henri, talking to one of the Polish ambassadors, stands on a high platform in front. It is amusing to note that both this Pole and Henri de Navarre, at the foot-jousting, wear a silk of practically the same design as the velvet worn by an angel in the Spanish State Apocalypse (cf. p. 73), a lion couchant in glory, with eagles and doves; but here, if there is any reason at all for the choice of the pattern, and quite probably it was selected by sheer accident, it could only be that the lion and eagles were emblems of royalty.

Catherine presides over her court in the background. On the lawn before her four couples (one hidden behind the spectators on the left) are dancing the Pavane. The orchestra is mounted on a high artificial rockery, evidently a favorite device, for it was also used for the orchestra at the Tuileries banquet. There are six women, three with bass viols, a lute, a flute, and a lyre.

[178]

PLATE XXVI

ONE OF THE FÊTES OF HENRI III. Brussels, 16th century
Italian Government Collection, Florence. See p. 178

The Pavane was so characteristically the court dance of this period that it was often called the *grand bal.* It was very stately, with only gliding motions, none of the leaping and twirling of the more lively steps like the Gaillard or the Moresque. Highly formalized, the character of the movement was supposed to have been derived from the dignified strut of the peacock (*pavo*), hence the name.

The dance, at the moment chosen for the tapestry, has only just begun. Before beginning, the couples paraded in a solemn promenade, then advanced before the Queen to salute her. They then took their places at opposite ends of the lawn, and are now in the opening figure, each pair of couples moving in an arc to the right to change places. In the next movement they will advance four steps toward each other, each man will circle with the lady opposite, and then they will return, each with his own partner, to their original places, the man behind, holding his right hand forward that the lady may clasp it with her left. Arrived at their places they will take one step on their toes and bow. In the third movement each man alone will advance in an arc of four steps, bow and return. Then in the coda the couples again advance, but this time not holding hands, bow to each other, and each man bows to his own lady. All this is done in the pavane step as the tapestry shows, in two-two time; on the first beat the right foot is glided forward, with both knees bent, then on the second the left is advanced and pointed. The next step is the reverse, beginning with the glide of the left, and so they proceed.

And meanwhile they are singing the song of the Pavane:

> Love who holds my soul
> Captive 'neath thy eyes,
> Who my spirit stole,
> Thief in smiling guise,
> Come, save me from my death.
> Revive me with thy breath.
>
> Why dost thou follow me?
> Why art thou at my side?

When in thy eyes I see,
I lose my inmost pride.
Such grace and lure thou hast,
My will will not hold fast.

Thy beauty and thy charm
And thy divine allure
Have made my being warm.
No coldness can endure.
My heart glows into flame
In ardor at thy name.

My spirit yearns to be
Free from passion, calm;
But love has seized on me.
My soul will have no balm.
Love pierced me with his dart,
Transfixed my faith and heart.

Then come to me, my love.
Then come to me, my dear.
No longer shouldst reprove.
Thy heart should know no fear.
My soul is all amiss.
Give me just one kiss.

I die, my love, my sweet,
I die in kissing thee.
When lip to lip we meet
My dazzled senses flee,
I hearken for thy call.
Love has me in his thrall.

The tides will cease to flow,
The mountains cease to stand,
The sun and stars to glow,
Verdure to clothe the land,
Ere my dawning love
One whit less will prove.

[180]

CHAPTER XI

RUBENS AND THE SEVEN-TEENTH CENTURY

IN the sixteenth century Flanders had been able to produce acceptable tapestries for the whole European market because her artists had assimilated the one style in demand at the time, that of Rome. In the seventeenth century she was still able to meet the taste of all of her clients, from England to Sicily, but now it was because she herself set the one universal fashion, that of Peter Paul Rubens (1577–1640). Hers was the great master, the outstanding personality, who both epitomized and determined the taste of the age.

Yet the triumph of Rubens was by no means the fall of Italy, for Rubens came to his paramount place on the shoulders of his Italian predecessors. Not only Rome, but also Venice contributed fundamentally to his style, so that spiritually he was the pupil of both Raphael and Titian, the one, through Giulio Romano whom he greatly admired, instructing him in the ingenuities of invention and the formulae of composition, the other inspiring him to glowing warmth and richness of color, though Rubens freshened the Venetian palette and intensified it with pure, unmediated surface colors in the Flemish taste. The Roman style of figure drawing he had already learned in his apprenticeship; heavy shoulders, thick biceps, corded calves and bossed knees, exaggerated volumes and massive frames. In Rome, and later in his own collection, he perfected his studio mannerisms by a direct study of the classical originals.

But though Rubens was thus imbued with the Italian spirit, and through Italy with her Roman heritage, he was, himself, wholly and typically a Fleming. He was a good, sound citizen, handsome in a large, robust way, and he always took good care of his health. Industrious, orderly, dependable, punctual, throughout his life he was a devoted family man, preferring at home a prudent life, well within his means, with a very regular régime. He was good natured but firm, ruling his pupils to absolute obedience, but always keeping on the best of terms with them and every one else, so that he was universally popular.

He prospered mightily because he had a good commercial intelligence. His studio was organized on modern shop principles, which enabled him to exploit his capacities to the full, accept every order that came, and make a good deal of money. He systematized the work by means of a skilfully assigned division of labor. A pupil or assistant — for he also employed qualified masters as the demand for his work mounted beyond all bounds — would be adjudged, within a short time of entering the atelier, as particularly talented in a specific line, and thereafter he did just that one job. Thus a painting was not merely divided into landscape for one group and figures for another but it was subdivided, so that the landscape would be apportioned according to the categories, architecture, animals, land, sky, water, woods. In this he was merely carrying to its logical limit the basic principle of his native school, for practically every Flemish painter of this period was a specialist, forcing to its utmost a capacity for one type of work, almost to the exclusion of every other kind of subject. Rubens himself made the preliminary sketches, supervised the development, and put on the last touches.

Moreover, Rubens's natural commercial intelligence functioned not only thus in the organization of his art, but also in driving a good bargain when the chance came along. He was asked to act as negotiator between Spain and England (1625–26). The Duke of Buckingham, representing the latter, was naturally anxious to have Rubens as friendly as possible. He offered the painter a hundred thousand florins for his art collection. It was a very good price. Rubens promptly took it. Flemish common sense came, in Rubens, to its epitome.

In attempting to combine his Italian education with his strong Flemish national characteristics Rubens was facing the same problem that Bernard van Orley had had to face a hundred years before. But there was this difference: Rubens, just by virtue of the completeness, intensity and fully coherent consistency of his qualities, was a great man. Van Orley suffered the uncertainty of the second-rate. Van Orley and Rubens, both being Flemings, were both frank and sensuous materialists, loving deep plush, shining satins, yielding furs, soft, firm flesh, warmth and abundance. Rubens, in his strength, could let his sense of touch become a passion, almost a lust. Van Orley could never revel in his enjoyment. Again, Van Orley, not quite a gentleman, had to be carefully well bred. He pictured ladies and gentlemen. Rubens, equally bourgeois, was swept by his inherent force and the self-confidence that it bred into the upper class, and so could be robustly common and exuberant without risk. And in their assimilation of their acquisitions from Italian art it was the same thing. Van Orley, having an ordinary mind, was cautious and so adhered to the facts, without, in consequence, ever controlling the underlying principles of the Renaissance. But Rubens had the assurance of inexhaustible vitality which crashes over all bounds. With this lack of inhibition he combined the intelligence to understand the essentials. Free to take and knowing what to take, he made himself master of the Renaissance style, not merely in some one aspect, but in its most fundamental and universal concepts, yet without ever conceding to it any relinquishment of his native and personal qualities.

And that is why Rubens did epitomize and determine the taste of the Baroque period, because he could infuse into the forms of Italian knowledge the vitality of his Teutonic, crass good health, mental and physical. For the Baroque style is, in its most obvious characterization, artistic thinking, whether for sculpture, architecture or the graphic arts, in the materials of the third dimension; but this is muscular thinking, which can be done most vividly and impressively by a man of physical strength and of such wholesome animal equipoise that his instincts are normal and are correlated with, and richly fulfilled in, his bodily life.

Every aspect of the third dimension was incorporated into

[183]

one compound structure by any fully competent painter of the seventeenth century as a matter of course, but he had these resources to hand only as the heritage of a long evolution. Mediaeval Europe, in common with the East, had designed paintings in terms of lines, and of planes which were surfaces of color. The latter were inflated, in the thirteenth century, into simple volumes. The next and complementary expansion of the concept attracted the attention of the painters to distance. The growing scientific interest of the Renaissance amalgamated these two elementary phases into the more complex and so more specific manifestation, perspective, with the minor concomitant, which so fascinated the fifteenth-century Italian draftsmen, foreshortening. With these three factual problems under control, volume, distance, and perspective, the way was open for their exploitation as an expressive vocabulary. The incorporation into the painter's education of a study of Roman sculpture and bas-reliefs accelerated the exploration of these possibilities and exaggerated their importance, so that in the seventeenth century, painting presupposed a manipulation of solid contours, the bulk and mass that lie behind them, cubical space relations both filled and empty, the mechanical interplay of these volumes and weights, and the emotional effect of the kind of pressure they exert, their quality of movement, their feeling and, perhaps most important of all, of the memory images of muscular experiences which they evoke. Rubens, not of course by theory, but by the assumptions of his training, automatically composed with these elements, and he was supreme in the use of them because his own physical soundness and bodily vitality made them a spontaneous medium of expression.

In making explicit all aspects of the third dimension, the Baroque style had created a rich material, fecund in possibilities both of physical beauty and of emotional excitement, but by that same token it was refractory and dangerous. It had to be harnessed and held to a pace, else the canvas would be crowded with confusion. And here again, in ordering and focussing the multiple complexity, Rubens was supreme precisely because he invigorated the knowledge of Italy with

[184]

magnificent Teutonic health. The Renaissance had perfected a set of formulae for controlling design, first by a plan developed simultaneously in the several constituent elements of a painting, and second, by the maintenance of a rhythm as marked as the rhythms of measured music. A completely unified organization was effected by, first, the interrelation of the lines into a consistent pattern in which no feature was either irrelevant or accidental; second, by the organization of the planes and the volumes contained within those lines to a correlative and equally determined cohesion; third, by the arrangement of the directions of motion, including the implied motion of the major lines of interest, to re-enforce the coherence already obtained by the first two systems of composition, and finally by the calculated use of color to the same end, re-echoing the unification of the linear, spatial, and movement schemes. Moreover, when Rubens adopted these categories of invention and expression, they had been further specified to the Baroque conception of a theme. The design, whether of line, mass, movement or color, must conform throughout to one motive, though according to the taste of the time, the greater the variety and the more flexible and cunning the adjustments, the more successful the development. The favorite Baroque motive was the " S " which gave play to the voluminous curves which this opulent century loved.

The rhythm, which ran through the composition, further tying it together, had to be appropriate to the form of the chosen motive, animating but restraining it. And this rhythm had to play clear and undeviating in a consistent flow throughout all the other aspects of the design, so that the same movement would swing, beat, pause, and resume its rush, in the interplay of the lines, the surfaces and the bulks behind them, in all of the implied and actual activities within the picture, and in the tonal variations, including the lights and shadows.

These principles, intellectually acquired and academically applied, resulted in a clever but tortured and unconvincing art. Rubens, predisposed to spatial feeling and motor realization by the easy sureness of healthy muscles and the pulsing beat of vigorous vitality, swept his designs into natural rhythms

[185]

of great force and swing, so that his forms roll and toss and sway through their exuberant S-curves, often cutting across and weaving in and out in energetic diagonals. But, however driving the force, there is never any violence, any excess or taint of hysteria. Rubens was balanced, physically, nervously, and rhythmically.

Rubens was, moreover, the perfect master of the Baroque style because he was never tempted to constrain its essentially physical potentialities to the expression of intellectual subtleties or spiritual abstractions beyond its inherent limitations. He had a good mind but only a very limited intellect. God never stirred from Rubens's Heavens, and the world was very right for him. He was an intelligent voluptuary, perceptive, understanding, shrewd, but essentially unsophisticated, so that he did not evolve; he only perfected his skill. His was the triumph of the physical normality of the Germanic races, the perfect antithesis of Theotocopoulos, El Greco.

Rubens was the most popular artist of his day because he was the consistent embodiment of his moment of history. The intellectual enthusiasm of the Renaissance had filtered down, in the fashionable world, to the stale dregs of convention, the partisan fanaticism of the Protestant struggle had provoked a reaction of routine orthodoxy, and after the shams and shattering uncertainties of the romantic imperial ambitions of the sixteenth century, the various countries had relaxed with relief into the limitations of a comparatively orderly local life. Flanders, recovered from a half-century of murderous, disruptive religious conflicts, was rejoicing in peace and expanding in busy prosperity. France was coming into her great age of affluence and strength. The English fleets were helping to fill English coffers. The German principalities, relieved of the menace of Catholic domination by the House of Austria, were going about their daily work soberly and competently. America, on the one hand, and the Eastern trade on the other, were yielding earned riches. On all sides there was growth and increase, and the wealth was soundly gained by effective activity. The poison of unearned increment was not yet numbing minds and weakening character. Rubens, healthy, normal, hard working and successful, and setting forth all these qualities in rich paint, was an outstanding symbol of the qualities of the age.

Rubens's studio produced, under his direction, four series of tapestry cartoons. In 1618 a Genoese noble family ordered a set of ten panels illustrating the Life of Decius Mus. The subject was very sympathetic to Rubens. For him, Antiquity was Rome. He knew Latin well, had a good library of Latin literature which he kept fresh in mind, had a large collection of Roman sculpture (when he designed this set he had recently bought Sir Dudley Carleton's collection of Antiquities), and was proud of the precision of his archaeological knowledge, famous for rendering accurately the details of Roman costume. In the painting of the Decius Mus cartoons Van Dyke seems to have collaborated with him, but the best opinion attributes not only the conception and the general arrangement, but even the specific development directly to Rubens, and even considers the designs especially personal and typical.

Three years later (1621–2), while Rubens was decorating the Gallery of Marie de' Medici, Louis XIII commissioned him to make a set of twelve cartoons for the Paris shop run by Comans and Van den Planken (cf. p. 262), illustrating the History of Constantine. France was not, at the moment, rich in artists who could make the needed designs, and the prestige of Rubens would add lustre to this official enterprise. Rubens turned the cartoons out quickly and easily. It is highly improbable, of course, that he ever touched brush to canvas for them, yet they were truly his production none the less. When he sent the first four to Paris, word went around the French capital that some new works of the great Rubens had arrived, and all the fashionables and the fashionable pseudo-learned hurried to express their opinions. Rubens was extolled for the accuracy of his classical costumes, even the nails in the shoes being just right, according to these erudites; but about the style they were far less enthusiastic. The legs, they said, were too curved. Rubens did not straighten the legs.

His next tapestry order came four years after this (1627–8), from the Archduchess Isabella of Spain. She wanted a set illustrating the Doctrines of the Eucharist (sometimes called

[187]

the Triumph of the Church) for the convent of Santa Clara at Madrid. Rubens made fifteen cartoons. The first five pieces were adaptations of one of the favorite themes of the Renaissance, the Triumphs. The subject had first become popular with the Triumphs of Petrarch, and then had been extended to endless other allegorical abstractions. The original form was always the same, following the Roman Triumphs; the Virtue, or personified concept in question, rides on a chariot drawn by symbolic animals, accompanied by the appropriate heroes and heroines from history and legend, while the wheels of the vehicle and the feet of the triumphant crush the traditional enemies. This standard version is used in the Triumph over Ignorance in this set. The Church, a woman in a satin cope holding aloft a monstrance, about to be crowned by an angel with the papal tiara, rides on a chariot drawn by heavy muscled horses with crimped manes and tails, led by women, armed with swords and staves. A second angel acts as charioteer, the dove of the Holy Ghost flies above, and a cloud of cherubim is in attendance. On one of the horses rides still another angel carrying a royal umbrella, with the crossed keys of Saint Peter on the ferrule, satyrs are bound to the wheels, and devils with serpentine locks are ground beneath them. The scene is not an event but a theatre tableau, with columns and swags defining the proscenium, which serves as a border, and the stage covered with a fringed carpet.

The next four pieces, representing the Old Testament antitypes of the Eucharist, were taken from a standardized program for the propaganda of the Eucharist, formulated at the beginning of the sixteenth century. The General conception of antitypes was, however, much older than this, dating from the ninth century. An antitype is an Old Testament story interpreted as the anticipation of a New Testament principle. The underlying theory is that God did not wait until the Messianic visitation to reveal truth to mankind, but embodied it both in the world itself, so that all manner of natural phenomena are really symbols of the Redemption, and in the Old Testament, where it is shrouded in allegory, subtly disguised, yet is so absolutely specific, that every moment in the New Testament is

[188]

PLATE **XXVII**

SCENE FROM THE HISTORY OF ACHILLES after a cartoon by Rubens.
Brussels, 17th century   *Boston Museum of Fine Arts.* See p. 189

exactly paralleled by at least one, or ideally two, episodes of the Old. For example, insight discloses that Jonah's adventure in the whale and his eruction really meant the Resurrection. This method of amalgamating to one idea, which has been accepted as absolute truth, other beliefs by means of ingenuity in rereading them, was in essence a revival of the Alexandrian gnosticism (cf. p. 10). The antitypes for the Eucharist could have been expanded almost indefinitely, for the ceremonial meal, as the physical counterpart of spiritual union with, or participation in the divine, is common to a great many cults, including some of the most primitive; but the official proselytisers selected four of the events of Judaic history — the meeting of Abraham and Melchisedech, the Gathering of the Manna, the Sacrifice of the Old Law, and the Prophet Elias in the Desert, and it is these that are shown by Rubens. The remaining subjects in the Eucharist set were devised to meet the needs of this occasion, and show signs of being arbitrarily and effortfully invented. The Christian mind was no longer naturally or easily expressing itself in allegory.

The small sketches for this set, which are now in the Prado, are finished with the greatest care, and many have been judged to be by the master's own hand; but the large cartoons fall far short of the conception. Clearly they were done by less talented members of Rubens's shop and were insufficiently supervised. The energetic rapidity with which Rubens's vigor inspired most of the work done in his atelier, degenerates here into mere haste, and some of the figures are shockingly awkward and formless. The first four pieces are by far the finest. Triumphs were sympathetic to Rubens's temperament, giving scope to his love of ample sweep and unchecked gusto.

The fourth set of tapestry cartoons, made between 1630 and 1635, illustrated the History of Achilles in eight scenes (Pl. 27). It seems to have been produced to the order of Charles I for the Mortlake looms. England was not going to be outdone by France. If the Paris shops were to have Rubens cartoons, so too must the factory of the British crown.

In all of these cartoons Rubens unreflectively applied his habits of three dimensional composition, thereby carrying to the limit the trends that had already characterized the tapestry of the preceding century. The landscape details which had presented the third dimension in the tapestry designs of his predecessors are now practically eliminated, leaving the figures in almost empty space; yet Rubens always managed to indicate limitless air circulating around them. His figures have grown to colossi, and their round modelling is inflated to the utmost spherical plasticity just for the exploitation of bulk and protuberant forms. As a necessary corollary of these latter developments, the number of figures is sharply reduced, many of his cartoons having only three or even two personages, and some only one.

The tendencies that Rubens thus exaggerated are directly contrary to the natural requirements of tapestry; yet Rubens's characteristics were not all unsympathetic to the medium. His lack of intellectual subtlety and his direct, sensuous interest in material facts, were both advantages; his skill in manipulating compositional schemes could have made a significant contribution, and his rich depth and range of pure color was a reform to be hailed with joy after the thin pallor or flat opacity of much of the sixteenth-century production. But as Rubens actually contrived his cartoons, not all of the merits that might be expected were realized. Rubens's materialism did not focus on things and their forms and colors, but on surfaces, the feeling of them and their tones in changing lights. Consequently, there is none of the detail that gives a varied and closely covered design, inexhaustibly amusing, to most of the fifteenth-century tapestries. Furthermore, in most of his cartoons Rubens exerted his ingenuity in composition only perfunctorily, and his color, though deeper and more satisfyingly saturated than that of the majority of his immediate predecessors, is disappointing in tapestry because it is a painter's color.

And there lies the real defect of Rubens's work for tapestry. Rubens was a painter, so instinctively and completely an oil painter that he defied tradition and rendered his large cartoons, not in tempera, but in oil. Oil paint was essential to the fulfillment of his greatness because its qualities as a material and its potentialities as a medium were the concomitants of the kind of physical and mental experience that constituted his aesthetic perception. When Rubens encompassed the essence of an object with the use of a keen eye, supplemented by vivid muscular responses, and by the vibrant feeling that those responses stirred, both his sensations and his emotions were such that, transmitted through his facile but well controlled gift, they flowed undeflected into his richly charged and exquisitely manipulated brush, immediately and completely externalized in the fat pigment, spread smoothly and viscously to make an unctuous surface, richly lustrous.

But this sleek, evenly free flowing, glossy medium is in direct antipathy to hairy, twisted wool in heavy ridges; and the imperceptibly graded transitions of a well laden, soft brush, swept with a cunning adjustment of the wrist, have only a specious and forced resemblance to hatched threads in irregular comb edges, interpenetrating in a direct contrast. Rubens asked a bobbin to become a brush, demanded that spun and dyed wool convert itself into malleable pigment carried in thick flowing oil, required the straight shoot of weaving to take the modulations of a swinging arm and turning hand. Raphael had, unaware, assumed the right to expect this of the men at the looms to a certain extent; but Raphael had qualities as a decorator quite independent of his medium. For the weavers really to follow Rubens it would have been necessary for them to be, not merely painters, but painters who thought, felt, and had their being in paint.

The Flemings were arrogant craftsmen with an old and stubborn pride in their skill. They did what Raphael asked of them, and did it so well that the best weavings of his cartoons really are superior to the cartoons themselves, which is as it should be. Then, having had to learn many difficult tasks which painters who knew not the bobbin had casually imposed, they were confronted with the new and graver perplexities of Rubens's oil cartoons. And they did what Rubens demanded, almost; but in just that fractional difference beyond which wool could not go in imitating paint, the greatness of Rubens was lost. The turbulent energy was there, the cleverly managed diagonals, the strong, well juxtaposed tones, but the pure paint surface, integral to those forms and to the feeling of them, and essential to their fulfillment, the genius of technique so great that it is itself a source of aesthetic emotion, these died on the loom.

The merits that remain are those that Rubens's pupils of sound talent could, under his thorough training, achieve with equal success. Indeed, some of the cartoons of these lesser men make better tapestries than the designs of the master himself; first, because, being lesser men, such commissions were more important to them, so that they expended a more thoughtful invention on the work; and second, because, not having the passionate genius of the brush, their results were less wholly dependent upon their medium.

Jakob Jordaens (1593–1678) produced cartoons that have, at their best, a grace, a delicacy of detail and a respect for the flatness of the surface that make them superior as tapestries to Rubens's work. They do not burst out of the weave in the tumultuous rhythms which Rubens inevitably swirled about in his designs, but are rather patterned on a full and varied surface. The finest pieces are in the series of Maxims, a set of eight designed in 1644 for three Brussels weavers, Jan Cordys, Franz van Cottheim, and Baldwin van Beveren, illustrating proverbs and popular sayings. All of them were adapted from paintings that Jordaens had already made, with little or no concession to the new medium, but in spite of this, some, notably the first of the set, really are tapestry, not just woven paintings. The figures are in almost flat silhouette, in expressive outlines that also make a continuous tracery, without too much overlapping, and the interstices are filled with minor decorative elements.

Seven years later (1651), Jordaens made a set of seven cartoons known as the Riding Lessons of Louis XIII, destined, by the very nature of the subject, to be far less successful, for horses are too obviously sculptural in their hard bulk to be treated tactfully as textile decoration by a pupil of Rubens. A third set of eight pieces depicts country life. These are the typical genre episodes of the period, specifically fitting in tapestry only as the subject happens to give an agreeable effect, yet

[192]

at no time offensively a betrayal of the medium, save, perhaps, in one night scene.

The qualities that render Jordaens's designs sympathetic to the medium, such as compactness and continuity of texture, are probably to be attributed, first, to the ascendance of the Flemish elements of his style over the Italian influence, for tapestry has always been primarily a Flemish art, only accidentally and by effort Italian; and second, to the circumstance that, unlike Rubens, his talent was not essentially interrelated with oil paint, but could function successfully in water color, which he used for some, at least, of his cartoons. Jordaens's chief defect, too, the thick, inert opacity into which his color degenerated, was no handicap when working for the weavers, for the palette of the finished product would be independently determined by the quality of the dyes at hand. In short, Jordaens's tapestries, while they are far from being great and can even properly be derogated by the exacting, are exceptionally good of their kind.

Concurrent with this school of Rubens a more purely Flemish tradition was maintaining itself, in spite of the world dominance of the great master. These thoroughly Lowland cartoons illustrate scenes of peasant life, and the determining practitioner was David Teniers, the Younger (1610–1694). In the fifteenth and early sixteenth centuries the peasantry had been a romantic fiction with a moral attached. In general, this moral was a sentimental yearning for the simple life, an escape philosophy so artificial in its aspirations that it seems scarcely sincere, a pretty pose. But even the most sentimental of the tapestries are often enlivened with the more natural Gallic savour of the risqué. Some of the doggerel on the shepherd and shepherdess pieces does not bear translating. In the sixteenth century this pastoral tradition was continued in painting, but with a sudden sharp alteration in character through the eccentric but powerful genius of Pieter Breughel the Elder (1530–1569). His peasants, also, are invested with a moral, but in place of deliberately naïve charm and Rousseauesque sentimentality, they convey a biting satire. Breughel patronizes his peasants, hates them, scorns them, spits on them in disgust, but respects them as a kind of fact, correlative with the brute truths about life. They are a more genuine performance than the fifteenth-century peasants dedicated to wistful hopes, but they are relentless, so that Breughel peasant scenes are often raw lechery.

The seventeenth century steered a course between these extremes because it was not utilizing the peasants for any didactic end, but was simply presenting them for themselves. The innate Flemish interest in fact and illustration came into its own, so that the affectations or suggestiveness of the fifteenth century on the one hand, and the brutality of Breughel, on the other, underwent equal changes, resulting in peasants that are a frank demonstration of healthy animality. The peasants of Teniers almost always royster in licence or even in lust, but it is always in a normal and sound exuberance. Teniers was competent, industrious, experienced. He had not a flicker of genius, not even a notable talent. He was wholly satisfied with common-sense observation, never suspecting that there is such a thing as aesthetic perception. But because he did accept his limitations without either struggle or pretence, probably unaware of them, he tilled his small field thoroughly and, the most important merit for this kind of subject, honestly.

It is easy to expound the deficiencies of Teniers's work, but it is more illuminating to see how bad it might have been if he had not had his solid Flemish virtues, and how shockingly bad it surely would have been if he had abandoned his native quality and scrambled after Rubens. For Rubens, also, painted a peasant festivity, the Kermesse that hangs in the Louvre. As in many Teniers scenes, the gaieties are well advanced, so that the peasants are hot, drunken, and lustful; but in Rubens's picture they are not just strong, earthy Teutons, scarcely human, only a bit above the farm beasts that are their daily intimates. They have turned into Italianate voluptuaries, with creamy, luscious flesh. Their abandon is not compulsive but conscious, and so vicious. Their sexual exhibitionism is not instinctive but contrived, conveying deliberate excitement. Rubens, in short, was not painting peasants. He was relieving his own surcharged mind.

[194]

PLATE XXVIII

THE INN after a cartoon by David Teniers, the Younger

P. W. French & Co. See p. 19

Not, certainly, that Rubens was an erotic. The large, deep-bosomed, healthy women of most of his paintings bespeak only the interest of a very full-blooded, strong, thoroughly normal man. But Rubens was in his early fifties when he painted the Kermesse, had reached the age when the urgency of the dying sex impulse suddenly impels men of instinctive energy to an almost frantic grasping of every possible expansion of sex experience, regardless of standards and taste. Driven by this anxious, insistent sense of haste, Rubens, because he lived so much of his life directly in paint, took to painting pornography. He produced at this time a series of pictures, at first only suggestive, then more and more devouringly lascivious. The Kermesse represents the ultimate pitch of this temporary psychosis. Because Rubens's painting was the kind directly relevant to simple sensations and instincts, and because one of the most basic instincts was here at a moment of ebullient intensity, this is a great painting. If it were even a slight degree less great it would be indecent. .

It is as surprising as it is fortunate, that Teniers did not follow Rubens, for the two men were intimates, and it is said, though without evidence, that Teniers studied for a time with his older and far more important friend. Certainly his father, David the Elder, who was very probably David the Younger's first master, had worked with Rubens. But Teniers went his own characteristically Lowland way, producing, according to a formula which he modified only in details, nearly seven hundred pictures. There is no record of how many cartoons he designed. Certainly a good many in his style are only adaptations from his paintings, or imitations, and his son, David III (1638–1685), must be partly or even wholly responsible for others; but the style is so consistently that of David II that he must be considered as the spiritual author, even when he is not the actual painter, of these peasant tapestries that are almost as numerous as his canvases.

Teniers painted a good many interiors with peasants but most of the tapestries follow the better known outdoor scenes (Pl. 28). The arrangement varies but certain elements are constant. At one side or the other is a steeply gabled inn, often with a flag fluttering from a pole projecting from the attic window. Against the sky are massive but feathery elms. In the inn yard are groups of celebrants, a half-dozen at a table, toasting and guzzling, couples flinging themselves about in rustic dances to the tune of a musician mounted on a barrel, lovers fondling each other in frank desire, a drunken man or two, a mother trying to enjoy herself in spite of having to shepherd the children, and often a little group of gentlemen and ladies come to get a vicarious release. Sometimes there are only a dozen figures, sometimes half a hundred or more. Everyone in the picture is living with his whole heart, not with the conscious anxiety to seize the fleeting moment of the theoretical romanticist, but with the animal enjoyment of stupid vigor.

The weavers who wove the tapestries after the cartoons of Rubens and his pupils and their numerous inferior imitators, or of Teniers and his disciples, were almost wholly Brussels men, for the city was still far and away the most important centre of the industry. But new families had come to the fore. The Reymbouts, for instance, were of major importance. They had been weavers at least since the fifteenth century, and by the seventeenth century the family shops were prosperous and productive under Martin (active 1576–1619), who also carried on business in Antwerp. Many sixteenth-century cartoons were still in use in his shop, including the Pomona set (cf. p. 142), the History of Paul, and the Scipio Africanus (cf. p. 160). His son, Nicolas, succeeded him on his death in 1619, but the days of the shop's importance were already over.

The Reydams family maintained their position from about 1629, when Heinrich appears in the trade, to about 1720, and were closely associated with the Leyniers, Daniel, Urban, and Everard. The output of these two factories, both separately and jointly, was enormous, the names appearing on countless sets, including many of the Teniers type, and also many of lesser importance in the current styles, standard products for the general market. Both the Reydams and the Leyniers on occasion collaborated also with members of the Van der Borght family, also called Castro, beginning with Jakob in 1676 and followed by his sons Gaspar († 1742), and Franz (Dean 1727–1761). Gaspar's work was carried on by his sons Johann Franz († 1772) and Peter († 1763), who were in turn succeeded by another Jacob († 1794), the son of Johann Franz. Of equal importance were the Van den Heckes, beginning with Franz who was Dean of the Guild in 1633–34, and who wove Rubens's Triumph of the Eucharist from the original cartoons, followed by his son Jan Franz. He was succeeded by his two sons, Franz and Peter, of whom the latter († 1752) became more conspicuous in the industry, though both held the office of Dean in the Guild, the former in 1697, 1707, and 1713, the latter in 1703 and 1711. The Van den Heckes' closest associates were the Raes, who first became prominent when Jan was the head of the family, about 1613. His sons, Franz, Peter, who became master in 1643, and Jan the Younger, followed him. The work of all of these men, and of numbers of lesser weavers, would be indistinguishable were it not for the shop indication in the selvages, usually recorded during this period with the name written out in full. The same cartoons were used by now one, now the other factory; the same designers worked for them all; wool, dyes, detail of weave, style, and qualities are uniform throughout. The industry was thoroughly standardized, so that the differentiation of the work of one from another has only a futile antiquarian interest.

CHAPTER XII

THE LESSER LOOMS

THE tapestry industry was so integral and deeply rooted an element of the economic life of the Low Countries, at least from the fourteenth century on, that it ranks as an indigenous occupation and resource, but everywhere else in Europe it existed only as an imported, artificially initiated enterprise. The possible exception is Paris, where there was a well founded trade during the fourteenth century, which was successfully re-established in the seventeenth; yet even there it had, in the first instance, a close reliance on Arras, and in the second, was recreated, and for a time sustained, by Flemish weavers. In the other countries it was, at its inception, frankly and completely an alien novelty, and as such it had, as a rule, only intermittent existence that depended on special fostering.

Usually such shops were brought into being at the behest of a ruler or official, either because he was seeking another medium of ostentation or, especially in the later centuries, because he was bent on economic reconstruction and had faith in the luxury industries. But sometimes looms were set up by a wandering weaver who had left his native country in the hope of bettering himself, or had simply started out on an impulse just because he was restless, to an indefinite destination. For travel, which had been a temptation to most Europeans of all classes throughout the Middle Ages, became such a passion in the fifteenth century that it was actually an economic problem and danger. All manner of excuses were exploited. The constant embassies back and forth kept huge trains of people on the move, since an emissary of any importance took with him a complete retinue. Pilgrimages were a pretext open to all classes.

Fairs and markets gave merchants and their associates opportunities for change and variety. Students could always find a
good excuse for trying another university, and the recently
liberated apprentice was called a journeyman. Even wars might
serve as a reason for going somewhere else. And so, too, master
craftsmen shifted about. Such itinerants wandered into almost
every city of Europe of any size during the fourteenth or fifteenth century, but their work could rarely, if ever, have been
important. Often they were employed only for repairs or, if
they did weave new tapestries, these were usually coarse utili-
tarian pieces, bench covers, mule blankets or the like, ornamented only with shields of arms or simple floral patterns.

Every now and then, however, one of these roaming craftsmen succeeded so well that a significant achievement followed.
Such was Rinaldo Boteram who had a checkered career but
attained consequence, and participated in a shop that won a
worthy reputation. Boteram came from Brussels to Siena in
1438. He was a refugee from hard times in his own country,
and in serious financial straits. He begged from Siena a sub-
vention, in return for which he agreed to train at least two
apprentices. He was granted a modest sum for two years, and
then the contract was renewed for another six. Then Boteram
began to profit by princely patronage, inspired by the display
and prestige motives. Leonello d'Este (1441–1450) called him to
Ferrara, together with two other Flemings, Bernard and Lievin
of Bruges, son of Giles, to supplement a weaver already on his
payroll, Piero d'Andrea, whom he had inherited from his father,
the fat, jolly, and lustful Niccolo III (1393–1441). Niccolo had
maintained weavers at his court for minor services, notably
repairing. From Ferrara, Boteram went to Mantua, where he
worked from 1449 to 1457 for Lodovico Gonzaga, Leonello
d'Este's brother-in-law. Then he returned to Ferrara, but by
this time he had prospered so greatly that he was functioning
as a dealer rather than a mere weaver, supplying Duke Borso
(1450–1471), who had now succeeded his brother, with panels
showing Solomon in the Midst of His Court and The History
of Achab. After that Boteram appears to have been a free lance,
maintaining, however, his relations with the Gonzagas at

Mantua. In 1466 he went back to Brussels to make purchases, but he apparently spent his last years in Mantua, dying about 1481, and in 1483 war with Venice finished the Mantua shops.

Under Duke Borso, the Ferrara factory became of primary importance, but the weavers were still imported, usually from Flanders, occasionally from France. In 1464 the city undertook to train local craftsmen, bringing in as teachers two Tournay weavers, Jean Mille and Rinaldo Grue, but the Ferrarese did not take kindly to so exacting an occupation. The Ducal factory continued under the régime of Borso's half brother, Ercole (1471–1505), but began to wane toward the end of his life, and under his successor, Alphonse I (1505–1534), it lapsed, to be revived, however, on an even more important scale by the next Duke, Ercole II (1534–1559). Two new weavers came from Flanders, probably about 1517, Nicolas and Jean Karcher, and in 1536 the Duke established a more complete atelier, with the collaboration of eight additional weavers summoned for the purpose.

It is not known whom Leonello selected to make his designs. His favorite artist was Pisanello, who would have been an ideal cartoon painter. With his fresh, clear detail, his clean, vivacious silhouettes, his instinct for patterning in terms of two dimensional forms and his pure singing colors, he could have created some of the greatest tapestries ever conceived. But, alas, there is no evidence that he did.

Under the next two Dukes, Borso and Ercole I, the chief designer was Cosimo Tura (1432–1495), with Gherardo Costa (active c. 1432–1495) a close second. One Agolino, also made some designs for Borso. There are four tapestries which must on stylistic grounds be assigned to this period of the Ferrara shop. The first, a Lamentation in a New York commercial collection, is clearly after a cartoon by Cosimo Tura. Tura had been a fellow pupil of Mantegna and had developed an even more extreme degree of the glyptic discreetness that distinguishes Mantegna's draftsmanship. There is no sweetness, softness or atmosphere. Chiaroscuro, emphatically employed, only accentuates the firmness of the surfaces. Fact without mitigation is exalted, with the kind of frankness which assumes that truth is truer in proportion as it is ugly. In the Lamentation tapestry the muscles of Christ's body stand out in distorted and isolated relief. The face is twisted in anguish. The features of the Virgin are strained in a frenzy of grief. Mary Magdalene, a heavily modelled, ugly woman, is wracked with emotional pain. The misshapen face of John is contracted in a rigid scowl. Joseph of Arimathea, clutching the nails, is a bestial creature with an abnormal elongated, cleft chin. A powerful registration of nightmare horror, the hard, determined drawing is intensified with clear, definite colors and rendered in a beautifully fine, firm weave.

The cartoon of the second panel, in the collection of Mr. Martin Ryerson of Chicago and formerly in the Spitzer Collection, if not by Cosimo is by a colleague imbued with the same essential qualities. The subject, the Annunciation, demands a milder treatment, but the same hardness is evident. The angel is solidly built with a long chin and thick arms. The Virgin has a rigid, expressionless face, the features all a little drawn. Both have very small eyes like many of Cosimo's women, with straight brows fitted close above them. The angel's hair is a flaxen wig, an effect evident on many of Cosimo's men. The angel's cloak and gown billow and flutter, but the multiple ripples are fixed with starch. The Virgin's cloak is a carefully folded sheet of tin. Yet in spite of this effortful, stiff-handed drawing, this tapestry is exceptionally beautiful, thanks to the richness of the color, the exquisiteness of the rendition, lavishly inwoven with gold, and the variety and interest of the detail. The pavement is of multicolored veined marble, exquisitely streaked and mottled. The Virgin's portico is carved and gilded, every inch adorned. At the back of the terrace are a rose trellis, lovingly wrought, and an urn of pinks. A peacock parades his arrogance across the foreground above a row of flowering plants, each a painstaking but endearing botanical portrait. In the background of both this and the Lamentation is a landscape, conscientiously carved out in multiple hard, clean minutiae. Both cartoons are deeply indebted to Flanders. Roger van der Weyden had not tarried in Ferrara in vain. The Annunciation bears a Gonzaga shield of arms.

The third, which shows the Pentecost, is in the church of Santa Maria della Salute, and here again the style of Tura is evident in the exaggerated types of the Apostles, with salient facial muscles, conveying hysterically intense expressions, and the elaborately arranged, crackling folds of the mantles, though an associate may very well have been either partially or even wholly responsible for the actual cartoon. As in the other examples, the details of architecture, landscape, floriation, and fauna are elaborate, and are drawn in a tense, implacable engraving style. The peacock again trails his gaudy tail, this time followed by his dowdy hen. Duke Ercole II made, on the outskirts of Ferrara, a garden, the Barco, which was famous for its peacocks. On the opposite side there are a metal-cast deer and a clumsy mongrel setter.

The fourth, the presentation of the head of Pompey to Caesar, in the Paris Musée des Arts Decoratifs, must also be after a cartoon by someone close to Tura (Pl. 29). Caesar sits on his high throne with four members of his entourage symmetrically disposed in pairs on either side of him, one offering him the head on a charger. The drawing is less tense than in the other two pieces, the garments less stiff and studied, but the types are characteristic in every detail of Cosimo's work. Both the peacock and the richly veined marble of the Annunciation are used here too, but the landscape is closer to that of the Lamentation. A little Maltese dog crouches at Caesar's feet and an angry cat climbs up the back of his chair, spitting at the soldiers below, by far the most successful cat in tapestry. The wide borders of the Caesar are exceptionally interesting. They show Caesar's Triumph, in eight sections, in grisaille. It is noteworthy that Tura's colleague, Gherardo Costa, made cartoons of Triumphs in the antique manner for the Duke, though these were sent to Flanders to be woven, and also that he was skilled in grisaille, for he used this medium in a loggia at Belfiore. The two last pieces are notably inferior technically to the first two.

A triumph in the same style, though not in grisaille, is shown on a set of five tapestries formerly on loan in the Boston Museum of Fine Arts. Evidently the work of the designer of the Caesar

PLATE XXIX

POMPEY'S HEAD OFFERED TO CAESAR. Ferrara, 15th century

Musée des Arts Décoratifs, Paris. See p. 202

border, or perhaps of one of his pupils, the central scenes show the same rigid, stone-carved draftsmanship and an identical distortion of the figures, with tiny heads on tall bodies, the legs abnormally long from the knee down. The composition is skilful, thanks to lessons learned from Roman reliefs, and the silhouettes, owing to their very exaggerations and awkwardness, are decoratively striking. The dry meagre colors are, moreover, perfectly adjusted to the hardness and impersonality of the delineation. They are not ingratiating tapestries, nor even pleasant, but they are excellent architectural elements for a severe impersonal interior.

The relation between the character of these tapestries, on the one hand, and the personalities of the reigning Dukes and the situation in Ferrara on the other, is very curious. Within the tapestries themselves there is a contradiction. Two, at least, of the four are fashioned of the richest materials. The Annunciation is exceptionally fresh and lovely in color, a primaveral innocence of tone. The workmanship exhausts the possibilities of finesse, and in all four pieces every elaboration of elegant detail is lavishly exploited. This was to the taste of both Borso and Ercole I, for they liked things to be showy, elaborate, expensive, and impressive. But the spirit of the tapestries is the direct antithesis. The mildest, the Annunciation, is unyielding and uncompromising. The most extreme, the Lamentation, is frantic and macabre. The other two are tense, aggressively ungracious, with a bitter tang, and in this they contradict directly the characters of the Ducal patrons that made them possible, for Borso was a rollicking soul, like his father a robust Hedonist, but free from his brutality, peace loving and good natured, while Ercole I was equally sensual and peace loving, but more intellectual in an emotional and even mystical way. The Dukes and their gay and brilliant court were not, however, all of Ferrara. Revolt rumbled just under the glittering surface, the poison cup and the assassin's dagger were necessary now and then to keep the peace that the Dukes desired, and it was in Ferrara that Savonarola (1452–1498) was born and lived the first twenty-three years of his life, breeding in his bowels the passionate hates that burst out in the fanatic asceticism of his

preaching, and culminated in the frenzy of the Florentine bon-
fires. The Lamentation, with its morbid figures, revelling in
the pathological excitement of their evilly colored emotions,
is the psychological portrait of the soul of Savonarola.

During the Karcher régime under Ercole II, many Italians
supplied cartoons but the most constant collaborator was
Battista de Lutero known as Battista Dossi (1548), and to him
must be attributed the outstanding series of this time that
remains to us, the Puttini, formerly in the possession of the
Baronne Worms in London, now in the Gulbenkian collection
in Paris. The series was made for the Cardinal Hercules Gonzaga of Milan, who was named Cardinal in 1527 and died in
1563. Every piece bears his arms at the top and on one, one of
the putti is writing on a tablet HER (cules) Man (tuanus).
The set was still in the possession of the Gonzaga family in the
middle of the seventeenth century. Each panel shows a grape
arbor or a bower of trees, usually fruit trees, with a score of
naked winged erotes, playing about in all sorts of pranks and
antics. Though the conception is the conventional Alexandrian
formula (cf. p. 16), the children are quite different from the
usual pudgy and characterless puppets. They are, rather, muscular little boys of marked personality that have, in spite of
their wings, a decided gamin quality. In the foreground in each
case are handsome decorative birds. One panel shows Venus in
the stern of a high curved, richly carved bark. The color is
blond and fresh, the whole conception vivacious and entertaining, instinct with joy and charm, and the rendering is rich
without being either ostentatious or heavy. The set is distinctly
of the Renaissance, but as purely and properly tapestry as anything of the preceding period, and with a gaiety and elegance
that only Italy at this moment could have produced. A closely
related series by the same designer illustrating the Metamorphoses of Ovid (designed 1545) is far less elegant, though it
is hard to judge, as the only accessible example, in the Paris
Musée des Arts Decoratifs, is dirty and worn, so that the effect
is seriously compromised.

No contrast could be more sudden and more extreme than
that between the tapestries of the Tura period and these frivo-

PLATE XXX

THE ASCENSION OF THE VIRGIN after a cartoon by Giuseppe Arnobaldo.
Ferrara, 16th century   *Boston Museum of Fine Arts.* See p. 205

lous and graceful panels. They have in common the material beauty of fine silk and gold, clear pure dyes and perfection of weave, but in spirit the one is the violent rejection of the other. Moreover, by a queer inversion of fate, Dossi is as irrelevant in quality to his Duke as Tura had been to his. Indeed Dossi should have painted for Borso and Ercole I, while Tura would have done well for Ercole II; for Ercole II was a constricted, melancholic personality, and his court was a morass of gloom and hate with his Duchess, Renata, daughter of Louis XII, first loathing Ferrara because life there was so niggardly and dull after the gaieties of France, and then turning ardent Protestant. How perfectly Tura could have expressed the discontent and spite, the anxiety and antagonism of the unhappy household, how ironical are Dossi's self-indulgent, mirthful loves.

The beautiful fineness and generous but discreet metal enrichment which distinguishes the Puttini is repeated in a panel belonging to the Boston Athenaeum but exposed in the Boston Museum of Fine Arts, portraying the Assumption of the Virgin (Pl. 30). The Virgin rises into the clouds, seated on the crescent moon and escorted by gambolling cherubim. Below, the Apostles are gathered around the empty tomb in attitudes of surprise and adoration. The cartoon for this was clearly painted by Giuseppe Arnaboldo of Milan who designed, between 1561 and 1570, the three scenes from the life of the Virgin in the Cathedral of Como.

Garafolo and Camillo Filippi (c. 1500–1574) supplied a number of cartoons of which a set illustrating the History of Saint Maurilius is in the possession of the Cathedral of Ferrara. The Filippi belonged to the Dossi school but their cartoons show neither the aristocratic ease nor the lucidity of Battista's. They seem to be making a conscious attempt to imitate the current Flemish style, with a group of large figures in the foreground and heavy classical architecture in the upper register. A Haarlem painter, Lucas Cornelitz, had come to Ferrara and designed some cartoons for the atelier, especially backgrounds and borders, including the border for this series, and it looks as if he had deflected the Filippis' native taste. After the death of

Ercole II the factory deteriorated rapidly until, before the end of the century, it was quite dead.

Milan did not develop any atelier, which is surprising, for the city had long been an important wool weaving centre and her Dukes were proud of their wealth, sophistication, and enterprise. But in the nearby town of Vigevano the Trivulzio family usurped this honor. Gian Giacomo (1438–1518) established an atelier sometime between 1503 and 1518 which produced a set of the Months that still hangs in the Trivulzio Palace. The weaver was Benedetto da Milano, who must have learned his trade elsewhere, probably in Flanders, and the cartoons are attributed to Bramantino (Bartolommeo Suardi, b. c. 1450). In each panel the personification of the Month stands or sits on a dais in the centre, sometimes under a portico or baldachin, while a group of courtiers is arranged in careful symmetry on either side. Every cartoon is thus a deliberate composition, artificial and contrived, without any attempt at illustrative naturalism to clothe the structure. In short, the conception is not pictorial but architectural, and this treatment is intensified by the emphatic architectural settings, varying in each case, but always of equal importance with the figures. The figures, too, are consistent in character with this basic idea, congealed in their calculated poses and treated with hard outlines which isolate each one, even when there is superimposition. This interpretation of tapestry in terms of colored bas-relief, which is what these cartoons amount to, is theoretically impossible to defend, given the extreme opposition in character of the media, yet enough concession has been made in this instance to the textile feeling, notably in the richness of some of the costumes of lustrous velvet, and in the draping of most of them, to justify the innovation. Especially if seen in the proper setting of a stone hall, this series would be a strong decoration, integrated with the structure to a degree not even imagined in any other tapestry designs until the eighteenth century (cf. p. 280).

The second major factory of Italy, a Medici enterprise at Florence, was also, like those at both Ferrara and Vigevano, initiated as part of a program of lordly art patronage. Founded

[206]

PLATE XXXI

SCENE FROM THE HISTORY OF JOSEPH. Florence, 16th century
Italian Government Collection, Florence. See p. 207

in 1546 by Duke Cosimo I (ruled 1537–1574), the first employes were two of the Flemings who had already worked at
Ferrara, Nicolas Karcher, and Jean Rost. The former seems to
have stayed only seven years in the Medicean service, but Rost
remained to become the outstanding weaver in Italy, and one
of the most notable of his age. Like many of his race he enjoyed his little joke, using as his signature a spitted chicken
(Rost = roast), sometimes combined with the letters F. F.
(fatto in Firenze).

The Medici looms profited by the cartoons of painters of real
merit, notably Agnolo Bronzino (1503–1572). Indeed it appears that Karcher and Rost were first brought to Florence
specifically in order to weave some cartoons which Bronzino
had begun in 1545, two of a set illustrating the History of Joseph: Joseph Selling Corn to his Brothers, and the Capture
of Joseph. The rest of the Joseph set, seventeen more pieces,
he did not design until 1540, and for these he had the help of
Raffaelo dal Colle, called dal Borgo (b. c. 1490). The series
is divided between the Palazzo Vecchio in Florence and the
Quirinal in Rome. At about this same time he also designed
cartoons illustrating Justice Liberating Innocence and the
Triumph of Flora, which are in the Uffizzi. Bronzino's cartoons represent the Italian equivalent of the Flemish cartoon
style of the time. Large, heavily modelled, posed figures, that
look as if they had been drawn from inferior sculpture in the
Roman tradition, fill the foreground, and inert, correct architecture completes the composition (Pl. 31).

Two of the Joseph series, Jacob Learning the Death of His
Son, and Joseph Leaving His Cloak with Potiphar's Wife, were
executed by Bronzino's master, Pontormo; but superior as
Pontormo was as a painter, he was not a success as a cartoon
designer, and so was never again commissioned for such work.

The third collaborator on this series, Francesco Dei Rossi
Salviati (1510–1563) who painted one piece for the set,
Pharaoh's Dream, had better fortune, and received a number
of further orders, a Pietà and an Ecce Homo in 1549 and a
History of Lucretia, not to mention a History of Alexander
which was woven in Flanders for Pier Luigi Farnese.

But the most important painter for the Florentine shops, judged by the fitness and effectiveness of his designs, was Francesco d'Ulbertino, il Bachiacca (1494–1557). Here was an artist properly chosen for the work, not a pictorial painter with the habit of altar pieces, but a decorator, son of a goldsmith. He designed a series of Grotesques and a set of the Months, examples of which are in the Uffizzi (Pl. 32). The Grotesques hold true to type, but the elements are daringly varied in scale. Naturally this type of invention never is constrained by any respect for realistic scale. A pavilion may be scarcely larger than a hare, and this is correct, for in such an assemblage the motives have no factual relation to each other; but Il Bachiacca is ruthless, not only with his naturalistic, but also with his decorative scale. Thus, at either side of one piece is a putto two-fifths of the height of the whole panel, while in the center medallion is a peasant harvesting, whose whole height is scarcely more than the length of the putto's leg from the knee down, and two other putti, flying in the clouds above, are not as big as the heads of the first pair. Yet surprisingly enough this is not shocking. The spectator reconciles the conflict by an unconscious interpretation. The marginal figures, including the big putti at the sides, some masks and swags above, and an addossed goat and ram on a dais below, all in the large scale, are interpreted as a frame through which the spectator looks at the interior ornament as if into a peep-show box, with an exaggerated recession of perspective, so that the central medallion gives the effect of a lens through which the tiny scene is transmitted like the remote image in a reversed opera glass. Too conscious an application of this assumption, however, destroys its efficacy, and the incongruities of size become, for the first time, offensive. The structure of these Grotesques is very simple, consisting of a centre motive framed in a rectangle, with flanking verticals, a far less ingenious scheme than many other designers have contrived. But the beauty of the work is in the details; exquisite yet firm, refined yet definite and courageous, they have the quality of metal work. Il Bachiacca was not the son of a goldsmith in vain.

The Months show the same exquisite yet firm delicacy in a

Plate XXXII

The Autumn Months after a cartoon by Il Bachiacca. Florence, 16th century

Italian Government Collection, Florence. See p. 208

pictorial application. They are the Italian equivalent, in anticipation, of the Teniers cartoons, and there is just the difference
between the two that the contrast in racial quality would lead
one to expect. Il Bachiacca's peasants are aristocratic fictions
that exist, not for the expression of vitality, but for decorative
grace, consequently they are grouped in effective stage tableaux
which have nothing to do with their occupations. They work
in a landscape that is a painted, theatre curtain scene, elegantly
romantic figurines on the classical formula, as unconvincing as
the libretto of an Italian opera, but as agreeable as they are
indifferent, because they cannot be taken seriously and the
line patterns are beautiful in an empty way.

Under the next Duke, Francesco I (1574–1587), the factory
continued, but the deterioration in artistic quality was sudden
and serious. The chief designer in both this and the succeeding
reign of Ferdinand I (1587–1609) was Alessandro Allori
(1535–1607), Bronzino's pupil, who carried into his work the
master's faults with few compensating merits. Allori's designs
are, again, the Italian equivalent of the Flemish style of the
late Renaissance, more ingratiating because southern, but
speciously so, with a meretricious grace obtained by the use of
elongated bodies topped with too small heads, the torso swaying in languorous or too rhythmic curves or twisted to give
expressive movements as fictitious as the gestures of aesthetic
dancing. For Allori elegance is affectation. Outstanding examples are five episodes from the Old and New Testaments
in the Duomo of Como. The ambiguity to which self conscious
mannerisms inevitably lead is especially evident in the Last
Supper. In attempting to be dignified yet moving, he succeeds
only in being theatrical. Wishing to be strong yet expressive, he
fashions a style that is both stiff and soft, severe yet cloying.
Throughout, he is trying to have his cake and eat it too. The
result is, as always, an unacceptable dishonesty.

By this time the head weavers and many of the subordinates
were Italians trained under the Rost régime, but toward the
end of his reign Cosimo II (1609–1621) found it necessary to
reinvigorate the factory by bringing in more foreign workers,
of which the most important was Pierre Fèvre, a French weaver

who, during the following reign of Ferdinand II (1621–1670) brought the factory to a period of great productivity. But the Renaissance was over. The painters that could be called on for cartoons were third rate practitioners of an inflated style, especially ill adapted in its grandiose vacuity to the needs of tapestry. The figures are characterless and formless, the compositions perfunctory, there is no distinction.

During the period of Cosimo III (1670–1723) the looms were far less productive but the quality of the work was, allowing for the taste of the time, somewhat better, a strong French influence making itself felt. Spiritually the cartoons are vacant and pretentious. Artistically they are obvious, the clouds too dramatically thunderous, the light too strikingly radiant, the garments too excitedly billowing, the gestures too expressly emotional, but they have at least an academic competence.

During the reign of the last Duke, Jean-Gaston (1723–1737), the most important cartoons of the preceding period were repeated, though various painters did create new cartoons of mediocre interest, and occasionally a more striking design was achieved; for example, a portrait of the Archduke Franz Stephen, now in the Uffizzi in Florence, which is a dashing picture of swaggering pride. At the death of Jean-Gaston the factory was closed. Subsequently the Lorraine successor of the Medici, François III, kept a few weavers busy for four years (1740–1744), but they produced only some negligible pieces.

When the factory was dismantled most of the weavers found work at Naples where the Duke established a factory that lasted about thirty years, producing uninspired imitations of the French tapestries of the period. Other employes went to Turin, where Carlo Emanuele set up a small shop with less than a score of artisans. It was intended only to provide tapestries for the royal palace, but it lasted nearly half a century and created quite a number of sets. The industry was revived for the first thirty-five years of the nineteenth century. The cartoons of the first period were almost all on the basis of designs by Claudio Beaumont (1694–1766), the chief series illustrating the lives of Alexander, Caesar, Cyrus, and Hannibal. The designs have all of the deficiencies of the period, a vacant pseudoclassicism with pompous compositions, inflated figures, and no illustrative significance. The work of his successor, a Venetian, Giovanni, Battista Crosato (1695–1756), was more airy and somewhat more graceful, but equally lacking in genuineness. He contributed a set on Aeneas and Dido. Minor additions to the repertoire of the shop were made by a half dozen other mediocre painters. In the nineteenth century most of the productions were Italianized imitations of eighteenth-century Flemish types, especially verdures with rather small figures.

Meanwhile the third important tapestry atelier of Italy had been developed, at Rome. The papal city was a century behind Florence in entering the field, two centuries behind Ferrara. True, Nicolas V (1447–1455) had had one famous set illustrating the Creation of the World woven at the Vatican, but the weavers were dispersed when this work was done, and no regularly organized shop was established until 1635. Then the initiative came, not directly from the Pope, Urban VIII (1623–1644), but from his nephew, the Cardinal Francesco Barberini, who imported for the purpose a weaver of uncertain origin, Jacques della Riviera. The shop was short lived, for in 1644 Urban VIII died, his nephew was banished, and work on the looms soon ceased. Quite a number of tapestries were produced, however, notably an Aeneas series by Giovanni Francesco Romanelli (1610–1662). His designs are in the convention of the period, crowds of large empty figures rendered in excessive modelling with exaggerated high lights, quite lacking in force because so flamboyant, the grand gesture with, of course, no grandeur.

After more than half a century a new factory immediately under the patronage of the Popes was founded by Clement XI (1700–1721). The Pope brought his first weaver to Rome in 1710, a Frenchman named Jean Simonet, and set him to work with a few assistants in the Hospice of San Michele, providing at first a regular salary, but substituting later remuneration on a piece basis. The principal painter during this time was Andrea Procaccini (1671–1734). During the papacy of Pius VI (1775–1799) the shop was very active. The Director at the time was Felix Cettornai and one of his kinsmen, Philip Cettornai, was evidently master weaver, for a portrait of him in the Victoria and Albert Museum, dated 1790, shows him actually working at the high warp loom. On the whole, the Roman tapestries are technically competent, though the colors are sometimes feeble, but as tapestries or even as woven paintings most of them are, in their cheap and theatrical sentimentality, offensive.

In spite of the fact that the shops of the Italian Renaissance were all founded and largely sustained by Flemish workmen, the tapestries that they produced were truly Italian. For Italy had a highly developed and markedly individual art, which was so sustained by the confidence of prestige that it remained dominant in the collaboration between Flemish weavers and Italian painters. Moreover, the Flemings were able to do full justice to the cartoons supplied them, translating them without any distortion of the style, because these had some affinity with the mannerisms to which they had already been accustomed in their native workshops. In the earlier period of the Ferrara atelier the chief designer, Tura, had, whether by accident of personal disposition or by direct influence, or more probably by a combination of the two, a distinctly Flemish quality of spirit. In the Renaissance designs, on the other hand, the style was the purer prototype of the idiom on which the weavers had been nurtured at home. Only in the Vigevano cartoons and the Ferrara Triumphs, both of which were constructed on a bas-relief convention, did they encounter the unexpected, and there their unfamiliarity is evident in various infelicities. For the rest, the collaboration was easy and natural, and the outcome was, in the fifteenth-century Ferrara examples that remain, the strongest and soundest tapestry produced in Europe outside of Flanders, worthy to be ranked with the best Flemish work of the period as a fitting and expressive adaptation of the technique, while the sixteenth-century work of both Ferrara and Florence, but especially of the latter, includes lucent and graceful decorations of exceptional charm.

In Germany, on the other hand, where numerous Protestant weavers migrated during the religious persecutions of the middle of the sixteenth century, there was no such authoritative school of painting; hence there the Flemings determined the character of the work. The result is that much of the output of the many small ateliers sustained by the various Princes and Dukes is indistinguishable from the contemporary Lowland work unless marked or documented. Apparently the weavers commonly carried with them a stock of cartoons on which they relied, at least for the first years after their removal, but in some instances cartoon painters accompanied them, so that they had at hand a source of new patterns when needed. Thus some of the Van Orleys appear in Germany, notably Nicolas who, with the weaver Jakob Carmes, was employed by the Duke of Württemberg when he was building his new palace near Stuttgart about 1566, and Everard who at the opening of the seventeenth century was with a group of workers in Frankenthal, where a colony of Protestant weavers, primarily from Tournay, had been settled since 1549. The tapestries produced under these conditions are not German in any proper sense of the word.

When, on the other hand, there was neither a Flemish cartoon in stock to meet the order, nor a Flemish painter to execute one, German painters were employed, and the result was a hybrid style which has no character except the specious primitiveness of incompetence. Yet the clumsiness of this type is not offensive but is rather, like many similar productions of Germany, childlike and amusing.

One enterprise, however, in which German cartoons were executed kept on a decidedly higher level than this. Seeger Bombeck (active 1545–1557) who was a German but must have learned his trade in Flanders, directed shops at Leipzig and at Weimar from about 1545, in which German designs were made into interesting and distinctive tapestries. To be sure there are still, in spite of the excellence of the weaving, traces of the awkwardness which so deflects most of the Flemish-German collaborative work. But in this instance it is not sufficient to obliterate the serious interest of the tapestries. Nor is the reason far to seek. Bombeck's outstanding productions are in the field in which German painters did have at that time a sufficiently individual talent and secure capacity to impose their character on the weavers. They were portraits. The tradition of which Holbein and Cranach were the standard bearers fostered the secondary gifts of many lesser men so that they turned out admirable portraits, well drawn and effectively presented, likenesses of character as well as of features. Painters of this calibre assisted Bombeck to create a series of portraits in tapestry which are of unusual interest historically, and have genuine aesthetic merit as well.

A portrait is an anomalous hence dangerous subject for any textile, but from time to time tapestry weavers have been tempted to undertake them, either by pride of virtuosity or to meet commercial demand. Heads were one of the commonest subjects of the more important tapestries produced in Egypt from the fourth to the tenth century (cf. p. 19 f.), but certainly not many of these attempted any real likeness. Most of them are merely conventional masks, some as abstract as the formal motives with which they are equated in the total design, though a few of the finer ones do give the impression of being individuals. In European tapestry on the other hand, human heads never have been common and do not appear at all until a later stage. Historians of the art have striven from time to time to find portraits in the body of illustrative cartoons, but, at least in the earlier periods, such efforts have been more ingenious than convincing. By the third quarter of the fifteenth century, however, one type of subject is introduced which may very well, in some cases, represent portraiture. This is the picture of the " Author," usually in a separate compartment fitted to the end of the first or last piece of a series (cf. p. 130). The identity of the Author is dubious, whether he was the literary man who contrived the scenario, determining the episodes, their sequence and the captions, or the artist who designed the cartoons. When he is specifically labelled " Author " it seems almost certain that he was the former, but similar figures are presented in the same manner without any designation, and some of these may well be the cartoon painters. Whether or not they are portraits, however, in any exact sense, it is impossible to determine. The earliest that has been noted, showing an elderly man with two younger men, presumably pupils, is attached to the famous Wars of Troy set. If this is the cartoon painter and two of his assistants, it is an interesting type of self portrait, for the three are in a

[214]

kind of workshop and are apparently discussing the design which, filling the rest of the piece, is unrolled before them.

A figure that is more obviously the self-portrait of a designer is introduced into the body of the composition in the early sixteenth-century Descent from the Cross in the Cinquantenaire Museum in Brussels. The signatory inscription "Philiep," which was the basis of the identification of Maître Philippe, (cf. p. 112), is inserted on the edge of the hood of a middle-aged bearded man, and to make the significance indubitable the man points to the name. Not all the figures, however, which carry such signatory inscriptions are self-portraits of the designers, for Jean van Roome, for example, has recorded his name, in the Carrying of the Cross in a series of the Passion in Trent Cathedral, on the tunic of a snub-nosed negro. The first emphatic and independent self-portrait of a designer is the figure of himself that Jan Vermeyen presents in the introductory panel of the Tunis set (cf. p. 139).

Portraits of donors introduced as well marked figures come nearer to true portraiture in a complete sense of the term. These are fairly common in German tapestries of the fifteenth century, though the figures in these can be called portraits only by courtesy, since they are mere effigies rather than individuals. In Flemish tapestry nothing of the kind is known before the very closing years of the century. Then donors with their patron saints do appear, notably the ecclesiastics who gave the Life of the Virgin series to the Collegiate Church of Beaume in 1472, and the Bishop who gave the Life of the Virgin to the Cathedral of Bayeux in 1498 (cf. pp. 93, 94). Or, again, there is Francis de Taxis who is in the very forefront of two scenes of the Notre Dame de Sablon set two decades later (cf. p. 154), while in an approximately contemporary tapestry expounding the doctrine of the Eucharist, in the Cathedral of Chalon-sur-Saône, the donor's whole family kneels in devout accord.

Such self-portraits are only incidental by-products of illustrative designs, but portraits were also made the specific subject of tapestry at about this same date, for in the inventory of Marguerite of Austria there is listed a tapestry portrait of herself. The earliest examples that remain, however, are those woven

[215]

by Seeger Bombeck several decades later, of which the most important, in the Dresden Schloss, represents Charles V (dated 1545) (Pl. 33). The Emperor stands in three-quarter view, his head almost in right profile, his body shown to the waist, against a shallow niche in a marble wall on which are displayed, above, two shields of his arms. He is in simple civilian clothes, a velvet tunic with puffed sleeves and flat beret, but he holds, in formal pose, the naked sword of his authority. The sword and the arm are too large for the body, and indeed the whole torso, even allowing for his portly figure, seems to increase irrationally in scale toward the waist, but in spite of this defect, which probably resulted from a lack of technical sympathy between the designer and the weaver, the portrait is convincing. Charles is revealed as a shrewd, self-contained, withdrawn personality, the cold type of Teuton.

Even more characteristically German is another style of portrait which Bombeck, as well as other tapestry weavers, made for various noble houses, representing genealogical descent in the form of a family group. While the earlier ancestors in such family-tree tableaux were merely conventional figures, the contemporary ones were often true portraits.

Although all of Bombeck's work is pleasant in color, rich in silk and metal thread, and excellent in tension and texture, some does show an ineptitude which reduces it to the status of the merely quaint. This is markedly true of a panel in the Altenburg Museum made about 1550 which is, however, in spite of the infantile uncertainty of drawing, interesting on account of the subject, an allegory of the struggle of the Reformation. The frivolities and corruptions of the organized religion, which had grown cynical from too much experience, are rebuked by Germanic moral rectitude. It was a grim contest, threatening the survival of many amenities which an implacable self-righteousness was ready to cast out as sin, disrupting the Empire, sowing destitution and death across the continent, yet it is enacted here by excessively tall, small-headed figures, a disproportion that always suggests degeneracy, who mince and coquette in affected dancing movements. They would be comical even without regard to the theme.

PLATE XXXIII

RTRAIT OF CHARLES V. Leipzig or Weimar, 1545   *Dresden Museum.* See p. 216

All trace of Seeger Bombeck's shop is lost in 1557. Thereafter a scattering of workers, singly or in twos or threes, appear in various towns, and to many of these can be attributed tapestries, usually by means of armorial bearings. But practically all of them show marked deterioration in practical skill, and neither they nor the documents indicate shops of any importance.

In the late seventeenth and eighteenth centuries, however, when the officials of various countries were enviously remarking the success and prestige of the Gobelins, several new factories were attempted in Germany. Thus at Berlin the Great Kurfurst employed a Frenchman, Pierre Mercier, in 1686, to weave a set of six panels depicting his military honors, directly imitated from the sets glorifying Louis XIV, and in a derived style, and production continued there until at least the middle of the century. Meanwhile Mercier had moved, in 1714, to Dresden, where he carried on his career until he died in 1726, and there, too, skilled compatriots continued the craft for another thirty years. Two other contemporary German shops manned with Frenchmen achieved an output of some importance, one in Wurzburg and the other in Munich. But, again, there is no sound reason for calling any of these enterprises or their work German. Culture in Germany at the moment consisted of the most convincing imitation of French mannerisms that the race could manage, so that the noble patrons were only too delighted to have tapestries that were unadulteratedly French. To be sure, many of the cartoons were painted by Germans, but they were Germans who had qualified as artists in proportion as they had ceased to betray their origins, and if there are clumsy passages where a Teutonic taint might be suspected, still the cartoon painters of France were themselves at that time not exempt from such lapses.

Sweden contributed even less than Germany to the work of the Flemish weavers who settled there, having no painters of sufficient character to make any impression on the work. The first weavers were summoned by King Gustave in the middle of the sixteenth century, but organized shops were not established until his son Erik, who became Erik XIV (1533–1577), set up an independent court as Duke at Kalmar. Erik was a true prince of the Renaissance, given to intellectual amusements, luxury, and fêtes. The shop, with perhaps ten or a dozen imported weavers and some native apprentices, was at first at Kalmar, but soon was moved to the capital, and when Erik became king the enterprise, though still catering only to the court, was expanded and three major ateliers were maintained, the most important at Stockholm, the others at Kalmar and Svartsji. Under his successor, the weavers were dispersed so that by 1570 only three tapestry makers remained on the royal payroll. The weavers dismissed from the royal service scattered through the country, making their living where they could under lesser patrons. Thus the industry practically died out before the century ended.

In the seventeenth century, Sweden, like France, benefitted by a ruler, Charles IX (1550–1611), intent on a conscious program for the development of industry, including textile manufacturing. Tapestry was part of his plan, so to this end he invited to his capital foreign tapestry makers. The King personally interested himself in the work, even in trivial details, doubtless because his queen, Christine of Holstein, was herself an amateur in the art. The major atelier, at Eskelstuna, lasted for a time after his death, but this was the last shop of any importance in Sweden. From time to time the court made an effort to re-establish the industry but every undertaking was abortive. The tapestries attributed to all the Swedish shops are purely Flemish in style, characteristic products of the standardized taste of the time, showing no effect whatever of the change of locale.

Curiously enough, the eastern end of the Low Countries, Holland, did not enter the tapestry field on any serious scale until the end of the sixteenth century, and there the industry was no more indigenous than it was in Germany or Sweden. The only shop of primary status was established by an Antwerp weaver, François Spierinx, in 1592, in Delft. He had as collaborators two painters of some note, Hendrik Cornelisz Van Vroom (1566–1640), and Karel III Van Mander (1579–1623). The former painted seascapes, thanks to an accident rather early in his career, for he took to this type of subject only after having been shipwrecked on the Portuguese coast. His most famous cartoons illustrated the Defeat of the Spanish Armada (1588). The tapestries were destroyed when the Houses of Parliament were burned in 1834, but accurate records of them remain in engravings made by John Pine. The designs were as varied as the limited subject would permit, with the ships laid out in a different geometrical scheme in each piece, against conventionalized water, pleasing if somewhat thin decorations that avoid any shocking contradiction of the illustrative purpose. In the border are portraits of twenty-eight British naval officers. Van Mander's best known set is a History of Alexander in a standard Renaissance style that is, however, enlivened with rather more than the usual degree of Lowland naturalism. There were also small shops at Amsterdam which produced little pieces, including occasional portraits (cf. p. 223) characterized by substantial drawing but feeble in color.

England's dependence on foreign countries for the luxuries and embellishments of life, which had forced Henry VIII and Cardinal Wolsey to buy their tapestries abroad (cf. p. 138), continued in the next reign. The English lady stitched with a skilful and industrious needle, but the weavers undertook only the simpler fabrics, and indeed none of the decorative arts really rose above the level of substantial utility, however satisfying the solid tables and honestly wrought iron may seem today. While a few of the rich bought tapestries in Flanders, they were a comparative rarity even in the finest houses, most of the walls being hung with painted canvas simulating the more costly woven materials. In the middle of the sixteenth century (c. 1561), however, a country squire, one William Sheldon of Worcestershire, undertook to establish looms at Barcheston Manor, taking advantage, like his German contemporaries, of the Protestant exodus to secure Flemish weavers whom he put under the direction of an Englishman, Richard Hicks. The factory continued through many vicissitudes to the middle of the seventeenth century (c. 1647), but it never attempted a large output and rarely undertook ambitious designs, so that the existing examples are comparatively few in number and almost uniformly of meagre artistic interest. The outstanding exceptions are four maps, two of which exist in two weavings, while of another only two fragments remain. These show English Midland counties with a wealth of topographical detail pictorially rendered. While they are delightful as maps and have the antiquarian charm that infuses all old geographical records with an interest beyond their true significance, as tapestries they are mediocre. A second set, the Seasons, with disproportionate classical figures awkwardly rendered, have a certain specious attraction, like many fictitious primitives of provincial art, but they really demonstrate quite shockingly the ineptitude of the weavers. For the rest, the shops produced commonplace verdures, often with shields of arms, and many small panels, especially cushion covers, clumsily executed. In short the enterprise never rose above the country-gentleman limitations.

Royal patronage, however, assured a more worthy standard and more honorable achievement to the next English enterprise in the field, a national factory established by James I at Mortlake in 1620, in imitation of Henry IV's industry in Paris. Again Flemish weavers were imported to initiate the work, fifty arriving together with all their families, including some masters of the craft of established reputation, notably Philip de Maecht, a Middelburg man, though originally from a Brussels family, who had worked in the Comans shop in Paris. He was appointed overseer. The factory struggled in almost constant financial insecurity throughout the seventy-three years of its existence, for the Crown provided more promises than pounds, but in spite of this it produced many large and expensive hangings, technically excellent. None of these sets, however, can justly be called English, for though woven on English soil the only English participation was that of the financial administration. The weavers were to the end Flemings, with possibly a few minor exceptions. The cartoons were either series that had already been in use in Flemish shops, of Flemish or Italian design, or, in the few cases where they were specially made, they were the work of Flemish painters. Mortlake tapestry, in short, is Flemish tapestry, transferred across the Channel but in no way naturalized.

PLATE XXXIV

GROTESQUE in the style of a "Coromandel" lacquer. England, 18th century

Victoria and Albert Museum. See p. 221

One set from the shop is distinctly English, however, in subject. This is the series of three in Hampton Court Palace illustrating the Battle of Solebay, an encounter between the English and Dutch fleets. The theme is ill adapted to tapestry as water realistically treated makes a monotonous surface and the tones of sea and sky are too pallid for the material. But the massed sails of the fleet have the savour that attaches to all ships, so that the tapestries are pleasing beyond their artistic merits. Britain records herself ruling the waves, though actually the engagement was indecisive.

In the successive periods of acute distress to which the Mortlake workers were subject, owing to the unsound financing, various weavers undertook to establish themselves independently. Many of these ventures were so ephemeral and so insignificant that no record of them remains, and they produced only copies of the Mortlake cartoons or adaptations of Flemish designs, so that all of their work, with the exception of one type, is indistinguishable from the contemporary Flemish weaving, save sometimes for a certain hardness of color.

The one exception is a group of Chinoiseries in a style imitated from the lacquer screens that were being imported by the East India Company and were much in vogue. On a dark ground are little islands of grass, posed at different levels to make an irregular and open powdered pattern, and on these are clumps of tropical trees, or fantastic pavilions in the oriental taste, or little pagodas, with personages, birds, and beasts of Eastern or jungle style (Pl. 34). They are a very special version, really, of the verdure conception, or perhaps, rather, the offspring of that conception mated with the idea of the grotesque. Themes are commingled without any attempt at consistency, Chinese, East Indian, American Indian, and merely queer. It is a fantasy world that is equally outside of space and of logic, very entertaining and very well adapted to the aims of tapestry. The best of the type, and possibly all of them, were woven by John Vanderbank, a Fleming established in Soho.

Wandering Flemings appear in different Spanish cities at various times in the fifteenth and sixteenth centuries, but none of these have left any traces except Joan Ferrer, who in the middle of the sixteenth century was working in Barcelona and there made some tapestries for the Cathedral of Gerona which still hang in the chapter rooms of the Cathedral. The series is noteworthy only for its technical incompetence. Voluminous draperies in multiple folds that have no meaning or form, clothe misshapen figures that increase in scale in a progressive descent so that narrow heads are fitted in an impossible articulation on heavy shoulders, which pass into an expanding torso, that is, in turn, set on enormous legs of dropsical modelling. The color is thick and ugly, the weaving coarse, the borders mishandled in every detail. Joan Ferrer should have been a navvy. It is depressing that he could have remained in business even for the decade or so in which he seems to have been active.

Russia was as dilatory in establishing a tapestry industry as in the introduction of all other Western institutions, but when, in the eighteenth century, France was accepted by the upper classes as the arbiter of fashion, a tapestry factory was one of the first innovations. Founded by Peter the Great in 1716, it was manned by a dozen weavers and half as many dyers from the Gobelins. In three years most of the Frenchmen, discouraged by poor living conditions and bad pay, returned to France, and by 1732 only two of them remained, the rest of the workers being Russians who had learned the craft. For forty years the factory barely managed to exist, but in 1756 the undertaking was reawakened to life by an order for a series of panels for Empress Elizabeth's new winter palace, commemorating her accession to the throne. But the stimulation was temporary, for Elizabeth went into a decline and died (1761).

With the accession of Catherine the Great (1729–1796), however, the factory at last really became active, and for thirty-eight years continued a steady production. The work is technically excellent but most of the pretentious endeavors are tiresome if not positively offensive, weak imitations of the current French mode or ingenious and hideous copies of paintings in the Hermitage. Even the barbaric vulgarity that makes the bad taste of most Russian art of this period amusing, is lacking. Two types of work, however, achieve some interest, cushion covers in a local style of design, often rather coarse in weave and almost always raw in color, but energetic and genuine, and portraits.

Tapestry portraiture which had been tentative and incidental in Flanders until the end of the sixteenth century became increasingly important in the seventeenth. The Fêtes of Henri III, made in Brussels from French cartoons late in the sixteenth century (cf. p. 177) show many members of the court, but they are not really portraits in the most limited sense, but rather are records of court life that involve group portraits. It is only in the next century that separate portrait heads appear in Lowland weaving. One of the earliest known, in the collection of Mr. Frank Gair Macomber of Boston, depicting Joachim de Montagu of Toulouse in the sixty-fifth year of his age, in 1628, was probably woven at Amsterdam (cf. p. 219). The Mortlake works wove a portrait of the Director, Sir Francis Crane, about 1630.

In the eighteenth century the Gobelins brought this phase of the craft to an unsurpassable degree of perfection. Bobbin and thread, thanks equally to the skill of the dyer and of the weaver, became almost identical in results with brush and paint. Artistic legerdemain has, in this instance, the justification of success, for what that is worth. Outstanding examples are the portraits of Louis XV and of Maria Lesczinscka.

The Saint Petersburg portraits are but another phase of this Gobelins achievement, since the workers there were either Gobelins men or their pupils. Historically one of the most interesting is an oval tapestry depicting the Countess Catherine Dashkov, sister of Elizabeth Voronzov, Peter's mistress whom he would have liked to put on the throne in his wife's stead. Catherine lured the younger Voronzov girl, then only nineteen, to her side of the quarrel, and when her coup succeeded and she was the all powerful Empress, she never forgot the Countess. The portrait shows a woman neither handsome nor distinguished, in fact decidedly commonplace, and quite stupid looking. It is said to be after a canvas by Conte Pietro dei Rotari (1707–1762), a Veronese nobleman who turned painter and spent the last five years of his life in Russia, painting many members of the court.

But by far the most significant production of the Saint Petersburg looms is a full length portrait of Catherine herself (Pl. 35). She stands, in all the pomp of her imperial robes, a monument of velvet, ermine, and jewels, as German as Queen Victoria but with genuine power to justify her complacent self importance. Fine in weave, pure and strong in color, accurate in representation, the tapestry is a masterpiece in workmanship and a significant record of a moment in history and of a phase of taste.

Of all the scores of shops founded in the various countries of Europe outside of Flanders and France, none endured for any period as an economically self justifying industry. All depended on patronage, and most of them, even with subsidies and repeated official orders to aid them, were constantly in financial jeopardy and proved eventually to be of short duration. Some, at least, of these countries could develop among their own natives the requisite craftsmanship. All had access to the same raw materials as Flanders and on the same footing, for Flanders also had, for the most part, to import both wool and dyes. In Italy there were more talented and more distinguished painters to make the cartoons. Every centre could supply skill in financing and in administration, and marketing resources. But, for some reason that is not evident in any of the explicit facts, only Flanders could, generation after generation, produce tapestry as a paying commercial occupation. Even in France the factories had to be fostered by the State. Tapestry was, both artistically and industrially, specifically the accomplishment of the Lowlands.

PLATE XXXV

PORTRAIT OF CATHERINE THE GREAT OF RUSSIA. Russia, 18th century

P. W. French & Co. See p. 224

CHAPTER XIII

THE FAR AND MIDDLE EAST

DURING all this time another social order had been growing up on the other side of the world, in the Far East. Or perhaps it was not really an independent evolution. Perhaps the cultures of both China and Mesopotamia had branched from a central root somewhere in the heart of Asia. It is a striking coincidence that the soberer Chinese historians have placed the beginning of their civilization, of an adequate control, that is, of the basic equipment of organized life such as agriculture and wheeled vehicles, at 2800 B.C., a few centuries after the earliest Sumerian date or the beginning of Egypt in an equivalent cultural sense. Chinese chronology is, however, notoriously ambiguous and Chinese archaeology has still most of its fundamental work to do.

The history of Chinese art does not begin to be at all clear until two millenniums later, but in the centuries just preceding the Christian era a fairly definite idea of Chinese life does emerge. At that time the Chinese already lived comfortably in adequate houses with well constructed furniture, ate off handsome pottery, travelled in a leisurely fashion in carriages and boats, and carried umbrellas. And they could write letters to each other in a fully developed script on bamboo tablets scratched with a stylus. In essentials, that is to say, they were not so very different from their contemporaries at the other end of the earth.

But one thing the Chinese had of which Western civilization had not yet heard. They had learned to take the peculiar cocoon of a certain worm (*Bombyx mori*), dissolve it, separate it into strands, spin it and weave it to make a material, fine and smooth, glossy and supple, lasting but luxurious. How long

[225]

they had enjoyed this pleasantly slippery stuff it is impossible to say. With the arbitrary precision that makes their legends such a delicious parody of history, the Chinese fix the date at 2640 B.C., and credit the idea to Si-ling, wife of the Emperor Huang-ti. She personally raised the worms, reeled the fibre, and conceived the notion of the very first loom.

The West had learned about this textile luxury by the time the Classical civilization was well established in Greece, and Aristotle describes the worm, emphasizing its horns, and the process of using its cocoon. He could have got his information, however, only at second hand, for China guarded closely the control of silk production, so that none of the worms were brought to the West until five hundred and fifty years after Christ.

The silk itself, on the other hand, came out in great quantities, for both Greece and Rome were ready to buy all and more than they could afford. The island of Cos was famous for a very sheer silk gauze which the Greeks loved because it so beautifully revealed the human form, while Rome insisted on silk even when it cost its weight in gold because it represented luxury and display. Emperor after Emperor contested the dangerous trade, which helped to drain the resources of the capital unproductively from the West to the East, but the Roman Patrician and his self-willed, clamorous wife demanded at all cost elegance. Through more than a thousand years China exported her worm-spun product to the West, both in its raw and woven forms, sending it in bales and bolts across Turkestan, a long, hard trip through the hostile deserts, made possible only by the maintenance of way stations along the weary road.

It was in one of these way stations that was found the first known tapestry of silk. With other, shuttle-woven textiles, it came to light in the desert region of Central Turkestan, in Loulan. All that part of the silk route, including this site, was abandoned shortly after the Christian era, so that this tapestry presumably dates from somewhere about that time. Thus it represents work of the Han period in China, provided, indeed, that it really is Chinese, for the pattern is Iranian in iconography. Perhaps it was made in China or in Turkestan, near where it was found, to appeal to the Persian market, for the Chinese have always been flexible craftsmen, quick to make export wares to meet foreign specifications.

The design, wrought in seven colors, two browns, another purplish brown, blue, two greens and crimson, shows a sacred tree composed of symmetrical scrolls of a classical type, with a central bird's head finial. The hawk in Iranian mythology was a magic bird nesting in the Tree of Life. On either side, confronted in the manner derived from Mesopotamia, are compound animals with the head, wings, and tail of a bird and the forequarters of a horse, a kind of equine griffon. The whole unit is repeated in a horizontal band, alternating with a simple scroll, and above and below are border stripes with a repeated conventional flower, also showing Hellenistic character.

A millennium, more or less, passes, and then silk tapestry reappears, again in Turkestan, but this time at Ton Huang which is quite a bit further east than Loulan, closer to China. Several fragments have been found, all of which probably date between the eighth and the tenth century. They have only repeating designs. One, on an orange ground, shows a quatrefoil composed of vine leaves, applied to the sides of a flattened oval, with a duck in profile in the center. This is a very finely woven slit tapestry (cf. p. 303) in yellow-green, blue, white, and brown, enriched with inwoven strips of gilded paper, a typical Chinese device. Other less interesting bits show angular quatrefoils or small floral spots. Figural designs do not appear in tapestry, but there is embroidery with elaborate pictorial themes.

The investigation of another group of sites in Turkestan yielded a few more bits of tapestry, probably from the immediately succeeding centuries, the tenth and eleventh; and here again the more elaborate, figural compositions are rendered in embroidery, while the tapestries have only rather simple, repeating motives. Some of these are very attractive, however. A lovely little scrap shows a yellow duck floating on a dark blue pond among red and yellow pond-lily leaves. On another piece, a roaring lion is drawn in dark blue outline and lighter blue shading on a beige ground. Unfortunately the piece that must have been by far the most sumptuous is so torn to bits it is impossible to reconstruct the design. The ground consists of an imbricate pattern in rose and a gold weft, which is a rather wide, flat strip of membrane covered with gold leaf. Against this are scrolling vines in two shades of violet, green and yellow, and blue and white. In all the pieces from this area the warps are vertical and there are no slits, the wefts being, apparently, interlocked (cf. p. 304).

There is again a lapse of five or six hundred years and then silk tapestry reappears in the Far East, the technique, which the Chinese had probably never ceased to use, being employed both for wall panels and for fine garments. A few of these tapestries, commonly called *k'ssus,* can definitely be identified as work of the Sung Dynasty (A.D. 960–1280). Thus the mounting of a landscape scroll by Mi Fei (twelfth century) in a collection of Mrs. William H. Moore includes a *k'ssu* about a foot square which can with confidence be accounted Sung because the painting has never been remountèd. It shows a spray of peonies on a pale gray ground, with one full-blown purple flower, and three half-open buds, one of these also purple, another blue, and the third streaked purple and white. The foliage is in two shades of green, there are minor details in lacquer red, and the stems are gold, as are also the outlines, which have been inserted with a free bobbin in double rows. The gold is still a gilded paper or membrane, but now it is wrapped around a core of silk. The warps are vertical and there are marked slits.

There are a few *k'ssus,* too, that can be attributed to the Ming period (A.D. 1368–1644), but the great bulk of the existing pieces are certainly Ch'ing (A.D. 1644–1912), many, doubtless, from the reign of Ch'ien Lung (A.D. 1736–1795), but most of them still later, for the production continued well down into the nineteenth century and has been resumed in recent years. In the inferior examples details, especially faces, are often painted.

The garments are of three main types, court robes, robes of officials of lesser importance, and ladies' coats. The court robes have a standard symbolic pattern. Great dragons, five-, four- or three-toed, according to the wearer's rank, coil above a conventional band of waves out of which rises the sacred mountain, and interspersed among the waves and the formal clouds that cover the rest of the ground are bats for happiness and multiple emblems of good fortune, both Buddhist and Taoist, or, in rarer examples, the twelve attributes from the Book of Rites dedicated to the Emperor himself. Officials' coats display the dragons less conspicuously, if at all, but have again the talismanic motives and, in addition, a square on breast and back, designating, according to fixed rules, the owner's status. The ladies' costumes, on the other hand, are freer in design, with a happy play of flowers, birds, and butterflies, patterns that closely resemble those on the painted porcelains of the time. Indeed one somewhat unusual style seems to be a direct and conscious imitation of porcelain, for the ground is milk white, while the flowers are rendered only in three or four tones of blue. Thus a coat in the collection of Mrs. William H. Moore has peonies and marguerites in this blue and white convention, and the hatching from one tone to another reproduces as closely as possible the effect of the shading in the porcelain painting.

The wall hangings, also, fall into three main classes, the commonest being sets of four tall narrow panels, each usually divided into three sections, the top and bottom ones with floral or still life subjects, the latter composed of symbolic objects, and in the middle a figural scene illustrating a popular romantic or poetic episode. In general the drawing of this type is inferior, closely resembling the style of the mirror painters. The somewhat larger and much rarer panels in the format of wall paintings, mounted, like paintings, on brocade and rolled, are usually of much better artistic quality, the designs evidently of really well trained artists. These almost always present bird and flower subjects, such as peonies springing from rocks, and pheasants. While the ordinary pieces are merely naturalistic decorations of rather perfunctory invention, a few fine examples are true lyric portraits of the subject, with a delicate presentation of a fresh insight into the essential quality of that kind of beauty. The third style is very large, more nearly approaching in dimensions the Western idea of a tapestry, but the weave is too fine to obtain a true tapestry effect in the Western sense. The bird and flower designs, which are again common in this type, are usually still under the domination of silk painting, but sometimes they show, rather, a relation to the painted wall-papers, achieving a bolder scale and a more sweeping decorative breadth of composition. Thus a large square pair in the Metropolitan Museum has splendid big phoenix flying above peonies. Still another version of these large wall panels, however, seems to follow the example of the brocades, with subjects, usually gods and saints, arranged, not illustratively, but formally. The cartoons for these seem, judging from their general character, to have been rendered by the same grade of craftsman that made the huge painted temple banners. In all of these types, whether garments or wall hangings, small or large, the colors are, in general, rather light and clear, in keeping with the quality of the thin silk and the fineness of the texture.

An exceptional piece in the collection of Mrs. Christian Holmes, probably from one of the earlier Ch'ing dynasties, is stronger in texture and color and bolder in treatment (Pl. 36). It is a large wall panel showing a hunting party in a mountainous landscape, with pure blues and vibrant reds supplementing more neutral ground tones, and there is quite a marked tapestry grain. Here again there is an enrichment with gold, especially for outlines.

In addition to all these purely native styles there is one tapestry woven in China which meets all the Western expectations. It is in wool, fine but still sufficiently coarse to have the characteristic tapestry texture. The scale is quite large (it is eight and a half feet high and a little over twelve feet wide), and the cartoon presents a fully developed illustration. There is, moreover, a border, an unprecedented feature in Chinese tapestry. Obviously it was copied from a French tapestry border, for it simulates a carved and gilded frame rendered in three tones of yellow. The piece, which is in the home of Mr. John Long Severance in Cleveland, shows a large social gathering with numerous figures about half life size. A blue brocade curtain is draped across the top and side of the composition, revealing a handsome room. The back wall is a beautifully carved lattice, partly covered by a large hanging of white silk brocaded with

PLATE XXXVI

HUNTING SCENE. China, 17th or 18th century
Collection of Mrs. Christian Holmes. See p. 230

gold bats. A heavy carved table in front holds a blue and yellow porcelain vase of flowers, a dish of sweetmeats, a bronze sacrificial vessel, a mirror and a casket, and it is flanked by handsome standard lanterns. On the side wall is a Chinese flower painting, and under this is a lighter table with a few decorative objects. The patriarch of the family, in a rich dark blue coat, and his consort and older descendants are seated about a round table, eating, while some of the younger children are gathered about a square table to the left. At either side, on a red lacquer stand, is a blue and white jar holding a blossoming peony plant. Ladies and children of the household, graceful or comical figures as the case may be, are scattered about, and servants are bringing in the viands. The colors, which are very varied, are for the most part blond in tone, lacquer red, pale rose, pale yellow, blue-green, dark blue, pale blue, dark brown, tobacco-brown, beige, gray, and white. The palette might be too light for the wool surface were it not weighted by the solid gray of the floor, and enriched by a dark blue valance across the top, with a pattern in medium blue. The weaving is very skilful, adequate to every demand, the food on the table constituting a very delicately rendered still-life study. But from the Western point of view it is surprising in one respect. The warps are vertical. The Far Eastern technical habit could not be set aside.

The French Government sent the Emperor Ch'ien Lung a present of Gobelin tapestry (cf. p. 279), and perhaps that prompted this experiment, for the Chinese are adept at just such imitation, and the piece was clearly the product of some exceptional circumstances since no other resembling it is known. Moreover, the border of this piece and that of the Gobelin piece that belonged to Ch'ien Lung are almost identical. The subject is sometimes identified as Ch'ien Lung's Birthday Fête, but this is pure speculation.

Wool tapestries were commonly made in Korea, but with a wholly different kind of design, purely decorative motives, of naturalistic origin but highly conventionalized, especially flying cranes converted into slanting lines and sharp angles. They are quite coarse, limited as a rule to three or four colors, and are used as rugs. Possibly some of them date from the eighteenth century but most of them are of the nineteenth or are quite contemporary.

The tapestry of Japan, called *tsuzure,* or when it has a metal thread ground, *tsuzure-nishiki,* maintains more consistently the character of the craft than most of the Chinese *k'ssus,* both in the texture of the weaving and in the style of the design. For in place of the excessive fineness which makes almost all the *k'ssus* closely resemble clothwoven silk, the *tsuzure* have the substantial body and marked rib of true tapestry, the warp being usually a fairly heavy cotton and the weft a flexible but solid silk; and instead of the ultra delicacy of painted porcelain patterns or the brittle thinness of wallpaper, usual in the Chinese work, the Japanese cartoons have the sweep and strength of their screen compositions or of their lacquer decorations. The result is a highly individual style of tapestry which is striking and effective, but which also has, in the best examples, the grace of movement and the subtleties of relation that distinguish Japanese invention.

Japan learned tapestry weaving from China about the beginning of the fifteenth century, and it is quite possible that the superior strength and energy of the weave in Japan is but a perpetuation of the quality current in China at the period when the technique was transmitted from there. A colonial derivative often preserves an earlier phase of an art, submerged in the mother country by successive changes of fashion, just as many American idioms have retained a seventeenth- or eighteenth-century form which has dropped out of the current speech of England. Moreover, the Holmes *k'ssu,* which is comparatively early as the Chinese wall tapestries go, has somewhat the same quality as the Japanese *tsuzure.* The craft was first established in Japan in the Nin-Naji Temple near Kyoto, but it soon spread, becoming even a fashionable pastime among the nobles, a certain crown prince of the Ashikaga line having won great renown for his skill. In the sixteenth and seventeenth centuries the Japanese conception of the art was expanded by the importation of European examples, so that large panels were now produced, the most famous being those made to decorate the festival cars of a Shinto temple, the Gion-Jinsha, in Kyoto. In the eighteenth century the industry made great advances. Priest robes, hangings, *fukusa* (the squares in which to wrap gifts), and tobacco pouches and other small bags were produced, and famous artists, especially of the Okio and Kano schools, painted the cartoons.

Western collections are poor in *tsuzure* but there are occasional examples of quality and interest, notably two pieces in the Moslé collection. The more important historically is a hanging made for a festival car, from the temple of Otsu near Berra lake, the cartoon being attributed to Kano Motonobu, and the weaving also being identified as of the seventeenth century. It shows the traditional Chinese theme of the Thousand Children, innumerable pudgy little boys amusing themselves, in this instance in a landscape of jagged mountains so highly conventionalized that they constitute almost an abstract, formal pattern. The second piece, a priest robe or *kesa* of the Tendai Buddhist sect, has a more elegant design of musical angels (*Tennin*), birds, plants, and conventional waves. *Kwacho* painting, the decorative yet naturalistic depiction of birds and flowers, has been maintained in Japan at a high level of excellence in both design and execution until the present day, with a concomitant production in *tsuzure* that are very charming and effective. Thus a *fukusa* in the possession of Mrs. Louis Ledoux has lotus and cranes rendered with delightful decorative grace.

While the Far East was developing these various types, the Middle East also was exploiting tapestry technique in a number of different styles adapted to different purposes. The earliest piece known from this region, found in Southern Russia and now in the Hermitage, is purely Sasanian in design and probably was made in Persia in about the sixth century. It shows a brilliant cock in blue, green, and yellow on a red ground, framed in a yellow circle. There was an important cock in Iranian mythology named Parodash. He flapped his wings and crowed at dawn to rescue humanity from the demoness of sloth, Bushyansta. A very similar bird, also enclosed in a circle, the characteristic Sasanian pattern unit, decorates a Sasanian silk in the Vatican.

No other tapestry can be attributed to Iran for four or five centuries. Then a second piece appears, quite different in character, however, and silk. It was found in central Persia, but judging from the style it must have been made further east, probably in Khorassan on the edge of Turkestan. A sphinx, with the body of a lion and the head of a princess, wearing curling locks and a high crown, is caught in the toils of a serpent, which is twisted about the victim in long undulations that spurt flames, while the hissing, venomous head is reared dangerously. The figure, which is in yellow and red on a blue-green ground, was repeated four times, when the panel was complete, confronted and feet to feet. It is drawn simply, but it has a sophisticated vitality and rhythm. In it is resumed a basic Iranian religious idea, quite possibly here Manichaean, which had been likewise the underlying motive of the Mesopotamian cults (cf. p. 4), the struggle between good and evil, the moral dichotomy of the universe that splits asunder every phase of existence and living.

With the advent of the Safavid Dynasty in Persia in the sixteenth century, tapestry reappears. During this period, especially under Shah Abbas, tapestry weaving was used for carpets of an ostentatious quality. Often enriched with gold and silver, they show the same patterns of palmettes and lotus, lanceolate leaves and arabesques that cover the knotted pile carpets of the time, especially those in silk often erroneously called *Polonais*. One, however, in the Bavarian State Collection, adds to the conventional repertoire figures of angels; but they are not a great success, either artistically or technically. The weaver was not even able to render their features, so that the faces are unpleasant blank pink ovals.

It is the more surprising, therefore, to find one tapestry of this period, in the collection of Mrs. William H. Moore, that does portray, skilfully and beautifully, an illustrative scene (Pl. 37). It is the transcription in magnified scale of a miniature of the second quarter of the sixteenth century, judging from the costumes. Against a cerulean sky, over a rolling country rendered in fawn, tobacco, and aubergine, a company of mounted hunters dash after their prey. Their costumes are light and dark blue, orange, terra cotta, emerald green. A white cheetah paces warily out from a clump of waving reeds. A frantic hare leaps desperately to safety. A startled, milk-white ibex pauses and turns on the crest of a hill, clear cut against the clear blue sky. It excels in beauty of color any tapestry of any origin that is known, and the restraint yet vivacity of the varied silhouettes, the skilful distribution of the design and the finished perfection of the weave make it one of the outstanding achievements of all periods of the art.

Silk tapestry, often enriched with metal thread, was also used in Persia to make bands for trimming garments, little bags of various kinds and other small personal objects. The trimming bands usually have repeating floral designs, the bags simple geometrical patterns in which the slits are emphasized as part of the outlining. In coarse wool the technique has been used down to the present day, for rugs, with rudimentary geometrical designs, not only in Persia but also in Turkey, the Balkans and parts of Russia, but though often effective in color, they are scarcely a contribution to the history of the art. Tapestry in the Near East, as everywhere else, is irrecoverably of the past.

CHAPTER XIV

PERU AND MEXICO

FROM a comparatively early period the Far East and the Mediterranean countries were aware of each other, and however independent most of their history was, there were, from time to time, interchanges by means of which each deflected and enriched the other. Both, however, were wholly unaware, not only of the existence, but even of the possibility of still another civilization which was flourishing in a section of the universe inconceivable to their minds, the other side of the world. Yet the remote peoples of South America, working out their separate destiny, arrived at some of the same technical accomplishments, notably tapestry.

Though Asia was so entirely unaware of them, this race was very probably of Asiatic stock. The migration was presumably accomplished about the beginning of the first millenium B.C. But in Peru there is no evidence, as far as present knowledge goes, of any culture prior to the Christian era. Within a century or two thereafter, however, three areas there were producing interesting and even beautiful crafts, two on the coast notable for their handsome, varied and technically excellent pottery,— in the north Chimu, in the south Nazca, and the third to the south and east, inland in the mountains, at what is now Tia-huanaco in Bolivia.

A few textiles evidently of this early period have been found at Nazca and at Ica, a closely related contemporary center, but they are embroideries, not tapestry. These consist of a panel about four by twelve feet, when complete, with a black ground on which are set, in staggered horizontal rows, usually giving the effect of a large checked pattern, single figures about five to nine inches high, in red, blue, and brown. Across the bottom

and sometimes up one or even both sides is a red border, with
the same figure in a single continuous row. The entire panel,
both the ground and the design, is solidly embroidered with
wool, in coarse stem-stitch in varying directions, on a basis of a
loosely woven cloth of natural brown cotton. The figures are
either anthropomorphic or a fantastic cat, both probably deities.
The anthropomorphic motive is quite realistically rendered,
a man in a fringed *uncu,* or shirt, that comes below his knees,
an elaborate headdress and anklets, usually carrying a staff in
one hand, and a shrunken trophy skull in the other. The Peruvians were accustomed to carry about with them the mummified
heads of their conquered enemies, for purposes either of magic
or of display, or, more probably, from the two motives combined. In some pieces, for example a fragment in the collection
of Mrs. William H. Moore (Pl. 38a) , this man or deity is swimming, and so that there can be no mistake about what he is
doing, there is, above him, a rectangle of conventional water.
This is probably the god that continues to appear for another
thousand years, a creator god who evidently changed certain
attributes from time to time, and certainly bore different names
in the various localities and in successive periods, but who
maintained his essential identity down to the Spanish Conquest.
He embodied fundamentally the fertility principle, he was generally associated with the sky, in one type a radial headdress indicated his connection with the sun, he wept tears of rain. The
most famous representation is on the monolithic sun gate of
Tiahuanaco, but he is shown in even more complete detail on
some of the pottery. He stands affronted, rigidly symmetrical.
The rays of his headdress are often tipped with the emblems
of his attributes, the head of a cat, the head of a bird, apparently
one of the Raptores, a certain flower, and a tripartite plant.
The bird heads appear again as ornaments at either side of his
belt, and cat masks are dependent therefrom. He almost always
holds staves, which sometimes have similar finials. It has been
suggested that they represent spears and spear-throwers. He is,
in almost every detail, startlingly reminiscent of the fertility
god of the Ancient East.

The cat deity in the Nazca embroideries is remarkable for

the eccentric tricks employed in the conventionalization, which are, in principle, the same as devices employed by the Scyths centuries earlier. The creature is dismembered and then reassembled on a flat plan. Additional heads are appended, too, wherever the form suggests such a possibility. This latter trick, of equipping a fetich with multiple heads at irrelevant points of the anatomy, also appears in the Ancient East, notably in the Lurestan bronzes. The typical Nazca-Ica cat has a strangely painted mask, a fan shaped headdress and a protruding tongue which curves up and ends in a face. His body is flattened out to a rectangle, usually in two sections, the second enclosing a semi-circle indicating the rump. The legs and tail are variously fitted to this. Thus in one example in the American Museum of Natural History, one foreleg comes down under the mask in a comparatively normal position, but another is attached above the first section of the body. The hind legs are, as a rule, on either side of the semicircular rump, laid out like an animal skin rug. The tail, which has scalloped edges, and also terminates in a mask, is affixed to the middle of the back. One or two long fluted ribbons hang down from under the chin, and these again end in faces which also have protruding tongues. Minor masks are often inserted where the tail and these ribbons join to the body, or are simply applied to the back-bone. The resultant effect, dramatic and decoratively striking, suggests that the figure was adapted, not from the real animal, however remotely, but from a ritual costume to be worn by a man representing that animal god. Later, in the Incaic period, at a great annual festival at the capital in honor of the Sun God, the emissaries of the different provinces wore costumes representing the animals that were their totemic ancestors, and it is most probable that this was a preservation of a far more ancient rite.

That the cat deity would appear in such a totemic pageant, not in his own simple semblance, but with fanciful trimmings, is suggested by the mummy of a puma found buried with as much pomp as that accorded to a notable personage. The beast wore tufts of feathers on his head and tail, bangles on his forepaws, and chains about his neck, and two long streamers, such as appear in a number of the embroidered figures, hung under his chin. The body was wrapped in a sumptuous feather garment. But that the Nazca and Ica embroideries do not represent a real puma dressed up in this fashion is indicated by an embroidery of the next period, in red and blue on white cotton etamine, in the collection of Mrs. Moore, for the figure here has the tufts on his head and back and pendants under his chin, but clearly he is a real puma, in spite of the block conventionalization, and he is quite different from the Nazca cats (Pl. 38b).

The feline deity appears again in a number of interesting variations on an important textile, evidently approximately contemporary with the Nazca embroideries, found at Paracas. This covering or curtain, an oblong rectangle with a border on all four sides, is not tapestry in any part either, but brocaded cloth, with a border composed of figures in the round made with a crocheted core and a knit cover. The pattern of the centre is a mask in a hooked rectangle repeated thirty-two times, in eight rows of four each. In the border there are about ninety figures of three main types, the usual god in human form in several different representations, the feline deity, and various human beings. The most interesting figure of the god shows him explicitly in a fertility aspect, holding a large flowering branch over his head. But the feline god also evidently had a fertility connotation, or had, at least, plant associations, for in a number of these figures he, too, has a flowering branch, held in his mouth, in some instances a branch of the cantu tree with its marked red blossoms, while in at least one instance, where he is shown not in an elaborate costume adapted to a human form but as an almost wholly realistic quadruped, he carries on his back a whole tree identifiable as the pacae tree.

The earliest remains of the mountain settlements, consisting of masonry ruins and a little pottery, show no relation in methods or ideas with the coast centres; but a later culture in the same place, which attained a far more developed life and has left richer records, had clearly absorbed many contributions from the coast, especially from the Nazca people. Having assimilated these borrowings, however, the mountain community then in turn imposed its style, not only on the coast populations, but also over a wide neighboring area, from Colombia to the

[239]

Argentine. This society, called by the anthropologists Tiahuanaco II, flourished in the Middle Ages of Peru, roughly
from about 500 to 900 A.D.

The mountain people who dominated this civilization were
great stone builders and carvers, and it was this glyptic preoccupation that shaped their decorative and pictorial idiom.
Their unit of form was the square. They conventionalized in
terms of the block and the right angle (Pl. 39). It might be said
that they elaborated, also, in these terms, for their designs consist of a multiplicity of squares, or sections thereof, compounded
into larger squares. This elaboration, which is the outstanding
quality of the art, is founded on repetition, not merely a random repetition, but one organized in arithmetical relations,
the same motive recurring at fixed intervals in the sequence,
every other one, every third one, or in more complex systems,
such as permutations on three and two. Moreover, a major
motive is often repeated in one of the minor interior motives
or, considered from the opposite angle, a minor motive that is
repeated is subsumed in the major motive, a principle that
shows a highly evolved aesthetic reasoning. Finally, consistent
with the quadratic basis of the style, bilateral symmetry is
usually maintained.

Anthropomorphic and feline deities are again the most conspicuous features of textile design, and now they are rendered
in true tapestry. The god in human form is simpler than in the
preceding period, with a plain square headdress surmounted
with a hornlike ornament. He is usually affronted, though
sometimes the body is affronted while the head is in profile
(Pl. 38c). A second god associated with him on the monolithic
gateway of Tiahuanaco is also frequently seen on the tapestry.
He wears a feather crown and has great wings which often ter-
minate in animal heads. He, too, carries a staff, tipped sometimes with a symmetrical three-branched plant. In contrast with
his associate he appears in profile, running.

The feline figures are now far less fantastic than in the Nazca
embroideries, realistic in conception, in spite of the block system of drawing. The coastal peoples also depict many fish, for
they worshipped them as part of a cult of the sea. Detached,

PLATE XXXVII

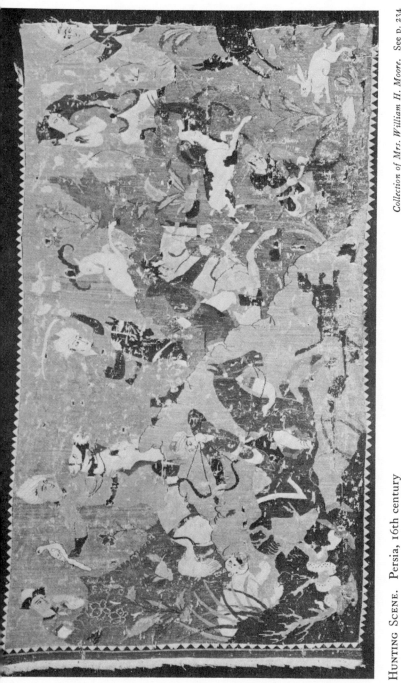

Collection of Mrs. *William H. Moore*. See p. 234

HUNTING SCENE. Persia, 16th century

PLATE XXXVIII

THREE DEITIES. Peru, a) probably early Christian era, b) and c) Middle Ages *Collection of Mrs. William H. Moore.* See pp. 237, 239, 240

PLATE XXXIX

A SEATED DEITY. Peru, Middle Ages   *Collection of Mrs. William H. Moore.*   See p. 240

PLATE XL

SCENE OF TREE WORSHIP. Peru, Middle Ages

See p. 241

affronted heads without even a neck are also characteristic of this period, a motive that recalls a favorite Egyptian design (cf. p. 20).

An especially interesting tapestry panel found at Ancon seems to be a scene of tree worship (Pl. 40). The tree is highly conventionalized, the mass of foliage represented by a black square, with separate leaves indicated by an interior powdered cruciform motive in red, but the trunk is firmly drawn and the proportions are just, so that the figure does give a fine impression of a dignified, spreading, deciduous tree. On the trunk is applied a feline mask and at the foot is a bird. Spread on the ground under the tree is a black and white rug, and over it is a canopy, apparently trimmed with a pair of huge tassels, drawn, in an awkward attempt at perspective, as an irregular pentagon. To one side are a huge jar on a low stand and a big pot, attended by a man. Above is the usual figure of a god, and all about are men and animals. Such complex illustrations are rare in Peruvian textiles.

Another plant motive that appears quite often at this period has three blossoms and two leaves, and the root is clearly drawn. It is often associated with the god who wears the radial headdress topped by the horn ornament, and is probably the same flower that on the pottery sometimes ornaments the rays of the god's headdress. On some of the tapestries there is a face in each blossom. The type has been found at both Chimu and Pachacamac. Other tapestries, probably somewhat later, from Pachacamac and Ica, have a conventional maize plant.

The stone cut style of square patterning could be transferred to tapestry with little or no concession to the change of medium because rectangular forms are natural to this weave. Other angles and curves are, as a matter of fact, portrayed in tapestry only when the technique is constrained to the purpose by the weaver's skill. The rectangularity of the Tiahuanaca II designs did not, however, relax the demand on the weaver's competence, for the complexity of the details required both deftness and accuracy in manipulating the bobbins. The colors were sombre in the highlands, but on the hotter coast, where the pottery of the earlier period had already shown a taste for rich polychromy, there is a gay and varied palette of yellows, browns, red and pink, green and purple, as well as black and white.

Toward the end of this period (about 900) some dire catastrophe, which cannot be defined, befell these people. The disaster, whatever it was, was especially damaging to their capital in the mountains, practically obliterating it. The coast communities evidently suffered less, so that they continued the culture for two hundred years more, but with the destruction of the capital, the source of their inspiration and standards, there was a change and degeneration in their art. Memories of glory remain, but the mentality has deteriorated.

Not so, however, the weaving skill. The craftsmanship is still under perfect control. Moreover, with the decline in thinking, technique increasingly dominates design. The result is the most effective primitive textile decoration that is known. The same motives continue: the god with the horned headdress, though he is comparatively less conspicuous; the felines, always now the actual animal; birds, especially water and shore birds, geese, ducks and pelicans; and fish, which are very important. But in all these figures, conventionalization now completely overrides respect for the object until they are mere symbols of men, animals or birds, with no lingering pretence of illustration. A human being becomes a compound of geometrical units, without regard to proportion in the human sense, though with a fine feeling for distribution as woven pattern. The emphasis of values has been reversed, so that the designs are no longer natural forms geometrically treated, but have become geometrical forms which have simply retained some natural reference; and many designs are pure geometry.

In the degeneration of the natural forms the typical processes of progressive decadence have taken place. The motives had already, in the preceding period, been treated with a high degree of simplification. Now, pursuing the tendency beyond its limit, there is considerable elimination. A profile of a human figure is reduced to an enormous nose, while in the affronted human faces the nose and mouth are represented together in one spot. In a number of figures the body no longer exists. There are only head, arms and legs. Owing to this elimination, exaggeration passes all bounds. All that remains of a pelican is a huge head that dwindles away to an angular scrawl. Human heads are often enormous, and in both men and beasts the eye sometimes consumes the face. In the logically final stage of this elimination and exaggeration, one finds the use of the part for the whole. This is especially true of a few pieces from the mountain districts. A puma persists only as a claw, a condor as the beak, a whole creature as an eye.

But though extreme simplification thus controls the representation of natural objects, the resulting patterns, on the other hand, are highly complex, both in the structure of the individual motives and in the arrangement of the repeats, for most of the textiles have repeating patterns. The two basic geometrical units on which the designs are now built are the square, which these weavers had inherited from their predecessors, and the diagonal which becomes the dominant principle. The diagonal put into the square gives the triangle, which plays an important part. The diagonal applied to the square gives the hexagon, while a quadrant outlined by diagonals in two directions provides the stepped lozenge. The stepped lozenge can, in turn, be subdivided and recombined to make other figures, for instance a stepped hourglass. Thus the idea of the square plus the diagonal expands in various directions to produce a very typical grammar of ornament. Naturally these craftsmen did not actually work out their designs by these steps of conscious invention, but this is the implicit logic which controls and explains their results.

The most notable development, however, of the principle of the diagonal or the oblique, and the one that contributed most to the very marked individuality of this textile art, is the idea of the reciprocal. The simplest reciprocal is created by a series of alternate diagonals, making the serration or zigzag, the angle at the peak being subject to variation. The section of the zigzag is the Z. The multiple zigzag is the chevron. And from these there are many stages and variants of elaboration into numerous angular spirals and meanders. These are used in every possible combination. Thus four sections of a spiral applied to a square makes a kind of swastika. Moreover, these figures are also adapted to naturalistic motives, individual features of an animal being emphasized to give an opportunity to introduce them. For example, the fur down the spine of a cat will be drawn as a reciprocal, or a bird will be given a huge crest that develops into a meander. Again rows of separate condors, on a piece in the Boston Museum of Fine Arts, are silhouetted and spaced in such a way as to suggest a zigzag reciprocal, even though they do not constitute one.

But there is also a more subtle development of the reciprocal principle which is especially notable in Peruvian art. This is the scheme of the reversible unit, of which there are three main types, usually composed of representational motives, though they may also be purely geometrical. In the first, the identical figure is repeated, though with a possible change of color, side by side and each upside down to the other, sometimes with a light connection between the two (Pl. 41). In the second, less obvious arrangement, the reversed units are on top of each other and fitted together, so that they interlock to form a coherent geometrical unit. Conventional birds are most successfully treated in this way. In the third, the motives are fused to make a single, but double ended, geometrical unit. For instance, the Peruvians use a face with the eyes in the middle and two noses and mouths balancing, or a square body is completed with a head and arms at either end.

In addition, moreover, to this application of the reciprocal principle, all versions of the upside down arrangement, still another scheme is also employed. This is the addossed relation. There are addossed quadrupeds, presumably llamas, of which the two bodies have been merged, and also addossed protomes of birds, both common motives in Ancient Eastern art. An interesting special, but very typical development of this kind of unit in Peruvian tapestry is a pair of addossed birds conventionalised into a Z with a head at either end.

The problem of composition, the system of repeat, was solved with varied ingenuity but almost always, again, by means of phases of either the square, or the diagonal, or the two combined. The most elementary form, vertical stripes, with the repeats spaced above each other, is sometimes employed. This

PLATE XLI

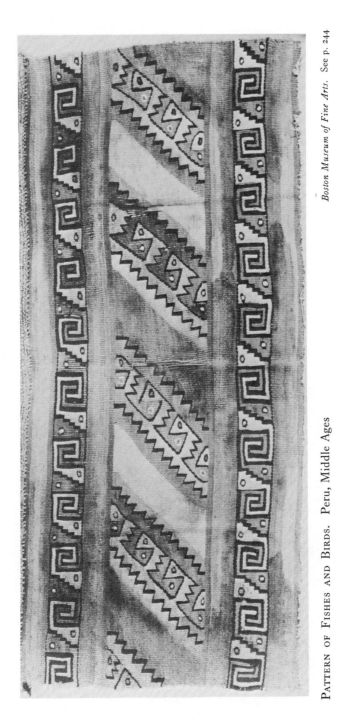

Boston Museum of Fine Arts. See p. 244

PATTERN OF FISHES AND BIRDS. Peru, Middle Ages

is a development of the square, because it is implicitly a series of superimposed blocks with the dividing lines erased. Vertical stripes are the most normal textile scheme, involving the minimum demand on both thinking and digital skill, because, in simple weaving, they can be obtained in stringing the loom just by changing in regular groups the colors of the warps. Simple vertical stripes, however, rarely occur, owing to the Peruvian taste for elaboration. They almost always have at least reciprocal edges. An interesting and typical form has marginal serrations in groups, but staggered in the opposite sides, making a very striking jagged outline. In other designs a plain vertical band alternates with one divided into blocks, or a plain stripe is split into two colors by a stepped outline, with the repeat at alternate levels on either side of this division, or this dividing outline may assume the more complicated form of a reciprocal meander.

The equally basic device of horizontal rows is more common and this, on the contrary, usually occurs in its simplest form, with the units in straight lines, not staggered, though sometimes there is an overturn. The zigzag horizontal stripe or chevron occurs, as might be expected, frequently. The check, which is a combination of vertical and horizontal striping, is also widely used, most often with fancy interior developments. Thus steps are used to split the checks in halves of contrasting colors which may carry either the same, or entirely different repeats. Such a triangulated block sometimes alternates with a solid block which has a single interior figure. Or in a very elaborate form of check, one set of blocks is divided into horizontal chevrons while the alternate set is cut into plain horizontal stripes.

Diagonal stripes, almost always with serrated edges, reflect the interest in the oblique. Finally, the diagonal striped check, which is the lattice, is used in different forms. Sometimes the simple lattice is combined with the step principle to make the stepped lozenge lattice, and the hexagonal lattice also occurs.

The repeats usually fall into groups of three, or of its double, six. Three is a unit naturally sympathetic, apparently, to the human mind, even in its most primitive forms, probably because it echoes the marked bilateral symmetry that is involved in the balance of the human body itself. In the blocks divided into horizontal bands, alternately straight and chevron, there are three stripes in each square. Again, in a pattern with separate blocks set on a plain ground, though the squares are evenly spaced, they are made to fall into groups of three by the color sequence. Cats, in a horizontal row, each of a different color, are in groups of three followed by a space which is almost as long as the three together. A very common design is three conventional, affronted men holding hands, like folded cut-out paper dolls. But the most interesting triadic form is a tripartite, asymmetrically centrifugal section of a kind of meander, which is used as a larger repeat to carry smaller repeats.

The use of six units begins in the first period in which decorated textiles are known and continues into the Incaic art. The early Paracas brocaded cloth has already a highly evolved application of a scheme in terms of six and three, based on ingenious permutations in the arrangement of six colors. In the post-Tiahuanaca, pre-Incaic patterns (c. 900–1400) the application is usually in a simpler form, merely a regularly recurring arrangement of six color combinations in straight rows of patterns, but in the Incaic period complex developments again appear.

The range of scale in these textiles is quite wide. The repeating patterns are frequently minute, a half an inch or even less in both diameters, but even repeating figures may be a foot or even a foot and a half long, while occasional single figures attain almost a yard. The commonest repeats, however, are in units of about three to six inches. This variation in scale, moreover, is not effected merely by adjusting the size, but involves also a change in treatment, the very large motives, especially, being developed with a breadth that gives them genuine monumentality.

Many of the textiles of this period are in only two colors, light red and white being a favorite combination. But exceedingly polychrome arrangements also were contrived, evidently in an effort to enrich the effect. The available dyes were only fairly satisfactory and not remarkably varied. The basic colors, in addition to the white cotton and black, which was sometimes human hair, were blue, which was good, pure, clear, varied in shade and very durable; brown which is often corrosive; red which is apt to be heavy and thick, with a purplish cast; yellow which varies greatly in quality; green, of which there are a light and olive shade, but which is rare and often faded; a rather dull purple from murex and, in addition, some light pink, tan, and gray. The only way to get a really rich effect with this palette was by extreme fragmentation of the colors so that, as a rule, the areas are broken into very small sections with rather marked contrasts, a device that is aided by the use of reciprocals. A special resource is " jewelling," the arbitrary application of small spots varying in size, shape and color, essentially the same solution, though in less elegant form, that the Sasanian weavers devised when working for coloristic effects (cf. p. 23). In addition, also, to these exceedingly polychrome designs, there are more restrained styles that can be strikingly effective. One type uses pastel schemes, for example pink, white, and pale blue, set off with the sharp contrast of black dots. Another works in neutral compositions, gray and brown, or a very sombre tonality of black and brown.

Most of the finest patterned textiles of this period are true tapestries, though there were a number of other weaves in use, and also a high development of embroidery, including some complex stitches. The warp is always cotton, either natural brown or white, which were both produced locally, both rather poor in quality, but skilfully spun. The weft is wool from the llama, which is coarse but long and easily spun; from the alpaca, which is stiff, or from the vicuna, which is short, but so soft and lustrous that it is almost like silk. For pure white a cotton weft was sometimes introduced. The wefts are usually straight, though when they are adapted to the contour of the pattern they are often handled very freely. Plain, dovetailed and interlocked tapestries were all used. The Peruvian weavers seem, moreover, to have had a talent for developing the inherent features of a technique into positive artistic assets. Thus they often utilize the slits very effectively to emphasize outlines, or even exaggerate them to produce a lacy quality. In an exceptional piece in the American Museum of Natural History, the perforated effect is carried beyond the intrinsic character of the weave, the textile being composed of narrow solid strips, alternating with strips composed of holes alternating with semi-transparent checks. Again, the talent for exploiting technique is seen in a solution of the slit problem evolved in Peru. An extra, dark-toned weft is dovetailed back and forth across the slit, laced as it were, holding the two sides firmly together and making a dark line between the color area which, skilfully employed, emphasized the strength of the design. Another peculiar Peruvian device, however, contributes nothing to the aesthetic effect. This is the use of an extra cotton weft carried, in cloth binding, the full width of the loom between every two rows of tapestry wefts. The tapestry is always perfectly finished on both sides and the wefts are very firmly and skilfully fastened, so that every piece is reversible.

The process of thinking that lies behind the various forms of the reciprocal principle, an emphatic interest in the symmetrical relation of opposites, is equally manifest in another group of inventions in which two weaves are produced independently, one functioning as the positive, the other as the negative factor. The simplest form of this conception is the double cloth which was very popular in Peru, usually in a rather coarse open weave in brown and white, indigo and white, or red and white. The logical principle is fulfilled here since the fabric is reversible, each side being the contrary of the other. It is again this purpose that dictated an unprecedented variation of tapestry technique in a piece in the Boston Museum of Fine Arts. The textile is double, a cloth ground and, on top of that, entirely independent but one with it, a meander pattern in stripes, in tapestry. The pattern is defined by areas in which the cloth is exposed, producing practically the same quality of texture that creates the character of voided, uncut velvet.

The survival of so many Peruvian textiles is due to the burial customs. The dead was dressed in his best clothes, placed in a sitting position and wrapped in a large cloth. In the grave with him were interred his most personal possessions, including vessels and implements. The tapestries that we have are either the straight, plain tunics worn by men and women alike (*uncus*),

[248]

or the straight pieces that the women wrapped around their hips as a skirt. Capes (*yacollas*), also, were used, especially in the mountains where it was colder, but these are much less common. Girdles are sometimes very elaborate, as are some of the numerous bags (*chuspas*) that have come down to us. The latter were used to carry the cocoa leaves, which practically the whole population seems to have chewed. The corpses and their possessions, including the textiles, have been remarkably preserved because on the coast there is practically no rain. In some localities saltpetre in the soil has also acted as a preservative. Since these conditions do not prevail in the mountains, however, textiles from that region are rare, having survived only when an accidental disposition of rocks chanced to protect them.

Well filled graves have been found all along the coast and in the adjacent valleys, but certain centres have proven especially rich. The embroideries of the earliest period are from Nazca and Ica on the southern littoral, and the adjacent small peninsula of Paracas has yielded related textiles of great interest, also largely embroideries. Many of the finest examples of the Tiahuanaco style, with figures of the Sun God in block conventionalization and related motives, all in a strong, glyptic silhouette, were unearthed at Ancon in the middle coast district. The neighboring site of Pachacamac also has provided examples of this style, though less splendid ones, while others, some of importance, have been found both as far north as Chimu and as far south as Ica. The most important single site for the diagonal-reciprocal style of the last pre-Incaic period has been Pachacamac, also in the central coast area. But essentially the same type has been found, not only at a number of other sites in that same region, notably Ancon, which is quite as rich in material of this later period as in the earlier type, Chancay, Lima, and Infantas, but also in the northern area around Chimu, and far in the south at Mollendo, which is below Nazca. Among the sites in the Chimu region where finds have been recorded are Chimbate and the Santa Valley, Paramonga and Horca, Cosima, Moche and the Chicama Valley. Nazca has perhaps been the most abundant source of this late style on the southern coast, but Ica also has produced quite a number of specimens. Unfortunately the origin of only a relatively small proportion of the textiles that have been found has been recorded, for most of them have been recovered, not by archaeological expeditions, but by natives who have disposed of them commercially. Consequently the material that is dependably labelled is too limited to permit any safe theorizing about local variations in style. In general the immediate pre-Incaic pieces from the north coast seem to be broader and less complex than those from the central and southern coasts, which cannot be distinguished. In other words the late Chimu style apparently maintained more of the block character and comparatively open spacing of the Tiahuanaco tradition. Yet even this generalization cannot be consistently maintained, for there are examples from the Chimu region as angular, intricately dentated and closely interlocked as anything from Pachacamac or Nazca, while, on the other hand, some later pieces from the Ancon necropolis could easily be attributed on stylistic grounds to Chimu. The fact seems to be that the relations between these communities were too close for the maintenance of any definite distinctions.

It is only at this point in the history of Peru and its arts (c. 1400) that the name appears which, for the world at large, stands for primitive Peru and its romance, the Incas. The Incaic center also was in the mountains, but it was some distance to the north, in the region about the modern city of Cuzco. The coastal settlements, however, also continued to be important throughout this period. Moreover the Incaic culture seems to have spread over a wide area, with local variants, into the modern Ecuador, Bolivia, Chile, and the Argentine, reaching its height not long before the Spanish Conquest (1531).

It is true that the people of the Incas were remarkable, but it is also true that their relative significance has been exaggerated, owing to our more complete knowledge of them than of some of their predecessors. The Incaic civilisation was built on that of their forerunners, and perhaps the finest aspect of their accomplishment was their preservation of the already existing values when they effected the transmutation which was necessary in order to organize their wider power. They found, in the fertile valleys, family communities, formed in the patriarchal system, practising quite a varied agriculture that yielded a contented comfort. They used these as the building unit of their government, imposing from above the pinnacle, the Great Chief, the Inca himself. The result was a monarchial communism in which there were no unemployed and no leisure class, no destitution and no great private wealth, for the riches of the Inca, his family and his court, were not their personal right, but the appanage of their function in society, and when that function, no matter how high, did not comport with indulgence or display, the emoluments of the office were limited. Thus the High Priest, second in status only to the Inca and usually his own brother, dressed in a plain gray wool garment and cloak, ate only vegetables, drank water and did not appear at the secular festivals. His glory was in God; unfitting, then, that he should clothe himself in mere earthly magnificence. Functioning in his sacerdotal duties, he was encrusted with symbolic plates of gold, both honoring God and figuring him to the people. But in his personal existence his values were spiritual, his life, in consequence, ascetic.

The Incaic Government, in accepting the family units, changed them only enough to standardize them for ease of administration, limiting each community to a hundred families, and adding an officer of the crown whose chief duty was to make certain that every individual had proper sustenance. Ten such "villages" (*pachacas*) made the next higher unit, the "county" (*huaranca*), with a higher officer from the central government. If any village met catastrophe, certain other villages had the obligation, predetermined in anticipation of the possible need, of lending the sufferers aid. If the catastrophe were more widespread, a whole county would be aided by other counties whose responsibility also had been defined in advance. The counties were grouped into "states" according to natural geographical divisions, and each of these also had an official appointed by the Inca. Four states made a "province," each province having, under the later Incas, a Vice-regent. Thus just as, economically, the Incaic state was a monarchial communism, so administratively it was a monarchial federation; for the centralization of authority had been effected, not by annihilating local autonomy, but by organizing these autonomies, each of which was kept centripetal, into a succession of groups in a hierarchy, every step of which was a compound of the units below.

Doubtless the system grew out of practical needs and was not established all of a piece on a theoretical basis, but nevertheless it implied thinking of a high logical order. Such logic was not, however, an innovation to be credited to the Incaic people, since essentially the same kind of thinking had already been manifested by their predecessors in their textile designs. For just as the Incas took small economic units and developed them without any sacrifice of their local characteristics into a great central government, so their predecessors had in their patterns, taken two simple geometrical units, the square and the diagonal, and created from them complex forms by exploiting their inherent characteristics to the full in every possible combination and extension. And just as in the Incaic administration a complex multiplicity was united by a rigid enclosing skeleton, which was, however, but a larger expansion of the same form of organization already present in the village or even in the family, through a hierarchy of intermediate units, so, too, the schemes that hold the repeats together in the textile designs are just wider developments of the same principles that are inherent in the pattern units themselves. In both the Incaic social system and the designing of the earlier Peruvians, invention proceeded from the simple to the complex, not by the addition of new and varied factors, but only by the explication of the inherent possibilities and implications of the original simple element, without distortion of its character. The big and elaborate outcome is the small, uncomplicated starting point writ large, yet it is not simply inflated, but is truly evolved.

Within the villages each individual was given three units of land, for each had a triple responsibility. One-third of the total yield was for his own household, one-third for the state, and one-third for the gods. Within his household his obligations were defined according to age, so that there would be neither shirking for the able bodied nor anxiety for the old. Similarly, the yield of the communal flocks, under state shepherds, was apportioned into three parts, the head of each family being assured of one pair of llamas for breeding, the surplus stock being distributed between the state and the church.

The family life was divided between work and recreation, the latter taking often a formalized, ceremonial character, the great moments of each individual's life being marked with a festival which was at once an entertainment and a rite. Birth, christening at the end of the first year, weaning, puberty, marriage, each had its elaborate and standardized solemnity, gaiety and feast, and the burial customs were very elaborate. The ceremonies at puberty were both communal and familial, and there were also other public rejoicings at intervals throughout the year, of which the greatest was the Harvest Festival. Thus life was balanced between production and realization, the family and the larger community.

The Incaic practice of encouraging the continuance of local habits resulted in a multiple worship that doubtless varied greatly from district to district. The Incaic creed itself was an astral religion, with the sun as the central deity, the Inca as his earthly representative and son, lesser astral bodies completing the pantheon. This sun deity was in essentials a continuation of the creator-fertility god of the earlier civilizations. It seems probable that above this official cult there was also a belief in a Supreme Being, the ultimate creator, a concept certainly inaccessible to the people at large, but understood by the intellectual aristocracy. The people worshipped, in addition to the official gods, various agricultural patrons and spirits, and there were also tribal gods of totemic type, conceived as the progenitor of the clan. Finally, each individual had his own household god, his immediate guardian and hope, who doubtless in daily life played the most important role.

While the ordinary weaving was certainly done by the women of each household, there was also a special class of nuns who devoted their life to the Great God, producing, as part of their service, fine and beautiful fabrics. These Virgins of the Sun, the *Acllas* or *Mamaconas,* were chosen as young girls by state officers, and lived in communities to be educated for their high destiny, learning, together with their religious duties, weaving and sewing. After three years of novitiate, those who were accepted for service were consecrated with elaborate public rites to lifelong chastity and devotion to the gods. And weaving and sewing were for the rest of their lives their major occupation. The total production of these women must have been very considerable, for at one time there were in Cuzco as many as three thousand. Every year they were all required to present their work at the Harvest Festival. The finest pieces, always of vicuna wool, were for the Inca himself and his family, the next finest for his military nobility. The lesser products, of llama wool or cotton, were distributed among the celebrants. Moreover, in addition to these, there were also professional men weavers, *cumpicos,* who produced especially fine fabrics for the upper classes, notably the *cumpi* worn by the Inca and his court, possibly the finest grade of tapestry.

It was necessary to have these two special classes of professional weavers because quantities of fine textiles were needed, not only in the royal household, but also in religious rites, owing to the use of garments and beautiful fabrics as sacrifices to the gods. This was no Incaic innovation, for similar offerings had certainly been made in preceding centuries by the coastal peoples, but under the Incas this aspect of the cult was very important, so that much of the wool from the community flocks assigned to the church went into such textile offerings. Thus on the first day after the full moon ten red and white garments were sacrificed, two to the sun, two to the moon, two to the sea, two to the great god, Viracocho, and two to the earth, while thirty were dedicated to the Sun God. These were burnt, but in some instances the garments simply accumulated, along with other offerings, in the temples. Moreover textiles and garments were also used to pay taxes, and these were stored in great state warehouses to be issued to the troops and government employes, each of whom had a right to certain requisitions according to his status.

The tapestries of the Incaic period show a combination of a continuance of the ancient Tiahuanaco block style with a new naturalism. The resurgence of the block style suggests that it had never disappeared from the mountain districts, but had been carried on there with only minor concessions to the angular, diagonal style of the later coast work, disappearing from our ken in the intermediate centuries only because no textiles from the mountain culture of that period have survived. Thus it was ready again to dominate the textile arts when the people of the Incas, mountain tribes, extended their power, culturally as well as politically, over the coast populations.

The preference for squares is most specifically manifest in the varied use of checks. Thus checked *uncus* were a conspicuous feature of the uniform of the royal troops. When the Inca Atahualpa entered Cajamarca to meet Pizarro, there was one Peruvian detachment of a thousand soldiers dressed in shirts with red and white squares like a chessboard, and the finest *uncus* of this period that have been found have checked designs at the neck and waistline, or around the bottom, or sometimes over the whole surface.

The assumption of the square as the unit of design is, moreover, also evident, though less directly and consistently, in the rendering of the naturalistic motives, resulting in a broader style with simpler, less detailed forms. Thus the birds, fish, and animals are blocked out in open plain areas of color becoming, in the coarser work, flat and rather empty.

The naturalistic tendency in the Incaic tapestry even went so far as to produce a few illustrative scenes, again a phase of the art that had been developed, at least to some extent, in the Tiahuanaco style (cf. p. 241), but had since disappeared, suggesting that this tradition, too, had been part of the mountain culture and had been kept alive there. Of these illustrations the most interesting and important is one found at Pachacamac which presumably dates from just about the time of the conquest of that region. In the centre is a column with seven Maltese crosses carved on the face. It is erected on a mound composed of a pile of stones or hummocks of earth. Above, on either side, is the deity as he has appeared in all the successive centuries in Peru, rigidly affronted and wearing the residual horn headdress, and below and on either side are a number of

[255]

men in profile, standing or kneeling, apparently offering gifts. The column, the seven crosses, the mound and the way it is constructed, and the association with the god are again all startlingly reminiscent of the Ancient East. Stone worship, of which column worship is a more evolved derivative, had prevailed generally throughout Peru for centuries, and in some localities was of great importance, so that the Incas, true to their policy, permitted it to continue, though subordinating it to the official sun cult.

The growing realism was also sympathetic to the expansion of the decorative vocabulary, the outstanding novelty being bird feathers rendered with exquisite accuracy, but very formally arranged, laid flat side by side in straight rows. There are, too, new plant motives, but these also, may have been used without interruption in the mountains, for they seem to be in a continuous descent from the plants sometimes included in the earliest coastal pieces under Tiahuanaca influence (cf. p. 241). They have either a cup type of flower or rosette blossoms. The drawing is always stiff and is still somewhat conventional, in a symmetry that is usually triadic, with one flower between two leaves or, in a more complex development, with a crest of three flowers in a straight row, and below on either side, a stem which is also triadic. Another design shows complete trees in a triple stylisation, the flat leaves side by side the full length of the branches, the trunks close together so that the whole surface is covered with the foliage, a thick deciduous wood.

In general the colors of the Incaic textiles are lighter and the combinations are more delicate. A usual scheme is a yellow ground with the design in rose-cerise and white, sometimes with accents of black. The work from the coast regions is apt to be rather coarse and the distribution of colors simple and spacious, as compared with the work of the preceding period. In the district adjacent to the capital, however, quite a different quality is displayed. The Incas were deliberately ostentatious, yet in the textile arts they were hampered in any attempt at luxury by the lack of the richer materials, linen and silk. To compensate for this deficiency and achieve the sumptuous effect desired, the weavers of the capital developed exceedingly fine textures and very brilliant color arrangements. Thus a large unbroken area of some extremely vivid shade, intense red or a bright medium blue, may be pitted against extremely fragmented contrasting colors. Such a scheme is usually either further intensified with sharp accents of black, or refreshed with white spotting.

The weave of these fine pieces, which have been found in the vicinity of Lake Titicaca, a number on Titicaca Island, is exceedingly close and firm, suggesting that they are the famous *cumpi,* the textile *chef-d'oeuvre* of the time. This assumption is further supported, moreover, by the fact that the *cumpicos,* also called *cumpicamayos,* lived in just this area, the province of Capachica.

In 1531 strange men appeared in Peru out of an inexplicable space. The Spaniards had come in search of adventure, territory, and treasure in the name of Charles V, Holy Roman Emperor, champion of the Prince of Peace (cf. p. 139) . The Incas were rich in gold. Their sacerdotal robes were plated with it, their idols were solid cast in the pure metal, their ornaments, cunningly wrought in symbolic shapes, were of the virgin, gleaming substance. Charles V had need of gold. His German princes had formed a Lutheran coalition against him. His Flemish burghers kept their thick-fingered, thrifty hands tight clutched on their money bags. His Spanish subjects, ever suspicious, were bitterly hostile to this foreign ruler. Charles had spilled great wealth in constant wars with François I. He was facing another, more desperate war, with the Germans, the Pope, and Henry VIII allied. He must have money. The Spaniards seized the Incas' gold and wrecked a civilization.

The Conquerors established a centre at Cuzco and forcibly imported there the most skilful craftsmen they could assemble, including tapestry weavers, whose dexterity was now devoted to meeting the demands of their new masters so that they produced wall hangings in European format. These were usually almost square, about five feet in a side, with a centre motive, frequently a shield of arms, almost always on a red ground, and multiple borders of varying width in which European Renaissance ornament was modified by Peruvian habit and combined with native designs. Further to complicate this *mélange,* small personages in a crude conventionalization are often introduced. Some of them are recognizably Spanish with fantastically exaggerated costumes. In some instances the middle of the panel has an all-over floral pattern and the tiny human beings, together with little animals and birds, are fitted in among the relatively gigantic blossoms.

Another type, probably later, of the end of the sixteenth or beginning of the seventeenth century, is clearly the product of collaboration between Spanish painters and Peruvian weavers. Less than a half-dozen specimens of this class are known, all architectural in conception. Thus one piece has a design of Renaissance arcades with cherubim heads in the spandrels and within the arches a conventional floral lattice on a yellow ground, while on an outstanding piece in the collection of Mrs. Holbrook Walker, the central panel is filled with a large urn holding a formal bouquet, flanked by rampant lions, under a trellis, and the border carries a floral scroll with birds, all in red, yellow, and black on a white ground (Pl. 42). The rendition of the florid Spanish Renaissance ornament in a rigorously geometrical, pseudo-primitive drawing and limited but contrasted palette, and the exceedingly fine firm weave creates a piquant decoration with a charm that, however accidental, is legitimately delightful and is unique in the history of the art. The weave of these pieces is as fine as that of the best quality of *uncus*.

A group of the people of which the Peruvians were but one branch, settled in Honduras and began developing there a significant and individual culture, probably about as early as 500 B.C., though it did not come to its height until the first century of our era. By the fourth century A.D. this Maya civilization was terminated and abandoned, but meanwhile it had spread northwest into Yucatan and north into the great valley of Mexico. Here it survived, more or less, to serve as the basis for a second strata of culture, introduced about 700 A.D. by the Toltecs, another branch or tribe. Their society persisted for about three centuries, spreading meanwhile to subordinate centres in the south and east, Tobasco, Chiopas, and Yucatan, and there it was carried on, so that when the central communi-

PLATE XLII

DECORATIVE PANEL. Peru, 17th century *Collection of Mrs. Holbrook Walker.* See p. 258

ties lapsed, there was still a deposit of tradition to contribute to the basis of the third strata of culture, established in the great Mexican valley about 1400 by still another people, the Aztecs. Their dominance, spreading over a wide area, with many tributary relations, was likewise extinguished by the Conquest.

We know that all these peoples had a highly developed textile art. The Maya sculpture shows complex repeating patterns which were probably woven, and ornamented borders which may have been embroidered. The Aztecs received some of their tribute from subordinated communities in the form of patterned cloths and had a taste for elaborate designs. The importance they assigned to the textile arts is shown by the many well made, effectively decorated spindle whorls that have been found, and by the fact that they had a special goddess as patron for weaving and spinning. But owing to the climatic conditions throughout these regions, none of their textiles remain.

In all probability, however, their traditions contributed to the later Mexican weaving which includes tapestry, though the commonest technique is double cloth, in blue, red, black, or brown and white. The patterns, though the specific motives are frequently of Spanish derivation, show the same tendency that was dominant among the Peruvians, to oblique and reciprocal geometrical forms. These are, however, less ambitious and far less varied. The most frequent are different Z forms, various less evolved meanders with the saw-tooth sometimes incorporated, and the related lattices. The double cloths, two-colored and reversible, lend themselves especially well to reciprocals.

In the motives borrowed from the Spanish, two predominate, the double headed eagle and the tree flanked by symmetrical animals. The latter is often arranged in bands with a vertical overturn, so that the beasts are alternately confronted and addossed. This device, together with the crudity of the invention, gives these textiles an unexpected and attractive comic effect.

That other South and Central American cultures produced textiles, possibly including tapestry, is highly probable but the archaeological research in these regions is only just beginning. In sites where the climate has been favorable to the survival of textile material new phases of the art may some day appear.

CHAPTER XV

THE PERIOD OF LOUIS XIV

DURING the reign of Louis XIV (1638–1715) all of the arts were bent by the royal will to the royal exaltation, tapestry, especially, serving the monarch's self-glorification. For Louis XIV was the supreme egoistic absolutist; absolutist because of his consuming ego, egoist because he was absolutist, and justifying both qualities by a theory of the State which found its reflection not only in every French institution, but also in literature, the theatre, painting, and even the cartoons for tapestry.

Louis XIV was the last of three French kings to conceive of monarchy as the unification of the kingdom, but each constructed his unity on a different principle. Charlemagne built his in terms of an idea, the Holy Roman Empire. Louis XI (1423–1483) built his in terms of fact, the economic and political interdependence of the land. Louis XIV built his in terms of the only idea and the only fact he was interested in, himself. His was the Copernican state; he was Sun King.

The three different solutions were the answers to three equally different problems. Charlemagne was faced with a complete dispersion of authority. There was no inner unity to develop. The parts could be brought together only by a system external to them all, imposed from above. Louis XI, on the other hand, confronting the fully evolved feudal system, had to deal with a power that was basically unified in that every part of a feudal society is reciprocally interdependent with every other, but with the authority distributed. In the notion of the country, France, he found a means of centralization which embraced the whole system at the same time that it took precedence over it. Louis XIV's situation represented the third stage of the problem, an inherent unity already effected and real, which had broken apart within itself, first in the conflict between Catholics and Protestants, and second in a class division, a contest for rights among the nobility, the bourgeoisie, and the Church. The warring factions all derived their claims from the State, hence only a revised conception of the State could reknit the antipathetic elements. To hold all three classes in balance together there was only one kind of focus conceivable, a personality.

Louis XIV qualified perfectly for the function of re-uniting France in terms of a personality. His desire for power had been heightened to the almost morbid pitch necessary for such an undertaking by youthful experiences. He had seen the royal family cower in helplessness during the revolution of the Fronde (1648–1652), and had been personally humiliated by being used as a sop to quiet the rebellious militia, displayed to them, feigning sleep, like an inanimate pledge. The shame of this situation bit deep and undoubtedly sharpened his determination to control the mob, insolent in its chaotic force. Moreover, though he felt himself ready to rule shortly after this, he had to wait seven or eight years, chafing and irritated, unable to function because of his commanding mother and especially because Mazarin would not relinquish the authority. Hence, when Mazarin died in 1661, Louis was ardent for a personal, immediate domination that would not even brook a minister.

Louis had, too, just the right degree of mentality to manage a dictatorship — sensible intelligence without intellect. Real intellect may be an embarrassment to a dictator, for critical reason turns on itself, breeding the hesitation which sends a quiver through public confidence. Louis was, moreover, a personable man, which served the double end of nourishing the conceit that carried him on and making him a decorative figurehead. As Saint Simon says: " He was, it seemed, made expressly for the role of majesty, for in any company his stature, his carriage, his graciousness, his handsome appearance, and the grand manner that took the place of good looks as he got older, and which affected not only his natural grace and dignity but even the tone of his voice, marked him out, to the day of his death, as the King of the bees."

Louis owed the opportunity for his self-advertisement in tapestry to the constructive work of his immediate predecessors, for the state shops that wove his tapestry monuments had been first conceived and set on foot by Henri IV (1553–1610). The Fontainebleau looms (cf. Chapter VIII) had been only a palace enterprise, dependent on the caprice of the monarch. Consequently they had died out by about 1540. The establishment of Henri IV, on the other hand, was no gesture of kingly extravagance, but a device of governmental economic policy, one of a group of national factories to which France owes her pre-eminence in the modern world as the centre of luxury production. Henri IV had thought of creating a tapestry factory in his own domain of Bearn even before he came to the throne, but that project was not realized. After becoming King he made several false starts with French workmen, then realized that the only sound plan was to import experienced artists, and so at the beginning of 1601 he settled a colony of Flemings in the old dye factory of the Gobelin family, headed by Marc Comans and Franz van den Planken, the former from Antwerp, the latter from Audenarde. The Flemings were given financing, privileges, and protection in return for which they were required to train French apprentices and also to supply the tapestry needs of France at prices no higher than those of the Flemish factories. The contract provided that at least eighty looms be kept active, and twenty to twenty-five apprentices be in training.

By far the most distinguished set undertaken by the factory during this period was the History of Constantine, designed by Rubens (cf. p. 167), but almost as important was a series of twenty-four illustrating the History of Artemisia, part of the set originally designed for Catherine de' Medici (cf. p. 169), but now thriftily adapted by the officials to honor the contemporary royal widow, Marie de' Medici (1573–1642). Marie de' Medici did not have such dramatic reasons for being grateful for widowhood as Catherine had had, yet she could hardly regret very keenly the murdered King. She, too, had been married by political negotiations as an unconsulted puppet, a human voucher of debt cancellation between Florence and the French crown which, as a legacy of the religious civil wars, owed a vast

[262]

sum to Florentine bankers, and throughout her married life her husband had been, to the scandal of the public, the enslaved dupe of the unscrupulous Madame de Verneuil. Marie was, however, too obtuse and indolent to seek the compensations that Catherine enjoyed when death made her Regent. She had sense enough to rejoice only at one phase of her liberty, the chance to spend as much money as she wanted on whom she she wanted, which meant her Italian favorite. She did not even take an interest in her son, the youthful Louis XIII. Thus the Artemisia series was quite irrelevant to her, not only in specific episodes, but even in general spirit. But just because she was so stupid, lazy, and wholly negligible, she merited only a make-shift, ready-made record.

The official painter for the factory entrusted with the execution of all the large cartoons was Henri Lérambert (active from c. 1608), but in 1609 he died, and at once four men applied for the post, — Guillaume Dumée (active 1601–1626), Laurent Guyot (active 1600–1644), Gabriel Homm, and Martin de Hery (active 1609–1630). The first two won, with a set of eight pieces based on the romantic tragi-comedy by Jean-Baptiste Guarini (1537–1612), Pastor Fido, a highly artificial pastoral invention. The set is a verdure with figures, and the treatment is typically Baroque, for the landscapes are not forest scenes at all, but theatrical settings, with artfully contrived groups of large dark trees artificially spaced to give symmetrical vistas and to constitute a screen of branches at either side, the " wings " of the stage. Essentially the same style of woodland scene was one of the stock properties of the theatre down through the nineteenth century. The figures, too, of the Pastor Fido, are equally of the theatre, for despite the bucolic theme, they are no peasants and their girls in homely garb, but pseudo-classical goddesses complete with chignons and vaguely flowing robes, together with curly headed gallants in stage costumes of no particular epoch, and naked Loves. The pastoral, born in a romantic ethics, has now run away from realism altogether and become a classical theatrical convention.

Van den Planken died in 1627 and his son Raphael founded a rival establishment in the Faubourg Saint Germain des Près, while the original factory was carried on by the Comans sons. The Van den Planken studio continued to use the Rubens Constantine cartoons, but they had also a number of designs exclusively their own, notably a set of eight illustrating the History of Achilles by Claude François, known also as Frère or Père Luc (1615–1685), a set of nine with the story of Theagène and Cariclée after the paintings by Ambroise Dubois (c. 1543–1614) at Fontainebleau, and a Playing Children after Michel Corneille (1642–1708). The first two sets are not known. The last is a commonplace performance with clumsy children, some in pseudo-classical costumes, others in the court costume of the period, disporting themselves laboriously. By 1662 the factory was of no importance at all, and by 1680 it had disappeared.

Meanwhile, the original establishment at the Hôtel des Gobelins had become increasingly important, until in 1662 Colbert took it over, gathered together there the weavers from several minor looms that had been struggling along in various places, and put it under the direction of Jean Jans, a Fleming who had been settled in France for thirteen years. Finally, in 1667, it became specifically a Royal Factory.

Thus the enterprise was made ready to the uses of Louis XIV, and it was immediately set to its monarchial task, the official painter, Charles Le Brun (1619–1690) being commissioned to design a set of eighteen panels illustrating the History of the King (1662–1673). The landscapes and vistas of cities were rendered by François van der Meulen (1632–1660). The set begins with the Coronation, illustrates thereafter His Majesty's marriage, and takes him then through four diplomatic episodes and seven battles. The next piece is of utmost interest for the history of tapestry, for it shows the King visiting the Gobelins. The Gobelins establishment, it must be remembered, had all manner of shops in it; hence Louis is inspecting not merely tapestries, but also carpets, fine furniture, and massive metal work. The impressive monarch, tall and exhibiting his grand manner, stands apart, truly regal with his thick falling curls, his sweeping plumes and long, straight legs. He is attended by his ministers and members of his court, while the various artists hurry forward to present their masterpieces for the all-important approval, obviously strained and anxious. The King receives them with condescension, but indifferently, thoroughly official. The next five pieces by Le Brun show various minor episodes in the monarch's life and then follow seven other panels which were made by several lesser designers in 1710 to complete the set.

The series, in spite of the fact that it ran into twenty-five pieces, was not enough to satiate the royal conceit, so, the available episodes in both his public and his private life having been exhausted, a set was now consecrated to the Royal Residences (1668). There were twelve subjects, one fitted to each month of the year. Le Brun was again the main designer, with the collaboration of another Flemish landscape painter, Abraham Genoels (1640–1723). It was a trying commission, for an architectural elevation, however skilfully rendered, is a meagre theme for a tapestry. But Le Brun met the dilemma ingeniously by making the motive only an excuse, creating, really, a series of formal designs. The building is in the distance and across the middle distance moves a group of personages, the royal coach dashing up, or a riding party cantering forth for genteel exercise. But all that is only a vista seen through an architectural framework which fills the foreground and constitutes the major decoration. This is a classical colonnade in rich materials, garlanded with flowers, with potted plants set about, pieces of sumptuous stuff carelessly draped, handsome animals and vivid birds wandering around, and one or two personages theatrically posed to enliven the effect. Given the problem and given, too, the pompous and rigidly limited taste of the time, Le Brun was reasonably inventive, but the results are rather thin and very forced, and the series seen as a whole is repetitiously monotonous.

Charles Le Brun was the ideal designer for Louis XIV because he was the perfect official painter, the impersonation of authority, system, and correctness. He was not, that is, an artist, but an administrator who happened to function in the realm of painting. His mediocre talent was developed by determination. His drawing is always purposive, not in the sense that it is

[265]

impelled to a predestined end by a vision or an idea, but in the sense of deliberate and unremitting effort. He is, in short, an artistic grind. As might be expected from such a temperament, he had no sense of color. His paint was applied to his drawing to finish the work, adjectives inserted afterwards into a description.

Le Brun marks the decisive end of continuity between painting and the crafts. Up to his time painters had been but one kind of skilled artisan, trained in an apprenticeship like a leather worker or a tinker. The establishment of the Academy, with Le Brun as the first Director, isolated the Fine Arts from the industrial arts. Thereafter, when a painter concerned himself with decoration he would, like Le Brun, function as a superior, directing from a social and professional eminence the actual craftsmen, fallen into the dependent role of workmen. Le Brun at the Gobelins had under him shops for metal work, furniture, carpets, and various other textiles; but he was not one master among many. He was the Director, the reflection of his patron in that he also was the absolute and unapproachable monarch in his own domain.

The old guild method assumed that an artist learned to do by doing, that muscles trained from childhood to precise co-ordination would provide the immediate outlet and formative expression for any aesthetic purpose. Le Brun and the Academy, all academies, take for granted that the arts are practised by the understanding, that the fingers follow the mind. A picture is the solution of a problem contrived by manipulating elements which can be formulated and defined. The older method understood that creation is an immediate process of the whole personality, closely knit by internal relations so that there are no such deliberate and exterior functions as plans, arrangements, schedules or even self-consciousness. Le Brun and his kind are so wholly outside of any true experience of creation that they do not even suspect the difference between aesthetic invention, on the one hand, and, on the other, analysis, classification, and all the other budgetary mechanics of the lesser, practical phases of the human mind. Le Brun, discoursing on Expression, seems to promise, for a moment, to say something.

[266]

PLATE XLIII

LOUIS XIV ON THE BATTLEFIELD. Beauvais, 17th century

P. W. French & Co. See p. 267

" Expression . . ." he writes, " is essential and enters into every aspect of painting; . . . it is that which displays the true character of a thing." This is the beginning of wisdom. And then he turns to a treatise on physiological psychology as it was understood at the time, ending with detailed formulae for " registering" each emotion, whether " simple " or " compound," giving specific information on just how to arrange eyebrows, pupils, nostrils, and the corners of the mouth to designate jealousy or joy.

While Le Brun was enshrining in various media, including tapestry, the taste, spirit, and person of Louis XIV, another tapestry factory was working in a different style, primarily to another end. At Beauvais a shop had been established (1664) by one Louis Hinart who had long had an interest in the industry in Flanders. This factory, also, was State subsidized but it was intended, like the first Gobelins under Henri IV, not to supply the crown demand, but to work to private order as a commercial investment. Hinart directed this enterprise for twenty years (1664–1684), but he produced only verdures of varying quality, and at the end of that time he was, in spite of liberal government assistance, in such financial straits that he had to retire. The direction was then taken over by a Tournay weaver, Philippe Behagle, who at once launched into far more ambitious projects and succeeded in the measure of his daring, for he ran the factory for twenty-seven years (1684–1711) with very little financial assistance from the government, and produced many important sets.

Despite the fact that the Beauvais works were not supposed to cater to the court, as soon as they attained prominence they were diverted to the glorification of the God-decreed monarch, in a series called the Conquests of Louis the Great (Pl. 43). The Beauvais looms, however, even when working for the royal patronage were still independent of officialdom, so that they were spared the intervention of Le Brun. The cartoons for this set were painted by van der Meulen, or possibly by his pupil Jean Baptiste Martin (1659–1735). The scheme is essentially the same here and in the battle scenes in the Le Brun set woven at the Gobelins. In both, the King, almost life sized, regally attired and nobly mounted, is in the foreground on rising ground, attended by a few officers, while the battle is seen spread out in a far sweeping panorama on the plains below. The general disposition is the same as that which Vermeyen had used more than a century and a half before for his battle scenes. But though the composition in the Gobelins and the Beauvais sets is thus practically identical, the similarity really ends there; for the Gobelins figures are only large puppets that have been moved into place and posed, often on wooden horses propped up in a galloping attitude. Their curled wigs and rich clothes are more important than they. The stage is set with papier mâché rocks and cloth plants, and the battle scene beyond is a backdrop that no one is expected to believe. The Flemings, on the contrary, were old hands at realistic illustration, so that, although the Beauvais series does violate almost every canon of tapestry design, it is, nevertheless, within its purposes, competent, vital, and effective. Louis is no dressed up doll, but a dominant personality, and his attendant officers exist convincingly. The soldiers in the middle distance are animated with vigor, and the far scene is patterned into a neat, illustrative relief map, with precise and interesting details. The color, too, is strong and energetic. Thus even in these two state factories of France in the seventeenth century, the final supreme award for tapestry designing and weaving must go to the ancient traditional masters of the craft, the Lowlanders.

The third French state factory, on the other hand, was wholly French in personnel and history. A certain number of tapestry weavers had been active in both Aubusson and Felletin, at least since the beginning of the sixteenth century, and even prior to that there are occasional names associated with the craft in the local archives. Thus the industry was of a respectable antiquity in that part of France. Despite that, however, it had never achieved any standard of quality, the output having been limited almost wholly to verdures, evidently for the most part of the coarsest quality, until the end of the sixteenth and beginning of the seventeenth century, when a certain number of illustrative sets appear in the records. These, however, must also have been very crude, for all of the pieces that can be at-

PLATE XLIV

CHINESE FANTASY. Aubusson, 18th century   *P. W. French & Co.*   See p. 269

tributed to both Aubusson and Felletin from the middle of the seventeenth century, are clumsy in drawing, dirty and faded in color, and coarse in weave.

In 1665 the Aubusson factory was given an official status, and from that time on had the right to use a fleur-de-lis in its mark and the inscription, " Manufacture Royale d'Aubusson," which was variously abbreviated. The pretentious title, how-ever, did not mark any great improvement in the work, which continued to be without artistic merit until 1732, when the whole enterprise was reorganized by a new decree. Thereafter, though the cheaper quality of work was continued, a few more interesting sets were also kept in production, notably various gay and pleasant, if trivial, *Fêtes Champêtres* in the style of Huet, a number of effective designs in the Chinese taste (cf. p. 277) (Pl. 44), and a really distinguished Don Quixote set in an unusually rich semi-naturalistic verdure background which smacks suspiciously of Flemish taste.

CHAPTER XVI

THE PERIOD OF LOUIS XV

SINCE Louis XIV had established the precedent of embodying his majesty in a series of tapestries, it behoved Louis XV (1710–1774) when he succeeded, to have his fame perpetuated by the Gobelins, too. But to find in the royal record events to illustrate was an embarrassing problem. Louis did, however, hunt, and personages of state before this had had their hunts depicted. So it was decided to create a series devoted to the Hunts of Louis XV, and Jean Baptiste Oudry (1686–1775) was selected as designer.

The subject was sympathetic to Oudry and he was tactful in making the most of it. For Oudry was especially an animal painter, and the mounts of the king, his court and attendants gave him a chance to show every attitude, pace, and contour of sleek thoroughbreds, while the pack of hounds, prize specimens in the pink of condition, offered him another opportunity to present animal vitality in cleanly modelled bodies. Not, to be sure, that he attains the revelation of animals as such, or even of life as such, which the Persian miniaturists delicately outlined, or Far Eastern painters shadowed onto silk. Nor does he feel the tender sympathy that stirred the Mediaeval Indian painters. Only Orientals can transmit animals with that nervous subtlety. Indeed, though Oudry was a portraitist, he did not even create portraits of animal subjects, for he had not enough communion with them to endow them with responsive personalities. His finest creatures are the dogs, but they are not so much the dogs of a dog lover, as show specimens whose points are thoroughly understood. Similarly, in depicting animal movement, he renders, not the excitement of speed and litheness, or of life and supple force which the Orientals convey as a clear, incorporeal emotion in their intensified portrayal of animals, but only the well observed muscular interrelations of superbly efficient living machines. He simply made records, but they are actual and convincing, the product of the aptitudes of a competent and conscientious man fostered by an inheritance, through his master Largillière, of the merits of the seventeenth-century Flemish animal and still life painters. From these artistic ancestors he had acquired a literal but enthusiastic regard for fact, an appreciative respect for substance, able craftsmanship in rendering it solidly, and a dominant sense of order and tidiness. And thanks to the last quality he organized his designs into compositions which, while not profound, since profound design requires not merely neatness but rhythm, are agreeable and especially appropriate to tapestry.

The landscapes in which the hunts are set are admirably conceived for tapestries. The forest is symbolized, though with an air of realism, by patterned trees that embroider the surface and fill the space, reducing the area of vacant sky and cutting off too distant vistas, sometimes with the aid of hills in the middle distance. Moreover, Oudry has had the wit to make his people large in scale, realistically speaking, but not too large in scale for the decoration of a room. And here again Oudry's great debt to Flanders is manifest. In these particular cartoons he is the direct descendant of Bernard van Orley (cf. p. 149), freed, however, from too self-conscious an awareness of design. Certainly these tapestries judged as tapestries, as flat, closely covered decorations that are at the same time illustrations, are among the finest invented subsequent to 1525.

Though this series belonged to the Gobelins and was always woven there, most of Oudry's tapestry designing was done for the Beauvais works, to which he was attached as official painter in 1726, de Mérou being then Director (1722–1734). One of the first sets he made after the appointment was also devoted to Hunts, but these, not being records of specific facts, are more in the conventional, romantic style of the period, with too lovely peasants and too picturesque groupings, too much the *tableau vivant*. During de Mérou's régime he created also a set of Pastoral Amusements, and four panels illustrating the Come-

[271]

dies of Molière, while for the next Director, Nicolas Besnier (1734–1753), he designed eight Metamorphoses, ten Verdures with animals, and his most famous series, the Fables of La Fontaine. Moreover during this period, Oudry actively participated in the direction of the establishment, not only controlling with a firm hand the weavers, but even taking responsibility in the business administration, until his power was so great that the Beauvais factory was known as "Oudry's Kingdom." When the next Director succeeded, André Charlemagne Charron (1753–1780), Oudry was to all intents the dictator of the enterprise, but he survived only one year.

The many times repeated Verdures and Fables of La Fontaine show Oudry again as landscape and animal painter, embodying the same qualities as the Hunts of Louis XV in a more limited and more concentrated form; but the Comedies of Molière reveal new aspects and new merits. The first shows the Lovers' Quarrels; the second, the School for Husbands; the third, the Imaginary Invalid, and the fourth, the Doctor in Spite of Himself. Here is the eighteenth-century theatre in its artificiality, its charm, its grace, its wit, its essential Frenchness. But the Imaginary Invalid is something more. It is a delightful genre scene, a staged genre scene, to be sure, but none the less a moment of bourgeois life, presented with a directness and an inviting intimacy that Oudry again owes to Flemish predecessors.

Oudry, however, in spite of the fact that he executed the cartoons for the official illustration of the reign, was by no means the typical cartoon painter of France of this period, for he rendered the facts in his own way, which had no real affinity with the spirit of the time. The intimate revelation of the mental and moral quality of the society of Louis XV was recorded by a painter of quite different talents, François Boucher (1703–1770). Boucher's father is said to have been an embroiderer, which is interesting if true, for Boucher's paintings have always something of the quality of embroidery, the creamy tones of sleek floss laid shallowly on the surface in skilfully shaded gradations. When Boucher was seventeen he entered the studio of Lemoine, the fashionable and facile decorator, but even before he left Lemoine's tuition he had to turn his trade to profitable account, for painting was a very necessary means of earning his livelihood. He took to producing the religious subjects for which there was a quick popular market, but the work was so obviously unsuited to his talents and temperament, that he abandoned it as soon as he found another source of income. This was painting scenes at the Opera, a sympathetic job, which affected his style for all the rest of his life. Meanwhile, Boucher's pictures were so attractive to the taste of the time that he readily won patrons outside, gaining increasing fame until he was named Academician in 1734. Yet this event was far less momentous in his career than a casual episode four years later, his presentation to Madame Lenormant d'Étioles. For the lady became, by virtue of the favor of the King, Madame de Pompadour, virtually Queen of France, arbiter of taste and devoted and powerful patron of Boucher.

Boucher won the place of favorite artist of the Pompadour for the same reason that the Pompadour had become the dictatorial mistress of the King, because each met the other's requirements. Louis XV was King by accident. The Dauphin, the only legitimate son of Louis XIV, died in 1711, and in the next three years two of the Dauphin's three sons died. The third, middle son, Philip, was already excluded from succession, having been installed in Spain. Meanwhile, the elder of the two grandsons of the Dauphin had died also, leaving only Louis XV, a child of five when his great-grandfather bequeathed the crown to him. He had been fourth, fifth, or even sixth in succession, yet he was King. Louis was a frail child, and he became a nervously feeble man. Some fundamental biologic flaw made him so lacking in psychical energy that he could not focus his attention sufficiently to carry on even the routine business of state. He was constantly sunk in a lethargy which was paralleled by his supine character, suffering acutely from this psychasthenic inertia and from the concomitant ennui. The one aim that he could pursue was some kind of compensation, and, as in most cases of this type, the immediate and successful antidote was sex excitement.

The Pompadour prevailed (1745–1764) because she was

[273]

capable of providing, by one means or another, the effective kind of sexual stimulation. The Pompadour was only ordinarily pretty and had had just the standard feminine education of France of the time, a training in the arts of civilized seduction. But she did have an unusual advantage for her purpose. She was so sexually deficient that she made no demands for her own physical satisfaction, and she was shrewdly intelligent. It was doubtless this physiological frigidity which made it easy for her to modify her role, when Louis's satisfaction in her was flagging, from mistress to procuress, thereby securing her influence to the day of her death. But though she herself was subnormal in sensuality, it was part of her perspicacity to understand it in others and to enjoy for herself the external accessories of an erotic temperament. It was this understanding of the life of pleasure, which emanates from and focusses on sexuality, that made her, on the one hand, a skilful royal panderer, and, on the other, the patron of Boucher.

Boucher himself was, as a matter of course, a sexual hedonist. His normal Latin male instinct, more active than profound, was not checked by scruples or counterbalanced by intellect. Consequently, he divided his time between the easel and the couch, with the same pretty women his companions for both, and no change in the quality of experience from the one to the other.

> "Never cease to fear the fair,
> Even at rest their lure they keep,
> Love watches with unceasing care,
> Cupid never is asleep."

Boucher was, then, ideally suited to be the official painter in a court which was devoted to the escape from ennui by the cultivation of erotic delights. The selfishness of eroticism shut out love, even as a trivial regard for another specific individual. The absorbing aim was, not a relation to any person, but the stimulation and pleasure of the experience, and even these were not the tumultuous and overwhelming physical emotions of

[274]

stormy sexuality. Unlicensed practice, together with a consciousness of elegance, had exhausted healthy animal lust so that all that remained were cultivated thrills and tremors which had to be evoked. Boucher's business was to help evoke them.

His purpose was not without precedents. One hundred and twenty-five years before, a great painter had swept canvas after canvas with the glowing surges of physical enjoyment. Boucher could learn from Rubens and Boucher did learn from Rubens, but he was a bastard pupil and inevitably so, for the sensations and feelings that were the material of his art were the emasculated experiences of enfeebled personalities. The rhythm that was an animating principle of Rubens's compositions was a profoundly organic quality of the movement of richly realized substances. Boucher painted primarily rhythms, too, but they are the shallow ripples that flow and float in a light surface contact. The deep stream of sensation that sweeps and swings through Rubens's enthusiasm expands in the rolling interplay of solid forms, but the galvanic current of Boucher's stimulation passes over the forms, not through them, the forms being chosen not because they are intrinsically satisfying, but only to suggest grace, seduction, and complaisance. Similarly, while Rubens's color bursts and thunders, Boucher's is a delicious, creamy skim.

Rubens, in short, was painting the passion and satisfaction of the body, Boucher the titillation and recreation of the senses. And he did it with appreciation, cunning, and *savoir faire*. His compositions play along with the carelessness of gay but happy accident, frankly making the most of coquettish but skilful ingenuities, yet ever flowing with unhindered sensory ease in a smooth continuum in which the accents are crescendos and diminuendos, with no breaks and no shocks, undulating, pausing, getting a little faint in some sweet, far tone of the distance but never dying out; swaying back until, in the more important compositions, the movement rounds back on itself with a flourish to a complete experience and pattern, though in the lesser, transitory designs the incident is often allowed to fade out in a relaxed vagueness.

[275]

" On dirait que pour peindre,
Instruit par la nature,
Boucher ait à Venus
Dérobé sa ceinture."

The types that Boucher chose to portray are of the same quality as the experience that he was conveying. Rubens responded to the warm, substantial flesh of mature, abundant women, rich in instinctive vitality, but Boucher was excited by the silky skin of plump young girls, pretty little frolics of ready delight. Or, when he did go beyond the easy and trivial tremolos of adolescence, he chose the type of woman that exists for charm, not mere sex commodities, but the professionally provocative of a sophisticated world, with the wittily affected elegance of French women, the epitome of French *chic*. He provides them, too, with all the accessories of the successful kept woman, a distracting clutter of smart and pretty things all daintily useless, the "*fouilli*" which became a standardized feature of his designs and for which, indeed, the word was originally invented. These and the myriad silly, delightful ornaments of the costumes and of the capriciously fictitious landscapes, give many of his lesser compositions the vivacity of a light-headed woman's chatter.

The subjects that Boucher was called on to depict, in both paintings and tapestries, were all consistent with the character of his mind and style. His first cartoons were made for the Beauvais works, in 1736. Oudry was Associate Director of the factory at the time, but he had no talent for figural decorations of any scope, so he called on Boucher for assistance, and the latter provided a set of half a dozen romantic country scenes, called the Italian Fêtes. At intervals during the next twenty-four years Boucher executed other orders for the factory, creating five series altogether, all amatory episodes in one guise or another. Meanwhile, in 1749, he had begun to work for the Gobelins also, painting in that year two cartoons expressly for the King's apartments at La Muette, the Rising and Setting Sun, the usual languishing nude, or still more suggestive half nude, men and women, swooning together on feather bed clouds in a mist of

PLATE XLV

SCENE FROM THE LOVES OF THE GODS after a cartoon by Boucher.
Beauvais, 18th century   *Duveen Bros.* See p. 277

intoxicated cupids. Eight years after this he was again called on for cartoons for the Gobelins, furnishing illustrations of the Loves of the Gods, for a series on which a number of painters collaborated, that was woven also at Beauvais (Pl. 45). He made, too, several lesser cartoons of his usual plump, lascivious erotes. Later he expanded the Gobelins' repertoire still further with two sets in the same taste, one known as the Elements, the other as the Metamorphoses, and some of the cartoons made for Beauvais were also executed at the Gobelins.

One other set that Boucher prepared for the Beauvais works is of special interest because it is the outstanding masterpiece of a style that is pungently characteristic of the mentality of the upper classes at this time. It portrays in five panels fantastic scenes that are supposed to be Chinese. Chinese decorations, especially silks and embroideries, porcelains and lacquers, became a raging fashion in France in the second half of the seventeenth century, and French artists hastened to take advantage of the mode by publishing engravings and illustrated books of Oriental subjects, while French manufacturers of textiles and faïence undertook to meet the alarming competition by imitative designs. The Oriental treasures of the French court were largely augmented in 1686 by lavish gifts sent by the King of Siam, but " *lachinage,*" as Eastern curiosities were called, could also be bought at the fairs and in certain shops of which the most famous, dealing in all manner of oddities, was on the Cité. Even Mazarin, who had an extensive variety of Chinese textiles in his catholic collection, did not scorn to import Chinese lacquer for public sale.

In most of the decoration of this period it was the genuine Eastern object that was the desideratum, so that European copies aimed at accuracy. Consequently, the first tapestries in the Oriental taste, a set of six designed for the Beauvais works between 1711 and 1722 by Guy Louis Vernansal (1648–1729) with the collaboration of Jean Baptiste Belin de Fontenay (1653–1717) and Jean Joseph DuMons (1687–1779), are illustrations of Chinese life as convincing as the painters knew how to make them. They seem today fantastically imaginative, with their mixture of unbotanical tropical vegetation and fancy-

[277]

dress figures of indefinite ethnography, but the contemporary public had too little information to be worried by any discrepancies. Similarly, Boucher's set designed in 1743, which also consisted of six panels, represents presumably veracious scenes of Chinese life in much the same manner, though rendered with more elegant grace.

Meanwhile the Eastern elements and qualities had been adapted to the fashion for grotesques which had been revived from the Renaissance (cf. p. 147). The great master of grotesques, the crisp and inventive decorator Jean Berain (1637–1711), created a set of tapestries of this type early in the history of the Beauvais works (1684–1711), firm and vivacious designs composed of unstructural architectural units draped with flowers and tasseled silks, with little comedy personages and animals in the foreground, not really Oriental but of an Oriental savour (Pl. 46).

The first interest in the Orient was undoubtedly due simply to a normal intellectual curiosity about the unfamiliar. The world was expanding and men's minds with it. To be sure, the Far East had been explored and described many times in the preceding centuries, but such travellers' tales were accepted as romances utterly remote from the real life of Europe. Now, however, the East was entering into the actual existence of the West in the form, not only of luxury articles, but also of such increasingly familiar commodities as tea. Naturally, everyone of a certain economic status wanted to participate in this enrichment of experience.

But especially in the eighteenth century, other motives reenforced the movement, above all the eagerness for novelty which was a reaction from the ever looming spectre of ennui. Novelty was exciting, particularly such queer and unexpected novelties as China could afford, and anything that could give a filip of stimulation to flaccid spirits was prized. Moreover, the anxiety of boredom invested the East with still further interest as a refuge from reality. Life had become a nuisance and effort to so many of the wealthy, that any promise of escape was a beacon light in their desperation. This strange new world of Asia that defied all anticipations was sufficiently far away to

PLATE XLVI

See p. 278

GROTESQUE after a cartoon by Berain. Gobelins, 18th century

seem to offer surcease from the weight of existence, while the imaginary universe created in its name by artists was certainly outside of both time and space, providing an unlicensed freedom, unlimited even by rationality.

Finally, underlying these overt motives and sustaining them, was an economic interest, for Cardinal Mazarin was frankly a dealer in Chinese importations, while the Pompadour, who always had her feet on the ground, owned stock in the Compagnie des Indes, and between these two and subsequent to them there were a number of other personalities of the great world whose incomes fluctuated with the returns from the sales of Asiatic cargoes.

The same motives, moreover, awakened an interest in that other strange and distant world, America, and this, too, was met with a set of tapestries, as early as 1687. It chanced that that year the low loom shops of the Gobelins found all their work finished and nothing ahead. More cartoons were needed. One of the officers of the Crown connected with the factory bethought himself of eight great paintings in the warehouse, which Prince Maurice of Nassau had given to the King some time before, showing scenes in Brazil, not attributed to any artist, but said to have been painted on the spot. They were brought forth, adjudged fit for the purpose, though in need of repair, put in good order by some of the Gobelins painters and arranged for the looms, with the title The Indies. The set was evidently a success, for five years later it was decided to weave it on the high looms, and François Desportes (1661–1743) was called on to make the cartoons. In 1738 Desportes reworked the themes to an entirely new set of cartoons which also had a successful career. Evidently the French Government considered the series a fit present to the Emperor of China, with a vague notion that all things exotic amounted to the same thing, for when the Palace of Yuen Ming Yuen was looted in 1861, the Animal Fight, from the first set, was found in the store-room, bearing the inventory mark of Ch'ien Lung and the date 1771. The panel now belongs to the Ashmolean Museum. It shows a bloody scene of animal ferocity, leopards attacking a boar and a tapir, a lioness killing a sheep and a fox, a crocodile devouring an-

[279]

other sheep, two white ostriches screeching in excitement in the background, the pool in the foreground alive with fish and crabs, and the branches above noisy with vivid birds, parakeets, macaws, a flamingo, an owl, a red-headed blackbird, an aigrette heron. Tropic abundance makes a lush decoration.

The French tapestries of this period, and especially Boucher's cartoons, initiate a new conception of the art. For the first time tapestries were being designed as one element among several in a decorative ensemble. Up to this time tapestries had been adapted to the buildings in which they were to be hung, simply because both the cartoons and the architecture, being contemporary productions, were products of the same taste. But now the tapestry was planned expressly to fit into a special type of room, often, indeed, into a specific apartment, and usually it was actually set into the panelling, as integral to the ornament as the mouldings and the chimney piece.

This meant that the style of the tapestry took precedence over the theme. Hitherto, when a great lord ordered a series made to his personal command, the specifications stressed primarily the subject. Now, on the contrary, the subject was contrived as a deduction from the character of the place where the piece was to hang. So when the Rising and Setting Suns were rendered in tapestry for the King's apartments at La Muette, it was not really a subject that had been selected, but only a title for an effective display of the kind of elements, principally clouds and nude flesh, that would harmonize with the furniture and with the spirit of the place. In short, tapestry, an art of decorative illustration, from being primarily illustrative had become primarily decorative.

Moreover, the type of room for which tapestries were now being made was an innovation of this period. Up to the eighteenth century tapestries had always presupposed great state halls. The only small scale pieces were bench or cushion covers or an occasional antependium or hanging for a private chapel. Even bedrooms were high ceilinged and spacious. The personal habits of Louis XV, however, had introduced the fashion of intimacy. The basic sense of inadequacy from which he suffered made the grand display of pomp and authority intolerable

[280]

to him. The setting of life had to be reduced to a smaller scale and a personal manner which would not crush him nervously. The result was moderate sized rooms and an elegance that avoided rigor. These tendencies were furthered also by the importance of women of the courtesan type and the wanton pleasure seeking of the society. Preceding monarchs had been as dependent on their mistresses as Louis XV, and court debauches had been at times more shamelessly licentious. But either the mistress had, like Diane de Poitiers, functioned primarily as a person, occupying the place of sex companion only as one phase of a more complete relation, or the damsel and the festivities of indulgence over which she presided were theoretically considered only recreative lapses, however much of the monarch's time and strength they might actually consume. Hence the lady of pleasure had never controlled taste. But now the relative values were reversed. The royal mistress might use her charms as political bait, but she existed expressly for the satisfactions that those charms procured to His Majesty, and such satisfactions were not peccadillos of a moral holiday but life itself. So the palace architects and their colleagues the tapestry designers recast their theories, and created the essentially feminine and frivolous style of the boudoir.

Dignity made way for charm, ideas gave place to entertainment. Straight lines relaxed to graceful curves. Nothing could be monumental, heavy, rigid or commanding. Everything had to be inviting, seductive if possible, and light. Since a room could not be rich in any impressive way, it had to attain luxury by excessive delicacy and varied complexity of exceedingly refined detail. In such a room there was no place for color that was sumptuous, only that which was lovely. The pastel sheen of silk brocades, the pale translucence of the neutral tints, this was the range and hence, necessarily, the palette of the tapestry cartoons too. It was a precarious style, trembling on the brink of triviality, menaced with confusion. But the French clarity of understanding, with its concomitant sense of relations and unity, controlled it and gave it form and order, creating rooms that were aristocratic and exquisite. It is only in such rooms, for which they were intended, that the tapestries of Boucher and his contemporaries can be seen. Torn out of their setting they can be appraised but not appreciated.

This intimate relation between the architectural setting and the tapestries is explicitly incorporated into one style of cartoon in which a *décor* of mouldings and pure ornament plays a role of equal importance with the illustration, which is reduced to a miniature inset. Some of Boucher's sketches were used in this way, the Metamorphoses and the Elements, but the most famous example of the type antedates Boucher by a good quarter of a century, having originated during the Regency when the close unity of all phases of interior decoration was first imposed. The set, by Charles Coypel (1694–1752), illustrates the romance of Don Quixote. The ironic adventures of Cervantes' (1547–1616) romantic exponent of *el honor* in the chivalric style were repeatedly depicted in tapestry, though the subject did not make its way into this field until a century after the author's death, appearing first about 1725 in a Brussels set in the Teniers style. Shortly after that (1735), Charles Joseph Natoire (1700–1777) made a set for the Beauvais works. This is entirely different in conception from the Flemish presentation, showing, really, a series of stage scenes so that the tapestries are interesting primarily for the light they throw on the French theatre of the period. Three other series appear at the end of the eighteenth century, two of them closely related, both being semi-realistic verdures with moderate-sized personages, though one was woven in Flanders and the other in Aubusson (cf. p. 269). The third series of this period is that designed by Procaccini for the Santa Barbara factory (cf. p. 288).

Of all these sets, however, that designed by Coypel for the Gobelins (1714–1721) is the only one that attains really primary importance in the history of the art. Coypel was a wholly orthodox exponent of the style of the Academy, to which he was elected when only twenty-one years old (August 31, 1715). His father, Antoine (1661–1722) was also a standardized painter of this period and a tapestry designer, and Charles was both his pupil and his collaborator, having provided the cartoon for the last of eight panels with Old Testament scenes painted by his father in 1710; and again having added, thirteen years later, one piece to a set of five illustrating the Iliad which his father had designed in 1717. Charles Coypel's work is well instructed, thoughtfully rendered, skilfully composed, and carefully finished, the performance throughout of a man of intelligence and high standards who lacked only the individuality of personal inspiration. He was thus wholly adequate to tapestry designing, and his Don Quixote series is effective, entertaining and altogether delightful, sounder than most of the later tapestries of the eighteenth century in that the illustrative interest is equally balanced with the decorative, not submerged by it. He depicted twenty-eight scenes and they are varied, graceful and expressive, showing an excellent theatre sense. The original decorative framework, an elaborate composition of mouldings, swags, cartouches and triumphal panoplies on a checkered ground, was designed by Belin de Fontenay, pupil of the Fleming, Jean Baptiste Monnoyer and his successor as official ornamentist of the Gobelins. A few years later (1721) Claude (III) Audran (1658–1734) designed a second framework with the same elements on a diapered ground, with the addition of animals and erotes, the latter after designs by Coypel himself. These are lighter and more gracious than the Fontenay frames, and they are in perfect equilibrium with the illustrative panels, rich and varied enough to sustain an independent interest comparable to the literary interest of the scenes, without being so large in scale or so confused that they overwhelm them, as the earlier ornamentation had tended to do. The design did not, however, come to its full perfection until much later (1760), when the ground was changed to a pattern of crimson damask of a pure and vibrant tone, strong enough to hold the ensemble together perfectly and to sustain the energy of the whole design. The outstanding examples of the finest rendition of the set are in the State Collections of Spain and Sweden, the collection of the Duke of Rutland in Belvoir Castle, and the collection of Mr. Clarence H. Mackay of New York.

As the eighteenth century waned, elegance declined into prettiness, and grace and charm assumed a simper. Jean-Baptiste Huet (1745–1811) studied with Boucher, but the qualities that made Boucher great could not be taught. Hence

[283]

Huet went on painting pink cheeked blonds, but they are too mild to be interesting, hand-painted bisque dolls framed in wreaths of China silk flowers. Their most appropriate occupation seems to be to sway daintily in a swing. The same spirit was also applied to the Oriental themes which continued in popularity, notably in a set of four that Amedée Vanloo (1719–1790) made for the Gobelins (1772–1776) called *Le Costume Turc*. Lifeless wax figures, vacantly pretty, are arranged in affected poses amidst artificial scenery. Orientalism assumes more of a tang in the cartoons made for the Aubusson works by Joseph Vernet (1714–1789), for ships and sailors and cargoes, his specialties, have a fresh, salty romanticism even when Eastern circus costumes are intruded. And finally, the academic tradition was also sustained in a Gobelins set composed (1782–1787) to the memory of Henri IV by François-André Vincent (1782–1787), a pretentious series of scenes that manage only to be unsuccessful costume pieces. The day of the French state factories was past. They would continue to produce, but to their increasing dishonor.

CHAPTER XVII

THE TAPESTRIES OF GOYA

B Y the opening years of the eighteenth century every important country in Europe either had or had had at least one tapestry factory that was more or less official, and Spain, where several small, informal enterprises had struggled and failed (cf. p. 221), could not be left out of the running any longer. So in 1720 a shop was established under the patronage of Philip V (1683–1746) and his Minister, Cardinal Alberino, called, because it was housed in a building near the Santa Barbara Gate, the Santa Barbara Factory. As usual a Fleming was employed to initiate the work, John Vandergoten. For more than half a century the shop labored at imitative commonplaces. Then the genius of Goya was put at its service, enabling it to produce the only tapestries of the eighteenth century that are, both as tapestries and as works of art, of primary significance.

In general, Spain is the country of the striking second rate. Because her types and customs, art and architecture are so instantly impressive, it is not immediately obvious how specious they are, but this very effectiveness is part of their meretriciousness. For it is won by exaggeration. Everything is overdone. Facts are not stated but insisted upon, and instead of reserve there is repression. In this manner every style that Spain has borrowed in her eclectic history has been cheapened in the translation. "Moorish" architecture in Spain is Persian building become showy and unsound in its extremity. The subtle gleam of Persian lustre faïence turned, when the Iberian potters adopted the technique, into a broad blaze and then, in the seventeenth century, into a hot copper splash. The religious tenderness of the late Italian Renaissance, already oversweet, is in Murillo an ostentatious and cloying exuberance. Even Venetian velvet designs when woven on Spanish looms developed fat curves and an intrusive superfluity of gold loops, while the Renaissance architectural elaboration of Italy was debased into the specifically Spanish *plateria* style, which shamelessly plastered façades with thick butter and sugar modelling. All this shows the common failure to realize that a quantitative variation makes a qualitative change, the error of supposing that if some of a quality is good, more is proportionately better.

Yet intensity in other lands has been consistent with greatness and beauty. Persian architecture of the Shah Abbas period is more continuously embroidered with pattern than any Spanish building, and the decoration is rendered in a medium that adds brilliant and varied polychromy to the complexities of design. Syrian glass, unstintedly embellished with enamel and gold, has none of the distressing appearance of display of most Spanish faïence. Turkish velvets are bold, emphatic, rich, but are untainted by vulgarity. Pathos is explicit in the Avignon Pietà of the Louvre, but it does not seem exploited. Sumptuous elaboration and burning emotion elsewhere have been, not detrimental to the arts, but the material of their supremacy. Why in Spain did they carry the stigmata of the underbred?

Because extreme expression of any kind is justified only as the inevitable manifest of genuine passion. But passion is the absorption of the whole co-ordinated personality in one compellent emotional focus that obliterates contest, creating a vivid, tense poise. The Spanish mind, not only in the race at large but also in the most typical individuals, has no such unchallenged aim to drive it to a direct and conclusive objectification. It has intense emotion, but this emotion does not, unquestioned, dominate. For the Spanish character is sundered in twain, with a cold, unflickering sense of actuality confronting the swift storms of feeling. The inescapable, factual lucidity of the Latin persists, despite the onslaughts of a chaotic excitement reminiscent of the ancient Orient, and the two are relentlessly balanced, so that the one, implacable, is irritated to a vicious cynicism, the other is exasperated almost to hysteria.

[286]

Why, then, if there was no true passion to compel vivid expression, have the Spanish almost always attempted exaggerated intensity? As a race, they have had an exceptional amount and degree of talent and skill, and these, combined with the Latin sense of order, could have produced original, competent, and agreeable works of art. But success of this quality could not satisfy them, for it represented only half of their mind. The fierce and undisciplined emotion demanded its due. Consequently, the artists, baffled by an accomplishment insufficient to the impulse of their feeling, have tried to force their work to surpass itself through emphasis. As a result, much of Spanish art has ended in inflation, excess or bombast.

Not once a century in the history of Spanish painting have the conflicting phases of the Spanish mentality united into the complete personality necessary for genius. Indeed, there is no figure of genius in the Spanish graphic arts until Velasquez (1599–1660), and only one other equal, Goya, three hundred years later. In these two men emotion and objectivity are unified, not merely coexistent and adapted the one to the other, but really fused. Both men saw and unhesitatingly presented the emotion of the fact. Both are typically Spanish, more alike for all their obvious dissimilarity than either could be to any foreign master, despite the external lessons that each learned and accepted. But they are the two extreme phases of the Spanish personality. Velasquez was the painter of the aristocracy, dazzled by the glamour of *el honor,* Goya was ever the peasant, whatever official recognition and titled mistresses he won, with the bitter tang of peasant literalness, Don Quixote and Sancho Panza.

Before Goya was engaged as cartoon painter for the Santa Barbara looms, the cartoons woven there exemplified every current style of official mediocrity. The dozen tapestries that are known from the régime of the founder, Vandergoten, who lived only three years, are all on Flemish cartoons, a peasants' festival in the Teniers' style (cf. p. 193), for example, a set of hunting scenes, and a young man with a dog and an ape at a window. In the first nine years after his death the factory, carried on by his five sons, languished almost to the point of lapsing, owing to the fall of both of the inspiring patrons, Philip V by abdication and Cardinal Alberino by banishment in accordance with the peace terms after the War of the Quadruple Alliance (1722). The enterprise was kept going only in a rather precarious fashion, by the superintendent who represented the Crown, a certain Cambi, until 1733, when the Monarch again resumed the full responsibility.

Foreign cartoons were still in use during this period, the chief productions being a History of Telemachus designed by the Court Painter, a Frenchman, Michel Ange Houasse (c. 1680–1730), who wielded a dilute and clumsy version of the style of Le Brun (cf. p. 265), and a series of ten panels illustrating the Adventures of Don Quixote on cartoons painted by Andrea Procaccini (1671–1734), aided by Domingo Maria Sani. Procaccini had had experience with tapestry, for he had helped Pope Clement XI establish a factory in Rome (cf. p. 211). The Quixote series shows an effort to imitate Teniers, but the Flemish quality is incongruously deflected by the Italian hand. The Telemachus was woven on vertical looms set up by a Frenchman named Lainger who had been brought from the Gobelins in 1727 for the purpose, but who lived only seven years, dying in 1734 after a riotous life. The Don Quixote was woven by the Vandergotens on the horizontal looms they had always used. Lainger was succeeded by another Frenchman, Gabriel Bouquet, also a high loom weaver, and one of the Vandergotens, too, perfected himself in the vertical loom technique, so that from that time on the two were used indiscriminately in executing orders, a set sometimes being produced half in one shop and half in the other.

After the deaths of Houasse and Procaccini, Sani supplied cartoons, a series on Tunis and another on the Life of Cyrus (after 1743). During the reign of Ferdinand VI (1746–1759) the factory was very active. The country was peaceful and rich and the Queen, Barbara de Braganza, was interested in all the royal factories for the industrial arts. Many series in the Teniers style were woven, the cartoons being rendered by the court painters, Louis Michel Vanloo (1707–1771), Andreas de la Calleja (1705–1785), and Antonio Gonzales Ruiz († 1785), a pupil of Houasse. But the outstanding productions were the Four Seasons by Jacopo Amigoni (1675–1752), a facile practitioner of a sweetened and Frenchified Tiepolo style, and the Life of Solomon by Conrado Guiquinto (b. *c.* 1699), who was a typical follower of the Italian Baroque, a Neapolitan who expanded his eclectic manner with borrowings from Rome and Venice and was given to pretentious, dispersed compositions. In the rendition of his designs Guiquinto personally directed the weavers in order to get the most perfect translation of his intent.

During the reign of Charles IV (1748–1819) the output of the Santa Barbara factory was large, a half dozen painters producing a number of cartoons, all of them minor men turning out ordinary stock designs, with the exception of Ramon Bayeu y Sabias (1746–1793), Goya's brother-in-law, and Goya himself. With Bayeu and Goya the factory at last arrived at an authentic Spanish style.

When the last of the Vandergotens died (1786), the shop passed into the hands of a young relative whom they had brought from Flanders, Lievin Stuyk y Vandergoten. In the invasion of 1808 foreign troops seized the buildings and committed extensive vandalism, but with the restoration of Ferdinand VII (1823), the factory was re-established, and for a hundred and thirty years, down to the present day, it has continued work under the direction of members of the Stuyck family. During that period the only important products have been based on the Bayeu and Goya cartoons.

Francesco Bayeu y Sabias (1734–1795) was trained by Antonio Gonzales Velasquez. He did many church fresco decorations and enjoyed considerable prestige among his contemporaries, receiving in 1788 the appointment of Director of the official Spanish Academy of San Fernando, but the comparative judgment of history has long since evaporated his reputation, sparing only his tapestry cartoons. These do have a genuine interest, due to their marked Spanish character. Their distinction can be credited primarily to the hard Spanish insistence which is attained equally by emphatic silhouettes, isolated by firm, unbroken outlines, combined, as a rule, with a few underscored angles, and by exaggerated highlights. Such tricks of definition are characteristic of the meretricious methods of much Spanish painting down to the present day (Bayeu is, for example, artistically a grandfather of Zuloaga), but they are more acceptable in Bayeu's tapestries than in the usual Spanish painting, because he combines with them a good sense of informal decoration. Probably, too, the seasoning of Spanish romance helps make these tapestries palatable; but that is admissible also, for an illustrative art has the right to call in a literary interest, and a decoration that is not pretending to take itself seriously is justified in exploiting even a puerile charm. Indeed, any art should occasionally be play.

Goya, between his first order in 1776 and the last work that he did for the factory in 1791, produced forty-five cartoons. All are genre scenes. The genius of Francesco de Goya (1746–1848) was true and complete, but it was not steady. Emotion and intelligence sometimes broke away from each other, neither willing to abandon the field, the disparity augmented by the equality of the contest. Thus in most of the Caprices the mind is functioning, not for insight into objects, but for the keen apprehension of a theory, and the emotion is a bitterness, sometimes sardonic, sometimes snarling, which guides neither the eye nor the hand, but seethes and explodes while the agitated artist struggles to keep up with his own perturbation. Yet this is only one Goya, truly he but not by any means his whole self. In the Havemeyer Balcony in the Metropolitan Museum all the tension of his emotion, strained yet not out of control, is focussed in the retina and forearm, so that a rather simple fact becomes more acutely real than anything in solid space could ever be, and the light and air that are the medium of this superactual world are themselves sharp and taut. This is the utmost Goya, all living, at his peak; but intermediate between the two extremes he can function, as true to himself but more casually, can note facts still with heightened perception and with a twang of emotion, but with a detachment that permits of humor, not with a smile — the Spaniards do not smile in humor — but with a chuckle that has a harsh note.

It was this Goya, still young, who painted the tapestry cartoons. Goya was as instinctively of the people as Velasquez was of the Court. When he was working on the level of illustration his genius turned with the same unconscious naturalness to the gaieties of farmers and shopkeepers on holiday as Velasquez' did to royal children. Only Velasquez, slave to a conception of himself, could never relax. Goya's mind did not get soft, his judgment functioned grimly on, but his spirits could, at the same time, mount intuitively into the abandon of common men tossing a silly puppet or of a girl flying up perilously in a swing. He knew in his own experience the reckless animal gaiety of the lower classes, a lighter aspect of the brutality of the bull fight.

All this is in the tapestries. They present real fact that is a little more real than fact itself, but not embarrassingly real like the group on the balcony, for a decorative art has no business to be insistent. They convey the gusto of deeply excitable people using every minute to exhaust themselves in pleasure in order to compensate for their usual exhaustion of work. And they are instinct with Goya's intense vision of everything as part of the stimulation of life, its drive and its ultimate futility. The swagger does not cover the sneer, but the sneer is not at his subjects but at himself, and the spectator of acuity is forced to share that sneer, equally at his own expense. This is the will to live commenting on its own folly and its necessity. It is all said with laughter, albeit laughter with a clangorous ring, and it is all said with grace, though jerked into sudden awkwardness to give it point.

In his earlier cartoons Goya was so little accustomed to the requirements of weaving, especially to the necessity for tactful color juxtapositions and transitions, that the weavers were forced to modify the models considerably. But later he learned to adjust himself to the weavers' needs. True to his irascible independence, however, he granted no concessions whatever to the current fashions in cartoons in other countries. He was rendering *Fêtes Champêtres,* but he made no obeisance to France. He was drawing peasants, but he never flicked a glance at Teniers and his school, although cartoons in the style of Teniers had been one of the chief resources of the factory prior to this. He went about the work in his own way, nervously but directly, with an irritable disregard of tradition that makes the cartoons acutely personal.

Nor could these designs be anything but Spanish. They are so flatly factual, they are intensely, exaggeratedly actual. They do not portray individuals, and when really analysed, they reveal a complex of conventions, both literary and pictorial. Yet they manage to give the effect of being blatantly specific. The impudence with which Goya introduces a wooden doll, unskilfully jointed, or a creaking gesture, somehow heightens the vividness of the scene as a real episode. An intelligent man is perpetrating a gauche picture card in order to be deliberately insulting, flaunting in the spectator's face, meanwhile, the vicious proof that these foolish mannequins are more real than he. If these paint figures do not and could not exist, they ought to, and their world is more bitterly genuine than that in space and time. By this same token too, though all of the cartoons are conspicuously costume pieces, because of the heightened inherent existence they do not date.

The immediate effect is due, partly, to the lack of composition in any expected sense. Most of these designs reject the academic proprieties of balance, compensation, echo or even unity. But many of them come so close to standard formulae that the last-minute refusal to conform gives a satirical twist. So in Flying Kites, the group of figures almost repeats the lozenge outline of the kite itself, and attention is audaciously called to this fact by the placing of the apex figure as a sharp vertical in the exact centre of the panel (Pl. 47). But the seated woman, who throws her head back and hitches her shoulder up with mechanical clumsiness, emphatically contradicts the plan. She is like a tongue suddenly stuck out in the spectator's face. Moreover, the design has the truly Spanish quality of exaggeration and over-intensity which is not overtly present in any of the obvious ways, but is attained largely by the acute angularity of the underlying geometrical figure, though in some other cartoons the same effect is obtained by a challenging sudden jump from a vertical to a horizontal line.

But perhaps the most fundamental basis of the arresting in-

PLATE XLVII

FLYING KITES after a cartoon by Goya. Madrid, 18th century
Spanish State Collection. See p. 292

tensity is the character of the rhythm. It is the diametric antithesis of the rhythm of Rubens. There is no sweep of unctuous, irresistible curves, no flow even of continuity. Everything is broken, spasmodic, dashing. It is the rhythm of the Habanera, guitar chords thumping disparately, a bony hip twitching out of balance, the stamp of a thin foot. Everything is sharp, decisive, sudden. This is the theme of the Spanish spirit, extreme, scorning both compromise and transition, seeking to escape fact in excitement, but still held by fact and so torn between the two.

CHAPTER XVIII

THE NINETEENTH CENTURY

IN 1782 the implicit power of coal was successfully put to
work. The steam engine was a practical fact. By 1803
knowledge applied ingeniously had devised machines that,
animated by the steam engine, would sweep shuttles back and
forth, fashioning with unfaltering speed the woven textiles that
for five thousand years and more had been wrought by skilled
and patient human hands. Tapestry, too, could be made with
this inhuman ease and regularity, this indefatigable rapidity.
Surely tapestry as a craft, a personal art, was now doomed.

Moreover, practical imagination had now perfected many
other productive outlets for the energy bursting from coal in
hot, invisible steam, so that most of the things needed in ordinary life were being turned out with relentless inpersonality in
increasing quantities, leaving the craftsman who had held the
chisel or burin, manipulated the bobbin or spun the potter's
wheel, to starve, with his wife and children, or, if he were lucky,
to snatch a dreary sustenance tending a lever, watching iron arms
devouring his work. This was the third tumultuous change to
shake modern European society, and it had upheaved life more
suddenly and more shockingly than any event in remembered
history, casting it in a turmoil of unprecedented problems.
Half a millennium before, the European mind had been jolted
from its grooves by the Humanism of the Renaissance and its
reflex, the Reform of orthodox religion. A thousand years before that, the Roman Empire, with its pride of peace and commerce, had dropped apart into formless fragments. Each time
men's lives had been riven, men's minds both baffled and
excited, but neither of these confusions had been at once so
basic and so blind, so lacking in guiding clues to its own

resolution as the Industrial Revolution of the nineteenth century.

The Renaissance was at once less cataclysmic and more clear-headed. The mechanisms of existence, its means and practical relations, were only incidentally touched. The continuous progress, already long under way, in the institutions, the state, the church, the political and economic order, the family, and the place of women, was only shaped and deflected, not broken off or jerked suddenly askew. The innovations were primarily in the motives and emphases of life, hence the novel situations, because they were not only self-conscious but even theoretically formulated, carried in themselves their own means of adjustment. Again, while the fall of Rome had disrupted the organization of life, shattered the state and commerce, confused society and left the individual in institutional ambiguity, it had been paralleled by a new emotional apprehension of aims and values, the spread of Christianity which brought a compensating ethical definition. The Industrial Revolution of the nineteenth century, however, while it equally dislocated the structure of living so that men could not go on automatically in an habitual pattern, did not bring with it any insight into purposes and ideals. Jarred out of all routine, men had to consider by what means they would live, in what manner, and even why, and the changes that disturbed them could give no direction in the inescapable problems, for the aims served by this upheaval, the rapid indiscriminate production of things to the sole end of profitable sale, contributed nothing to a program of standards or of morals. Life had taken a new course on which it was destined to rush at ever more frenzied speed, but whither no man could say. The scientific thinking correlative to the mechanization of industry weakened the force of Christianity. The social system that took shape inevitably in the wake of the economic revision made a mock of Christian ethics. For the first time the human animal was in control of enormously powerful means for which he did not know the end.

The definition of ends and the clarification of values is never the business of more than a tiny fraction of any society. The priests, the philosophers, and the artists are always a numerically negligible minority. In the nineteenth century, as at every time, the mass of men went their uncritical way of self preservation and procreation, but even they, however little they may consider them, must have ends and values and sanctions. All those whose profession it was to preserve the intrinsic, to illuminate the lives of these others, were in a quandary.

Most men faced with a problem beyond their powers seek an evasion, and the commonest evasion is recourse to the past, prior to the emergence of the dilemma that is defeating them. So while manufacturers accumulated vast fortunes through the new power of coal, and the unemployed starved or rioted according to temperament, and children died of factory exhaustion before puberty, the community at large practised a consciously ostentatious Christian piety. The priests had closed their eyes to the embarrassment of irrelevance.

Nor did the philosophers acquit themselves in their field much more serviceably. The subtleties of Aristotelian logic had long since been spun to gossamer. The basal logical insight of Plato had been given its most fundamental formulation by Kant and that had, in turn, been developed to the utmost, in one direction of metaphysical theory, by Hegel. The interest in natural science stimulated restatements of Materialism, but they were too naïve to be serious contributions. For the rest, philosophy became the history of philosophy and the reformulation of the creeds of schools. Nor in this recasting of already accomplished ideas did the philosophers really grasp and deal with the new problems of life peculiar to their age. They were using the same evasion as the priests, escaping the difficult present by continuing, without regard to appropriateness, the preceding conventions.

Some of the ethical philosophers, however, did struggle honestly and courageously with the confusion. The Utilitarians, deprecating the waste and suffering, looked for a way out, but their formula of the Greatest Good for the Greatest Number was hardly more than a statement of the question, leaving ambiguous both the nature of the good and the way modern society was to achieve it. A group of English idealists, Green, Caird, Bosanquet, gave a mature and cultivated expression to

[296]

an ethics based on the concept of the complete and coherent individual, which offered some guidance to the intellectuals, but the most immediately distressing problems inherent in the social disorganization were not effectively within their scope.

But of all of the purveyors of intrinsic values it was the artists who suffered the most damagingly; for the arts are all, in one form or another, the presentation to immediate intuition of the aspirations, the appreciations, and the realized values of human experience. When a generation has befogged its values, confused its appreciations, and misdirected its aspirations, the real artist exists only as a lone wolf, howling futilely in a pariah's isolation, but the imitation artists may be legion, reproducing the externals of their art without its revelation or high communication. And such were the bulk of the nineteenth-century artists in all media, versifiers, story tellers in words, paint or tunes, turning the tricks of their trades for the satisfaction of a public that had so completely lost the awareness of ultimate values that they did not even know when they were lacking.

Yet even at this period of aesthetic depression there were still artists too able and sincere to meet their problems by any such evasion. Such, for example, were a number of French painters of a series of schools or groups, who realized the full perfection of their various styles, exploring and exposing the sensory qualities of the world around them, or the constitutive essence of simple objective experiences, from one point of view and then another. In so far as they went beyond sensory fact it was only into the domain of literary romance or lyrical sentiment. The intense aesthetic appreciation of facts could not be disturbed by the social and economic earthquake that had changed the face of so much of life, and the circumstance of dimmed values and muddled purposes was no embarrassment to them since they were devoted neither to profound insight nor to the correlative deep emotions.

Among these French painters there were a few who could have provided the Beauvais and Gobelins works with successful tapestry designs, for both of these factories, as well as several others subsidized by governments, continued to function, in spite of machine competition. Bureaucracy always tends to be self-perpetuating. Especially Gauguin and Rousseau le Douanier could have made splendid cartoons, for both of them had an instinct for the use of flat pattern richly filled with original but not shocking silhouettes, and especially in Gauguin's work there was an effective development of overlapping forms to create striking segments. Both, too, compensating for the spatial thinness of their forms, used deep, solid colors, which were ideal for wool.

But it was not these men who were called on to make the cartoons for the ateliers of the French Government. Officials were in control. The work of one painter of merit was used, but it was one whose style was as completely ill adapted to the medium as possible — Odilon Redon, whose gossamer pastels and evanescent dreams could be only feeble and irritating in woven wool. For the rest, the cartoons were either candy box decorations with simpering women swirling in shapeless, suggestive petticoats, or chromo-lithographs, obnoxious with forced sentiment in meaningless drawing. Without exception, the nineteenth- and early twentieth-century designs for the French state factories are so objectionable aesthetically that they are, no matter how innocuous the subject, disgusting.

Nor were the standards better outside of France. The Roman factory continued to produce conventional sentimentalities, and the other shops that struggled on with failing strength against increasing machine competition and public indifference were engaged largely in repeating cartoons inherited from earlier successes. The one conspicuous exception was in England, where William Morris (1834–1896) and his associates not only attempted to revive tapestry and clothe it in a new style, but undertook to confront and combat the evils of the century. Following an initial clue from Ruskin, they deplored the ugliness of a machine age, were shocked by the carelessness of life, the indifference of industrialism to depravity, horrified by its denial of basic human values. They were, moreover, men of skill, of talent and training in the arts. Since they were honestly taking account of the situation and apprehending it with emotion, might they not become the priests of a new faith, reviving

[298]

ideals and standards in a form responsive to the problems of modern life?

William Morris had the intelligence, the vigor, and the high-mindedness for the great task. But this was not enough. Really to transmute the shattered ideas and perverted purposes of the nineteenth century into the lofty revelation that would purify and re-illumine the social soul, it was necessary to have the depth of insight of a Plato, or, in another vocabulary, of a Beethoven; or at the very least it would have required the intellectual grasp of a Kant. William Morris was too thoroughly English to have any such capacities. He was inexhaustible, determined, righteous, and he had brains. But they were English brains, so he did the typically English thing. He began to act.

He saw the evils of machines. Machines made things. With simple-minded obviousness he tried to right the wrongs of industry by doing the direct opposite, make things by hand. The assumption was that action, sincere and busy, would repair the devastation of values. The more desperate he felt the situation to be, the more he acted. He designed decorations, he painted, he wrote, he supervised the making of furniture, he directed the building of a house, he messed in dye vats, he wove, and he encouraged others to paint and embroider, beat copper, press leather, keep doing, furiously and earnestly. But he thought only as a secondary and subsequent corollary to his doing.

Because in all this work he emphasized digital accuracy and prized a neat line and open spacing, the performance gives the illusion of clarity; but really it is the epitome of muddling, this striking out in all directions to do something and coming to ideas only belatedly. And the ideas that he came to were as superficial, confused, and sentimental as might be expected from such a process of pseudo-ratiocination. He espoused an infantile, romantic Socialism.

In his literary way he formulated his theory in a fiction, an historical fiction, claiming that he and his followers were trying to bring back a golden period of craftsmanship and brotherhood, which had never existed, of course, but which they quite arbitrarily located in the fifteenth century. Thus, honest as Morris had been in facing facts at the beginning, through his native defect in intellection he had arrived at essentially the same evasion as his contemporaries in religion and philosophy. He, too, had taken refuge in an attempted revival, regardless of inadaptability, of the past. Acting, as a substitute for thinking, was almost bound to result in such a retreat, for action undirected by thought must needs fall, for the individual, into established habit patterns, and for the race, into familiar traditions. Morris's originality lay in selecting the particular period to which he wished the world to revert, and then imparting to that period his own variety of sentimental fantasies.

Tapestry weaving was one of the many artistic crafts in which Morris earnestly dabbled. In 1871 he founded looms which, in 1877, were moved, along with his other shops, to Merton Abbey, so that the factory has ever since been known by that name. In the first nine years only verdures were undertaken, with, at the most, a single figure; but in 1890 a complete pictorial composition was attempted, the Adoration, designed by Burne-Jones. The first weaving became the property of Exeter College, Oxford, but the cartoon has been repeated a number of times. Morris, himself, also created a design that year, the only one, except verdures, for which he was personally responsible, the Orchard (Pl. 48).

Two years later the most ambitious undertaking of the shop was initiated, a set of six pieces, also by Burne-Jones. The subject was typical of the romantic and somewhat pious antiquarianism of the group, Mallory's version of the Quest of the Holy Grail. The profane aspect of the same mediaeval romanticism is represented in an episode from the Roman de la Rose, likewise designed by Burne-Jones. This mediaevalism has been equally conscientiously practised by Burne-Jones' successors, notably Mr. J. H. Dearle; but in recent years the repertoire has been extended to Renaissance imitations, representing a somewhat uncertain compromise between Van Orley, Peter Coeck, and the habits of the Morris traditions.

With the exception of these recent variants, all of the work of the shop maintains a strong family resemblance, and even these pseudo-Renaissance cartoons are sugared with the same quality. In a carefully and intelligently composed conventional verdure,

Plate XLVIII

The Orchard after a cartoon by William Morris *Victoria and Albert Museum.* See p. 300

in which every serration of a leaf and each blossom had its justification, the Merton Abbey designers placed, with a well informed respect for the laws of composition, the finest type of paper dolls, hand painted and artistic. The sweet, refined girls who have no substance and no existence, pose gracefully in attitudes of gently appealing purity. Everything is thought out and well thought out. Every minute detail is correct.

The flowers are rendered with exquisite accuracy, the drawing is firm and clear, and the color as clean and saturated as could be obtained, a salutary antidote to the contemporary vogue for dilute and blurred tones. The weaving is even and sound. There is an intelligent appreciation of the problems of tapestry, and a proper solution at every point. William Morris had a sound theory of the integrity of material and of the importance of taking advantage of the specific qualities of each substance and each technique, again a corrective reaction against the current taste, which took pride in disguising everything possible as something else. Compared to the offensive things that were being turned out in France at the same time, these tapestries are meritorious. But the world would have been no poorer if no one of them had ever been conceived. Indeed, these well bred corpses have perhaps been more vicious than the unqualified vulgarities of the Gobelins, for the simulation of artistic merit has enough superficial success to seduce those who substitute taste for aesthetic perception.

Beginning, as he did, with an apprehension of his own period, strongly colored with emotion, Morris might have made a genuine contribution to the art. But to have done this he would have had to face his insight through, come out the other end of the experience with a more complete grasp of the whole vision and an impelling feeling about his revelation that would have fused the perception immediately with the expression. Because he sidestepped his first flash of appreciation in a verbal theory of the past, he had in the end no genuine penetration to make explicit. He had only a message to expound, a set of propositions to illustrate. He excoriates the contemporary painters for being anecdotal, but his art of uplift was equally anecdotal with a different theme. The others illustrated episodes, he set forth maxims, even when he was drawing only leaves and flowers. Everything he does is a demonstration of the right, the good and the admirable, never a flash into the essence of a poppy or the stern grace of a curled and serrated acanthus. As an artist his only superiority lay in the fact that he had an intelligent decorative program guiding his pictorial expositions; but this was a slight superiority, for here again the program was external to the work. It was a set of rules drawn up clearly by the understanding, not a felt necessity fused into the hand.

Morris began with an ethical insight; continued, in the English fashion, by acting busily about it, and English-wise ended by moralizing on it. His tapestries are harbingers of sweetness and light. The art had been embalmed in syrup.

THE TECHNIQUE AND AESTHETICS OF TAPESTRY

THE kindergarten child plaiting a mat is only a little short of weaving tapestry. The Navajo Indian manipulating thick woollen strands into blankets is often already practising the art. For tapestry is but two short steps removed from the simplest and most inevitable type of weaving. When one set of threads, the weft, is woven alternately in and out of another set of threads, the warp, as in darning stitch, the result is cloth. When the wefts are compacted so that they completely cover the warps, the first characteristic of tapestry is produced. When, instead of shooting these weft threads the full width of the loom, each color is passed back and forth only over the area where the pattern requires that color, the technique of tapestry is fully developed. Thus in polychrome-patterned tapestry, unless there is some point at which the ground is a solid color clear across, there are no wefts at all that are carried the total width of the warps, a technical eccentricity peculiar to tapestry.

This discontinuity of all the wefts creates a problem, for at the point where one color stops, turning back on itself, and another starts, turning back on itself in the opposite direction, there are no wefts crossing from warp to warp. Hence, where there is a straight line parallel to the warps between two color areas, between the two warps that define these two color areas, there is a slit. This defect in the technique can be dealt with in any one of four ways. First, it can be simply left open. If the slit is not too long this is quite feasible. Nor are these slits necessarily an artistic deficiency. As a positive factor in the design, indeed, they can become a very subtle device when the weaver is ingenious. Second, the opening can be sewed together with a needle. This strengthens the fabric but is a makeshift, leaving still a structural weakness, for the sewing inevitably breaks apart in the course of use, and adds nothing to the artistic resources of the craft. The only real solution must develop in the weaving itself, and the two other possibilities are of this type. The point of juncture can be dovetailed, with a certain number of wefts of the first color passed from one side over the marginal warp, alternating with a series of the other color of weft, woven over the same warp from the other side. This has an artistic merit in a conventional pattern, for it creates an interesting minor motive of its own, a serration that can be manipulated to enhance the effect; but in a representative design, unless the weaving is so fine that it is almost concealed, it is undesirable, for it interrupts the realism with too arbitrary a convention. The final, most complicated but most complete solution is the interlocked weave, in which the two different colored wefts are looped through each other at the point of contact. This leaves no slit, the fabric is equally solid and strong throughout, and the juncture is invisible, lending itself to the most finished realistic drawing. The Peruvian weavers invented two further solutions which remained, however, peculiar to themselves. The first of these is a special form of dovetailing, with an extra weft of another color introduced, dovetailed or laced back and forth across the slit. This makes a striking outline and can emphatically fortify a purely abstract design. The second peculiarly Peruvian solution utilizes a concealed cloth woven weft, carried the width of the loom between every two tapestry wefts. In the strictest technical definition, the tapestry then becomes an eccentric type of brocaded cloth.

Usually, whether the tapestry is slit, dovetailed or interlocked, only one side is intended for display, so that on the back the ends of the wefts are left hanging. But in meticulous work each end is wrapped about the warp where it terminates, and trimmed short, so that the finished piece is reversible.

Tapestry is woven on two types of looms, vertical or horizontal. In the more primitive version of the former the warps are attached to a beam at the top but are only weighted at the bottom, a number being grouped together and fastened to an object heavy enough to hold them taut. This kind of loom was current in the Classical world. The more evolved vertical loom has a beam below as well as above. Primitive looms have no device for separating the warps, so that the weaver has to pick them apart with his fingers for every passage of the weft. More adequate looms, however, have a system of looped cords, one around each warp, the other ends of which, in alternate series, are fixed to two bars, so that first the even-numbered warps can be drawn forward simply by pulling forward the bar, enabling the weaver to slip the bobbin behind them, and then the odd-numbered ones can similarly be lifted for the return shoot. These are the heddles or *lisses,* whence is derived the French term for such a loom, *haute lisse.* The horizontal loom, known as the *basse lisse,* is the same in principle, with the warps attached to beams at either end, the lower beam being necessarily a roller so that the finished web can be rolled up to keep the work within comfortable reach of the weaver, who is seated. The *lisses* in this instance, however, pass down under the warps and the two bars to which they are attached are connected with foot treadles, so that the shed, the space between the two sets of warps required for the passage of the bobbin, can be opened by depressing alternately these pedals, leaving both hands free to manipulate the bobbin. This permits greater rapidity, but the vertical loom assures more perfect results, for the weaver, who is working from the back of the tapestry, can at any moment see his work to check his accuracy simply by walking around to the other side. On the horizontal loom, on the other hand, he cannot look at what he has done until the whole thing is finished and so beyond correction. A mirror under the loom, which he can see by peering between the warp threads, gives him his only clue to the effect he is creating. And the greater rapidity of weaving, made possible by the pedal control, increases the danger of error. Consequently, *haute lisse* tapestries have been valued higher than *basse lisse,* though, actually, it is impossible to determine, without reference to any outside evidence, on which kind of loom a finished tapestry has been made.

In the purest version of tapestry both the warp and weft are kept perfectly straight, at right angles to each other. But in certain primitive work, including some peasant weaving, the weaver has relaxed his medium to a more flexible adjustment, curving the wefts to follow the contours of the pattern and sometimes, too, slackening the warps to the same end. Still further adaptability is sometimes obtained also by the introduction of a "flying needle" or free bobbin that carries its thread in and out and round about through the regular weft, with the ease and variability of an embroidery needle. This is really a kind of brocading of the tapestry, but it is usually confined to outlines, drawn with a single thread. True brocading is sometimes introduced into tapestry, in a few Flemish Renaissance pieces, for example, to render the gold brocaded designs of a textile. The effect is almost vulgarly rich, as the metal thread is thrown into decided relief.

Other techniques also are sometimes compounded with tapestry, but less worthily; for example, embroidery, which is, on occasion, introduced, especially in peasant pieces, for the more difficult and delicate details, notably facial features. Indeed, at a low ebb of the craft these may be only painted. Even the well organized Brussels shops fell into this nefarious practice at one time in an effort to increase their already highly industrialized production, so that it was necessary for Charles V to issue an edict (1544) prohibiting with serious penalties such makeshift evasions of the standards of the craft. In China, on the other hand, painting seems to have been an accepted supplement to tapestry technique for fine details, at least since the eighteenth century, and quite possibly earlier, also.

A slight modification of the technique, rarely found but valuable in giving a change in texture, consists in treating two or more warps as one. Any combination would be theoretically possible, but actually this type of weave is found with an alternation of two warps and one, the wefts passing over two and under one alternately, or the reverse. When an especially rich effect is desired, metal thread is often woven in this way, the rest of the tapestry being woven with the standard technique. A particularly sumptuous, encrusted quality can be obtained with gold or silver by using a "basket" weave; for example, four wefts in succession pass over three warps and under one alternately, and then the next four wefts pass over the groups of three, of which the warps that the preceding wefts passed under are the middle threads.

A special type of tapestry employs a fundamentally different weave, but is still considered tapestry, because here, too, a polychrome pattern is made by wefts that stop short at the edge of each color area, with no wefts passing the full width of the loom. This is twill tapestry, that is to say, the weft passes over two or more warps and then under one, the next weft passing under the sets of warps immediately to the left or right of those under which the preceding weft has passed, in a regular échelon that gives a diagonal grain. Twill tapestry is always dovetailed or interlocked. This weave has been found in only one figural tapestry, an exceptional sixteenth-century Persian silk fabric in the Czartoricki Museum in Cracow.

There is no reason why tapestry technique could not be employed in any material that can be woven, and indeed, at some time or place, it probably has been used in every type of straw, reed, or threads; but the characteristic material in which it has reached its great artistic heights is wool, with silk, in certain periods, a close second. Linen and cotton have sometimes played a supplementary role, the former especially in Egypt, the latter in Peru, while gold and silver threads have been favorite enrichments. Naturally, the tapestry weave can be used for any kind of pattern, plain or striped, regular repeats or all over lattice work, but it more completely fulfills its possibilities in designs in which there is no repetition or necessary symmetry, and its ultimate perfection is attained in the rendition of pictorial compositions.

The more extensive and varied the range of a technique, the greater is the danger of virtuosity. Because tapestry can translate painted figural designs with almost absolute accuracy, cartoon painters and weavers have repeatedly undertaken to use it to that end, without regard to its limitations and qualities. In this they have been encouraged rather than deterred by their public, for the most usual response to a tapestry, even on the part, sometimes, of presumably sophisticated people, has for

[307]

generations been the exclamation, " Isn't it wonderful; it's just like a painting! " But any adaptation of a medium that, on the one hand, attempts to expand it beyond its own character, or, on the other, fails to exploit its inherent potentialities and character, is to that extent a perversion of the art. It is, of course, wonderful that the manipulation of a bobbin laying straight threads of dyed wool could achieve similitude to the blended tones of an oleaginous pigment applied freely with a flexible brush. But it is certainly even more wonderful that anyone should think it worth the trouble to make such a dry and rigid process do the work of a smoothly viscous, free flowing medium. It is remarkable that a weaver can almost, never quite, copy a painting, but it is dull and futile for him to try. The aesthetic purpose of a tapestry, when the technique is being used for its ultimate fulfillment in large scale pictorial decoration, is properly defined, first, by the requirements of good mural decoration, and second, by the merits and deficiencies in the very nature of the craft and its material.

The most basic prohibition insists that the flatness of the wall should not be sacrificed. The wall supports the ceiling, keeps it from crushing us, and however little we consciously consider this, under the surface we are aware of it. If this supporting structure looks as if it were bulging or buckling precariously, owing to the high modelling of the figures covering it, or if holes are knocked in it by remote perspectives, the mechanical integrity is disturbingly violated. Moreover, not only structural integrity but domestic intimacy, too, requires a cartoon that is largely on a single plane, for a personage too highly modelled is too insistently intrusive; his realism interrupts privacy; while the appearance of a hole in the wall destroys the protecting, enclosed feeling that is the essence of being at home.

The design should also be lighter at the top than at the bottom, or, if of even density, then with a definite upward movement, so that the feeling of a supporting construction is maintained. The horizontal distribution, on the other hand, profits by an equable dispersion. The ideal is at the opposite extreme from the concentrated focus of the easel painting. A tapestry is designed to cover the whole wall and to be seen from any place and any angle in the room. Hence like the room itself, it should be a continuum, without any gaps. A compromise may be made with a series of more or less regularly spaced centers of interest, at intervals across the hanging.

Though continuous, however, the pattern must have ready visibility, so that the occupants of the room will not be strained in the interpretation or irritatingly frustrated. Yet at the same time it cannot be either empty or obvious, for there must be sufficient complexity of interest and detail so that a closer examination will not be a bore. The cartoon painter is thus committed to a delicately adjusted mean between strength and fineness, a clear, bold scale and amusing minutiae. A similar nice balance should be contrived, also, between animation and immobility. If the cartoon is inert it will say nothing, if agitated it will be a tiresome companion. Gesture must be depicted at that instant when it tells the story yet does not demand completion, when it constitutes the epitome of the expression, but avoids the exasperating implication that in another instant the movement must go on. The ability instinctively to select this moment of arrested pantomime, conveying an idea or a feeling by silhouette, is the test of the decorative illustrator. As for the exact requirement of scale and range of color, those are dictated by the specific problem, for here tapestry technique has almost unlimited flexibility. It can be as coarse as burlap, with gigantic figures, splashed on poster-like in violent hues. It can be as fine as a lady's handkerchief and designed with pen-drawn miniatures in a restricted pastel palette. Theoretically, there is no limit in either direction, practically almost none.

But even if it is to emulate cambric flexibility, tapestry will be the better for not disguising its technique. Just as a sleek continuity is the beauty of satin or a thick resilience the lure of velvet, so the definite ribbing of tapestry, however fine, is its quality and its merit. Moreover, in a large scale wall tapestry the ribs fulfill an important function. Owing to the verticality of most of the elements in an illustration, such as the human figure, trees, and many architectural features, most compositions extended over a long surface are in constant danger of breaking apart into segments. The ribs of a tapestry, running horizontally, serve, like the string courses on a building or the mouldings of a room, to tie the design together, and it is for this reason that in most tapestries the ribs, which are the warps, are horizontal, in spite of the circumstance that this necessitates weaving the design at right angles on the loom.

Less conspicuous aspects of the technique can likewise be advantageously emphasized as features of the effect, notably, hatching. When a tone or color passes into another, instead of making the margin between them a straight line, it is modified into an irregular sawtooth, or better, comb edge. Thus there is a zone with the two tones alternating, the relations of the width and length of the tongue and groove strips varying constantly in order to avoid a mechanical regularity and to diminish the conspicuousness of the device. Effectively handled, these shifting color areas with their uneven lines can become an interesting contribution to the pattern. In a similar way the slits that are a natural feature of the weave in its simplest, normal form can be employed in the drawing, provided they are not too long, particularly to create shadows in the detail of a face. For example, the bistre under the eyes is most effectively indicated by a series of little holes, minute slits, stepped in a curving line.

The texture is perhaps the outstanding quality that must be respected and can be exploited. The usual European tapestry is a thick, heavy wool stuff, demanding as its appropriate complement an effect of substantiality in the drawing and of solidity in the colors. Figures that float or flutter too much seem either caught in the fabric like a fly in a spider's web, or unrelated to it. Dyes that look like water color washes have the appearance of a weak stain instead of being part of the substance of the material. The texture can also be deliberately employed to enrich the color by the use of contrast. The practice of interweaving metal threads, which was introduced very early into the art, is a sound extension of both the texture interest and the tonal range. Similarly, silk introduced into a wool fabric, especially for high lights, gives a legitimate relief, its sheen against the light-absorbing wool, imparting vitality. Its very effectiveness, however, requires that it be handled with tact, for too large an area proportionate to the wool results, not in contrast, but in ambiguity. The basic texture of the fabric may seem uncertain, and sometimes, if there is too much silk, the tapestry seems specious, perhaps because it is subconsciously adjudged as a silk textile adulterated with wool, instead of as a wool weave enriched with silk. An all silk tapestry, on the other hand, can profit by its lighter quality to exploit more trivial subjects and a more airy style, with paler tones and, in general, a more feminine effect. The eighteenth-century French tapestries were for the most part designed by men to whom textiles meant brocades. Really their only proper medium is silk. But to render a fifteenth-century battle scene in silk would be to caricature it, while to put into silk one of the Crucifixions of that time would be a sacrilege.

Exceedingly fine silk tapestries can exploit their very fragility, for tapestry is the lightest weave possible to a polychrome-patterned textile. A cloth with a two-colored pattern must have at least one extra warp or weft, be at least three threads thick, or a brocaded textile must have as many extra wefts as there are colors in the design at the points where the motive is introduced. A tapestry, on the other hand, can show an unlimited number of colors without ever having more than one warp and one weft at a given point. It is always, in short, only two threads thick. The Egyptian weavers of the earlier Muhammadan periods took advantage of this extreme thinness to render crisp, minute designs, sometimes almost microscopic, but firm, and saved from any charge of finickiness by the clarity and contrast of color and the precision of the outlines. Again the Mogul Indian weavers made use of this quality to render flowers with exquisite delicacy, exact, but intimating evanescence. The Chinese *k'ssu* weavers found it appropriate for the same kind of slight, brittle pictures that they painted on porcelain, the ceramic equivalent, in its hardness and thinness, of this silk tapestry.

Thus the potentialities of tapestry range from one extreme of textile character to the other, and almost every possible quality has been developed at some time in the course of its long history.

APPENDIX II

GUILD REGULATIONS

THE first Paris laws relative to tapestry workers were established in 1302 for the guild of Tapissiers Sarrazinois, but the regular tapestry weavers, or *haute lisseurs,* belonged to this same organization. The meaning of this term, *tapisserie sarrazinoise,* has been actively but inconclusively disputed. The statutes make it clear that the work was done on a horizontal loom, for it is forbidden to pregnant women to be so employed lest they suffer injury, a danger possible only with a horizontal loom; and in a slightly later revision of the statutes the term *à la marche* is specifically used. But the question remains unsolved whether the textile was, first, some kind of shuttle weave, or, second, a pile fabric, or, finally, tapestry, distinguished from ordinary tapestry only in that the latter was made on vertical looms. The possibility of a shuttle weave is conclusively eliminated by various later inventory items specifying that *tapisseries sarrazinoises* had illustrative themes, which could hardly have been repeating patterns. The theory that they were a pile fabric is most logical since pile *sarrazinoises* were one of the outstanding importations from the East, and hence the nomenclature would be explained. There would be no reason for calling a tapestry *sarrazinoise* simply because it was woven on a horizontal loom, because it is not the horizontal but the vertical loom that is characteristic of the Orient. On the other hand, a knotted pile fabric could be made on a horizontal loom, there are specimens of illustrative themes of the fifteenth century actually rendered in this technique, and in the documents the distinction that is made usually contrasts *tapisserie sarrazinoise* and *tapisserie nostrez,* the latter having apparently been the velvet type of pile weaving, the pile composed of loops, cut or uncut, made by passing a warp or weft over rods.

But whatever the *sarrazinois* workers made, the important fact in this connection is that in Paris their guild, and hence the relevant laws, embraced, in the opening years of the fourteenth century, the regular tapestry weavers. The regulations concerning the *haute lisseurs* specify only that no work shall be done by candle light, since it is apt to fall below the standard, and that they may have an apprentice eight years in service and charge a fee of 100 sous.

The first Tournay law on record regarding tapestry dates from 1377. It forbade merchants to deal in old and new goods together and to sell at the Saturday market. The second, in 1380, requires that every weaver mark his work, and also that he have the lead seal of the city affixed. The third, in 1397, repeats the conditions of the law of 1377; specifies qualities of materials and workmanship; defines the seal to be used; forbids work on certain holidays; limits every master to two apprentices; and fixes apprenticeship at three years. The fourth law, in 1408, covers essentially the same points, but limits apprentices to one, and reduces apprenticeship to two years. The fifth law, in 1472, specifies that the only women apprentices shall be wives and daughters of masters; limits again other apprentices to one but extends the time; names the entrance fee for new masters; and to the holidays and hours during which work is forbidden, adds days of freezing weather. In 1496 the apprenticeship was fixed at three years and each master was allowed two apprentices, while weavers who had fulfilled all apprenticeship requirements in another free city were also allowed entry into the guild as masters. In 1499 some of the stipulations were re-enacted, and in 1502 a city tax was imposed on every piece of work, according to three grades of quality.

The fifteen master tapestry makers (*tapytwevers*) of Ghent, having been limited by law to two workers apiece, protested, in 1452, that they could not meet the orders of their greatly expanded business, and complained that most of their workers were leaving to work in the shops of the Vieux Bourg, which was outside the town. The Magistrates responded favorably to their plea by revoking the restriction, giving them the right to have as many workers as they wished and to employ workers without the franchise if they could not get enough with the franchise. But if there were any franchised workers unemployed, these had prior right to positions. Every Ghent master had to pay a fine for the support of the guild chapel. Nonattendance at meetings was fined twelve deniers.

In Brussels the tapestry weavers or *tapytwevers* formed part of the large and very influential guild of cloth weavers, until about 1448, when they organized their own society, the *Legwerckers Ambacht*. Even then, however, the brotherhood was still connected with the cloth workers under the protection of the same patron, Saint Lawrence. A few years after this (1450–51), the first statutes for the trade were formulated. To assure the maintenance of craft standards work could be done only between the morning and evening bells. Inferior materials, such as cow's and goat's hair, were forbidden. Every piece had to be examined and sealed at the chapel of Saint Christopher's Hospital in Ruysbroeck Street, where the jury met three times a week. Work from other cities could be sold only at the Wood Market on Friday, and could never be shown with Brussels products unless a clear distinction were made. Moreover, to assure such a distinction every piece of Brussels make had to bear a mark twelve warps wide and twenty-four wefts high.

A journeyman could produce, even when working with his own materials for his own use, only if he had his master's permission. Mastership was open either to a citizen of Brussels who had learned the trade, or to an outsider who had learned in an apprenticeship of not less than three years in some other free city, but the latter had to pay a special fee. To become master, a fee was due on admission to apprenticeship and again on being accepted to full membership, except for sons of masters whose dues were hardly more than symbolic, the offering of a certain quantity of wine. The fees for the status of journeyman were much lower.

A master could have only one apprentice in addition to his own legitimate sons, and all apprentices were required to spend three years learning the trade, though the sons were required to work only three days a week. An apprentice could not leave his master nor stay away from work more than a fortnight, unless it were unavoidable, and in that case the master was required to notify the guild. A journeyman when leaving a master had to give advance notice.

Finally, there were stipulations of a less professional nature, a prohibition of adultery, admonitions of proper manners to the guild officers, insistence on keeping Sundays and fête days, and requirements of attendance at ceremonial processions, and for any violation fines were fixed.

Slight modifications of these laws were made in 1472. The required sealing was dropped. A specification was introduced forbidding subcontracting for more than one-third of the total volume of orders accepted by any one master. The great annual banquet was no longer to be at the expense of the Corporation, and the wine tax was increased.

Additional laws passed three years later changed the arrangements for the examination of finished work, prescribing that the officers visit the shop to pass the pieces while still on the looms, and seven years was set as a minimum age for entering a master's son on the rolls of the corporation, eight as the earliest possible age for the admission of other boys to apprenticeship. At this time, too, a servant was instituted to take care of the corporation's property, such as furniture and silver plate, for the tapestry weavers of Brussels, in proportion as their fame mounted, were growing rich. They owned the Arbre d'Or, a house on the Grand' Place, and had an altar in the church of Notre Dame de Sablon where three masses a week were said.

It was about this time that the tapestry weavers and the painters had to arbitrate a delicate question. Some of the weavers were using paper cartoons, drawn in charcoal or chalk by draftsmen who were not authorized painters. Instead of taking the case before the magistrates, the two crafts conferred together and decided that tapestry weavers could design for each other textile designs and trees, animals, boats, grass and similar details for verdures, or could correct or complete cartoons with charcoal, chalk or pen and ink, but for any more extensive work they were bound to employ a painter.

By the end of the first quarter of the sixteenth century the Brussels industry had become so important that it was felt advisable to reformulate the regulations (1528). At this time a city mark was required for every tapestry over four square ells in size, the mark to consist of two B's (Brussels, Brabant), flanking an escutcheon. The shop mark also had to be woven in, the one on the left, the other on the right side of the selvage. Sixteen years later an imperial edict regulating the industry was promulgated, after more than four years study of the industry and the existing city laws governing it, and a mark for each city was therein stipulated, together with a shop mark.

It has been customary in histories of tapestry to cite these two provisions as the initiation of marking tapestries with signs or monograms indicating origin, but actually, as has been noted, Tournay had required weavers' marks from 1380, and the Brussels law of 1451 even specified the size of the mark, though whether that was a uniform city mark for all the shops of the town, or individual registered master marks is not clear. Doubtless these earlier provisions have been overlooked because whereas the marks subsequent to the 1528 and 1544 ordinances are conspicuous on many existing pieces, earlier weavers' marks have but rarely been noted. A few, however, have been recognized in the form of decoratively inserted inscriptions in the same style as the contemporary cartoon designers' " signatures." This indicates that at least in some instances such marks were put, not on the selvages, most of which have long since been destroyed, but in the body of the tapestry, suggesting that some of the conventional signs and designs incorporated on banners and tiles, for example, may also have been shop marks, though it would be difficult to prove this, and even more difficult, if not impossible, to identify any of them.

No important novelties are introduced into any subsequent legislation concerning the industry, but a French statute of the eighteenth century (1756) is interesting because of the high technical and artistic standard that it defines for a master weaver.

" All professions, it is said, presuppose in those exercising them relative and proportional talents; some even require somewhat distinguished powers. But how many are needed to make a distinguished tapestry weaver. In whatever style he may work, in ' sarrazinois ' carpets, in high or low warp, or even only in restoration, he should be master of all the rules of proportion, especially those of architecture and of perspective, of some knowledge of anatomy, of taste and accuracy in drawing, in coloring, and in shading, of grace in arrangement and grandeur in expression of all styles and classes, figures, animals, landscapes, palaces, rustic buildings, statues, vases, woods, plants, and flowers, of all kinds. He should add to these attainments a knowledge of sacred and secular history, and should be able to apply properly the rules of good manufacture, and to discern that which produces beauty of texture and of coloring."

SOME COLLECTORS AND COLLECTIONS

FRANCE reached the lowest level of depression and disorganization under John the Good (1319–1364). Her finest aristocracy was slaughtered at Poitiers (1356); the King fell into the hands of the enemy, the first monarch of the Middle Ages to be captured; England seemed about to seize half of the national territory; and the poverty and distress of the country at large was beyond exaggeration. Yet the four sons of this luckless and inglorious sovereign: Charles V (1337–1380); Louis I, Duc d'Anjou (1339–1384); Jean, Duc de Berri (1340–1416); and Philip (the Bold), Duke of Burgundy (1342–1404) were all brilliant figures with a lavish setting of the attributes and accessories of their rank, and notable collectors.

It is significant that the "Very large, very fine and best crown" of Charles V he had had made himself. Wars, ransoms and bad times had levied toll on the royal jewels. But what this crown lacked in tradition it made up in magnificence, with its "four great fleurons and four small, set with jewels," sixty-eight rubies; thirty-seven sapphires, cabochons and cut, square, long or round; twenty-eight diamonds; and one hundred and eighty-nine pearls, many of them enormous. Moreover, in addition to this, he had forty-seven other crowns, coronets and bandeaux, not to mention several score belts and collars, and as many buckles, sets of buttons and clasps, some in ingenious and effective forms: an Agnus Dei; an eagle with a jewelled crown; a griffon; a deer; a stork; a snake; a pair of clasped hands; two hands holding a crescent; and the device: *Bonne Foy*. And even more numerous were the rings, a hundred and twenty of them, all gorgeously wrought and set, except the Friday

SOME COLLECTORS AND COLLECTIONS

ring, emblem of Christian mourning, that the King never failed to wear in weekly commemoration of the Crucifixion, with a black cross on either side of a cameo, bearing the scene on Golgotha.

Then, of course, there were the crosses, reliquaries, figures of saints and other pendants, a round hundred of them, made of crystal, cameos and amber, enamelled and jewelled. Nor were all of Charles's pendants emblems of his faith. One represented an *écrevisse*. The plate of gold and silver, both for his chapel and his table, was equally abundant and rich, and again the finest chalice he had had made himself, with the Twelve Apostles enamelled around the bowl, and the foot and cover all jewelled.

The hangings for sixty rooms were of silk and velvet, many of them gold woven, many embroidered with armorial devices, fleur-de-lis, trees, flowers and birds. One of the more elaborate embroideries represented a lion, seated in a pavilion, bearing the arms of France, with birds scattered over the ground. Most of the silks were of Oriental manufacture. Then there were eight rooms hung with fabrics from England, probably wool embroideries, with parakeets, eagles, lions, one with wild animals and castles, another with savages.

But tapestries played their part, too. Two dozen sets had only conventional devices and armorial bearings, but as many more depicted illustrative scenes. The adventures of heroes of history and romance were displayed on several: the battles of Judas Maccabaeus at Antioch; the feats of Godfrey de Bouillon; the battles of the Duke of Acquitaine; the deeds of Girard de Nevers; the story of Florence of Rome; the adventure of Yvain and the Queen of Ireland; and the History of Amis and Amile. The Nine Heroes were displayed on two others, and two others had savages, while the Seven Arts and the Seven Sciences were both represented, the former in conjunction with the Seven Ages of Man, the latter twice, once with Saint Augustine, a piece of which it is especially noted that the King himself bought it. It was enriched with gold. The other piece with this subject had belonged to Queen Jeanne d'Evreux, the second wife of John the Good and Charles's step-mother. The Fountain of Youth claimed one piece, the Twelve Months another, and the Seven Deadly Sins a third. A large panel showed an allegory of Kindness and Beauty, while the subject of another is not clear: "*trippes.*" There was one piece with hunting scenes, ladies at the chase and hawking; and another piece with figures of women and a border of shields of arms of France and Burgundy was curious in that it was round. The religious subjects were Judith (*Judic*), a History of the Holy Grail, and a Passion. The Saints were Denis and Theseus. It is specified that the Judas Maccabaeus was of Arras workmanship, but no provenance is given for the others.

One panel, of which the subject is not noted, had been given to Charles by Philippe Gilier, one of his fiscal agents. Others he may have inherited from his next younger brother, Louis, who had predeceased him. Thus Louis had had four tapestries illustrating the deeds of Godfrey de Bouillon, and Charles's inventory, later by twenty years, shows two Godfrey tapestries. Louis had had two pieces of Heroes, one just called the Nine Heroes, the other more definitely described, with Charlemagne, Arthur and Godfrey, and Charles also had two Heroes. Both had one piece based on the romance of Amis and Amile. And both had a Judith tapestry which in each case is listed with the unusual misspelling "*Judic*," as if there were a garbled inscription on the tapestry itself.

Forty years later the tapestries of the next King of France, the mad and miserable Charles VI, were inventoried, and not one single piece of the collection of Charles V is to be found in the list. Charles VI was a minor when he succeeded and consequently he was under the guardianship of his uncles, men whose powers and ambitions outran their scruples, and voracious collectors, so that there may well be merit to the suspicion that some of the royal tapestries were diverted from the storerooms of the youthful King to the castles of his regents, especially as some of the subjects that Charles V had owned appear later in their inventories. There are two or three items in the inventory of the Duc de Berri that correspond in title with some of the royal pieces: the Seven Deadly Sins, possibly his Godfrey de Bouillon, and perhaps his Nine Heroes; and in the collection of the youngest of the four brothers there were three series that coincide with tapestries that his ward should have inherited, one presenting the romance of Florence of Rome, the second the Queen of Ireland, and the third the Life of Saint Denis, none of them common subjects; while in the estate of his wife, Margaret of Flanders, there was another Godfrey de Bouillon, though this she might have inherited legitimately direct from her brother-in-law, Louis.

Thus it would seem that at least a half dozen of Charles V's figure tapestries can be traced for another quarter of a century. Yet, on the other hand, it is possible that the whole accusation is sheer libel, and another demonstration of the weakness of circumstantial evidence, for Philip also had a Judas Maccabaeus, which might easily be assumed to have been the one Charles had left, but it certainly was not, for we have the record of his purchase of it in 1385 from Pierre de Beaumez. Either the two brothers had the same taste, or perhaps the coincidence was a result of fraternal rivalry.

In any case, in the next generation of the Burgundian collection all of these pieces had already disappeared, and today there exists only one panel that might conceivably, because of date and subject, have been owned by Charles V, the Arthur, presented as one of the Heroes, in the collection of Mr. Clarence Mackay.

Aside from the pieces that Louis d'Anjou may have left to his kingly brother Charles at the time of his death (1384), he had some two dozen figure tapestries, and he, too, favored romantic subjects. Two others, four in all, depicted the exploits of Godfrey de Bouillon; Roland and Oliver were on one piece; to the four sons of Aymon were allotted two, as also to Lancelot, who in one jousted with a knight, Margonde of the Black Castle who had been guilty of the gossip that Lancelot had been found with the Queen, while in the other Lancelot was conducting the Queen to the Castle of the Perilleuse-Garde. It would seem that the clerk who made the inventory was rather short on his knowledge of literature, for he had difficulty in making out the Queen's name, calling her " *Guemenie*," a mistake easily made in deciphering an unfamiliar name in Gothic miniscules. There was one tapestry with the legend of the Golden Apple; a pair

[321]

illustrating the Vow of the Peacock; and another single piece recounting the same tale in an abridged form; one showing the betrothal of the King of Armenia; and two others with no special title but with chivalric episodes, the assault on a castle defended entirely by black soldiers, and a tourney between knights and ladies. The religious themes were two episodes from the Vespasian legend, his cure by the sudarium, and the imprisonment of Pilate; a Solomon; a Daniel; an Annunciation; and a Crucifixion. The saints celebrated in this collection were George, who appeared on one piece fighting the Saracens, on a second taking a king, probably Rustam, prisoner in battle, and on a third piece that is not further specified; and Katherine — which Katherine is not indicated.

The Vow of the Peacock evidently went to his sister-in-law, the Duchess of Burgundy, and probably her piece telling of the Four Sons of Aymon also came from him, and perhaps the Saint George that appears first in the possession of Duke Philip and then in the estate of his wife also came from him.

Though the Anjou tapestries make a rather less imposing list than those of any of the other brothers, he is the only one of the four who has left a tapestry monument to posterity, and it is the greatest series that exists, the Apocalypse of Angers (cf. p. 66).

The other two brothers were the most important collectors of the family, and they represent two sharply opposed types. Charles's inventory gives the impression of a careless and random accumulation, as if he had acquired his vast treasures as a thoughtless part of regal lavishness and self-indulgence; but Jean de Berri, though he had an almost equal quantity and a much greater range of possessions, seems to have acquired most of them with a more considered preference, to have established with many of them a more intimate relation, and even to have brooded over his things as life shut in on him. For life did shut in on Jean de Berri, misshaping somewhat his innate constitution. He was naturally an extroverted type, active, able, organizing, typical even in his looks, with his broad, round face, short thick neck and tendency to pudginess. But his capacities were political rather than military (he ran away most shamefully at the battle of Poitiers, and his collection included almost no arms) ; yet he was restricted in the exercise of these political abilities, first because he was overshadowed by his older brother Charles, and then, after Charles' death, because the more vigorous brother Philip prevailed. Balked of other outlets, his energy was focussed more and more on his collection, consumed not only in extension, constant and varied acquisition, but even more in an intensity that drove Jean increasingly toward objects that he could make more concentratedly personal, either because they were so small (a large part of his collection was made up of little things, and he was, for example, the first coin collector of modern times), or because he could in some way put on them his own mark. If it were not his coat of arms it was, very often, his portrait, which he had represented on a variety of objects, or one of his two favorite animal emblems: the swan and the bear.

The youngest of the brothers, Philip, on the other hand, was more consistently and completely the man of action, for he was an enthusiastic and effective soldier, so that his success was predestined, especially in this period of national disorder. Consequently his collection was, not a substitution for more real satisfactions, but just an additional way of vaunting and exercising his expansive self. Not intimacy, but display was his uncriticized motive, and tapestries were a splendid medium for ostentation in a large way.

Jean de Berri, on the contrary, had tapestries only as part of the necessary equipment of his dozen residences, a merely incidental element of his collection, so that of the fourteen hundred items, more or less, of his inventories, only some seventy-five are tapestries. These include some of the usual illustrations of the popular chivalric fiction of the time: Charlemagne; King Richard; the Girard de Vienne; Bègue de Belin; Robert le Fuzelier; the Godfrey de Bouillon that he may have got from the King's estate; a Nine Heroes; a set described as the *féerie* series; and an exceptionally interesting set illustrating the History of the Great Khan.

Several Moralities were included: one on Good Repute; the Romance of the Rose; the Seven Deadly Sins; the Stories of

Hope and Confusion, and of Haste and Anguish, perplexing titles; and two Pilgrimages, which were probably allegories of human life. There were a certain number of scenes of daily life: playing checkers; and hunting, one being specified rather curiously as a *chasse à l'usage de Romme;* some conventional motives: his favorite swans; orange trees; a set with children; and one with trellises and the device "*ich hach mich,*" " I contest for the lady of my heart." Rather more religious subjects appear in his inventory than in his brothers': a Credo; a Trinity; a Death of the Virgin; a Coronation of the Virgin; an Apocalypse; a Magdalen; and two lives of Saints, Andrew and John. The Duke must also have had a set of Heroines to balance his Heroes, which he gave to his nephew, Charles VI, for it is listed in two pieces in the King's inventory, with the specification that they bear the Berri arms.

The Romance of the Rose was a gift to the Duc de Berri from his brother Philip who had bought the piece from Pierre de Beaumez of Paris in 1388, expressly to give to Jean. Philip, moreover, made other presents of tapestry to his brother Jean. a Pastoral that he got that same year from Jean Cosset of Paris, and two years before that two *sarrazinoises* tapestries, one with the Passion, the other with the Life of the Virgin, to go in Jean's chapel with two other chapel hangings that he had already given him. Perhaps the Robert le Fuzelier was a gift from his brother, too, for Philip bought one in 1386 which does not appear in his own inventory.

While none of the Berri tapestry collection has survived, as far as is known, there is one panel that is very adequately recorded, the Bègue de Belin, for it hangs on the wall behind the high table at which the Duke himself is dining in the decoration that heads the month of January in the calendar of the great Book of Hours at Chantilly. It is a symptom of his acute possessiveness that the Duke should have had portraits of his things made, along with the portrait of himself, in his chief book of devotion. The miniaturist has met the requirements so well that even in the tiny picture the name Bègue de Belin can be distinguished in the four verses across the top of the tapestry. There is, moreover, one tapestry in existence that is precisely of the same type, even to having essentially the same composition, the Jourdain de Blaye in the Museum of Padua, so that though we have no actual Berri piece, we have, at least, a certified first cousin. Perhaps, too, it was a first cousin in another sense, for in 1385 the Duke of Burgundy bought two pieces on this theme from Jacques Dourdin of Paris, an item which does not appear in the inventory made at the time of his death. But the Duke's Jourdain was a *tapisserie sarrazinoise* (cf. p. 312), so that it probably was not the same, unless the same cartoons were rendered in both techniques.

Philip the Bold had by far the finest tapestries of all the brothers, probably because his wife's domain (he married Margaret of Flanders) included such important centres of the industry; but doubtless, too, because he found them to his taste. In addition to the pieces that he may be suspected of having taken from Charles V's collection, he had, also, a Charlemagne, in fact two of them, one showing how Charlemagne went to Jerusalem and conquered the Saracens, which he had got in Paris through Jean Lubin in 1387; a piece showing the history of Guy de Bourgogne who was elected King in the absence of Charlemagne and then went to Spain and conquered the Saracens, which he got from Dourdin in 1387; one with Perceval le Galois which may have been a piece that he bought from Andry de Monchi to give to the Duke of York, Philip having, perhaps, changed his mind in the constant and sudden fluctuations of political relations; two pieces with Bertrand du Guesclin, one of which he had brought from Beaumez in 1386, and one of which was small; Hector which he bought from Dourdin in 1388, that was later cut in two; a Guillaume de Bomercy; a Harpin de Bourges; a small piece with the Comte de Santerre; a Jason; a piece devoted to Semiramis, who was one of the Heroines; and a King Arthur, in addition to a number of other pieces, also on romantic themes, of which we have records of purchase but which do not appear in his inventory: a history of Froimont de Bordeaux, and one of William of Orange, both bought from Cosset in 1384; a history of Octavian of Rome (a theme also called sometimes *Les Sept Sages*), which he owned already in 1385, for he had it moved that year from

Arras to Paris, and evidently it was a favorite, for in 1390 he bought another piece with the same subject from Michel Bernard of Arras to give to the Duke of York; a Troy which also was moved from Arras to Paris in 1385; a piece with the history of Fierabras of Alexandria acquired from Bernard in 1386; a piece with the story of the Golden Apple, a *tapis sarrazinois,* bought from Dourdin in 1386; a history of Begu who conquered the daughter of the Duke of Lorraine, bought from Beaumez in 1388; a Hero and Heroine set, noteworthy because it had Ten Heroes, though only the standard Nine Heroines, bought from the same dealer in 1388, but not completely paid for until two years later, and the Mackay Arthur may well have come from this instead of from the collection of Charles V, for it is specified that the figures of the heroes were large, and that each was accompanied by his coat of arms, even as in the Mackay piece; three pieces concerned with the history of the Roy de Frise, one showing how he was conquered by Aubry Bourguignon, the second a battle between the King and the Emperor of Greece, and the third illustrating the departure of his son to seek adventures; another piece concerned with the son of the King of Cyprus; an Amis and Amile bought from Dourdin in 1388; a Doon de la Roche which he got from Cosset in 1389; and the three pieces already mentioned, the Judas Maccabaeus, the Jourdain de Blaye and the Robert le Fuzelier, that he may have given to the Duc de Berri; and finally, one with the most unusual subject of all, which he got from Dourdin in 1386, showing the History of Mahomet. Moreover, in addition to this varied display of romantic subjects, his wife had others of the same type: two pieces depicting Meliant killing the Evil Beast; the story of William Shortnose; the episode of Mainfroy discomfited by Charles the Conqueror, Count of Anjou; the deeds of King Tristram Preudhomme; two that " spoke " of Doon de Mayence; the story of King Panthère; one with the deeds of Aymery of Narbonne and his six sons; and two giving Alexander legends.

Some of the same stories appear in the library of Philip and Marguerite: Hector of Troy; a History of Troy, apparently different from the preceding, and perhaps also covering the history of Jason, like a later edition prepared for Charles the Bold; the *Roman du Roy Artus et Lancelot du Lac; Aymery de Narbonne* and the *Voeux du Paon* which included the story of Alexander.

There were several moralities in the Burgundian collection at this time, and other allegories, also: the Romance of the Rose bought from Dourdin in 1386; two with Vices and Virtues, one of which the Duke had bought from Cosset between 1383 and 1385; one with the Seven Arts and Sciences also bought from Cosset in 1384; two with the *Chastel de Franchise* (was it Freedom or Candor?) ; one with the Lord of Kindness and Loyalty; and several that appear in the earlier records but not in the inventory: a Garden of Plenty (*Vergier de Souffisance*) which was mended that year because it had been torn by the men of Ghent when they got obstreperous; a Garden of Nature, which also had to be mended in 1385; and one with a most unusual design consisting of clouds and the Four Winds.

Among the scenes from daily life was one piece with sheep showing Madame d'Artois and Monseigneur de Flandres; another showing the marriage of a Lord's daughter; another with people playing the game of *hauce-pié;* another large green piece with a fountain and a young lady planting a pot of sweet marjoram; one with a lady standing between two lovers; another, already old and torn, with ladies defending a castle; and another with hunting, musicians and various diversions. Two similar pieces, which may be identical with some of these inventory items, are mentioned in the Duke's accounts: one with Knights and Ladies, bought from Beaumez in 1386; and one with ladies hawking and hunting game. There were, in all, ten pieces with shepherds and shepherdesses, so that it is impossible to identify which pieces came from which sources, there being four records of payment for such pieces between 1384 and 1388. In one they were dancing, and in another they were shown with the God of Love, a favorite theme in this collection for he appeared on another piece with Juno, Pallas and Venus (a curious mixture of the Roman and Greek names) ; in a piece belonging to the

Duchess; and several little Loves were seen gambolling with children on a piece in the Duke's inventory, an early anticipation of the Hellenistic theme of Playing Boys that became so popular in the Renaissance (cf. p. 204).

The religious subjects included a David and Goliath; a Jacob and Esau; a Resurrection; a Death of the Virgin; two Coronations of the Virgin, one bought from Cosset in 1389; a Crucifixion with the Four Evangelists, which was rare in that the ground was violet; and a Credo with Prophets which was bought from Beaumez in 1386, but fully paid for only in two subsequent installments, one in each of the two succeeding years. The Duke also bought a Passion in 1385 from Beaumez; another Passion with small figures in 1388; a piece with the Life of the Virgin in 1386, also from Beaumez, which may be the same as the Five Joys of the Virgin which recurs in the accounts five years later; and an Apocalypse, bought in 1386 and paid for again the next year.

The Saints honored in tapestry in this collection were George, a piece which the Duke bought from Cosset in 1385; Anthony, which he bought from Pierre le Comte of Arras in 1385–86; and Marguerite, which he got from Cosset in 1388. Some years before (1383–85) he had bought, also from Cosset, a history of Saint Jean; and in 1389 he owned a piece with the history of Saint Catherine, for he sent it to Dijon that year.

The Duke's own great victory of the Battle of Roosebeck was depicted in three pieces which he had got from Bernard in 1385; and finally, in addition to a good supply of the useful armorials, there were a few unusual examples of the less pretentious type, such as a blue piece with a large tree in the middle with a lion and an elephant tied to it; another blue piece, old, with white columbines and the arms of France; and, a very odd theme, four pieces showing lions walking up steps. Two other pieces that Philip bought to give away were: a hanging with the history of a king who went out hunting with a numerous company and lost his way in a wood, so that he was left alone without attendants or horses, and there he met a marvellous adventure with fairies, who condemned him to become a deer, as is recorded in the Bible (!), a piece that he gave to the Comte de

Vertuz in 1387; and a Crucifixion acquired in 1388 and presented to Monsieur de Bourbon.

Despite the dispersal of the collection of Charles V, and the increasing economic and political despair of France, Charles VI had a far larger and more important collection than his father had had. France was rushing headlong to a brink of disaster whence she would be snatched back only by the heroic hallucinations of a benignly obsessed peasant girl; yet the worse than useless sovereign could accumulate more than a hundred and fifty tapestries, more than a hundred of them the expensive hangings with personages. The collection can hardly be considered a reflection of the character of the sovereign, for he was too disintegrated a personality to effect any influence; but they do constitute a revealing cross section of the upper class taste of the time. There are still many of the romantic heroes: Clovis; Hercules; Mion de Beauvais fighting the pagans; Lion de Bourges; the Thebes legend; William the Conqueror; Bertrand du Guesclin; the Battle of the Thirty; the Heroines; and two typically chivalric subjects: the Jousts of Saint Denis, and those of Saint Inglevert. There were fewer of the allegorical subjects than usual: a Chamber of Good Repute, another called the Chamber of Honor, and another concerned with Fortune; but the scenes from daily life, on the other hand, were far more numerous. Some of these pieces showed simple contemporary groups with no specified occupation, but a half-dozen had hunting scenes of one kind or another, some described in considerable detail as: "a lady and gentleman going to the woods with two varlets, one leading their horses, and (probably to one side) people hunting water birds with falcons." One piece represented a tourney. On others were people eating cherries; or riding horseback; or, in one instance, a lady standing beside a fountain stirring the water with a stick; or two people playing checkers. A half dozen of these pieces represented children, in one case bathing in a stream; and three or four different sets, a dozen pieces in all, depicted courtly gallantries, variously described as Love Games, Love Petitions, or Love Personages, and in at least one case representing also the Goddess of Love. There were, too, a few of the standard religious subjects: a Passion; a

[329]

piece called a Judgment, which might have been the Solomon episode, or perhaps was the Last Judgment; and the Legend of Octavian.

To be sure, a number of these tapestries, some fifty or sixty, were small: bench covers, bed canopies or bed covers; and some twenty-five were coarse and hence probably of relatively little value; but, on the other hand, as many more were inwoven with silk and gold, the finest and most expensive type, so that the total cost of the collection was very high. Yet Agincourt was fought and lost, and France was ruined.

This inventory is useful, too, thanks to the conscientious details of the descriptions, for incidental information on the industry at this time. More than fifty tapestries are associated with Arras, including practically all that have silk and gold; only a little more than a dozen with Paris, and a number of these are described as being coarse. In short, the fine quality was Arras, the poor Paris. It is not, however, absolutely clear that the two grades were actually made only in the respective cities, for the phrase varies and is somewhat ambiguous. Sometimes the description runs: " *tapisserie d'Arras,*" or again " *de la façon d'Arras,*" but other items are described as " *de fille d'Arras,*" and the Paris pieces are also often similarly noted " *de fille de Paris,*" so that it has been suggested that these were merely trade designations for qualities, and had nothing to do with the actual place of weaving. But the fact that these terms had been thus formulated suggests that Paris did specialize in the cheaper products, and that its importance in the art has been overrated, owing to the association with it of the great Angers Apocalypse (cf. p. 66).

The collection of Charles VI was all scattered within a few years after his death, as the documents appended to the inventory painstakingly record. By the Treaty of Troyes (1420), the French throne passed to the English monarch, and since he was, at the moment, an infant, the Regent was the Duke of Bedford. Portable crown property had a sufficiently ambiguous status to be liable to diversion, and so the tapestries and other furnishings were rapidly absorbed into various collections, primarily that of the English Duke. Thus only a few months after the King's death the Duke of Bedford had got nearly a score of tapestries, not to mention a quantity of other stuffs, including the Clovis, which was one of the very rich pieces; the whole set of people playing checkers, comprising nine pieces; and a panel showing the Tour du Bois with a deer on either side. A year later he made another raid that delivered into his hands more of the outstanding pieces, the Annunciation, two Crucifixions, and the Judgment, with four less important pieces, and a quantity of silks and pile carpets. This seems to have sufficed him for seven years and then he appropriated almost everything of importance that was left, including the Saint Inglevert set, the Good Repute chamber, the *Chambre d'Honneur,* the Bertrand du Guesclin, the Girard de Commercy, the Heroines, the Lion de Bourges, some of the Love Games, the Penthesilea, William the Conqueror, the Battle of the Thirty, the Milon de Beauvais, the Fortune set, and thirty-seven other items, some of which were the simpler personage tapestries or ordinary verdures, while others were carpets, velvets and cloths of gold. A few years later the Duchess felt the need of a few more things, and then some lesser personalities attached to the English cause were given a chance to reward themselves with whatever bits were left, so that in less than ten years after the King's death the entire accumulation was wiped out.

While there is no known scrap that could be even hypothetically identified as part of this collection, there are a few examples of the period apparently corresponding in style to pieces that Charles VI owned. The less elaborate and valuable kind, described, for example, as " *tappicerie d'Arras, sur laine, a champ vert herbu, a deux personnages et feuillages,*" was very probably the type represented by five long narrow fragments, all of one series, in the Musée des Arts Décoratifs of Paris, badly repaired, but nevertheless sufficient to give an idea of the ordinary, rather coarse personage tapestries of the first quarter of the fifteenth century. These, however, are not on a " *vert herbu* " ground, but on " *pers,*" that is, dark blue. Again, there are small bits of verdures of this time, for example in the Victoria and Albert Museum, that correspond in general to such items as: " *Un dossier et demi-ciel, de l'ouvrage de Paris, a cinq bestes, ou il y a ung lion ou milieu, et a petiz arbres sur champ herbeux ";* or another, in the next item, with a unicorn in the middle. The *Chambre d'Honneur* recalls another piece that has survived from this period, formerly in a Viennese private collection, with a number of small personages, as the inventory says, with verses about Honor.

But the King's piece, or rather pieces for the set comprised nine items, were on a light red ground, instead of dark blue, and they were enriched with silk and gold.

The loss of one piece that the King had owned is especially unfortunate for that interesting branch of the history of art which unravels the reciprocal influences between the East and the West, for it had, on a ground of red and white undulating stripes, vine rinceaux, with lion masks on the leaves, a characteristic Persian pattern. This was one of a number of pieces sold to meet the expenses of the King's funeral.

The royal collection of France lapses into relative unimportance after this for nearly a century, but the House of Burgundy continued to pile up increasingly valuable and interesting stores of hangings. Of the tapestry acquisitions of Jean sans Peur little is known, for no inventory exists, and only occasional items recording his purchases have come to light. In 1412 he bought from André Rousseau of Paris a piece showing how God sent the fleur-de-lis to France, and they were given to Clovis. This he gave, as a New Year's present, to Louis, Duc de Guyenne, the eldest son of Charles VI. In 1414 he bought from Jean Renout of Arras a set of five pieces and valances that he gave to Robert, Duke of Albany, then governing Scotland. The design was a large figure of a woman, and small children, on a blue ground with a pattern, apparently, of greenish spots *(semée de persellis)*. Nothing of the kind is known. In 1415 he bought ten pieces from Laurent Champion which served as part of the trousseau of his daughter Marie, when she married Adolphe, Comte de Clèves et de la Marche. In 1416, after a conference with the representatives of the Emperor Sigismund and of Henry V of England, to get their consent to his claiming the French crown, he gave the German Ambassador, a Count in his company, and the Duke of Warwick who came from England, each a hunting tapestry.

It is rather a relief to find that of the sumptuous collection of Philip the Bold, eleven pieces were certainly transmitted to his grandson, Philip the Good, and perhaps three others also, to reappear in the inventory of Philip the Good in 1420. Here again is the Florence of Rome which may have come down all the way from Charles V. It is, indeed, specified in the inventory that it is old. And here likewise are the Godfrey de Bouillon that had belonged to the Duchess Marguerite and may also have come from Charles V. The other pieces that Philip still had from his inheritance are: one of the Charlemagnes; Perceval le Galois, with the additional title now specified, *Orgueilleux de la Lande;* a Bertrand du Guesclin; Jason; the Semiramis which had, by now, been cut into two pieces; the Doon de la Roche; the Chastel de Franchise; the Credo with Apostles and Prophets; and the great family monument, the Battle of Roose-beck. The other three pieces that may have belonged to his grandfather are: one with the Heroes and Heroines; a Death of the Virgin; and a Coronation of the Virgin; and perhaps, also, an old piece that Philip the Good had, with young men and women playing games, was the piece with the game of *hauce-pié* that had belonged to his grandmother. Three other pieces Philip may have inherited from his great-uncle Jean de Berri: a tapestry of Good Repute (*Fama*) , and two with illustrations of the Vespasian legend. There are two other pieces in the collection also described as old, so presumably from another generation: one representing Youth and Pleasure, the other illustrating the story of Regnault de Montauban. Louis II, Duc d'Anjou, the cousin of Philip's father, had bought a large piece illustrating this theme from Nicolas Bataille in 1396, so perhaps Philip had somehow inherited it from that source. Two other pieces, also, apparently came to him from other collections, one presumably from his father, since it represented Duke John and his wife hunting, ahorse and afoot; and the other from the Duke Antoine de Brabant, for it had portraits of himself, his wife and his children, evidently as donors, with the Coronation of the Virgin.

The nineteen other items of the inventory describing illustrative or elaborately decorative pieces presumably represent pieces of his own acquisition, though some may have come from his father. In this group romances play a small part. There are: one giving a battle scene from the story of Regnier; one illustrating the Conquest of England by William the Conqueror; and another with Nine Heroines.

There are three allegorical subjects: the Seven Sages (which may be the Octavian de Rome which his grandfather had); another with ladies representing Honor, Nobility, Generosity, Simplicity and other attributes; and a third, especially interesting and well described: "three pieces, interwoven with gold, showing the Church Militant, on one of which is seated in majesty the Holy Father, with a number of Cardinals grouped around him, and below, several princes presenting to him a church." At the time that the inventory was made, Philip had only just acquired this piece from Jeanne la Gaye, widow of the late Guy de Ternois, and Jean Largent. It was, perhaps, the realization of an ambition of Jean Germain, Chancellor of the Order of the Golden Fleece, who had invented a didactic treatise with the fanciful name, *Deux Pans de la Tapisserie Chrétienne* (1457). The text was part of the Chancellor's fervent campaign against the very real threat of Islam, and pandered, too, to the Duke's hope of leading an illustrious Crusade. The form, albeit necessarily a bit ambiguous in view of the propagandist contents, nevertheless does indicate that the author did aspire to see his pious injunctions glorified in actual tapestry. And indeed there exists a manuscript of the text with rough drawings that might well have served as a starting point for tapestry cartoons.

The episodes from daily life in this collection are commonplace: a scene of gallantry; children with trees, grass and rose trellises, the latter a rather unexpected feature so early, on a red ground; another red ground piece with a knight and a lady, and children in the corners; and three shepherd pieces, one interesting because of the surrounding design which consisted of a "double rinceau of lilies, and another double rinceau interlocked, with a wreath of roses in the middle" and the shepherd was in the centre of that, the whole pattern being on a blue ground. The design of a rondel framed in a wreath and enclosing a figural scene does not appear in any existing tapestry until a hundred years after this.

There was the usual scattering of religious subjects: one with the Coronation of the Virgin, the Resurrection and the Pentecost all together; another Resurrection on an altar piece; the Three Marys at the Tomb, with Saint John and Saint Anthony; and one unusual theme, Jesus in Majesty, with a King presented by a Saint. There was only one piece wholly devoted to a Saint, Saint Anne, and finally, there was another family memorial, the Battle of Liège.

Subsequently, in 1427, the Duke bought two more pieces from Jean Walois of Arras, one a bear hunt; the other striped green and white, with a scattering of roses on it, and against that, various figures. A set of three of exactly this type, but a quarter of a century later, is in the Metropolitan Museum of Art. Again seven years later the Duke got four more pieces from the same merchant, one with the Joys of the Virgin; the second with the Passion and the Crucifixion; the third with a bear hunt; and the fourth a verdure with birds; but these were used as presents, the first two for his cousin, the Bishop of Liège, the third for his brother, the Duc de Gheldre, and the verdure for another cousin, the Comte de Meurs. This dealer also sold the Duke a Resurrection of Lazarus, but the fate of that is not recorded.

About this same time he bought a set from the widow of Jean Baubrec of Tournay, with children going to school, while in 1459 he bought from Pasquier Grenier, also of Tournay, a history of Alexander; two years later a set of six, with the Passion; the hangings for a room, with trees and verdure and large figures of peasants and woodmen; the next year a history of Esther and a history of the Knight of the Swan; and four years later the hangings for two rooms: one with orange trees, and the other with woodsmen. We know that he owned also a life of Hercules, for he used it to decorate the banquet hall at the Vow of the Pheasant celebration at Lille in 1454.

But the great tapestry monument of Philip the Good was the

set made for the Order of the Golden Fleece, designed by Baudouin Bailleul, and woven in 1449 by Robert Dary and Jean de l'Ortie of Tournay. The chief hero of the history of the Golden Fleece, as it was here recounted, was Gideon. It is said that Jason had been the Duke's own choice, but that he was dissuaded from it by the argument that Jason had foresworn himself in not marrying Medea, so that he was not a fit model for Christian knights. Whether or not his contribution to the Golden Fleece myth was illustrated at all in this set is not clear, but it seems probable that it must have been included, for the series was very large, eight pieces in all, two twenty-two ells long and eight ells high, the other six, sixteen ells long and the same height; and Gideon, no matter how much the tale may have been artificially inflated, could hardly have supplied enough contents for that area of illustration.

The series had disappeared by the eighteenth century, leaving no trace or record of its fate. Because it was so celebrated in its own time, and because, too, it is so completely documented and hence has been so fully published in almost every work on the subject, every serious student in the field for the last hundred years has searched for even a bit of it. But no smallest fragment of any History of Gideon has ever come to light. Some fifty years ago, however, there passed through the art market a fair sized fragment with episodes from the history of Jason. It was of the period, and of the type that must be associated with Philip the Good. If Bailleul's Golden Fleece did include the Duke's first hero, Jason, this must have been part of it. But the problem seems dogged by an especially malign fate, for this piece, too, has now disappeared, leaving only a faded photograph.

Some of the Duke's other later acquisitions have been quite convincingly identified in existing tapestries, notably the Alexander which may be the Pallazzo Doria Alexander; the Passion, one piece of which might, judging from date and style, be a large panel now in the Cinquantenaire Museum designed by Piat van Roome; the history of Esther which can reasonably be associated with two fragments in the Museum of Nancy; and the Knight of the Swan of which two small bits exist, one

in the Wavel Castle in Cracow, and the other in the Museum
für Kunst und Industrie in Vienna.

Philip's interest in tapestry must have been a publicly recognized feature of his character, for not only did Jean Germain
perpetrate a literary invention intended for the Duke adapted
to the tapestry idea, but later in his reign some other, anonymous writer also evolved an elaborate allegory, presumably
based on some tapestries that he had seen in Vienna, and perhaps, indeed, actually a description of real tapestries, for the
subjects are characteristic: a debate at the court of Venus between Youth and Age; Honor; and the Condemnation of
Banquet and Supper, the last a theme that recurs more than
half a century later in tapestries that still exist.

It is unfortunate that there are almost no documents on the
tapestry acquisitions of Charles the Bold, only casual references
in contemporary chroniclers, and occasional records of sale;
for here again we come to a few more items that can be identified with reasonable confidence. Of the fifteen tapestries that
we hear about in these incidental records, seven seem to have
been inherited pieces that had already appeared in the family
documents: Jason, now in its third generation, which he displayed at his wedding to Margaret of York in 1486, and also at
the Conference of Trèves in 1473; Esther and Ahasuerus, which
was one of the decorations at the time of his marriage; the
Passion, also used at that time; the Alexander, which was hung
at his Hôtel d'Artois in Paris for the entry of Louis XI in 1461,
used at his marriage, displayed at Brussels in 1469 when the
men of Ghent came to apologize, and also hung for the Conference of Trèves; the Battle of Liège which was used for the
Conference of Arras in 1435, and also hung at his marriage;
the Golden Fleece, which he showed at the Hague in 1456, at
the entry of Louis XI, and also at his marriage; and also a
Bègue de Belin, which also was used at his wedding, and which
may or may not have come down to him in some way from
the Duc de Berri. Two of the romances of which there has not
been any previous record can be more or less conclusively connected with existing pieces: one with the Coronation of Clovis,
the renewal of his alliance with Gondebaut, and his marriage

to Gondebaut's daughter, used at Charles's wedding, which may perhaps be connected with the two pieces in Rheims Cathedral (cf. p. 79) ; and a History of Troy, which was bought by the city of Bruges from Pasquier Grenier of Tournay in 1472 to present to the Duke after his Château de Mâle at Bruges had burned. This is too early to be the actual Troy series of which pieces are scattered in many collections (cf. p. 81), but that series, which is only ten or fifteen years later, may have been a revamped version of the earlier one. Three other romances, one symbolic piece, and three religious panels that Charles owned cannot be equated with any known tapestries: a history of King Albe; a Hannibal, shown in Brussels in 1469; a Lucretia, used at his wedding; a set of Four Cardinal Virtues; a Life of Christ, used at Trèves; an Old and New Testament, also used at Trèves; and a piece that appeared at his wedding, showing God accompanying Adam and Eve in the Garden of Eden.

The records of sales to Charles concern only unimportant pieces, the subjects unspecified, but presumably armorials or verdures. Thus, while still Comte de Charolais he bought a wall hanging and bench covers from Camus Dujardin of Lille. In 1469 he acquired a piece from Brice le Bacre of Middelburg, formerly of Tournay; and the next year he patronized Melchior de le Wede, also in Middelburg, and Jean le Haze of Lille.

Finally, there is one tapestry in existence unmistakably from the possession of Charles the Bold because it bears his arms and insignia, the flint striker, and his initials. These are displayed against a pattern of small, naturalistic floriation on a dark blue ground. The piece is in the Historisches Museum of Berne, and is usually supposed to have been part of the booty taken from the tent of Charles after the defeat of Granson. Other tapestries in the same Museum, the Julius Caesar (cf. p. 78), a large piece with the Judgment of Herkinbald, and an Adoration of the Magi, have often been asserted also to have been part of the loot; but this is apocryphal, though the pieces in question are of the correct period, and Caesar, along with Hannibal and Alexander whom he did have represented in tapestry, were Charles's favorite heroes.

That some of Charles's collection was lost to the enemy in

that fatal débacle is certain, but there must have been still a rich store to pass to his daughter, Marie, and her husband, the Emperor Maximilian I; but again there are no inventories, nor are we any richer in documents concerning their own acquisitions. We know only that Maximilian bought seven small verdure bench covers from Michel Nyettens of Brussels in 1480–81; that he and his wife bought from Philip le Sellier of Bruges in 1478 two pieces with the history of the Emperor Maximien, an Adoration of the Magi, and a history of Absalom; and that Maximilian got from Arnould Poissonier of Tournay in 1510 eight pieces with the Triumph of Julius Caesar, a set with the " *ystoire des gens et des bestes sauvaiges a la manière de calcut,*" and another set " *de toutes choses plaisantes de chasse, volerie et autrement*"; and from Peter Pannemaker in 1517 a Crucifixion, and four pieces from the story of David. Of these, only the Calcutta set can be identified, and three pieces of this are known.

The next generation marks another definite stage in the tapestry history of this family, for while there are existing pieces that can thus be associated with Philip the Good, Charles the Bold and Maximilian, these pieces are all scattered; but the existing pieces that belonged to both Philip the Fair and to his sister, Marguerite of Austria, form part, the foundation really, of the great collection that is the tapestry monument of the house, the Spanish State Collection.

Philip's collection started off well, aside from what he may have inherited, for in 1497 when he was just nineteen years old and had been married only a year to the Spanish heiress Jeanne, who came to be known as Jeanne la Folle, the city of Tournay gave him six sets. He had decreed that Tournay tapestries could not be sold in his domains, and the gift was part of the negotiations to obtain a repeal of this ruling. Nor did it suffice, for in addition, the Archduke put in a claim for a substantial sum of money, to cover outlays that he had made in the acquisition of further tapestries. Unfortunately there is no indication of the subjects of any of these. Four years later he bought from Colart Bloyart of the same city four large panels with the History of the Condemnation of Banquet and Supper, and from another Tournay merchant, Jean Grenier, another Banquet set in six pieces, a series with Vineyard scenes, and another with woodmen. In 1504 he bought from the same merchant a piece from the Portuguese in India set to give to a French gentleman. Both this and the Banquet and Supper sets were almost certainly the same as those that we know.

Despite the fact, however, that all of his important recorded acquisitions are thus associated with Tournay, the pieces from his ownership in the Spanish State Collection are all of the Brussels type, with the possible exception of one, the earliest piece in the whole collection, an Annunciation, which first appears in the inventory of Jeanne la Folle, and probably belonged to her, and possibly to her husband. This could be of Tournay manufacture. The other pieces that Philip owned are: a Life of the Virgin in four pieces with Old Testament and other antitypes, always described in the early records as " Old Brabant," because of a tiny gold lion on black embroidered in each corner, the Brabant arms; two pieces from another Life of the Virgin which Jeanne took with her into the retreat that sheltered her insanity at Tordesillas; and a Mass of Gregory, which probably belonged to Philip the Fair, for Matthias Guerlas of Brussels was his first official tapestry purveyor, and this bears, inscribed on the hem of a garment, the name Brussels and — ERLAS.

Though Marguerite of Austria's period of rule in the Netherlands produced such a definite and appropriate style of tapestry (cf. Chap. VII), there are relatively few documents directly connecting her with the industry, and still fewer existing pieces that can be immediately associated with her. On several occasions she ordered armorial tapestries at Enghien; in 1527 she acquired some unspecified pieces from Jean Ardsteene of Brussels; and in 1513, on the occasion of her visit to Tournay to see Henry VIII (they got on splendidly, and there was some question of a marriage), the city gave her a set of six pieces from Jean Grenier, illustrating the " Cité des Dames." The inventory made after her death shows, in addition to this set and a tapestry portrait of herself (cf. p. 215), two items which were possibly inherited from the Burgundian collection: a set of four with the story of Esther; and a single Alexander. Another Alexander, a Credo in three pieces, and a Life of Saint Helen in four pieces had come from Spain. She had, for a time, been Infanta (her second marriage), and probably she had brought them back when she returned. There was also a piece with the Carrying of the Cross, seven other pieces with Scenes from the Passion, and a piece with God the Father and the Holy Ghost that she got from Pannemaker.

The pieces which she owned that are now in the Spanish State Collection are two from a Passion, one showing the Carrying of the Cross as specified in her inventory, and bearing the signature of Jean van Roome, her court painter (cf. p. 133). Four other pieces with scenes from the Passion are also said to have belonged to her, though they are also said to have been bought by Charles V. The last is the panel with God the Father that she got from Pannemaker, which has come to be known as the Dais of Charles V. Marguerite bequeathed it to Charles, who is supposed to have stood under it when he abdicated.

Marguerite's successor in the Netherlands, her niece Marie of Hungary, also made contributions to this collection. In addition to the Hunts of Bernard van Orley which probably should be associated with her (cf. p. 150), and the Tunis series which she ordered (cf. notes p. 139), she bought in 1535 from Guillaume Dermoyen of Brussels a Hercules set; and from Pannemaker an Alexander. In 1544 she got the Seven Deadly Sins at Antwerp from Pierre van der Walle, and from Erasmus Schetz, a Scipio; and shortly after that she had, in her palace at Binche, in addition to the Scipio, a Vertumnus and Pomona series which she had got from George Wezler; a Judgment of Paris; and a Pavia set. The next year she bought another Pomona piece from Pannemaker. The Seven Deadly Sins and the Scipio are both in the Spanish collection, bequeathed to Charles V; and some, at least, of her Pomona pieces are there, too, for there are four different, incomplete sets in the collection.

Meanwhile her brother Charles V had not only made a significant personal contribution to the art by employing Jean Vermeyen to record his expedition to Tunis (cf. p. 139), but he had, too, been buying some of the regular products of his Lowland Dominions. In 1545 he bought a series of eight, illustrating the history of Jesse, from Jean Dermoyen of Brussels, but that set is not included in the collection. His additions to the collection as it now stands consist of an Adoration of the Magi in the Brussels style of which Bernard van Orley was the outstanding practitioner; one of the Vertumnus and Pomona sets; a series of five illustrating the Fables of Ovid; and a set of three called the Spheres. When, after his abdication, he went into retreat at Yuste, he took with him the Life of the Virgin in four pieces that he had inherited from his father, and the Adoration of the Magi that he had bought himself.

Most of the other pieces in the Spanish State Collection were added during the reign of Philip II. Philip himself bought a Saint Jerome; the Apocalypse; six Renaissance grotesques woven by Hector Vuyens; and the Life of Cyrus. Marie of Portugal brought with her, when she married him, three of the four Moralities; four pieces of the Seven Deadly Sins, of which a complete version had already been left by Marie of Hungary, became crown property when the goods of the Comte d'Egmont were confiscated in 1567, for while most of his property was sold, the Duke of Alba decided to take those back to Spain; and three more series, a history of Alexander the Great, the Battles of Archduke Albert of Austria, and a set with children, accrued to Philip on the death of Cardinal Granville. Another set, the Abraham, belonged to Princess Jeanne, daughter of Charles V; while some curious pieces in a pseudo-Breughel style were bought by Philip IV (1605–1665), though the cartoons must antedate him by three-quarters of a century. In all, the collection comprises four hundred and twenty-two pieces which, even granting that half are of only secondary interest, is a fitting bequest to the history of the art from the family that for nearly three centuries was the overlord of the industry.

NOTES

CHAPTER I

PAGE 1. In the grave of Queen Shub-ab at Ur sufficient disintegrated remains of the garments of the attendant ladies were found to indicate that they were red, but the stuff as a textile had long since ceased to exist. See C. Leonard Woolley, *Ur of the Chaldees,* London, 1929, p. 64.

PAGE 2. J. E. Quibbell, *Excavations at Saqqara,* Vol. V, *The Tomb of Hesy,* Cairo, 1913, Pl. XVIII, XIX, XXIII. Also ill. Heinrich Schäfer und Walter Andrae, *Die Kunst des Alten Orients,* Berlin, 1925, Taf. 1.

For the Cretan garments with the bucranium, etc., see Sir Arthur Evans, *The Palace of Minos,* Vol. III, London, 1930, p. 39, Fig. 23; p. 41, Fig. 25; p. 43, Fig. 36.

PAGE 5. The history of the Tree of Life has been traced in Phyllis Ackerman, *The Rockefeller McCormick Tapestries, Three Early Sixteenth Century Tapestries, with a Discussion of the History of the Tree of Life,* New York, 1932; and cf. p. 48.

PAGE 6. For the painting of the youth picking crocuses see Evans, op. cit., Vol. I, London, 1921, Pl. IV and p. 265. The illustration is, of course, a reconstruction from fragments, but these seem to have been reasonably complete and quite legible. For the court ladies see Evans, op. cit., Vol. III, London, 1930, Pl. XVII A and B.

PAGE 8. According to N. Kondakoff, J. Tolstoi et S. Reinach, *Antiquités de la Russie Méridionale,* Paris, 1891, p. 69, the fragments found in the Kuban are rep on one side and satin on the other. The details of technique are not given. But Otto von Falke, *Decorative Silks,* New York, 1922, p. 1, reports that they are tapestry woven, without citation, and this is also stated by Walter G. Thomson, *A History of Tapestry From the Earliest Times Until the Present Day,* 2nd ed., London, 1930, p. 12 f. with ill., Figs. 9 and 10.

For the definitions of all weaving terms, such as "compound cloth," see Nancy Andrews Reath, *The Weaves of Hand-Loom Fabrics*, Philadelphia (The Pennsylvania Museum), 1927.

The description of Helen's weaving is to be found in Andrew Lang, Walter Leaf, and Ernest Myers, *The Iliad of Homer, done into English*, Revised edition, London, 1927, p. 53 (Book III, 1.129 ff.). Hector's wife weaves a simpler design in the same technique, op. cit., p. 485 (Bk. XXIV, 1.229 f.). The same assumption, that the designs must have been tapestry woven, has been made in regard to the illustrative designs on garments shown on Greek vases, for example the François vase. See Falke, op. cit., p. 1 and ill., Fig. 1. But the design, which is pure silhouette without any interior details, is precisely of the type that could best be woven by this other technique, and it is, moreover, arranged in bands, which is the normal, almost inevitable, disposition for this style of weaving, but not at all normal to tapestry.

The account of "tapestry" in the earlier civilizations and in the East given by Eugène Müntz, *A Short History of Tapestry*, London, 1885, Chaps. I to VI, while interesting for the history of textiles, is misleading for the history of tapestry because of this loose use of the term.

PAGE 12. For a description of the early Egyptian tapestries see W. M. Flinders Petrie, *Les Arts et Métiers de l'Ancienne Égypte*, Paris, 1912, p. 170, ill., Fig. 139. They are also discussed in Hermann Schmitz, *Bildteppiche*, Berlin, 1919, S. 35 ff., ill. Abb. 6; George Leland Hunter, *The Practical Book of Tapestries*, Philadelphia and London, 1925, p. 7 f., ill. Pl. II a; Thomson, op. cit., pp. 6 ff., ill. op. p. 10.

By far the most varied and complete collection of plates of Egyptian tapestries is in O. Wulff und W. F. Volbach, *Spätantike und Koptische Stoffe aus Ägyptischen Grabfunden*, Berlin, 1926. Armand Guerinet, *Étoffes Byzantines, Coptes, Romaines, etc., du IV au IX Siècle*, Paris, s.d., gives a series of plates, some in color, after drawings, most of them very badly rendered and with wholly undependable captions. H. Ernst, *Tapisseries et Étoffes Coptes*, Paris, s.d., is a volume of plates in color, most of them apparently from hand-painted photographs and so reasonably reliable, though those not based on photographs are very badly done; but there is no text and the list of plates gives no information. Brief discussions are given by Schmitz, op. cit., S. 38 ff., and ill.; Gaston Migeon, *Les*

Arts du Tissu (Manuels d'Histoire de l'Art), Nouvelle Édition, Paris, 1929, Chap. I, pp. 7 ff.; and Thomson, op. cit., pp. 19 ff. A good small selection is published in M. S. Dimand, "Early Coptic Tapestries" in *International Studio*, Vol. LXXVIII, New York, 1923, pp. 245 ff. These tapestries are usually called "Coptic," but there is no proof that they were inevitably made by the Christian Egyptians and in any case there is nothing specifically Christian Egyptian in the style or character of any but a very small proportion of them, so that the term seems unfortunate.

PAGE 14. Alexandria's prosperity recurred, moreover, at intervals for several centuries. See W. Heyd, *Histoire du Commerce du Levant au Moyen-Âge*, Leipzig, 1923, T. I, p. 41.

The Lyons fish panel is ill. Raymond Cox, *Les Soieries d'Art*, Paris, 1914, Pl. I. There is a small fragment of the same textile in Paris, Musée Guimet.

PAGE 15. The Berlin peacock is illustrated in color in Wulff und Volbach, op. cit., Taf. 11.

PAGE 18. The Berlin dancers are illustrated in color in Wulff und Volbach, op. cit., Taf. 4, 5, and in black and white, Taf. 44.

PAGE 20. For Semi-realistic portrait heads illustrated in color, see Wulff und Volbach, op. cit., Taf. 16, 17, and in black and white, Taf. 42 (9247, 9246). For detached heads used as a powdered pattern in staggered horizontal rows, see Ernst, op. cit., Pl. 9.

The Bliss panel is discussed in Hunter, op. cit., p. 9 ff., where it is called a "Blessed Vesta" without explanation of the interpretation, and ill. Pl. II b.

PAGE 21. A splendid eagle of this type in the Kaiser Friedrich Museum is illustrated in color in Wulff und Volbach, op. cit., Taf. 13.

PAGE 22. The angel is in the possession of the author.

CHAPTER II

PAGE 24. An excellent discussion of Roman industry is given in Ferdinand Lot, *La Fin du Monde Antique et le Début du Moyen Âge*, Paris, 1927, pp. 72 ff. This does not mean, of course, that there was no tapestry weaving in Rome. The often quoted passage from Ovid's *Metamorphoses* seems to refer to tapestry, and to show that he had seen tapestry weaving. The passage is quoted in full in Thomson, op. cit., p. 15.

PAGE 26. The Fortunatus is referred to by Helen Waddell, *The Wandering Scholars*, London, 1927, p. 27, who refers to Carm. III, 13; VIII, 7; III, 7.

PAGE 28. The tapestry was found in the Church of Saint Gereon in Cologne and is usually called the Saint Gereon tapestry. One piece of it is in the Schlossmuseum in Berlin (29 inches high and 24½ wide), another in the Nürnberg Germanisches Museum (28 inches high and 57 inches wide), another in the Musée des Tissus of Lyons, and a fragment in the Victoria and Albert Museum. It is woven entirely of wool, dovetailed, the warps horizontal, according to the most complete description, in Betty Kurth, *Die Deutschen Bildteppiche des Mittelalters*, Bd. I, Vienna, 1926, S. 22 ff., 205. Ill. Bd. II, Taf. 1, 2. Less complete accounts are given in Müntz, op. cit., pp. 78 ff., ill. p. 79, Fig. 12; Jules Guiffrey, *La Tapisserie du XIIe à la fin du XVIe Siècle*, Paris, s.d. (1911 ?) (*Histoire Générale des Arts Appliqués à l'Industrie*, T. VI), p. 4, ill. Fig. 2; George Leland Hunter, *Tapestries, Their Origin, History and Renaissance*, New York, 1912, p. 33 f., ill. Pl. 35; Schmitz, op. cit., S. 51 f., ill. Abb. 20; Hunter, *Practical Book*, p. 13, ill. Pl. II e; Thomson, op. cit., p. 46, ill. opposite page.

For the Sumerian representation see G. Contenau, *Manuel d'Archéologie Orientale*, Paris, 1927, T. I, p. 474, ill. p. 448, Fig. 345. The Louvre relief is illustrated in G. Perrot et C. Chipiez, *Histoire de l'Art dans l'Antiquité*, T. V., p. 719, Fig. 438.

PAGE 30. The first complete account of the Halberstadt tapestries and the Quedlinburg carpet was given by Julius Lessing, *Wandtep-*

piche und Decken des Mittelalters in Deutschland, Berlin, s.d. A complete and systematic account is given by Kurth, op. cit., Bd. I, S. 38 ff., 205 ff. and ill. Taf. 3–11, 222a. According to Dr. Kurth the Abraham (3 feet 11 inches high by 33 feet 5 inches long) is all wool except for the bright white lights which are linen, the warps are horizontal, and the slits are either dovetailed or sewed, op. cit., p. 206. The Christ and the Apostles (3 feet 8 inches high by 29 feet 3 inches long) is the same, but with more of the slits sewed; and the Charlemagne (4 feet 10 inches square) is all wool, with vertical warps, both dovetailed and sewed, and is reversible. These pieces are also discussed in J. Guiffrey, E. Müntz et Al. Pinchart, *Histoire Générale de la Tapisserie,* II, Eugène Müntz, *Histoire de la Tapisserie en Italie, en Allemagne, en Angleterre, etc.,* Paris, 1878–1884, 2ième partie, p. 2, ill. p. 2; Guiffrey, op. cit., p. 4 ff., ill. Fig. 3, 4; Hunter, *Tapestries,* p. 34 f.; Schmitz, op. cit., S. 52 ff., ill. Abb. 22–27; Hunter, *Practical Book,* p. 13, Pl. II f.; Migeon, op. cit., pp. 190 ff.; Thomson, op. cit., p. 46 f., ill. opposite p. 48.

PAGE 32. The most complete accounts of the Quedlinburg carpet also are given by Lessing, loc. cit. and Kurth, op. cit., Bd. I, S. 208 ff., ill. Bd. II, Taf. 12–21, 226. Brief accounts are given by Müntz, *Histoire Générale,* 2ième partie, p. 2 and ill. p. 3; Müntz, *Short History,* p. 87 f.; Guiffrey, loc. cit., ill. Fig. 5; and Schmitz, op. cit., S. 60, ill. Abb. 25.

The origin of the Marriage of Mercury has long been recognized, but the suggested historical identification of the theme and the interpretation of the Charlemagne are the author's own. A charming brief report of the romance of Philip and Irene is in Charles Diehl, *Gens et Choses de Byzance,* Paris.

PAGE 35. A good account of the influence of memories of pre-Christian goddesses in Mediaeval Germany will be found in Lina Eckenstein, *Woman Under Monasticism,* Cambridge, 1896.

CHAPTER III

PAGE 40. This is obviously no place to consider whether, who or what the Scythians were. The " Scythian " and Sarmathian gold and bronzes of the Hermitage are a fact, the most compelling animal art the world has ever seen.

The Oseberg fragments are published in Hans Dedekam, *Baldesholtaeppet*, Christiania, 1918, pp. 48, 56; more completely in Hans Dedekam, " Odins Trae et Stykke Billedvaev fra Osebergfundet" in *Kunst og Haandwerk*, Christiania, 1924 (?) , pp. 56 ff.; and, from a special point of view, in Hans Dedekam, " Perspektivet paa Osebergdronningens Tapisserier" in *Kunstkulture,* Christiania, 1920, pp. 145 ff.

The *Months* are published in Dedekam, *Baldesholtaeppet,* pp. 40 ff., 58; Kurth, op. cit., Bd. I, S. 36 f., ill. Abb. 13; Schmitz, op. cit., S. 56 f., ill. Abb. 21.

PAGE 41. Gudrun's embroidery is described in The Volsunga Saga, c. 32, quoted Paul du Chaillu, *The Viking Age,* London, 1889, Vol. II, p. 363.

PAGE 42. Brynhild's embroidery is also described in The Volsunga Saga, c. 24, quoted Du Chaillu, op. cit., Vol. II, p. 363.

PAGE 43. Among the principal publications on the Bayeux embroidery are:

Smart le Thieullier, *La Tapisserie Conservée à la Cathédrale de Bayeux,* Caen, 1824.

Achille Jubinal, *Les Anciennes Tapisseries Historiées,* Paris, 1838, T. I.

Augustin Thierry, *Histoire de la Conquête de l'Angleterre par les Normans,* 5ième ed., Paris, 1839.

Frank Rede Fowke, *The Bayeux Tapestry,* London, 1898.

A. Marignan, *La Tapisserie de Bayeux,* Paris, 1902.

J. H. Round, "The Bayeux Tapestry," from the *Monthly Review,* London, 1904, pp. 109 ff.

L. Champion, *Les Chevaux et les Cavaliers de la Tapisserie de Bayeux,* Caen, 1907.

Suzanne Turgis, *La Reine Mathilde,* Paris, Bayeux, 1912.

Hilaire Belloc, *The Book of the Bayeux Tapestry,* London. 1914.

Victoria and Albert Museum, *Guide to the Bayeux Tapestry,* London, 1914.

A. Levé, *La Tapisserie de la Reine Mathilde, dite la Tapisserie de Bayeux,* Paris, 1919.

A useful illustration of the whole piece, in small scale but in color and very clear, after a drawing, has been published as a set of large folding postcards by a Bayeux bookseller, Charles Tostain (s.d.). A series of separate, smaller postcards published in Paris (s.d.), is also available.

The embroidery appears in any inventory of the Cathedral of 1476. In 1562, during the Calvinist uprising, the Chapter confided it to the Municipality, but it was later restored to the Church, where it was exposed on certain fête days. In 1724 M. Launcelot, a member of the Académie, found a drawing of it but could not identify the nature of the original, deciding finally that it represented either part of the tomb of William or stained glass. In 1729 M. de Montfaucon found the original. For details and further history cf. Fowke, op. cit., p. 1, N. I; Turgis, op. cit., pp. 81 ff; Victoria and Albert Museum, Guide.

An interesting contemporary (13th century) account of Anglo-Norman ladies' embroidery is given in G. G. Coulton, *Life in the Middle Ages*, Vol. III, Cambridge, 1928, Item No. 28, " A Rhyme of Fair Ladies," p. 52 f., p. 53 — "When they rise from table (I say not from meat, for they have eaten but little and yet have well dined) then go they to their bower to entertain each other with subtleties of needlework whereof they love to talk; then comes up the frilled work and the open-work, the German and the Saracen work, the pinched work, the scalloped and the wool-work, the perroun and the melice and the diaper-work, the rod-work, and the peynet and the gernettée; nor is the double samite forgotten, nor do they fail to handle again and again the redener-work. She who knows most of these things shall be their lecturess, to whom the rest hearken without sluggardy; none sleeps here as they do at mass, for all are cheerful companions in these lists of vanity." Some of the terms are now incomprehensible.

The Embroidery of Agnes of Blois is cited in Marignan, op. cit., pp. XIV ff.

The arguments from the Anglo-Saxon Ð and from the form of Bagias are made in Roger Sherman Loomis, " The Origin and Date of the Bayeux Embroidery," in *The Art Bulletin*, Vol. VI, Providence, 1923, pp. 3 ff., p. 3.

The English attribution is also advanced by W. R. Lethaby, " The Embroidered Story of the Norman Conquest at Bayeux," in Grace Christie, *Embroidery*, London, 1909, pp. 152 ff.

PAGE 44. The Höylandet Embroidery is described and illustrated in Erik Salven, *Bonaden från Skag*, Stockholm, 1923. Two other illustrative Scandinavian textiles of about the same period show no stylistic relation, but this may be due to the difference in technique since these are executed in a kind of crude wool brocade on linen, or perhaps a compound cloth. The description is not clear. M. S. Dimand, " Mediaeval Textiles of Sweden," in *The Art Bulletin,* Vol. VI, Providence, 1903, pp. 11 ff.

For a discussion of the sanctity of the oath among the Norsemen, cf. Du Chaillu, op. cit., Vol. I, pp. 553 ff.

PAGE 45. It has been repeatedly assumed that Turold is the page, often referred to as a " dwarf," who holds the horses in this scene, as the name is inserted above his head; but aside from the improbability that so humble a servitor should be named, it should be noted that this name, unlike any other in the embroidery, is between lines, separating it from the page, but framing it as a label for the soldier in red to the left. This same conclusion has also been reached by Fowke, op. cit., p. 41 f., who is responsible for the identification of Turold as Constable of Bayeux. Belloc, op. cit., p. 11, concurs that it is the messenger who is indicated by the name, not the dwarf, and Levé, op. cit., 43, accepts Fowke's conclusion. Turold has also been identified hypothetically as the Fool of Guy de Ponthieu but the emphatic introduction of such a character would have no point. Smart le Thieullier, op. cit., p. 27, n. 1. One odd hypothesis that was offered without any reason made Turold the designer of the embroidery. Agnes Strickland, *Lives of the Queens of England,* Vol. I, London, 1851, p. 59, quoted by Fowke, op. cit., p. 40 f. On the other hand, since Turold seems to be in a warning and instructing role, he might be the Turold who was William the Conqueror's tutor. To be sure this Turold died in 1035, but as this is a tale to illustrate a moral rather than an historical record, that would not have mattered to the author. Indeed, he might well have merged this Turold with the Constable of Bayeux.

The identification of Aelfgyva or Edwiga has been much disputed, but it has been most reasonably claimed that she was a daughter of William. Turgis, op. cit., p. 32, citing Madame Emma Lienard (no reference) . One far-fetched interpretation of the episode suggests that the scene has nothing to do with the story, but that Aelfgyva is one of the Anglo-Saxon embroideresses, and the clerk is the learned man called in to compose the inscriptions, who dallied in the intervals of his scholarly advice with the fair needlewoman, so that her companions put this in as a joke. Loomis, op. cit., p. 5.

PAGE 46. The primitive Norsemen held a solemn meal three times a year known as the *Gilde,* the origin of the name Guild applied to craftsmen's societies in the Middle Ages and perhaps one of the origins of the societies. All of the freemen of each canton gathered together for these festivities, which were both political and religious, devoted to toasting the gods and heroes and discussing the most important affairs of the commune, war and peace, truces and alliances. Felix de Vigne, *Recherches Historiques sur les Coutumes Civils et Militaires des Gildes et des Corporations de Métiers,* Ghent, 1847, pp. IX ff.

PAGE 49. It has been suggested that Harold carries his falcon merely as indication of his nobility. Smart le Thieullier, op. cit., p. 17. It is this same writer, p. 22, who first suggests that the changed position of the falcon in the seventh scene indicates humiliation. At this period the nobility were accustomed to carry their hawks with them, even into church, and they did constitute a kind of general insignia of rank. See, for example, William Stearns Davis, *Life on a Mediaeval Barony,* New York and London, 1923, p. 58 f. But since the other noblemen in the embroidery do not carry their hawks it would seem that the bird did have a special significance in relation to Harold.

The animal heads carved on the beam ends appear also on the Swedish textiles published by Dimand, op. cit., p. 11, and it is suggested that they were put there to frighten enemies, but this does not seem convincing.

The perils of imitation are well demonstrated in a modern embroidery based on the Bayeux embroidery illustrating the Legend of the Precious Blood of Fécamp. Border motives have been imitated from the Bayeux strip, literally, but without any understanding of their significance, so that, for example, when Isaac is consoled by the angel, in the border appear the Fox and the Raven, and the apparition of the mystic stage of Christ is accompanied by the lion, the heifer, the goat, and the sheep hunting the stag. See André-Paul Leroux, *Une Tapisserie du Précieux Sang de Fécamp,* Fécamp, 1927.

PAGE 51. For the Bangstrup pendant see Du Chaillu, op. cit., Vol. I, p. 245, Fig. 521.

For representations of Phoenician ships see bas reliefs of the Palace of Khorsabad, repeatedly illustrated, e.g., Contenau, op. cit., p. 75, Fig. 35.

For the Sanchi tope boat see James Fergusson, *Tree and Serpent Worship*, London, 1868, Pl. XXXI, Fig. 1.

PAGE 52. For a discussion of dragon banners see Ernest Ingersoll, *Dragons and Dragon Lore*, New York, 1928, p. 129 and pp. 148 ff. The description of Sigurd's banner is taken from the Flatcyjarbok, Vol. I, quoted Du Chaillu, op. cit., Vol. I, p. 107.

PAGE 53. The Norwegian King and Court is ill. in H. Grosch, *Altnorwegische Bildteppiche*, Berlin, 1905, Taf. 10.

PAGE 54. The four commonest Norwegian peasant tapestries are discussed by Hans Dedekam, "Tapestry Weaving in Norway," in *The American Scandinavian Review*, Vol. XV, New York, 1927, p. 205 ff., and Grosch, op. cit., Taf. 11. The Adoration of the Kings, and Taf. 8. The Marriage at Cana. The Three Kings and several versions of the Wise and Foolish Virgins are also ill. Röhsska *Konstslöjdmuseet Tielfällig Utställning*, XLV, Aldre Norska *Tapisserievaevnader*, Gothenburg, 1922, Figs. 2 and 4–6. The Wise and Foolish Virgins are also ill., Thomson, op. cit., opposite p. 414. A group of Scandinavian tapestries is published in A. F. Kendrick, *Catalogue of Tapestries* (Victoria and Albert Museum, Department of Textiles), London, 1924, pp. 63 ff., Nos. 58–62B, ill. Pls. XXXI–XXXIII.

Norwegian Renaissance tapestries are ill. in Grosch, op. cit., Taf. 2 *et passim*.

PAGE 55. The Måås-Fjetterström tapestry is ill. Dedekam, op. cit., p. 291.

The History of the Swedish Royal Factory is given in Böttiger, op. cit., Vol. IV, pp. 4 ff., and summarized in Schmitz, op. cit., S. 325 f.

For an illustration of Swedish compact floral verdures see Böttiger, op. cit., Vol. I, S. 15, Vol. II, S. 131.

PAGE 56. The complete and systematic history of the German tapestries of this period is given in Betty Kurth, *Die Deutschen Bildteppiche des Mittelalters*, Vienna, 1926. A quite adequate account is given by Müntz, *Histoire Générale*, pt. 2; Schmitz, op. cit., S. 72 ff.; a reasonably complete statement in Thomson, op. cit., pp. 126 ff.; and brief statements in Müntz, *Short History*, pp. 108 ff.; Guiffrey, *Tapisserie*, pp. 64 ff., Hunter, *Practical Book*, pp. 205 ff.; Migeon, op. cit., Chap. VI, pp. 304 ff.

Excellent illustrations of Swiss tapestries are given in R. F. Burck-hardt, *Gewirkte Bildteppiche des XV. und XVI. Jahrhunderts im Historischen Museum zu Basel,* Basel, 1923.

The Nuremberg tapestries are specially discussed and illustrated in Duke Luitpold, *Die Frankische Bildwirkerei,* Munich, 1926.

PAGE 57. For the Hunt of the Unicorn see Kurth, op. cit., Bd. I, S. 118 f., ill. Abb. 59, 60, Bd. II, Taf. 98–99. The later rendition was in the Louis Germeau Collection, Paris, Hôtel Druot, February 11–12, 1905, No. 1375.

The legends of the unicorn are fully and delightfully discussed in Odell Shepard, *The Lore of the Unicorn,* London, 1930. There is also an excellent account of the history of the unicorn and the su-perstitions connected with it, with many citations from mediaeval texts in Léon de Laborde, *Glossaire Français du Moyen Age,* Paris, 1872, pp. 359 ff.; and there is a good summary in Heinrich Göbel, *Wandteppiche,* I. Teil, *Die Niederlände,* Leipzig, 1923, T. I, S. 130.

PAGE 58. The Upper Rhine caricature type is ill. Kurth, op. cit., Bd. I., Abb. 78–80, Bd. II, Taf. 160–161.

PAGE 59. The Fountain of Youth is ill. Kurth, op. cit., Bd. II, Taf. 124.

The early Nuremberg tapestry is ill. Kurth, op. cit., Bd. III, Taf. 238, and Schmitz, op. cit., S. 65, Abb. 26.

PAGE 60. The Nuremberg Prophets are ill. Kurth, op. cit., Bd. III, Taf. 240–241.

CHAPTER IV

PAGE 63. A hanging with scenes from the Apocalypse, probably em-broidered, was made in 1133 for Matthew of London, Abbot of Saumur, for the choir of his church. Achille Jubinal, *Recherches sur l'Usage et l'Origine des Tapisseries à Personnages,* Paris, 1840, p. 15.

PAGE 66. The intrusion of frivolity and even indecency in religious services was facilitated by the musical practice of the time, for a composer never undertook to invent a new melody in creating a mass, but always took a popular song on which to build his contrapuntal elaborations, just as Shakespeare took old tales as the basis for his plays. This theme, or subject as it was called, was carried continuously by the tenor, who often sang the original words of the song while the other voices carried the polyphony. The opportunities for obscenity were unlimited, and often exploited with gusto.

Several monographs have been devoted to the Angers set: Louis de Farcy, *Remarques sur la Tapisserie de l'Apocalypse,* Angers, 1912; Louis de Farcy, *Notices Archéologiques sur les Tentures et les Tapisseries de la Cathédrale d'Angers,* Angers, 1875; Louis de Farcy, *Histoire et Description des Tapisseries de la Cathédrale d'Angers,* Angers, 1889; Louis de Farcy, "Les Tapisseries de la Cathédrale d'Angers," in *Comtes Rendus de l'Association Française pour l'Avancement des Sciences, Congrès d'Angers,* 1903.

A more or less complete account is given in practically every standard publication. J. Guiffrey, E. Müntz et Al. Pinchart, *Histoire Générale de la Tapisserie,* T. I, Jules Guiffrey, *Histoire de la Tapisserie en France,* Paris, 1878–1885, pp. 12 ff., ill. p. 12, Pl. 2, 3; Müntz, *Short History,* pp. 100 ff., ill. p. 101, Fig. 15; Jules Guiffrey, "Les Origines de la Tapisserie de Haute et Basse-Lice à Paris," in *Mémoires de la Société de l'Île-de-France,* T. VIII, Paris, 1882, pp. 107 ff., 122 ff.; Guiffrey. *Tapisserie,* pp. 16 ff., ill. Figs. 7, 8, 10; Hunter, *Tapestries,* pp. 38 ff., ill. Pl. 39; Schmitz, op. cit., S. 68 ff., ill. Abb. 28; Betty Kurth, *Gotische Bildteppiche aus Frankreich und Flandern,* Munich, 1923, Abb. 1–7; G. J. DeMotte, *La Tapisserie Gothique,* New York, 1921–24, Pls. 2–14, inclusive; Heinrich Göbel, *Wandteppiche,* II. Teil, *Die Romanischen Länder,* Leipzig, 1928, Bd. I, S. 1 ff., ill. Bd. II, Abb. 1–13; Migeon, op. cit., pp. 196 ff., ill., pp. 197, 199; Hunter, *Practical Book,* pp. 21 ff., ill. Pl. III, e and d; E. Planès, *La Tapisserie Gothique,* Paris, s.d. (1929), pp. 6 ff., ill. Pl. I; Thomson, op. cit., pp. 56 ff., ill. opposite pp. 57, 58, 62.

The first complete account of Bataille was given in Jules Joseph Guiffrey, *Nicolas Bataille, Tapissier Parisien du XIVe Siècle: Sa Vie, Son Oeuvre, Sa Famille,* Paris, 1884.

For a discussion of the relation of the tapestry and the manuscript see Montague Rhodes James, *The Apocalypse in Art,* London, 1931, p. 69 f.; Jeanne Maquet-Tomlin, "Inspiration et Originalité des Tapisseries de l'Apocalypse d'Angers," in *Mélanges Hulin de Loo,* Brussels and Paris, 1931, pp. 260 ff.

PAGE 67. This identification of the initial figure was first made by Louis-Eugène Lefevre, "Les Sept Églises d'Asie et Leurs Évêques dans la Tapisserie de l'Apocalypse à Angers," *Gazette des Beaux Arts*, Ve Per., T. XI, pp. 206 ff.

PAGE 69. The Spanish State Apocalypse is fully illustrated in Conde Viudo de Valencia de Don Juan, *Tapices de la Corona de España*, Madrid, 1903, Lam. 82–89, and according to the account given here, Vol. II, pp. 65 ff., it was bought by Philip II in 1561; but according to Paul Saintenay, "Les Tapisseries de la Cour de Bruxelles sous Charles V" in *Annales de la Société Royale d'Archéologie de Bruxelles*, T. XXX, Brussels, 1921, p. 22, it entered the collection during the reign of Charles V. This dating would be more consistent with its style.

It has been attributed to Bernard van Orley, with the further suggestion that he was aided by his brother Gomar, Elias Tormo Monzo y Francisco J. Sanchez Canton, *Los Tapices de la Casa del Rey N. S.*, Madrid, 1919, p. 59. The set is also discussed in Alphonse Wauters, "Essai Historique sur les Tapisseries et les Tapissiers de Haute et de Basse-Lice de Bruxelles" in *Bulletin des Commissions Royales d'Art et Archéologie*, XVième Année, Brussels, 1876, pp. 394 ff.; XVIième année, 1877, pp. 194 ff., XVIIième année, 1878, pp. 149 ff., XVième année, pp. 402 ff.; J. Guiffrey, E. Müntz et Al. Pinchart, *Histoire Générale de la Tapisserie*, T. III, Alex. Pinchart, *Tapisseries Flamandes*, Paris, 1879, p. 120; ill. Guiffrey, *Tapisserie*, Pl. VIII; Göbel, op. cit., I. Teil, Bd. I, S. 156 ff., 417, ill. Bd. II, Abb. 128–129; Émile Mâle, *L'Art Religieux de la Fin du Moyen Age en France*, 2 ed., Paris, 1922, pp. 443 ff.; Migeon, op. cit., p. 266.

For other approximately contemporary pictorial defences of the Transubstantiation see Phyllis Ackerman, "Notes on the Doctrine of Transubstantiation as Illustrated in XVI Century Art," in *Bulletin of the Needle and Bobbin Club*, Vol. XII, No. 2, New York, 1928, pp. 15 ff.

PAGE 72. The Virgin being fitted with wings is illustrated in color, but very inadequately, in Tormo Monzo y Sanchez Canton, op. cit., Lám. XXII; the detail of the angel marking the foreheads in Lám. XXIII, and the detail of the Wedding of the Lamb in Lám. XXIV.

CHAPTER V

PAGE 76. The tapestries of the fourteenth and fifteenth centuries, and even some of the beginning of the sixteenth century which continue the earlier styles, are commonly called Gothic. This is really a misuse of the term. To begin with, the word itself is a philological bastard, for by the sixth or seventh century at latest the Goths had either been wiped out by subsequent invaders or had been completely merged with other populations. In the eighteenth century, however, their name was revived to designate anything barbarian. To the excessively refined, somewhat effeminate taste of that period, nourished on dilute imitations of classical models, the art of the thirteenth and fourteenth centuries seemed uncouth, especially the dark grey churches with their high pointed arches, crowded carvings and sharp pinnacles bristling with monsters, so remote from the neat white pediments and pillars that were then in fashion. This architecture was, therefore, derisively named Gothic and the name survived, the original connotation forgotten, even when a less prejudiced judgment had restored the great Cathedrals to their proper high honor.

Meanwhile the name had been extended to any works of art that showed the pointed arch or any flavor of the decorative style that developed with that type of construction. So it was applied to these tapestries, which reflect that general character even though many of them were produced well within the period that is usually called the Renaissance.

PAGE 77. Not, of course, that tournaments became popular only when opportunities for real fighting were diminishing. It would seem, indeed, that the more men fight the more they want to fight, for at the most disturbed period of the Middle Ages tourneys and jousts were a passion, in spite of the constant efforts of the Church to discourage them. See, for example, G. G. Coulton, *Life in the Middle Ages,* Vol. I, Cambridge, 1928, Item 39, " The Sin of Tournaments," p. 68.

In the fourteenth century tourneys sometimes attracted also bands of ladies of questionable status who, however deplorable socially, were nevertheless an asset to the pageantry, for they displayed themselves decked with effective fantasy. See Henry Knighton's Chronicle (1348) quoted in G. G. Coulton, *Life in the Middle Ages,* Vol. II, Cambridge, 1929, Item No. 40, " Tourney and Masquerade," p. 93 f. For a summary account of the place of Tournaments in the life of this time see Otto Cartellieri, *The Court of Burgundy,* London, 1929, Chapter VII, Jousts and Tourneys, pp. 119 ff.; or Georges Doutrepont, *La Littérature Française à la Cour des Ducs de Bourgogne,* Paris, 1909, pp. 106 ff.

PAGE 78. But Lalaing's Lady of Tears had a double reference, doubtless, to Marie de Clèves, the lady of his heart, who affected lachrymose emblems, notably a *chantepleur.* Jacquet has been made the subject of a set of tapestries. Cf. Phyllis Ackerman, *Catalogue of Tapestries in the Collection of Frank Gair Macomber,* privately printed, (Boston, 1928) , and D. J. Baird Wood, " The Hamilton Rice Tapestry," in *Art in America,* Vol. VIII, New York, 1919–20, pp. 302 ff. and ill. op. p. 47 in color.

The Caesar is described in most complete detail in A. Weese, *Die Casar-Teppiche,* Bern, 1911.

It is discussed in: Van Drival, *Les Tapisseries d'Arras,* Arras, 1864, p. 114 f.; Wauters, op. cit., XVième année, pp. 400 ff.; Pinchart, op. cit., p. 31; Guiffrey, *Tapisserie,* p. 51, ill. Figs. 24, 25; Hunter, *Practical Book,* pp. 89 ff., ill. Pl. V j; Göbel, op. cit., I. Teil, Bd. I, S. 68, 272 f.; Kurth, op. cit., Abb. 33, 34; Migeon, op. cit., pp. 226 ff., ill. p. 227; Thomson, op. cit., p. 101.

The Clovis series is published in M. Sartor, *Les Tapisseries, Toiles Peintes et Broderies de Reims,* Reims, 1912, pp. 58 ff., ill. p. 60, Fig. 9; p. 63, Fig. 10. For brief discussions see Guiffrey, *Histoire Générale,* p. 51 f.; Pinchart, op. cit., ill. Pl. II; Hunter, *Tapestry,* ill. Pl. 299; Hunter, *Practical Book,* p. 91 f.; Migeon, op. cit., pp. 232 ff.

PAGE 79. Charlemagne tapestries are discussed in Göbel, op. cit., I. Teil, Bd. I, S. 60. A scene in an early sixteenth century " Marguerite of Austria style " tapestry (cf. Chap. VII) has been identified as a Charlemagne episode, but the description is dubious. See Stella Rubinstein-Bloch, *Catalogue.*

The Troy series is ill. Müntz, *Short History,* p. 147, Fig. 29; and discussed in Guiffrey, *Tapisserie,* p. 34 ff., ill. Figs. 16, 17; Hunter, *Tapestry,* Pl. 59; Schmitz, op. cit., S. 196 ff., ill. Abb. 102, 103; Göbel, op. cit., I. Teil, Bd. I, S. 65 f.; Hunter, *Practical Book,* pp. 73 ff., ill. Pl. V a, b, c, ca, d, e, f, g, h; Amando Gómez Martinez y Bartolomé

Chillón Sampedro, *Los Tapices de la Catedral de Zamora*, Zamora, 1925, pp. 21 ff., 65 ff., ill. Lám. 7–10; Manuel Gómez-Moreno, *Provincia de Zamora*, (*Catálogo Monumental de España*), Madrid, 1927, T. I, pp. 129 ff., ill. T. II, Lám. 132–7; Kendrick, op. cit., pp. 25 ff., No. 11; Migeon, op. cit., pp. 235 ff., ill. p. 235; Thomson, op. cit., pp. 119 ff., p. 152 f., ill. op. p. 120.

PAGE 81. While Banquets are not often illustrated, except incidentally, in the tapestry of this period, the moral and hygienic reaction against banqueting was made the specific theme of a series of the early sixteenth century of which five pieces are in the Musée de Nancy and one in the collection of the Duque de Fernan Nuñez in Madrid. Here are depicted all the diseases and misfortunes of overeating in a complicated and active allegory, Pl. XI. The set is illustrated in Müntz, *Short History*, p. 142, Fig. 27 and discussed in Hunter, *Practical Book*, p. 71, ill. Pl. IV m; Göbel, op. cit., I. Teil, Bd. I, S. 89 f., 253, 280, ill. S. 89; Migeon, op. cit., p. 230 f., and ill. p. 229 with the erroneous caption " Esther et Ahasuère."

Some famous banquets of the time are described in Cartellieri, op. cit., Chap. VIII, Feasts, pp. 135 ff.

PAGE 83. The Saragossa Esther is discussed in Göbel, op. cit., I. Teil, Bd. I, S. 275 f., 409; Hunter, *Practical Book*, pp. 56 ff., ill. Pl. IV n, na.

The nef was used for the utensils, but also sometimes for spices and even, it would seem, wines. For a detailed account, see Léon de Laboide, *Glossaire Français du Moyen Age*, Paris, 1872, pp. 403 ff.

Another important feature of a well set dining table at this period was the table fountain. Representations of them are rare, actual specimens far rarer still, but the inventories give descriptions so detailed as to furnish a very definite idea of these varied and ingenious decorations. Louis I, Duc d'Anjou, had a mallard duck in silver, all enamelled, with a green neck, holding a fish in its beak, seated on a crystal pedestal mounted with silver, the whole within a great basin striped with green enamel and decorated with leaf designs and figures of wild animals. The water went in at the bird's tail and flowed out of the fish's mouth. De Laborde, op. cit., *Inventaire des Bijoux de Louis, Duc d'Anjou, dressé*, p. 19, No. 101.

The *espreuves* or *languiers* were an essential of an important person's table equipment, for any notable was always in danger of treacherous death, and these were tests of possible lurking poisons.

On the general and admirable principle that anything which had to be should be made as decorative as possible, the bits of serpent's tongue, unicorn's horn, bezoars, crapaudines, and other magic substances that served the purpose were mounted in fanciful contrivances, a tree (*Inv. Duc d'Anjou,* p. 50, No. 296; p. 83, No. 515; p. 84 f., No. 520), a castle (*Inv. Duc d'Anjou,* p. 50, No. 297).

The complete table service of a great Court in France at the end of the fourteenth or beginning of the fifteenth century included large deep dishes (*bassins*), platters (*plats* or *platteles*), trenchers (*tranchouers*), plates (*escouelles*), and sauce dishes (*saucières*). The vessels for liquid were very varied: ewers (*aiguières*), jugs (*pots*), quart jugs (*quartes*), pint jugs (*pintes*), pitchers (*cruches*); another wide-mouth type of jug (*brocs*), flasks (*flascons*), carafes (*bouteilles*), large, two-handled wine vases (*estamoies*); another type of large wine vessel called a *juste* and special water pitchers called *ydres,* probably from hydria, which were sometimes very elaborate. For example, a pair owned by Charles V (*Inventaire,* p. 66, No. 346) made of gold had a lion mask in relief in the centre, on either side a wildman holding a lance, and on the foot seven enamelled plaques, all with the royal shield of arms, except one that had a scene. The jugs were occasionally angular instead of round. For example, an interesting six-sided silver-gilt one in the collection of Louis I, Duc d'Anjou (de Laborde, op. cit., p. 13, Item 69), with enamelled decorations consisting of representations of six months of the year on the cover, and on the sides illustrations of various proverbs, with wild animals on the foot.

The flasks were sometimes in hydria form (*Inv. Duc d'Anjou,* p. 56, No. 334).

Some of the ewers were in naturalistic shapes, a fashion probably taken from the Orient, ultimately of Persian origin. Thus the Duc d'Anjou had one in the form of a cock with the neck, the wings, and the head enamelled in yellow, green, and blue while the head and tail were covered with pearls. On his back was a fox that had just seized the comb. The vessel stood on a stand on which were several children playing various games. De Laborde, op. cit., p. 13, No. 79. Another, No. 80, was a lion, while a few years earlier one appears in the royal accounts representing a man seated on a creature with the body of a cock and the head of a bishop holding a crozier. De Laborde, op. cit., p. 503, under "*sujets bizarres.*"

The drinking vessels were similarly varied. Goblets (*goubelets*), cups (*tasses*), another style of goblet (*coupes*), a kind of covered goblet on a high foot said to have been of German origin (*creuse-*

quins) , mugs *(choppines)* , another kind of flaring goblet called a *godet* and the shallow drinking bowls called *hannaps* which were of different forms, simple and low with no foot, on a foot, on a tripod base, with a lip, and covered or uncovered.

Bowls and goblets were elaborated by being set on complex stands. Thus in the collection of Louis d'Anjou there was a small bowl for holding water, of undefined use, on a base so complicated that the bowl itself had become only incidental. The piece consisted of a queen in a cloak enamelled with circlets in blue, green, and red, mounted on a two-footed, winged hybrid beast with the head and torso of a man and the tail of a serpent. The queen held in one hand a whip and in the other the decapitated head of a man wearing a large felt hat, and it was on top of this that the bowl was poised. The whole figure stood on a terrace enamelled with foliage and small animals (de Laborde, op. cit., p. 18, No. 90) . Similarly, a goblet in the same collection rested on top of an oak tree with leaves enamelled green and red, while at the bottom of the tree the trunk was straddled by a seated monkey dressed as a Bishop in a chasuble with blue enamelled orphreys and a mitre, holding a crozier and making a sign of blessing (de Laborde, op. cit., p. 15, No. 77) . Again, a goblet that belonged to Louis was made in the form of a columbine blossom surrounded by its leaves and set in a cluster of mandragore with one rose. The whole cluster was atop a masonry column with a succession of capitals, and gathered about this were three men, one playing the sarterion, the second the guitar, and the third the flute (de Laborde, op. cit., p. 23, No. 119) . The nineteenth century could not have imagined a more eccentrically incongruous composition.

There were also special vessels, notably a class of baskets and jugs *(corbeilles et pots à ausmône)* in which to put the remains of foods for the indigent; sweetmeat dishes *(dragouers)* , *thiphènes,* a kind of dish similar to the *drageoirs* that had originally had some association with Epiphany (see de Laborde, op. cit., p. 515) , little barrels or casks of various sizes to hold liqueurs and sauces, and sauce jugs (the *corbeilles à ausmône* are probably the origin of the modern silver bread basket; cf. de Laborde, op. cit., p. 225) . The cutlery consisted, in addition to the sets of carving knives, of smaller knives for eating, larger and smaller spoons, and larger and smaller forks, for though it is generally asserted that the people of this period ate with their fingers and their knives, the upper classes in France, at least, did have forks. The cutlery often came in sets which frequently included a tooth pick and sometimes an ear cleaner! For

[360]

particular purposes, or perhaps only for novelty, there were special kinds of spoons, with very short handles, or with a folding handle (Berri, Inv., p. 174, No. 66), with a spout, presumably to facilitate serving sauces (Berri, Inv., p. 297, No. 2807), or pierced, though the latter may have been a cooking implement.

The service, moreover, could be expanded with numerous elegant additions. Thus there were special platters for fruit, covered dishes designed expressly for serving eggs, Charles V had a gold plaque on which to put quince paste (Inv., p. 78, No. 477), while the Duke de Berri had a graceful implement that might well be revived, a crystal spear mounted with gold and set with pearls for eating strawberries (Inv., p. 167, No. 627).

The flat dishes were made usually of silver, silver-gilt, or gold, often with enamelled ornaments, and sometimes even jewelled, but both hard woods and earthenware were used also, for humbler persons or simpler occasions. A special luxury was a set of plates of enamelled glass from Damascus (Berri, Inv., p. 234, No. 2123).

The range of material for the hollow ware was exceedingly wide, for in addition to the metals, crystal, glass, and various stones also were used. The glass was evidently usually plain, but it was sometimes colored, notably red (Charles V, Inv., p. 223, No. 1974) or blue (Berri, Inv., p. 245, No. 2246), or tinted and veined to imitate agate (Berri, Inv., p. 215, No. 828). One goblet and ewer belonging to Charles V are specifically described as white Flemish glass (Inv., p. 228, No. 2043). Two flasks belonging to Louis d'Anjou were made of Damascus glass enamelled in blue with various, unfortunately unspecified, patterns, and set in elaborate silver mountings, and the Duc de Berri had a very small hannap of Damascus glass (Guiffrey, op. cit., p. 245, No. 2245).

A wide range of fancy stones was used, notably alabaster, serpentine stone, jasper of many colors, red, black, gray, or greenish, agate, porphyry and chalcedony.

The drinking vessels were commonly made of the metals, or crystal or glass, except for the hannaps, which were most often of hard wood called *madre,* although occasionally lignum is specified. One type of madre is described as white (Berri, Inv., p. 245, No. 2256). For a detailed discussion of madre see de Laborde, op. cit., p. 371. The fine ones were mounted with the precious metals. Occasionally goblets were made of ivory, and eccentric cups or goblets might be made of ostrich eggs or coconuts mounted in metal, a type that remained popular down into the seventeenth century, many of the later ones being extant.

[361]

There were earthenware jugs too, nor were these necessarily modest vessels, for faience of fine quality from the East found its way
to rich houses even at this date. Thus Charles V had two jugs, one
small, the other with a spout, of faience (terre) *en la façon de
Damas* (Inv., p. 241, No. 2202, p. 245, No. 2244). Whether or not
true porcelain from the East was also known in Europe as early
as this is a vexed question. Certainly many of the objects described
as *pourcellaine* were not porcelain. The generally accepted explanation is that they were mother of pearl, but on the other hand,
some other objects in this material sound more like real porcelain,
for example, two platters, four plates, and four sauce dishes belonging to Charles V (Inv., p. 247, No. 2276, and cf. p. cxxi f.). The term
is discussed at great length by de Laborde, op. cit., p. 465, but he
perhaps does not consider sufficiently the possibility of true porcelain at an earlier date.

The cutlery was naturally of metal, but crystal, ivory, ebony, or
the fancy stones were often used for handles, perhaps mounted with
gold or silver and sometimes jewelled or enamelled, or with the
owner's name inscribed. Rarely a spoon bowl might be made of
a stone, for instance, one in the possession of the Duc de Berri made
of serpentine stone with a crystal handle mounted with gold (Inv.,
p. 174, No. 660). A concrete record of the magnificence of the Duc
de Berri's table is beautifully preserved in the miniature at the top
of January in the Calendar in his Great Book of Hours in the
Musée de Chantilly.

PAGE 84. See Jules Guiffrey, "Un Bal de Sauvages: Tapisserie du
XVe Siècle," in *Revue de l'Art Ancien et Moderne*, T. IV, Paris,
1898, pp. 75 ff.; Migeon, op. cit., p. 320 and ill. p. 321, where it is
erroneously classed as French; Planès, op. cit. Pl. 21.

PAGE 85. The Hardwick Hall Hunts are discussed in Guiffrey, *Ta-
pisserie*, p. 37, ill. Fig. 18; Hunter, *Tapestry*, pp. 56 ff., ill. Pl. 57;
Schmitz, op. cit., S. 184, ill. Abt. 94, 95; Göbel, op. cit., I. Teil,
Bd. I, S. 84 f.; 270; Kurth, op. cit., Abb. 16–19; Hunter, *Practical
Book*, p. 101 f.; Thomson, op. cit., pp. 154 ff.; ill. (in color) op.
pp. 154 and 156.

PAGE 86. For complete illustrations of the Hunt of the Unicorn
series, see Phyllis Ackerman, "The Hunt of the Unicorn," in *International Studio*, Vol. LXXVI, New York, 1923, pp. 292 ff. It is also
discussed in Guiffrey, *Tapisserie*, p. 98, ill. Fig. 56; Hunter, *Practical

Book, pp. 95 ff., ill. Pl. VI, b-e; *Bulletin of the Metropolitan Museum of Art,* Vol. XXIII, New York, 1928, pp. 151–153; Migeon, op. cit., p. 326, where it is erroneously classed as French, and ill. p. 325; Thomson, op. cit., p. 126, ill. op. p. 124.

For a brief account of the history of the greyhound cf. Edward C. Ash, *Dogs: Their History and Development,* London, 1927, Vol. I, pp. 163 ff.

A popular superstition of the Middle Ages, current in varying forms in different places, was centred on the worship of a greyhound as a saint, with witchcraft rites. See Etienne de Bourbon (c. 1195–1261), *Preacher's Manual (Anecdotes Historiques, etc. d' Etienne de Bourbon,* ed. by A. Lecoy de la Marche, Paris, 1877). Quoted in Coulton, op. cit., Vol. I, Cambridge, 1928, pp. 92 ff.

Among the names that Jean, Duc de Berri, gave his numerous dogs were Prince, Lion, Chapelain. Guiffrey, *Inventaire,* p. CXXVI.

PAGE 88. The Nine Heroes, also called the Nine Worthies, first appear in literature in Les Voeux du Paon by Jacques de Longuyon in the fourteenth century. The heroines were first introduced by Eustache Deschamps. See J. Huizinga, *The Waning of the Middle Ages,* London, 1924, p. 60 f.

For a further discussion see Guiffrey, *Tapisserie,* pp. 31 ff., ill. Figs. 14, 15; Hunter, *Tapestry,* pp. 297 ff.; Göbel, op. cit., I. Teil, Bd. I, S. 67, ill. Bd. II, Abb. 82–84; Hunter, *Practical Book,* pp. 18 ff.; H. C. Marillier, "The Nine Worthies" in the *Burlington Magazine,* Vol. LXI, London, 1932, pp. 13 ff.

PAGE 89. The Mackay Arthur is ill. in colors in Phyllis Ackerman, "Tapestries of Five Centuries, I, The French Gothic Looms," in *International Studio,* Vol. LXXVI, New York, 1922, p. 48, ill. p. 41, and is discussed in Hunter, *Practical Book,* pp. 17 ff., ill. Pl. III a and b; and ill. in Göbel, op. cit., II. Teil, Bd. II, Abb. 14.

The Doria Alexander is discussed in Schmitz, op. cit., S. 190, ill. Abb. 98; Göbel, op. cit., I. Teil, Bd. I, S. 65, 67, 269 f.; Kurth, op. cit., Abb. 30–32; Hunter, *Practical Book,* pp. 83 ff., ill. Pl. V k, ka; Migeon, op. cit., p. 222 f., ill. p. 223.

For the relation of the Doria Alexander to two drawings in the British Museum, see A. E. Popham, "Two Fifteenth-Century Drawings for Tapestry in the British Museum," in the *Burlington Magazine,* Vol. XLV, London, 1924, pp. 60 ff., and letter, George Leland Hunter, p. 206, and reply, p. 250.

PAGE 90. Saints were often selected and associated with cities by miraculous episodes. Thus Eleuthère's connection with Tournay was revealed in a divine vision according to Heriman, Chronicle of Tournay, recounting a twelfth-century story, quoted in Coulton, op. cit., Vol. II, Cambridge, 1929, Item No. 10, " History by Revelation," pp. 14 ff.

The Tournay Piat and Eleuthère set is discussed in Van Drival, op. cit., p. 90 f.; Pinchart, op. cit., p. 17 f., ill. Pl. I; Müntz, *Short History*, p. 145 f.; Guiffrey, *Tapisserie*, p. 26, ill. Fig. 12; Schmitz, op. cit., S. 178 f., ill. Abb. 93; Göbel, op. cit., I. Teil, Bd. I, S. 234, 240; Kurth, op. cit., Abb. 9–11; Hunter, *Practical Book*, p. 25, ill. Pl. III e; Migeon, op. cit., pp. 210 ff., ill. p. 211.

PAGE 91. The Beauvais Saint Peter set is discussed in Guiffrey, *Histoire Générale*, pp. 42 ff.; ill. Müntz, *Short History*, p. 144, Fig. 28; Guiffrey, *Tapisserie*, 67 f., ill. Fig. 35; ill. Hunter, *Tapestry*, Pl. 363; Schmitz, op. cit., S. 196 ff., ill. Abb. 97; Kurth, op cit., Abb. 24; DeMotte, op. cit., Pl. 25; Marthe Crick Kuntziger, " A Fragment of Guillaume de Hellande's Tapestries," in the *Burlington Magazine*, Vol. XLV, London, 1924, pp. 225 ff.; Hunter, *Practical Book*, pp. 64 ff.; Migeon, op. cit., p. 241, ill. pp. 239, 241; Planès, op. cit., Pl. 23, 24; Thomson, op. cit., p. 124 f.; the piece from the set now in the possession of Mrs. William H. Crocker has been published by Crick-Kuntziger, loc. cit., and one of the scenes in the possession of Mr. Mallon is illustrated in the *Bulletin of the Metropolitan Museum of Art*, Vol. XXIII, New York, 1928, p. 149.

For a brief account of the Court of Love conception see Huizinga, op. cit., Ch. VIII, pp. 95 ff., and Ch. IX, pp. 107 ff.; or Cartellieri, op. cit., pp. 105 ff.

The antecedent of these "Court of Love" tapestries appears as early as the twelfth century in mural painting. " Beyond this was the lady's bed chamber, painted all over with shapes and colours most wonderful to behold. On one wall might be seen Dame Venus, the goddess of Love, sweetly flushed as when she walked the water, lovely as life, teaching men how they should bear them in loyal service to this lady. On another wall, the goddess threw Ovid's book within a fire of coals. A scroll issuing from her lips proclaimed that those who read therein, and strove to ease them of their pains, would find from her neither service nor favour." " The Lay of Gugemar," in Eugene Mason, *French Mediaeval Romances, From the Lays of Marie de France*, London, 1924, p. 8.

For an account of the highly organised " Court of Love " established by the Duke of Burgundy see Doutupont, op. cit., pp. 366 ff. The insistence on the purely romantic and symbolic character of the gallant relation in the Court of Love might well have been a reaction from the actual fact and from the kind of literature which exploited that fact, such as the *Quinze Joyes de Mariage* and the *Cent Nouvelles Nouvelles*. For good summary accounts of these, see Werner Söderhjelm, *La Nouvelle Française au XVe Siècle*, Paris, 1910, pp. 29 ff. and 111 ff.

For a discussion of the tapestries devoted to various phases of this chivalric devotion, see Göbel, op. cit., I. Teil, Bd. I, S. 77 ff.

PAGE 92. For a discussion of the Heroines see Göbel, op. cit., I. Teil, Bd. I, S. 67; Hunter, *Practical Book*, p. 104 f.

For the Angers Penthesilea, see Guiffrey, *Tapisserie*, p. 90, ill. Fig. 50; DeMotte, op. cit., Pl. 126.

For a set devoted to Lucretia see Stella Rubinstein, " Three Tapestries Representing the Story of Lucretia in the Felix Warburg Collection " in *Art in America*, Vol. XII, New York, 1924, pp. 291 ff., where they are erroneously attributed, somewhat tentatively, to the Valley of the Loire.

The Gobelin's Annunciation is discussed in Joseph Destrée, *Tapisserie et Sculptures Bruxelloises*, Brussels, 1906, p. 15 f., No. I, ill. Pl. I; Migeon, op. cit., p. 251, ill. p. 25; Planès, op. cit., Pl. 16.

PAGE 93. For the Bayeux life of the Virgin see Phyllis Ackerman, " The Reappearance of a Lost Bayeux Tapestry " in *International Studio*, Vol. XCVI, New York, 1930, pp. 17 ff. See also, Hunter, *Tapestry*, p. 70, ill. Pl. 71.

For a discussion of the Lady and the Unicorn series, see Guiffrey, *Histoire Générale*, p. 58 f.; Guiffrey, *Tapisserie*, p. 97 f., ill. Pl. IV; Hunter, *Tapestries*, pp. 48 ff., ill. Pl. 39; Schmitz, S. 276, Abb. 139; DeMotte, op. cit., Pls. 164–168 inc.; Hunter, *Practical Book*, pp. 98 ff.; Göbel, op. cit., II. Teil, Bd. II, Abb. 310, where it is erroneously attributed to Touraine; Migeon, op. cit., pp. 322 ff. and ill. p. 323, where it is erroneously attributed to France; Thomson, op. cit., p. 125, ill. op. p. 124.

In 1502 Pierre van Aelst sold a large set of six pieces, with gold thread, called the " Devotion de Notre Dame," clearly a set definitely different from the usual histories of The Life of the Virgin, or the Five Joys of the Virgin, Göbel, op. cit., I. Teil, Bd. I, S. 303.

The set was originally supposed to have come from the tent of
Zizem, brother of Bajazet and hostage of the Knights of Rhodes,
who was imprisoned by the Commander at his Château de Bour-
ganeuf. Cf. "Le Moyen Age et la Renaissance au Trocadéro" in
Gazette des Beaux Arts, 2ième période, T. XVIII, partie 2, Paris,
1878, pp. 969 ff., La Tapisserie, pp. 1005 ff. Darcel doubts the story.
The arms were at that time identified as belonging to the family of
Maillans d'Anglefort. George Sand admired the set and spoke sar-
castically of the attempts to interpret it. Quoted Guiffrey, *Histoire
Générale,* loc. cit. The arms were subsequently ascribed to the La
Viste family and for a long time the Lady was supposed to be an
unmarried daughter of this household.

The most recent interpretation is that the set represents the "Five
Senses," the sixth piece of the set being left unexplained. This was
propounded by A. K. Kendrick, "Quelques Remarques sur les Tapisseries de la Dame à la Licorne au Musée de Cluny" in *Actes du
Congrès d'Histoire de l'Art,* T. III, Paris, 1924, p. 662. It is repeated by Hunter, *Practical Book,* loc. cit.; J. J. Marquet de Vasselot,
Les Tapisseries dites La Dame à la Licorne, Paris, 1927; and Thomson, loc. cit. No such theme is known at the time and the theory
completely disregards the established symbolism of the unicorn. The
possible interpretation of a tribute to the Chastity of a Le Viste
lady is suggested by DeMotte, op. cit., p. 9, but the Five Senses
interpretation is really accepted.

For a summary of the romantic and chivalric symbolism associated with the Virgin see Émile Mâle, *L'Art Religieux de la Fin
du Moyen Age en France,* 2nd ed. Paris, 1922, pp. 205 ff. A more detailed account of certain aspects of this symbolism is the subject of
M. Vloberg, *La Madone aux Roses,* Paris, 1930.

PAGE 94. The Beaune Life of the Virgin is discussed in Guiffrey,
Tapisserie, p. 83 f., ill. Pl. III; Hunter, *Tapestry,* p. 68 f., ill. Pl. 69;
Kurth, op. cit., Abb. 60–63; Göbel, op. cit., II. Teil, Bd. II, Abb.
324, 325, where it is erroneously attributed to Touraine; Migeon,
op. cit., pp. 335 ff. where it is erroneously classed as French, though
with an ambiguous qualification; ill. pp. 334, 335.

A number of intimate scenes of the domestic life of the Holy
Family during Jesus' early childhood were current at this time,
known usually as the Joys of the Holy Family. See Mâle, op. cit.,
p. 153 f.

PAGE 95. For the Cluny Arithmetic, see Guiffrey, *Tapisserie,* p. 76, ill. Fig. 41.

PAGE 96. For names and mottoes of Guilds of Rhetoric cf. de Vigne, op. cit. For information on another aspect of the Chambers of Rhetoric see Doutrepont, op. cit., pp. 350 ff.

PAGE 97. For the Mather Procession see Hunter, *Practical Book,* p. 105 f.; Göbel, op. cit., II. Teil, Bd. I, S. 317, ill. Bd. II, Abb. 339 where it is erroneously but tentatively attributed to Touraine.

For an excellent study of the pessimism of this period and some of the devices of escape see Huizinga, op. cit., Ch. II, Pessimism and the Ideal of the Sublime Life, pp. 22 ff. One of the most character-istic poets of this pessimism was Jean Meschinot whose verses inevi-tably revert to the theme of death. See Pierre Champion, *Histoire Poétique du Quinzième Siècle,* Paris, 1923, T. II, p. 189 ff.

PAGE 98. For a discussion of tapestries of peasant life see Göbel, op. cit., I. Teil, Bd. I, S. 80 ff., 131 f., 281 ff.

This interest in the East was manifested at the Banquet of the Vow of the Pheasant given by Duke Philip the Good in 1454 in one of the *entremets* or table decorations which represented an Indian forest full of wild animals. Doutrepont, op. cit., p. 108.

For the Portuguese in India see Göbel, op. cit., I. Teil, Bd. I, S. 253, 278 ff.; II. Teil, Bd. I, S. 145 ff., ill. Bd. II, Abb. 118–121. One piece of the set is published in Kendrick, op. cit., p. 36, No. 19, erro-neously called "A Triumphal Procession" and classed correctly as Flemish, while another fragment is published p. 50, No. 42, classed as French!

PAGE 99. The Gypsy set is discussed in Göbel, op. cit., I. Teil, Bd. I, S. 259 f., 277 f.; Hunter, *Practical Book,* p. 102 f., ill. Pl. VI m; Planès, op. cit., Pl. 14.

The Lehman Hunt of the Deer is discussed in Göbel, op. cit., I. Teil, Bd. I, S. 131; Hunter, *Practical Book,* p. 71 f. For a discussion of the symbolic deer see A. Picot, "Le Cerf Allégorique dans les Tapisseries et les Miniatures," in *Société Française de Reproduc-tions de Manuscrits à Peintures, Bulletin,* T. III, IV, Paris, 1913–20, pp. 57 ff.;
The translation is the author's. The original verses are:

Gens de brief duree mondaine
Qu'a chasse mortelle et soubdaine

(Estes) comme cerf asservis
Considerez la vie humaine
Et la fin ou elle vous maine
Et les metz dont serez servis
Alors que serez desservis
De Jeunesse et aurez advis
Advisez a tel propoz prendre
Quem quant serez de Mort ravis
Et les vers seront au corps vifz
Que puissions a Dieu l'ame rendre.

A series of brief allegories and topical verses, many of them social or political satires from the point of view of the bourgeoisie, were composed by Maître Henri Baude who was exactly contemporary with Louis XI. No tapestries illustrating his themes are known, but a publication of the early sixteenth century includes a number of drawings that may have been petits patrons. See Champion, op. cit., T. II, pp. 276 ff.

PAGE 100. For a discussion of these Verdures see Göbel, op. cit., I. Teil, Bd. I, S. 97 ff.

Two shades of green were used for the ground of verdures at the end of the fourteenth century, *vert gay,* evidently a light tone, and *vert herbu,* dark grass green. Jules Guiffrey, *Inventaire des Tapisseries de Charles VI,* Paris, 1887, p. 40, Nos. 202 and 203–205. Black grounds were also used in the fourteenth century, at least for *personnage* tapestries, but none of these have survived. Guiffrey, *Inventaire Charles VI,* p. 41, No. 212. The piece cited was of Paris manufacture.

The beauty of flowers and the beauty of rich stuffs were readily associated in the mind of the time. So Michault Taillevant, poet to Duke Philip the Good of Burgundy, writes

A la terre ses couvertures
Et doucement assortissoient
De fleurs et de plaisans verdures
A sembloit velours sur velours.

Quoted in Champion, op. cit., p. 296.

Walter von der Vogelweide (Tc. 1229) has a delightful appreciation of spring flowers quoted in Coulton, op. cit., Vol. III, Item No. 8, "Flowers and Fair Ladies," p. 14 f.

CHAPTER VI

PAGE 102. It has been erroneously assumed, without any evidence, that the cartoons were made by miniature painters, and that miniatures commonly served as models. See, e.g., Göbel, op. cit., I. Teil, Bd. I, S. 230, 269.

It has also been too readily taken for granted that the large cartoons were not made by the artist responsible for the preliminary sketches. The fact that this was often the case later proves nothing for the fifteenth century about which we have no specific information. See, e.g., Göbel, op. cit., I. Teil, Bd. I, S. 231.

PAGE 106. For a discussion of the deciphering of these inscriptions see Phyllis Ackerman, "Recently Identified Designers of Gothic Tapestries" in *The Art Bulletin*, Vol. IX, New York, 1926, pp. 142 ff.; and Ackerman, *Rockefeller-McCormick Catalogue*, Appendix II. The results of the former have been corrected at points, and greatly expanded, by subsequent, largely unpublished research.

For another application of the signature method, see Phyllis Ackerman, "Three Scenes From the History of Perseus" in *Art in America*, Vol. XV, New York, 1927, pp. 117 ff.

The first adequate account of the early Paris shops was given by Guiffrey, "Les Origines de la Tapisserie de Haute et Basse-Lice à Paris" in *Mémoires de la Société de l'Histoire de Paris et de l'Île de France*, T. VIII, Paris, 1882, pp. 107 ff. They are similarly discussed in Guiffrey, *Histoire Générale*, pp. 5 ff. and the facts are brought together in a comprehensive restatement in Göbel, op. cit., II. Teil, Bd. I, pp. 1 ff. All of the standard books covered the subject more or less adequately.

For the references on Bataille see the notes to page 66.

PAGE 107. The Cinquantenaire Presentation is ill. Guiffrey, *Histoire Générale*, Pl. I; and discussed in Müntz, op. cit., p. 96 f., ill. p. 97, Fig. 14; Guiffrey, *Tapisseries*, p. 22, ill. Fig. 11; Hunter, *Tapestries*, p. 36, ill. Pl. 37; Schmitz, op. cit., S. 70, ill. Abb. 29; Kurth, op. cit., Abb. 8; Göbel, op. cit., II. Teil, Bd. I, S. 14, ill. Abb. 15; Migeon, op. cit., p. 205 f., ill. p. 205.

The basic publication on the Tournay shops is Eugène Soil, *Les Tapisseries d'Arras*, Arras, 1864. They are discussed in all the standard publications, notably, Pinchart, *Histoire Générale*, pp. 5 ff.; Göbel, op. cit., I. Teil, Bd. I, S. 219 ff.; Migeon, op. cit., pp. 210 ff.; Thomson, op. cit., pp. 71 ff.

The basic publication on the Tournay shops is Eugène Soil, *Les Tapisseries de Tournai,* Tournay et Lille, 1892. There are also more or less adequate discussions in the standard books, e.g., Pinchart, op. cit., pp. 73 ff.; Göbel, op. cit., I. Teil, Bd. I, S. 247 ff.; Migeon, op. cit., pp. 239 ff.

Tournai tapestries were first identified by M. Morelowski, "Der Schwanenritter-Wandteppich und sein Verhältnis zu den Französischen Teppichen des XV. Jahrh." in *Jahrbuch des Kunsthistorischen Instituts der K. K. Zentralkommission für Denkmalpflege,* Vienna, 1912, S. 118 ff.; and Dr. Betty Kurth, "Die Blütezeit der Bildwirkerkunst zu Tournai," in *Jahrbuch der Kunsthistorischen Sammlungen des Allerhöchsten Kaiserhauses,* Bd. XXXIV, Vienna, 1917, S. 53 ff. Dr. Morelowski only identified as Tournai work the one set under consideration, on a documentary basis, while Dr. Kurth attributed to Tournai a whole group on stylistic grounds, partly supported by more or less specific documentary evidence. Dr. Kurth's conclusions constitute the pioneer work in establishing the school, but, as is usual in new identifications, she made her class too inclusive. Dr. Göbel, op. cit., I. Teil, Bd. I, S. 409, suggests that one group of these pieces should be assigned to Brussels, which is undoubtedly partly correct, but also includes some errors.

PAGE 108. Further information on the Poissoniers is given in Phyllis Ackerman, "The Ferrets and the Poissoniers," in *Art in America,* Vol. XIII, New York, 1925, pp. 266 ff. The account is subject to minor corrections.

The documentary information on the Kiens (or Quiens, Chiens, etc.) is given in A. de la Grange et Louis Cloquet, *Études sur l'Art à Tournai et sur les Anciens Artistes de Cette Ville,* Tournai, 1888, T. II, pp. 69, 70, 71, 72, 77, 78. The identification of their work is made in Ackerman, *Recently Identified Designers,* p. 147 f., but the discussion given there is now subject to various corrections.

The documentary information on the le Bacres is also given in de la Grange et Cloquet, op. cit., *passim,* but the identification of their work has not yet been published.

PAGE 109. Again, the documentary information on the Le Feires is given in de la Grange et Cloquet, op. cit., pp. 69, 71, 72, 78, 79 and

the identification of their work is in Ackerman, *Recently Identified Designers*, p. 151 f., with a corrected account in the *Rockefeller-McCormick Catalogue.*
The research on the Bruges school has not yet been published.

PAGE 110. The identification of the work of Baudouin Bailleul also is not yet published. For a summary of the documentary information on this designer see Thieme-Becker, *Lexikon*, Bd. 2, S. 369.

PAGE 111. The basic reference on the Brussels shops is Alphonse Wauters, " Essai Historique sur les Tapisseries et les Tapissiers de Haute et de Basse-Lice de Bruxelles," in *Bulletin des Commissions Royales d'Art et d'Archéologie*, XVième année, Brussels, 1876, pp. 349 ff.; XVIième année, 1877, pp. 194 ff.; XVIIième année, 1878, pp. 149 ff. The summarized information is also given in all the standard books, e.g., Pinchart, op. cit., pp. 117 ff.; Göbel, op. cit., I. Teil, Bd. I, S. 293 ff.; Migeon, op. cit., pp. 254 ff.

PAGE. 112. The basic publication on Jean van Roome and Philippe is Joseph Destrée, *Maître Philippe*, Brussels, 1904. The subject was developed further, on the basis of the inscription method, by A. Thiéry, *Les Inscriptions et Signatures des Tapisseries du Peintre Bruxellois Jean de Bruxelles, Appelé Aussi Jean de Rome*, Louvain, 1907, wherein the confusion between the two van Roomes, as well as a number of other serious errors, was first perpetrated. The question of Philip's identity is inconclusively discussed in Guiffrey, *Tapisseries*, pp. 110 ff.; Schmitz, op. cit., S. 210 ff. follows in general Destrée.

Some of Thiéry's errors were repeated also in Phyllis Ackerman, "Tapestries of Five Centuries, II. The Flemish Gothic Looms," in *International Studio*, Vol. LXXVI, New York, 1922, pp. 119 ff., p. 121 f.; Göbel, op. cit., I. Teil, Bd. I, S. 410 f. identifies as Maître Philippe Philip van Orley.

For a discussion of Jean van Roome based on Thiéry and also subject to a number of corrections see Göbel, op. cit., I. Teil, Bd. I, S. 274 f., 304, 404 ff. The first attempt to disentangle the two Jean van Roomes is in Ackerman, *Recently Identified Designers*, p. 151. The identification of Maître Philippe is discussed in Ackerman, "The Final Solution of Maître Philippe" in *Apollo*, Vol. XIV, London, 1931, pp. 83–87.

For another application of the inscription method, leading to a further attribution to Jean van Roome, see Stella Rubinstein, "A Flemish Tapestry of the Early Sixteenth Century" in *Art in America,* Vol. VIII, New York, 1919–20, pp. 47 ff.

A valuable contribution to our scanty knowledge of the Brussels designers by an application of the inscription method has been made by Marthe Crick-Kuntziger, *Maître Knoest et les Tapisseries "Signées" des Musées Royaux du Cinquantenaire,* Liège, 1927.

It became fashionable in the early years of this century to attribute a number of the late fifteenth- and early sixteenth-century tapestries, especially the small scale verdures popularly known as *mille fleurs,* to Touraine, though there is no evidence whatever for the fiction. The nineteenth-century writers were quite clear on this point. See Guiffrey, *Histoire Générale,* p. 148, the error dating from the publication of L. Bosseboeuf, *La Manufacture des Tapisseries de Tours,* Tours, 1904. It has become current among many dealers, who have been principally responsible for its dissemination, but it is also stated as fact in a number of publications. Schmitz, op. cit., S. 269 ff.; Göbel, op. cit., II. Teil, Bd. I, S. 260 ff.; Migeon, op. cit., pp. 330 ff.; Thomson, op. cit., pp. 223 ff. For a criticism see Ackerman, Review of Göbel, *Wandteppiche.* Part II: *Die Romanischen Länder* in the *Art Bulletin,* Vol. XI, New York, 1929, p. 5 f.

The error of a French attribution, though the School of the Loire is only tentatively suggested, is also found in Stella Rubinstein, "Two Late French Gothic Tapestries" in *Art in America,* Vol. V, New York, 1917, pp. 27 ff., and the error of the French attribution concerning these two tapestries and also two other fragments in a crude version of the "Marguerite of Austria" style is again repeated in Stella Rubinstein *Bloch Catalogue,* Pls. III, IV, V.

A similarly erroneous French, though not specifically Loire or Touraine, attribution of a number of tapestries is found in DeMotte, op. cit., T. I., p. 4 f.; pp. 6 ff.

PAGE 116. For the Tournai arquebus shoot see de la Vignes, op. cit., p. 24 f.

CHAPTER VII

PAGE 117. The dealers, seeking a designation for this definite and consistent style, have called it Louis XII. The historians of the art, attempting to define it in the more specific terms of a designer's atelier, have called it, according to their personal bias, School of Jean Van Roome or School of Maître Philippe. The commercial name is somewhat justified at least in date. The historians' names are wholly unacceptable, for they presuppose that all of the hundreds of existent cartoons in this style, and the many hundreds more of vanished examples thereby implied, were the output of one man and his immediate followers, an impossible accomplishment.

That many of these tapestries were designed within the reign of Louis XII (1498–1515) is undeniable. Yet the designation in terms of Louis XII is quite irrelevant, in view of the fact that the tapestries are not at all French but entirely Flemish; and it is unfortunate, since they do not express in the least the quality of that frivolous and ostentatious king, but are wholly typical of the character of the Teutonic woman who governed the country where they were conceived and made. This is the style, not of the spendthrift Louis XII, snatching at the superficies of the Italian Renaissance to enhance his trivial luxuries, but of the substantial, sensible Marguerite of Austria, practical ruler of a competent, money-making bourgeoisie.

For the rape of Danaë see Göbel, op. cit., I. Teil, Bd. II, Abb. 109.

PAGE 118. Industry flourished in Flanders when France was still half barbarous, and by the eleventh century there was so much commerce that regular fairs were established with privileges and accommodations for foreign merchants, and free markets antedate even that. Thus Bruges and Courtrai both had a free market in 958, and by the thirteenth century, Flemish international trade was of prime importance. De Vigne, op. cit., pp. 37 ff.

PAGE 120. The standard publication of this set of tapestries is in Valencia, op. cit., but this gives arbitrarily and meaningless titles and presents the set in a haphazard order. The titles and plate numbers, following the order of the exposition, are: (1) Fortuna, Lám. 36; (2) La Fama, Lám. 34; (3) El Honor, Lám. 33; (4) El Fe, Lám. 32; (5) La Nobleza, Lám. 35; (6) La Justitia, Lám. 40; (7) La Prudencia, Lám. 38; (8) El Vicio, Lám. 39; (9) La Infamia, Lám. 37. The series is called Los Honores. The set first appears in the inventory of Charles V, 1544. Valencia, op cit., p. 23 f. considered that the style closely resembles that of Bernard van Orley, but notes that others see a resemblance to the work of Jean Gossart. Both suggestions are, of course, absurd.

It is also attributed to Bernard van Orley, with the further suggestion that he was aided by his brother Gomar, in Tormo Monzo y Sanchez Canton, op. cit., p. XIX. The set is also discussed by Pinchart, op. cit., p. 126; Guiffrey, *Tapisserie*, p. 141 f., ill. Fig. 74; Tormo Monzo y Sanchez Canton, op. cit., pp. 51 ff., ill. Pl. XIX (in color, very poor), and detail, Pl. XX; Göbel, op. cit., I. Teil, Bd. I, S. 117 ff., following another order and with another interpretation, and ill. Bd. II, Abb. 87, 88.

The iconography is discussed, but inconclusively, by Mâle, op. cit., pp. 340 ff., ill. Fig. 193. It is he who suggests that Jean Lemaire was the librettist, p. 342 f.

The discussion of Jean Lemaire's relation to tapestry is given in Göbel, op. cit., I. Teil, Bd. I, S. 100 f. The interpretation here given is the author's own. The translations from the Latin are very free.

Marguerite's period was not the first to esteem good repute sufficiently to extol it in tapestry. Charles VI of France had two items devoted to *Bonne Renommée*, one a series of six panels for the wall and the hangings for a bed of silk and gold, and the other a single piece of wool, of Arras make, that even more immediately recalls this set since on it were shown, among other exemplars, Solomon, Jason and Absalom. Guiffrey, *Inventaire*, p. 37 f., Nos. 172–180 (and cf. p. 333).

PAGE 131. Thus even in the first half of the seventeenth century Leon Mahelot designed a stage set combining a bedroom, a castle, a cave, a sea, a churchyard, a painter's shop, a garden and a mill, all fitted together in an architectural framework with formal perspective. See Karl Mantzius, *A History of Theatrical Art in Ancient and Modern Times*, Vol. II, London, 1903, p. 339 f.

CHAPTER VIII

PAGE 135. Charles was seven generations from their common ancestor, John the Good of France, through the House of Burgundy. François was five generations through the House of Orleans, Henry six generations through the consolation that Catherine of France, daughter of Charles VI, had found for her widowhood after the death of Henry V of England. Catherine of France was married to Henry V of England in 1420 as part of the campaign of Philip the Good, Duke of Burgundy, against the King of France. Philip agreed that by this marriage Henry should become King of France when the mad Charles VI died. After two years of marriage Henry died, leaving Catherine guardian of the infant Henry VI, and a lonely widow. There was, hanging around the court, a Welshman, Owen Tudor, with a quick eye to the main chance, no ancestry to speak of, but a strikingly handsome presence. By 1428 or 1429 Catherine had succumbed. Of the five illegitimate children, Edmund married Margaret Beaufort, also the issue of illegitimacy with one strain of mediocre origin, and they produced Henry Tudor who as Henry VII got the throne when the reigning house ended in confusion and murder.

PAGE 138. For the inventory of Henry VIII see Thomson, op. cit., pp. 245 ff.

PAGE 139. The Tunis set was actually woven to the order of his sister Marie of Hungary, but Vermeyen was taken with the expedition by Charles as official painter. It is completely illustrated in Valencia, op. cit., Lám. 56–65. It is also discussed in Müntz, *Short History*, p. 207 f.; Guiffrey, *Tapisserie*, ill. Pl. XII; Tormo Monzo y Sanchez Canton, pp. 95 ff., ill. Pl. XXXIV (in color, but poor); Ludwig Baldass, *Die Wiener Gobelinssammlung*, Vienna, 1920, Taf. 81–90; Göbel, op. cit., I. Teil, Bd. I, S. 144 f., 312 f., ill. Bd. II, Abb. 351; Thomson, op. cit., p. 203 f.

PAGE 142. The attribution of the Vertumnus and Pomona to Vermeyen was made by Marthe Crick-Kuntziger, "Tapisserie de L'Histoire de Vertumne et Pomone" in *Bulletin des Musées Royaux d'Art et d'Histoire*, 3ième série, No. 4, Brussels, 1929, pp. 74 ff. The set is also discussed in Müntz, *Short History*, pp. 198 ff., ill. p. 203, Fig. 46; Valencia, op. cit., Lám. 69–74; Guiffrey, *Tapisserie*, p. 139 f., ill. Pl. IX; Schmitz, op. cit., S. 234 f., ill. Abb. 121; Tormo Monzo y Sanchez Canton, pp. 89 ff., ill. Pl. XXXII; Baldass, op. cit., Taf. 146–154; Göbel, op. cit., I. Teil, Bd. I, S. 138 f., 333 f., ill. Bd. II, Abb. 103, 104, 105; Migeon, op. cit., p. 286 f., ill. p. 287; Thomson, op. cit., p. 204 f.

The Months is ill. Guiffrey, *Histoire Générale*, Pl. 33; and discussed in Müntz, *Short History*, p. 210, ill. p. 209, Fig. 47; Maurice Fenaille, *État Général des Tapisseries de la Manufacture des Gobelins Depuis Son Origine Jusqu'à Nos Jours*, T. II, Paris, 1903, pp. 337ff.; Hunter, *Tapestry*, Pl. 391; Hunter, *Practical Book*, p. 129 f., ill. Pl. XXII b; Göbel, op. cit., II. Teil, Bd. I, S. 143 ff., ill. Bd. II, Abb. 115–117.

Hunter, loc. cit., accepts the attribution to Lucas van Leyden and suggests that the set was made for Charles V shortly after his marriage in 1525, basing the hypothesis on a putative identification of the portrait medallions in the upper corners of the borders of the set belonging to Mrs. E. H. Harriman, as Charles V and his wife. Göbel, op. cit., I. Teil, Bd. I, S. 416 ascribes the cartoons to the Van Orley School, and Thomson, op. cit., p. 201, repeats this attribution. According to Pinchart, op. cit., p. 122, the set has also been attributed to Coeck and Floris. He states, but without evidence, that it was probably made originally for Ferdinand of Portugal. Wauters, *Bernard van Orley,* p. 92, cites an attribution then current to Bernard van Orley, but doubts that and suggests rather a pupil.

PAGE 143. The series of months imitating those of Vermeyen are illustrated in Baldass, op. cit., without titles and in the following pied order: Taf. 110, 117, 111, 113, 112, 114, 115, 116, 109; and one is ill. in Göbel, op. cit., I. Teil, Bd. II, Abb. 468a.

Two David tapestries have also been attributed, quite plausibly, to Vermeyen in Jos. Destrée, " Épisodes de la Jeunesse de David, Tapisseries Bruxelloises de la Première Moitié du XVIe Siècle " in *Mélanger Hulin de Loo,* pp. 128 ff.

Göbel, op. cit., I. Teil, Bd. I, S. 419 f. cites (without reference), but doubts, the attribution to him of the Creation of Man set and the João de Castro series. Göbel is undoubtedly correct in not accepting these attributions.

PAGE 144. Other lesser painters who made cartoons for the Fontainebleau looms were Lucas Romano, Charles Carewy, Francesco Cacciannuci of Bologna, Jean Baptiste Bagnacavallo and Bartolomeo Miniato of Florence.

An account of the Fontainebleau looms is given in Guiffrey, *Histoire Générale,* pp. 73 ff.; Müntz, *Short History,* pp. 230 ff.; Maurice Fenaille, *État Général des Tapisseries de la Manufacture des Gobelins,* T. I, Paris, 1923, pp. 89 ff., with illustrations; Guiffrey, *Tapisserie,* pp. 197 ff., ill. Pl. XIV, XV, and Fig. 96; Baldass, op. cit., Taf. 155–160; Göbel, op. cit., II. Teil, Bd. I, S. 37 ff., ill. Abb. 21–27; Hunter, *Practical Book,* p. 138; Migeon, op. cit., pp. 351 ff.

PAGE 146. Diana killing Orion is illustrated in *Tapisseries de la Renaissance, Catalogue des Pièces Exposées au Musée de la Manufacture Nationale des Gobelins,* Paris, 1929, op. p. 12. The verses on five pieces of the set are also given here, pp. 11 ff.; and the grotesque with the Death of Joab is ill. op. p. 14.

The Triumph of Diana is published in Phyllis Ackerman, *Catalogue of the Retrospective Loan Exhibition of European Tapestries*, San Francisco, 1922, p. 42 f., No. 37, ill. op. p. 46, and in Ackerman, " Tapestries of Five Centuries, III, The Transition to the Renaissance," in *International Studio*, Vol. LXXVI, New York, 1922, pp. 257 ff., p. 262.

A series of eight pieces known as the Hunts of François purport to illustrate episodes from his life. The existing examples are all of seventeenth-century weave but the personages wear costumes of the period of François I, indicating that the cartoons were of earlier date. The cartoons, however, show no quality whatever of the Fontainebleau school, but were evidently designed by a Fleming in close association with Bernard van Orley, for there are stylistic relations with the Hunts of Marie of Hungary, though his compositions show no such careful planning as Bernard's. See Fenaille, op. cit., T. I, pp. 241 ff.

PAGE 147. An interesting adverse criticism of this Fontainebleau School is given in Clive Bell, *An Account of French Painting*, London, 1931, Chap. II, pp. 43 ff.

CHAPTER IX

PAGE 149. The set is published and illustrated in full in Gaston Migeon, *Les Tapisseries des Chasses de Maximilien*, Paris, 1920; and discussed in detail in Wauters, *Bernard van Orley*, pp. 76 ff.

Van Mander's account is to be found in Karel van Mander, *Le Livre des Peintres*, translated by Hymans, T. I, Paris, 1884, p. 28; cited by Migeon, op. cit., p. 5. Van Mander wrote in 1604.

The attribution of the landscape to Tons is made by A. Felibien, *Entretiens sur les Vies et Ouvrages des Plus Excellents Peintres*, Paris, 1666, T. I, 2 partie, p. 349, cited Migeon, op. cit., p. 6.

The Hunts take place in the Forest of Soigne. It has been pointed out that they must have been designed between 1527 and 1538 because in the month of March the Chapel of Saints Philip and John is shown roofed with straw. The chapel was thatched in 1527 and the vault construction was begun in 1538. See Paul Saintenay, "Les Tapisseries de la Cour de Bruxelles Sous Charles V" in *Annales de la Société Royale d'Archéologie de Bruxelles*, T. XXX, Brussels, 1921, p. 25.

PAGE 150. The suggestion that these Hunts were made for Marie of Hungary was first made by Wauters, op. cit., p. 23 f.

The set is also discussed in Pinchart, op. cit., p. 121 f.; Müntz, *Short History*, pp. 204 ff., with an amusing adverse criticism, in essence quite fallacious; Fenaille, op. cit., T. II, pp. 299 ff.; Destrée, op. cit., p. 39 f., No. XVIII, ill. (in color, poor) Pl. XXI; Guiffrey, *Tapisserie*, p. 148 ff., ill. Figs. 77, 78, Pl. XIII; Stella Rubinstein, "A Tapestry from a Cartoon by Bernard van Orley," in *Art in America*, Vol. IV, New York, 1915–16, pp. 258 ff.; Schmitz, op. cit., S. 222 f., ill. Abb. 116; Göbel, op. cit., I. Teil, Bd. I, S. 102, 168, 316 f., 414 ff., ill. Bd. II, Abb. 70, 71, 276; Hunter, *Practical Book*, p. 129, ill. Pl. VIII d, da; Göbel, op. cit., II. Teil, Bd. I, S. 141 f., ill. Bd. II, Abb. 111; Migeon, op. cit., pp. 288 ff., ill. p. 289; Thomson, op. cit., p. 205.

For a summary of Bernard van Orley's biography see Alfred von Wurzbach, *Niederländisches Künstler-Lexikon*, Bd. II, Vienna and Leipzig, 1910, pp. 259 ff. The most careful consideration of van Orley as a tapestry designer is in Max J. Friedländer, "Bernaert van Orley, IV, Orley's Tätigkeit von 1526 bis 1540" in *Jahrbuch der König. Preuss. Kunstsamlg.*, Bd. XXX, Berlin, 1909, S. 155 ff., S. 163 ff., where the following tapestries or sets of tapestry are attributed to him, the list indicating roughly the chronological succession:

1. Lamentation over the body of Christ formerly in the collection of the Duke of Alba (ill. Friedländer, op. cit., p. 164, Abb. 47), with another weaving in the collection of Mr. Joseph Widener (Phyllis Ackerman, "Bernard van Orley as Tapestry Designer," in *Art in America*, Vol. XIII, New York, 1925, pp. 38 ff., where the writer mistakenly accepts Dr. Friedländer's attribution, and only partially corrects his other attributions);

2. The Last Supper in the Spanish State Collection (Valencia, op. cit., Lám. 66; Tormo Monzo y Sanchez Canton, pp. 43 ff., ill. Pl. XXI, and ill. Friedländer, op. cit., p. 165, Abb. 48), with another weaving in the Philip Lehman Collection, New York. Tormo Monzo y Sanchez Canton, op. cit., p. 55, repeat the van Orley attribution;

3. The God the Father from the so-called Dais of Charles V in the

Spanish State Collection (Valencia, op. cit., Lám. 25; also ill. Göbel, op. cit., I. Teil, Bd. II, Abb. 269) ;

4. The Christ in the Garden and the Carrying of the Cross in the Spanish State Collection (Valencia, op. cit., Lám. 28, 29; Tormo Monzo y Sanchez Canton, op. cit., pp. 31 ff., ill. Pl. XI) ;

5. The Adoration of the Magi in the Metropolitan Museum of Art (ill. Göbel, op. cit., I. Teil, Bd. II, Abb. 133), which is somewhat tentatively attributed;

6. The Sacrifice at Lystra in the Kronburg Collection, a little less tentatively attributed;

7. The Judgement of Trajan in a private collection (ill. Friedländer, op. cit., S. 167, Abb. 49; Destrée, *Tapisseries*, p. 43, No. XXIII, ill. Pl. XXVI; Göbel, op. cit., I. Teil, Bd. II, Abb. 377) ;

8. The series of the Foundation of Rome in the Spanish State Collection (Valencia, op. cit., Lám. 41–46; Tormo Monzo y Sanchez Canton, op. cit., pp. 47 ff., Pl. XVIII), in which van Orley's co-operation is said to be at least probable. Tormo Monzo y Sanchez Canton, loc. cit., repeat the attribution to van Orley;

9. The Battle of Pavia in the Museo Nazionale at Naples;

This last set of seven pieces was made for the Netherlands States General to present to Charles V, when he went to Brussels to convene the assembly in 1531. The set is discussed in detail by Mario Morelli, "Gli Arazzi Illustranti la Battaglia di Pavia Conservati nel Museo Nazionale di Napoli" in *Atti della Reale Accademia di Archeologia, Lettere e Belle Arti*, Vol. XXI, Parte Seconda, Naples, 1901, pp. 5 ff., and it is also discussed briefly in Wauters, *Van Orley*, pp. 70 ff.; Hunter, *Tapestry*, pp. 307 ff., ill. Pl. 309; Göbel, op. cit., I. Teil, Bd. II, Abb. 375, 376; Migeon, op. cit., p. 292;

10. The so-called Hunts of Maximilian;

11. The History of Abraham (Wauters, *Bernard van Orley*, p. 92, where the attribution was first made, though Dr. Friedländer does not refer to him; Valencia, op. cit., Lám. 75–81; Schmitz, op. cit., p. 228 f., ill. Abb. 118; Tormo Monzo y Sanchez Canton, op. cit., p. 101 f., ill. Lám. XXXV; Baldass, op. cit., Taf. 21–30; Hunter, *Practical Book*, p. 133, where it is attributed to Giulio Romano, ill. Pl. VIII; Thomson, op. cit., p. 202 f.) , presumed to have been a product of his later years;

12. A history of Jacob in a private collection in Schleswig.

13. The Triumph of David, formerly in the Ffoulke Collection and then in the possession of William C. Van Antwerp of San Francisco. (Destrée, op. cit., p. 41 f., No. XXI, ill. Pl. XXIV; Ackerman,

Catalogue of Loan Exhibition, San Francisco, p. 37, No. 21, ill. op. p. 38);

  14. A set of six Triumphs in the Berlin Schloss; and

  15. December, formerly in the Ffoulke Collection (Destrée *Tapisseries,* p. 41, No. XX, ill. Pl. XXIII).

Three of the sets referred to are not well known, the Sacrifice at Systra, the Jacob, and the Triumphs.* Of the remaining twelve, the attribution of four stands unchallenged, the " Hunts of Maximilian," of course; the Battle of Pavia set, which is equally unmistakable; the Metropolitan Adoration, and the Ffoulke December, of which the style seems clearly to be Bernard's. But none of the other series cited by Friedländer can on examination be accepted as Bernard's work. One, the Triumph of David, shows close relation to Pieter Coeck's work and is quite probably to be assigned to him, (cf. p. 159). Two others, the God the Father and the Abraham, are attributable to the other pupil Coxcie.

Two others, evidently by the same hand, the Trajan and the Foundation of Rome series, show a relation to Coeck but cannot actually be his work. Their character suggests that they were probably designed by some other pupil. A Peter Goes, for example, registered as apprentice with Bernard in 1517. This same artist must be accredited with a set of the Months, the known pieces of which are: January with Janus's banquet, Pan disporting himself outside, with the goddesses Juno and Iris in the upper corners, the Winds, Kucys and Eolus in the lower; February with the household gathered before the fire, the Winds, Boreas and Eolus, in the upper corners, and below on one side shepherds, and on the other a lady in a sleigh, both in a snowstorm; July with the Hay Harvest under the patronage of Humana Concine, with Pleuresis and Pestilence in the upper corners, Febre and Quinancie in the lower, all women armed for battle; August with the grain harvest under the patronage of Ceres, with Legessa and Circulina, and below peasants sacking the grain; September with the men trampling out the grapes in a great vat under the patronage of Bacchus, with Semele and Jupiter above, and below a pair of lovers; October with the peasants sowing under the patronage of Jupiter, with two winds in the upper corners, and below one peasant fishing and others picking apples. January and February are in the Palazzo Doria in Rome, ill. Göbel, op. cit., I. Teil, Bd. II, Abb. 444, 445. July was formerly in the possession of Jacques Seligman; Destrée, op. cit., p. 40 f., No. XIX, ill. Pl. XXII;

* At least not to the writer.

Göbel, op. cit., I. Teil, Bd. II, Abb. 446. August and October are in the Metropolitan Museum of Art, the latter ill. Göbel, op. cit., Abb. 447; and September is in the collection of Mr. William Randolph Hearst, ill. Laurvik, *Catalogue of the Mrs. Phoebe A. Hearst Loan Collection,* San Francisco, 1917, No. 403, plate op. p. 39.

The other three items in the list, the Alba Lamentation, the Madrid-Lehman Last Supper which had already been attributed to van Orley by Valencia (op. cit., T. I, p. 55) though Friedländer does not note this, and the Madrid Garden of Gethsemane and Carrying of the Cross, must also all be by one man, someone who, though in the same general school, is not as closely related as are the others. There is also another piece in the Spanish State Collection, the Pentecost (Valencia, op. cit., Lám. 67; Tormo Monzo y Sanchez Canton, op. cit., p. 63, ill. Pl. XXV, where they suggest that the cartoon was the work of a collaborator of Bernard van Orley), which must be attributed to this man. It may, moreover, prove possible to identify him, for on the Lehman tapestry, on the edge of Jesus' gown is inscribed IOAN/MEI/IM. Except perhaps for the IM, these cannot be fitted into any of the Latin inscriptions usually so employed, but seem quite clearly to indicate a Jean Mei. . . . On the tiles of the Pentecost are the letters MЯ. This could mean Maria Regina. Twining through the majescules, however, is a vague scroll which falls into the letters J–ye, which would make the total inscription J. Myer. While this might be accident, they seem too clear to be the result of chance, and the scroll pattern on the other tiles is quite different, much better drawn ornament. The semi-concealment of a name in such a way is, too, quite consonant with the fad of the time. (cf. Chap. VI). Such a "signature" would permit no conclusion if it stood alone, but in conjunction with the clear and careful lettering on the Lehman piece, it suggests very strongly that the designer was a Jean Meir or Meer. A painter of that name was Deacon of the Antwerp Guild in 1505. In any case the designer of this group of tapestries, when freed from the erroneous assimulation to van Orley, proves to be an interesting personality and should be studied further.

Tormo Monzo y Sanchez Canton, op. cit., p. XIX and p. 27, also attribute to van Orley the so-called Honores, i.e. the Morality (see Chapter VII), the Apocalypse (cf. p. 69), in which Valencia, op. cit., Vol. II, p. 65, sees van Orley's influence, and a series illustrating the Life of St. John the Baptist; but these suggestions do not require a serious refutation.

NOTES

PAGE 153. The Notre Dame du Sablon set is published in *La Collection Spitzer*, T. I, Paris, 1890, Nos. 10–16, pp. 165 ff. The last piece is illustrated in color, Pl. VII. There are additional illustrations in the volume of plates from the *Catalogue de Vente*, the second piece, Pl. IX; the fourth, Pl. XI; the seventh, Pl. IX.

Marthe Crick-Kuntziger, "Les Tapisseries de la Légende de Notre-dame du Sablon" in *Bulletin des Musées Royaux d'Art et d'Histoire*, 3ième série, 2ième année, Brussels, 1930, pp. 2 ff., p. 12, attributes the set to Bernard van Orley, an attribution previously made in Hunter, *Practical Book*, p. 127, and in Migeon, op. cit., p. 264, though Madame Crick-Kuntziger does not refer to them.

The first panel of the series is divided into four sections that have been dispersed. The upper left and entire right sections are in the Kaiser Friedrich Museum in Berlin, the lower left is in a Paris-New York Commercial collection. (Ill. Planès, op. cit., Pl. 51), while the centre is in the possession of Lord Astor in London. The second panel is intact in the Hermitage (formerly Stieglitz) Museum in Leningrad; the third is likewise partitioned, the left section being in the Brussels Hôtel de Ville, the remainder in the possession of Lord Astor, while the fourth piece is in the Cinquantenaire Museum.

Madame Crick-Kuntziger has accused the Berlin fragments and the piece in the commercial collection of being modern copies, but this has been conclusively refuted by Theodor Demmlei, "Die Zwei Teppiche der Sablon Legende im Deutschen Museum" in *Berliner Museen*, Jahrg. XLIX, Berlin, 1928, pp. 28 ff. Dr. Demmlei seems to accept the attribution to Bernard van Orley. The set has also been discussed by Müntz, *Short History*, p. 188, ill. p. 187, Fig. 39; Destrée, op. cit., pp. 36 ff., No. XVII, ill. Pl. XX; Hunter, *Tapestry*, pp. 77 ff., ill. Pl. 79; Schmitz, op. cit., S. 216 f., ill. Abb. 112; Migeon, op. cit., p. 263 f.

The procession of Notre Dame du Sablon came to eclipse entirely the two old processions of Brussels, that of Saint Michael and that of Saint John. It took place the Sunday before Pentecost and as this was the day of the annual kermesse it was an exceedingly brilliant affair. At two o'clock a play depicting one of the Seven Joys of the Virgin, in succession, was produced in the Grande Place. See G. Des Marez, *L'Organisation du Travail à Bruxelles au XVe Siècle*, Brussels, 1904, p. 433 f.

PAGE 155. The Somzée Adoration is ill. Göbel, I. Teil, Bd. II, Abb. 134.

The Cinquantenaire Anne and the Virgin was in *La Collection Spitzer*, No. 400, ill. Pl. X.

PAGE 156. Vasari's account of the Raphael cartoons reads: "The Pope also desired to have certain very rich tapestries in silk and gold prepared, whereupon Raphael made ready the cartoons, which he coloured also with his own hand, giving them the exact form and size required for the tapestries. These were then dispatched to Flanders to be woven, and when the cloths were finished they were sent to Rome (in 1519). This work was so admirably executed that it awakened astonishment in all who beheld it as it still continues to do; for the spectator finds it difficult to conceive how it has been found possible to have produced such hair and beards by weaving, or to have given so much softness to the flesh by means of thread, a work which certainly seems rather to have been performed by miracle than by the art of man, seeing that we have here animals, buildings, water, and innumerable objects of various kinds, all so well done that they do not look like mere texture woven on the loom, but like paintings executed with the pencil." Giorgio Vasari, *Lives of Seventy of the Most Eminent Painters, Sculptors, and Architects,* Edited and Annotated by E. H. and E. W. Blashfield and A. A. Hopkins, London, 1899, Vol. III, pp. 206 ff.

Marc-Antonio Michiel says of them in a letter dated Dec. 27, 1519: "After Christmas the Pope exhibited seven tapestries in his chapel, woven in the West. They are considered the finest work of the kind ever executed, notwithstanding the fame of other tapestries, those in the antechamber of Pope Julius III, those of the Duke of Mantua after Mantegna's cartoons, and those of King Alphonse or Frederick of Naples. The designs were made by Raphael d'Urbino, an excellent painter who was paid by the Pope 100 ducats apiece. They are rich in silk and gold. The weaving cost 1500 ducats apiece, or including everything as the Pope himself said, 'They have cost 1600 ducats each, though word has gone around that they cost 2000 ducats apiece.'" Quoted by Eugène Müntz, *Les Tapisseries de Raphael au Vatican et dans les Principaux Musées ou Collections de l'Europe,* Paris, 1897, p. 5.

Paris de Grassis, master of ceremonies for Leo X, wrote in his journal: "The whole chapter is amazed by these most beautiful and splendid things which, it is generally agreed, are the finest in the world." Quoted in Edouard Gerspach, "Les Actes des Apôtres d'après Raphael" in *Revue de l'Art Chrétien,* 11ième Année, 5e Série, T. XII, Paris, 1901, p. 110.

Some extravagant praise has been lavished on the cartoons in modern times, also. Thus Anton Springer has compared them to the Parthenon reliefs in that, as those represent the supreme achievement of Phidias and his School, so the cartoons were the culmination of the work of Raphael and his school, marking thus the apogee of the Italian Renaissance. Quoted by Hermann Dollmayer, *Raffaels Werkstätte,* reprinted from *Jahrbuch der Kunsthistorischen Sammlungen des Allerhöchsten Kaiserhauses,* Bd. XVI, Vienna, 1895, p. 23. Dollmayer himself, however, deplores this excessive praise, pointing out that after all, they are only school productions, marked with the deficiencies inevitable in co-operative work.

The set consists of:

1. The Miraculous Draft of Fishes
2. The Vocation of Saint Peter
3. The Cure of the Paralytic
4. The Death of Ananias
5. The Lapidation of Saint Stephen
6. The Conversion of Saint Paul
7. Elymas Struck Blind
8. The Sacrifice at Lystra
9. Saint Paul at Areopagus
10. The Imprisonment of Saint Paul

The six sets of cartoons are:

1. The original series, seven of which are in the Victoria and Albert Museum. This was woven seven times between 1516 and 1584 by Van Aelst. Examples are the first Vatican set, and series in Saragossa, Madrid, Berlin, Vienna, Paris, and the Gonzaga Palace, Mantua (formerly Schoenbrunn, returned by treaty, 1921). Between 1625 and 1708 it was woven twelve times in the Mortlake factory.

2. Cartoons of Jean Raes, Brussels, 1620. There were only nine pieces in this set and it was woven seven times. The cartoons are lost.

3. Gobelins cartoons, 1662, painter unknown. Also only nine pieces.

4. Italian cartoons, 1662, painter unknown. Also only nine pieces. Woven twice.

5. Académie Française de Rome cartoons, 1666–1694. Ten pieces.

Now at Gobelins. Woven eleven times at the Gobelins and twice at Beauvais.

6. Daniel Leyniers cartoons, Brussels, 1648–1673. Seven pieces. Cf. Kumsch, *Die Apostel-Geschichte,* Dresden, 1914, p. V.

At the beginning of this century a series of cartoons known as the Loukmanoff cartoons appeared on the market, and the claim was made, with some pretence of evidence, that these, and not the Victoria and Albert set, were the originals, but the claim was not sustained. See *The Raphael Cartoons for the Vatican Tapestries,* New York (*American Art Association*) s.d. (1901) ; and Vera Campbell, " The Loukmanoff Cartoons " in the *Art Journal,* London, 1903, pp. 103 ff. For an account of the set formerly in the Schoenbrunn Palace and now at Mantua, cf. John Rusconi, " The Tapestries of Mantua by Raphael " in *Connoisseur,* Vol. LIX, London, 1921, pp. 77 ff.

The series has been discussed repeatedly but the most complete and systematic account is given by Kumsch, op. cit. An earlier but very adequate treatment is in Eugène Müntz, *Les Tapisseries de Raphael, etc.,* as cited. A useful discussion with a just appraisal of their deficiencies and also of other tapestries attributed to Raphael or his pupils is given by Eugène Müntz, *Raphael, His Life, Works, and Times,* London, 1882, Chap. XIV, pp. 455 ff. Other accounts are given by Van Drival, op. cit., pp. 153 ff.; Müntz, *Histoire Générale,* pp. 19 ff., p. 87, ill. 2ième partie, Pl. 4, 5, 6; Pinchart, op. cit., p. 119 f.; Müntz, *Short History,* pp. 188 ff., ill. p. 191, Fig. 40, and p. 297, Fig. 79; Fenaille, op. cit., T. II, p. 43 ff; Valencia, op. cit., Lám. 47–55; Guiffrey, *Tapisseries,* pp. 129 ff., ill. Fig. 71, 72; Hunter, *Tapestries,* pp. 81 ff., ill. Pl. 83, 85, 89, 91, 93; Schmitz, op. cit., S. 220 f., ill. Abb. 113; Tormo Monzo y Sanchez Canton, op. cit., pp. 35 ff., ill. Pl. XII, XIII, XIV; Göbel, op. cit., I. Teil, Bd. I, S. 413; Kendrick, op. cit., p. 47, No. 41, ill. Pl. XXII; Hunter, *Practical Book,* pp. 130 ff., ill. Pl. VIII f, fa; Göbel, op. cit., II. Teil, Bd. II, Abb. 31; Migeon, op. cit., pp. 282 ff., ill. p. 283; Thomson, op. cit., pp. 192 ff., ill. op. pp. 192, 194.

According to Dollmayer the cartoons are to be attributed to Penni, either wholly or possibly with some collaboration of Giulio Romano. He is definitely opposed to the opinion that Giovanni da Udine contributed some of the details, notably the landscape. Dollmayer, op. cit., pp. 23 ff.

Tomaso Vincitore di Bologna (c. 1536) is connected with the Apostle series in some accounts, because he was sent to Flanders by Leo X in 1520 in connection with some tapestry business. See e.g. Campbell, op. cit., p. 106, who makes him the author of the Victoria and Albert cartoons, a view never seriously considered, and Colonel d'Astier, *La Belle Tapisserye du Roy et les Tentures de Scipion l'Africain*, Paris, 1907, p. 8, who suggests that Vincitore might have colored the cartoons and supervised the weaving.

Large sepia drawings after seven of the Raphael cartoons, made 1640–46, by John and Francis Clein, sons of Francis Clein (c. 1590–1658), Director of the Mortlake Works, are in possession of Wadham College, Oxford, and exhibited in the Ashmolean Museum.

But more genuinely apt both to Leo's temperament and tendencies and to the mannerisms of the Raphael school was the series of twenty panels with playing boys which Giovanni da Udine designed for the Pope a few years later. The wrestling, tumbling, disporting erotes, with their soft and gleaming flesh, the lustrous plumage of varied birds, the palpitant softness of furry animals and the succulent abundance of swags of fruit were all appealing to the taste of the patron and the virtuosity of the executant. See Ernst Diez, " Ein Karton der Guiochi di Putti für Leo X " in *Jahrbuch der Königlichen Preussischen Kunstsammlungen*, Bd. 31, Berlin, 1910, S. 30 ff.

PAGE 159. Hans Vriedeman de Vries published a half-dozen volumes of drawings of architectural elements and ornament between 1555 and 1577, with different styles of cartouches, columns, caryatids, grotesques, etc., all ready-made. These had a great vogue.

For a summary of the biography of Coeck see Thieme-Becker, *Kunstlerlexikon*, Bd. VII, S. 161 ff. The Paul series is attributed to Coeck by Max J. Friedländer, " Pieter Coecke van Alost " in *Jahrbuch der König. Preuss. Kunstsamlg.*, Bd. XXXVIII, Berlin, 1917, S. 73 ff., S. 88 ff., where he relates to Coeck also the Seven Deadly Sins of the Spanish State Collection (Valencia, op. cit., Lám. 97–106; Tormo Monzo y Sanchez Canton, op. cit., pp. 65 ff.; Baldass, op. cit., Taf. 39–45; and a Joshua series in Vienna, Baldass, op. cit., Taf. 31–38) .

The set is also discussed in Hunter, *Tapestries*, ill. Pl. 393; Tormo Monzo y Sanchez Canton, pp. 75 ff., Pl. XXVIII; Baldass, op. cit., Taf. 17–20; Göbel, op. cit., I. Teil, Bd. I, S. 418 f. A large cartoon for the decapitation of Paul is published in Destrée, op. cit., p. 44 f., No. XXIV, ill. Pl. XXVII, and a seventeenth-century weaving of it in Destrée, op. cit., p. 45, No. XXV, ill. Pl. XXVIII.

For Coeck as a book illustrator, see A. J. J. Delen, " Illustrations de Livres par Pierre Coeck d'Alost " in *Mélanges Hulin de Loo,* pp. 105 ff.

PAGE 160. The Scipio set is discussed at length in d'Astier, op. cit. See also, e.g., Valencia, op. cit., Lám. 90–96; Göbel, op. cit., I. Teil, Bd. II, Abb. 346.

For a summary biography of Coxie see Thieme-Becker, *Kunstlerlexikon,* Bd. VIII, S. 23 f. The only adequate account of the Wavel series is in Marjan Morelowski, "Arasy Waweleskie Zygmunta Augusta ich warto si i zu aczenie iv dziejach sztuki XVI wieku " in *Sztuki Piekne,* 15 Kwietna, Warsaw, 1925, pp. 293 ff. A summary of the information is given by Marthe Crick-Kuntziger, "Les 156 Tapisseries Bruxelloises du Château Royal de Cracovie et Leur Importance pour l'Histoire de l'Art Flamand au XVIe Siècle " in *La Revue d'Art,* T. 27, Antwerp, 1926, pp. 65 ff. A brief account is also given by Paul Ettinger, "Flemish Tapestries from the State Treasury of Poland," in *Burlington Magazine,* Vol. XLIII, London, 1923, p. 92 f. The attribution to Coxie had already been made by Tormo Monzo y Sanchez Canton, op. cit., p. 127. The Creation of Adam is illustrated, Lám. XLII. It is also discussed in Pinchart, op. cit., Pl. 19; Tormo Monzo y Sanchez Canton, op. cit., p. 127 f.; Guiffrey, *Tapisserie,* Fig. 91; Hunter, *Tapestries,* Pl. 19; Göbel, op. cit., I. Teil, Bd. II, Abb. 396; Luigi Serra, "Intorna ad una Serie di Arazzi Fiamminghi," in *Mélanges Hulin de Loo,* pp. 306 ff.

The Creation from this series is illustrated in Shepard, op. cit., Frontispiece.

A full sized cartoon showing Noah directing the animals into the ark appeared on the market in 1929–30 and was published by Marjan Morelowski, *Nieznany karton do arasow serij "Potopu" a Coxyen i Tons,* Krakow, 1930, who attributed it to Coxie and Tons; and by M. Crick-Kuntziger (reviewing the former) in *Bulletin des Musées Royaux d'Art et d'Histoire,* 3ième série, 2ième Année, Brussels, 1930, pp. 167, who justly questions the attribution to Coxie, suggesting his son or some other member of his school, and identifies a weaving of it in the Austrian State Collection.

PAGE 161. The Carrying of the Cross is illustrated by Göbel, op. cit., I. Teil, Bd. II, Abb. 388.

Göbel, I. Teil, Bd. I, S. 419 f., suggests the attribution to Coxie of the Spanish State History of Venus.

PAGE 162. For an account of the "acanthus thistle" verdures see Phyllis Ackerman, *Rockefeller-McCormick Catalogue.*

The thistle motive for verdures had also been used much earlier though no example of the early type is known. Thus Charles VI had a floor carpet, probably tapestry though this is not explicitly stated, with children and thistles on a blue ground. Guiffrey, *Inventaire,* p. 42, No. 230.

For a discussion of tapestries representing gardens, see Göbel, op. cit., I. Teil, Bd. I, S. 179 ff.

For the most complete account of the Gombaut and Macé series see Jules Guiffrey, *Les Amours de Gombaut et de Macée,* Paris, 1882. The set is also discussed in Guiffrey, *Histoire Générale,* pp. 98 ff., ill. p. 100; Müntz, *Short History,* p. 172; Fenaille, op. cit., T. I, p. 11, pp. 219 ff.; Guiffrey, *Tapisserie,* p. 194 f., ill. Fig. 93; Göbel, op. cit., I. Teil, Bd. I, S. 202 f., ill. Bd. II, Abb. 74; II. Teil, Bd. II, Abb. 43, 44; *Tapisseries de la Renaissance, Catalogue des Pièces Exposées au Musée des Gobelins,* op. p. 8.

There is a set of peasant scenes without verses but closely related to the Gombaut and Macé in the Austrian State Collection, ill. Baldass, op. cit., Taf. 69–76.

The translation is the author's. The original verses are:

Voyla comment en fin ira
Le Plaisir soudain finira
L'homme devient malade et vieux
Mais s'il peut parvenir aux cieux
Apres la mort il suffira

Vous ne Gaignez rien a fuyr
En fauldra-il en fin venir
Et passer par dessouz mes mains
A ce sont sujectz tous humains
Esperans aux cieux parvenir.

Cited Guiffrey, *Histoire Générale,* p. 101.

PAGE 163. For a discussion of the scenes from the lives of the Saints and the allegorical figures in the borders of the Acts of the Apostles see E. Gerspach, "Les Bordures des Actes des Apôtres" in *Atti del Congresso Internazionale di Scienze Storiche,* 1903, Vol. VII, Rome, 1905, pp. 315 ff.

The borders with scenes from the Life of the Apostle Paul and

the History of Leo X are attributed to Baldassare Peruzzi; Dollmayer, op. cit., p. 36.

Minerva's tapestry in the description of Ovid had an olive leaf
border, Arachne's flowers and ivy. Hunter, *Practical Book*, p. 15;
Thomson, op. cit., p. 15 f.

The statement (Göbel, op. cit., I. Teil, Bd. I, S. 438) that the
fourteenth- and fifteenth-century tapestries had no borders is an
error. Some fifteenth-century sets at least had borders; e.g., The
Saint Mark's Passion. See Phyllis Ackerman, "Antichi Arazzi Gotici
a San Marco in Venezia," in *Dedalo*, Anno VI, Milan-Rome, 1925–26,
pp. 441 ff.

The inventory of Charles VI of France (Jules Guiffrey, *Inventaire des Tapisseries de Charles VI*, Paris, 1889) gives two descriptions of early fifteenth-century borders. Thus a round blue tapestry
(p. 21, No. 37) had a design of fleur-de-lis and a border of knots.
A small dosseret or cover for a bench back with a scene from the
History of King Clovis (p. 28, No. 139) had a border of fleur-de-lis.

PAGE 164. The Bear Hunt with the allegorical border was in *Vente
de Madame Émile Gaillard*, Hôtel Druot, Paris, May, 1916, No. 191,
Pl. VII.

The practice of using decorative inscriptions to record authorship had not, however, wholly disappeared. Thus on a set illustrating the History of Cyrus, four pieces of which are in the possession of Bacri Frères of Paris and one in the possession of Mr. and
Mrs. John Franklin Forbes of San Francisco, there are four pseudo-
Naskh inscriptions on sword sheaths and garments that give,
in varying forms, the name Master, abbreviated as M or in one
place as MATR, I Tielt or Thielt. It seems very probable that
this refers to Jan van Tielt who became Master in the Antwerp
Guild in 1509 (Ph. Rombouts et Th. Van Lerius, *De Liggeren en
andere Historische Archieven der Antwerpsche Sint Lucasgilde*,
Antwerp, 1872, T. I, p. 71), but must have been Master before that
elsewhere since the year before he had already registered two apprentices, Hennen and Neelken van Walen. (Rombouts and van
Lerius, op. cit., pp. 69, 70). In 1516 he took another, unnamed apprentice. (Rombouts and van Lerius, op. cit., p. 87). The tapestries
show a combination of the standard Roman style with purely Flemish figures in costumes of about 1530–1540. Presumably Tielt had
come from Brussels, as a number of painters, including the
van Orleys, moved from the one city to the other at about this

time, most of them apparently Protestants fleeing religious persecution.

For a characterization of Antwerp painting see Louis de Fourcaud, "La Peinture dans les Pays-Bas Depuis les Successeurs des Van Eyck et de R. van der Weyden Jusque dans la Seconde Moitié du XVIe Siècle" in André Michel, *Histoire de l'Art*, T. V., Première Partie, Paris, 1912, p. 282.

PAGE 165. For a summary of the sixteenth-century Brussels weavers see Göbel, op. cit., I. Teil, Bd. I, S. 306 ff., or Thomson, op. cit., pp. 374 ff.

CHAPTER X

PAGE 166. The Pope matched this display by sending to Queen Claude Raphael's Holy Family, and to the King, Saint Michael Destroying the Dragon, delicate compliments, for Claude had just given birth to her second child and Saint Michael was the patron of François's royal order. Both of these pictures are now in the Louvre.

PAGE 167. The Medici power in Florence was being sustained by the Pope, Clement VII (Giulio de Medici). Hence when he was imprisoned by the Imperial troops, Florence found it easy to revolt (May 19, 1527).

PAGE 169. Catherine de' Medici carried her mourning even into the decoration of her own apartments. Her bed was of ebony trimmed with jet and silver with black velvet curtains embroidered with pearls. The rest of the furniture was of ebony with ivory inlays and the candelabra were jet. E. Bonnafé, *Inventaire des Meubles de Catherine de Medicis en 1589*, Paris, 1874, pp. 115, 121 ff.

To be sure Catherine de' Medici had many other tapestries, but the Artemisia set was the only one specifically invented for her. For a list of her tapestry collection, 129 pieces in all, see Bonnafé, op. cit., pp. 56 ff., 160.

The Artemisia series is discussed in Guiffrey, *Histoire Générale*, pp. 92 ff., ill. Pls. 10–13; Müntz, *Short History*, p. 172, ill. p. 233, Fig. 61; Fenaille, op. cit., T. I, pp. 7 ff., 109 ff., with complete illustrations; Guiffrey, *Tapisserie*, pp. 204 ff., ill. Figs. 97, 98; Göbel, op. cit., I. Teil, Bd. I, S. 186 ff.; II. Teil, Bd. I, S. 60 ff., ill. Bd. II, Abb. 32–38.

PAGE 172. The original of the epitaph on the tomb of Louis de Brézé is:

> Hic Lodice tibi Posuit Brezaee sepulchrum
> Pictoris amisso maesta Diana Viro
> Indivulsa tibi Quondam et fidissima conjux
> Ut fuit in Thalamo sic erit in tumulo.

Cited Helen W. Henderson, *Dianne de Poytiers,* London, 1928, p. 88.

PAGE 174. The relation of his poetry to the life of Charles d'Orléans has been succinctly formulated by M. Champion: "As for many prisoners, poetry became his habitual pastime.

> De balader j'ai beau loisir,
> Autres deduiz me sont cassez.

Charles amused himself like a child with the play of his thoughts, which were subtle and pretty. He gave them body and form beyond the requirements of the fashion of his time." Champion, *Histoire Poétique du Quinzième Siècle,* T. I, p. 20 f. In short, he, like all the rest of his family, was in search of amusement and he took to writing verses because it was the only amusement that was, under the circumstances, available.

PAGE 176. Henri may have been following the example of his mother, also. For while Catherine as Dauphine was suffering neglect and scorn, she had one recourse, one talent and opportunity that she exploited to the uttermost. Her few years in the Medici palaces, with one fête after another, had taught her to be a successful hostess, to play graciously her part in lavish festivities. This fitted in with her father-in-law's taste precisely, and thus she became an entertainer and woman of pleasure so that in later years, when she found herself in desperate difficulties of state, she would try to take refuge from her plight in a gorgeous party. After the murder of the Duc de Guise, when France was being torn asunder and soaked in blood by the civil war between Catholics and Protestants (1564), Catherine took the whole court on a tour around France, giving in every town the most exciting and handsome balls that she could devise.

A description of the Fêtes is given by Capefigue, *Les Héroines de la Ligue et les Mignons de Henri III,* Paris, 1864, p. 59.

The Fêtes of Henri III are ill. Pinchart, op. cit., Pl. 20, 21; and discussed in Guiffrey, *Tapisseries,* p. 154 f., ill. Fig. 80; Hunter, *Tapestry,* Pl. 355; Schmitz, op. cit., S. 242, ill. Abb. 124.

PAGE 179. The original of the Song of the Pavane is:

> Belle qui tiens ma vie
> Captive sous tes yeulx
> Qui m'a l'âme ravie
> D'un soubriz gracieux
> Viens tôst me secourir
> Ou me fauldra mourir.
>
> Pourquoi suis-tu mignarde,
> Si ie près de toy;
> Quand tes yeux ie regarde
> Ie me perds, dedans moy,
> Car tes perfections
> Changent mes actions.
>
> Tes beautés et ta grâce
> Et tes divins propos
> One eschauffé la glace
> Qui me gelait les os,
> Et ont rempli mon coeur
> D'une amoureuse ardeur.
>
> Mon âme voulait estre
> Libre de passions
> Mais amour s'est fait maistre
> De mes affections
> Et a mis soubs sa loy
> Et mon coeur et ma foy.
>
> Approche donc, ma belle,
> Approche-toi, mon bien.
> Ne me sois plus rebelle
> Puisque mon coeur est tien
> Pour mon âme apaiser
> Donne moi un baiser.

[392]

Je meurs, mon angelette,
Je meurs en te baisant.
Ta bouche tant doucette
Va, mon bien ravissant.
A ce coup mes espritz
Son tous d'amour espritz.

Plutôt on verra l'onde
Contre mont reculer
Et plutôt l'oeil du monde
Cessera de bruler
Que l'amour qui m'époinct
Décroisse d'un seul poinct.

Quoted, Desrat, *Traité de la Danse,* Paris, 1892 (?) p. 31 f., following Jean Tabourot, Canon of Langres who under the pseudonym Thoinot-Arbeau wrote the *Orchésographie,* the first serious treatise on the history of the dance published in France, which appeared during the reign of Henri III.

Henri III was more seriously and hence less veraciously presented in a series of twenty-seven panels known as the History of Henri III which the Duc d'Epernon had woven in the opening years of the seventeenth century in his Château de Cadillac near Bordeaux. Cf. "La Tapisserie de la Bataille de Jarnac" in *La Revue de l'Art Ancien et Moderne,* T. XLI, Paris, 1922, pp. 166 ff. including illustration.

CHAPTER XI

PAGE 182. For a discussion of Rubens's system see Louis Hourticq, *Rubens,* New York, 1918, p. 10 f.

PAGE 187. The Life of Decius Mus consists of:

1. Decius recounts his dream
2. He consults the auguries
3. Decius vows himself to the gods of the underworld
4. He sends the victors back
5. He and Manlius struggle against the Latins
6. Decius and Rome before the altar of Minerva

7. The battle of Veseris and the death of Decius
8. The funeral of Decius
9. The triumph of Rome
10. An entrefenêtre panel of trophies

Paintings of 1, 2, 3, 4, 7, 8, 9, 10 are in the Lichtenstein Gallery of Vienna. Cf. Max Rooses, *L'Oeuvre de P. P. Rubens,* T. III, Antwerp, 1890, pp. 195 ff.

For illustrations of the Decius Mus see Böttiger, op. cit., T. III, Pl. XVII, XXVIII, XXIX.

The Constantine set consists of:

1. The Marriage of Constantine
2. The appearance of the monogram of Christ to Constantine
3. The Labarum
4. The Battle of Constantine and Maximus
5. The Defeat and Death of the Tyrant Maximus
6. The Triumph of Constantine
7. The City of Rome Recovering her Authority
8. The Trophy erected to Constantine
9. Constantine Shares the power with his son Crispin
10. The Foundation of Constantinople
11. Constantine Honoring the True Cross
12. The Baptism of Constantine

The Gobelins' weaving of the Constantine set is discussed in Fenaille, Gobelins, T. I, pp. 245 ff.

PAGE 188. The Doctrines of the Eucharist set consists of:

1. The triumph of the Eucharist over idolatry
2. The triumph of the Eucharist over philosophy and science
3. The triumph of the Eucharist over ignorance
4. The triumph of the Eucharist over heresy
5. Divine love triumphant in the dogma of the Eucharist
6. The meeting of Abraham and Melchisedech
7. The gathering of the manna
8. The sacrifice of the old law
9. The prophet Elias in the desert
10. The four evangelists
11. The fathers of the Church and defenders of the dogma of the Eucharist
12. The dogma of the Eucharist confirmed by the Pope

13. The princes of the House of Austria
14. Angels glorifying the Eucharist
15. Another chorus of angels praising the Eucharist

Cf. Rooses, op. cit., T. I, pp. 53 ff.
Triumphs in tapestry are discussed in Göbel, op. cit., I. Teil, Bd. I, S. 103 ff.; ill. Abb. 72, 73, 75–81. The earliest set of Triumph tapestries known is that in the Austrian State Collection. See Baldass, op. cit., Taf. 1–6. Four early sixteenth-century Triumphs are published in Kendrick, op. cit., pp. 30 ff., Nos. 15–17, ill. Pl. XVI.

The adaptation of the convention of the Triumph to Christian dogma is described in Mâle, op. cit., pp. 279 ff.

The conception of the parallel between the Old and New Testaments is discussed in Mâle, op. cit., pp. 229 ff. For the development of the conception in tapestry see Göbel, op. cit., I. Teil, Bd. I, S. 147 f.

Some of Rubens's Triumph of the Eucharist cartoons were combined with additional cartoons designed in an imitation of his style to make an extensive set for the Church of the Grand Masters of Malta between 1697 and 1701, with a portrait of the donor, the Grand Master Perellos. The set was woven by Judocus de Vos. See Sir Ferdinand V. Inglott, *The Flemish Tapestries of the Church of the Grand Masters*, Malta, 1912.

PAGE 189. The history of Achilles consists of:

1. Achilles plunged into the Styx by his mother
2. The Education of Achilles by Chiron
3. Achilles recognized by Ulysses among the Daughters of Lycomedes
4. Thetis Receiving from Vulcan the Arms of Achilles
5. The Wrath of Achilles
6. Briseis sent back to Achilles
7. The death of Hector
8. The death of Achilles

Cf. Rooses, op. cit., T. III, pp. 36 ff.
For a discussion of Rubens's cartoons see Schmitz, op. cit., S. 246 ff., ill. Abb. 126; Göbel, op. cit., I. Teil, Bd. I, S. 206 f., 304, 423 ff.; Hunter, *Practical Book*, pp. 153 ff.

A somewhat different, though not contradictory, analysis of Rubens in relation to tapestry is given in Phyllis Ackerman, "Tapestries of Five Centuries, VII. The Tapestry of the Baroque Period," in *International Studio,* Vol. LXXVI, New York, 1923, pp. 470 ff.

PAGE 192. In consideration of the personality of Louis XIII and the political situation, it is not unfitting that the set of tapestries made in his name should represent only his riding lessons as a child. He is seen six times putting his rocking horse steed through various prances and paces. In order to eke out a series of eight, two more panels show Neptune creating a horse, and two Cupids leading horses to Henri IV and his wife, Marie de' Medici. Soon even the King's name was effaced from these rather feeble and futile themes, and the cartoons became a stock pattern under the title, The Great Horses. Cf. Max Rooses, *Jordaens Leben und Werke,* Stuttgart, Berlin, Leipzig, 1890, p. 188 f. The set is ill. Baldass, op. cit., Taf. 188–195.

Jordaens's scenes of country life are:

1. Hunters seated with a pack of hounds
2. A mounted falconer returning from the hunt
3. An old man bringing the cook and pheasant
4. The lute player and the lady
5. The wine drinkers
6. A maid plucking a fowl
7. A maid in a chicken yard
8. A night scene

They are ill. Baldass, op. cit., Taf. 196–203.
The list of Jordaens's designs as given by Rooses, op. cit., p. 194, is

1. Daniel in the Lions' Den
2. Another of the same
3. The revelation of Achilles by the judgment of Ulysses
4. The anointing of the Prophets
5. Achilles Wounded in the heel
6. Death of Achilles
7. Anointing of Jeroboam
8. The banquet of the gods
9. The dead Prophet
10. The sacrifice
11. Charon and Minerva
12. The battle with Neptune
13. The night battle

[396]

14. The carnival
15. Emmaus
16. A sacrifice with music
17. Battle of Jeroboam
18. The wife of Jeroboam coming to the Prophet
19. Bacchus and Mercury
20. Another of the same
21. Jupiter and Callisto
22. Narcissus
23. Jupiter and Io
24. The Milk maid
25. Cephalus
26. The red shepherd
27. Salmakis and Hermaphroditus
28. The shepherd and his dog
29. Pan and Syrinx
30. Verdure without figures

An account of all of Jordaens's cartoons is given in Rooses, op. cit., pp. 186 ff.; cf. also Schmitz, op. cit., S. 250, Abb. 128.

In addition to these outstanding sets Jordaens made a number of drawings for the Brussels weavers, some of which exploited the themes already rendered by his famous master, notably a series of five showing the Triumph of Religion, though the treatment is quite different from Rubens's. No woven renditions of these are known so it is possible that they were never used. Again, in a group of thirty drawings that Michael Wauters, a Brussels weaver, bought in 1678, there were three Achilles subjects.

PAGE 193. The Teniers type is discussed in Pinchart, op. cit., p. 126; Müntz, *Short History*, pp. 286 ff., with an amusing criticism sympathetically quoted from Charles Blanc, expressing shock at the peasant crudities; Destrée, op. cit., p. 51, No. XXXI, ill. Pl. XXXIV; Baldass, op. cit., Taf. 296; Göbel, op. cit., I. Teil, Bd. II, Abb. 311–315, 359, 365, 460, 462; II. Teil, Bd. II, Abb. 217; Migeon, op. cit., p. 291.

In concocting cartoons in the Teniers style, elements were sometimes repeated with only the modifications necessary to the change of title. Thus the landscape of one of the Teniers type Don Quixotes (cf. p. 282) is used intact in another Teniers style tapestry called The Smithy. Cf. Göbel, I. Teil, Bd. I, Abb. 290 and 365.

PAGE 196. For many documentary citations on the seventeenth-century Brussels industry see Wauters, op. cit., XVIIIième année, pp. 149 ff., and for a summary of the facts, Göbel, op. cit., I. Teil, Bd. I, S. 322 ff.

CHAPTER XII

PAGE 199. For summary of Flemish workers in Italy see Wauters, op. cit., XVIième année, pp. 196 ff.; and for a summary account of Italian shops Müntz *Short History*, pp. 150 ff., 215 ff.; Guiffrey, *Tapisserie*, pp. 60 ff., 165 ff.; Hunter, *Tapestries*, pp. 216 ff.; Schmitz, op. cit., S. 316 ff.; Hunter, *Practical Book*, pp. 213 ff.; Migeon, op. cit., pp. 294 ff.; Thomson, op. cit., pp. 131 ff., 229 ff., 409 ff.

The tapestry looms of both Italy and Germany in the sixteenth century are also discussed in Phyllis Ackerman, "Tapestries of Five Centuries, V. Transplanting Looms from Flanders," in *International Studio*, Vol. LXXVI, New York, 1923, pp. 443 ff.

A detailed history of the Ferrara looms is given in Gustave Gruyer, *L'Art Ferrarais*, T. II, Paris, 1897, pp. 453 ff., and a very complete summary in Müntz, *Histoire Générale*, pp. 16, 54 ff., 93 f.; Göbel, op. cit., II. Teil, Bd. I, S. 366 ff.

The Mantua shops, apparently always very small, were in such close connection with the larger Ferrara enterprise that it is impossible to distinguish the work of the two with any certainty, assuming that any of the Mantua productions have survived, which is open to doubt, for as far as the records show, these never were more than verdures and heraldic designs, for the most part small utility pieces such as bench covers, though a set inwoven with silk in 1469 seems to have been a more elaborate type of verdure, since Mantegna drew some animals for it. In spite of these limited indications, however, both the Spitzer-Ryerson Annunciation and the Gulbenkian series have been attributed to Mantua. Cf. Heinrich Göbel, " Die Wandteppich-Manufakturen von Mantua," in *Cicerone*, Jahrg. 16, Leipzig, 1924, S. 585 ff. A summary account of the Mantua shops is also given in Müntz, *Histoire Générale*, p. 77 f.

Other weavers working in the court looms were: Giovanni Costa, a Fleming who was active 1472–1482; Jean Mille, a Frenchman, 1474–1482; Rigo da Allemagna, 1472. Cf. Adolfo Venturi,

" Le Arti Minori a Ferrara Nella fine del sec. XV. L'Arazzeria," in *L'Arte,* Anno XII, Rome, 1909, pp. 207 ff.

PAGE 200. The attribution of the Lamentation to Cosimo Tura is advocated by A. Venturi, *Storia dell'Arte Italiana,* Vol. VII, Parte III, p. 565 and ill. Fig. 426.

The Spitzer-Ryerson Annunciation is ill. Müntz, *Histoire Générale,* Pl. 5; Müntz, *Short History,* p. 159, Fig. 32; *Catalogue des Objets d'Art et de Haute Curiosité composant la* . . . . *Collection Spitzer,* p. 71, No. 394; Göbel, op. cit., I. Teil, Bd. II, Abb. 389, where it is attributed to Brussels (?), and II. Teil, Bd. II, Abb. 426, where it is attributed to Mantua (?).

The Spitzer-Ryerson Annunciation was published erroneously as of Audenarde origin in Phyllis Ackerman, " Joas . . . of Audenarde," in *Art in America,* Vol. XIII, New York, 1925, pp. 188 ff.

PAGE 201. For a discussion of van der Weyden in Ferrara see Arnold Goffin, " A propos du voyage de Roger de la Pasture (van der Weyden) en Italie," in *Mélanges Hulin de Loo,* pp. 197 ff.

PAGE 202. The Venice Pentecost is ill. Müntz, *Histoire Générale,* Pl. 6.

The Head of Pompey is published in Müntz, *Histoire Générale,* pp. 17, 30, ill. Pl. I; and the borders are ill. Müntz, *Short History,* pp. 156, 157, Figs. 30, 31.

The cartoon is attributed to the Milan School of Butinone and Marco Zenale by Frida Schottmüller, " Der Europäteppich im Kaiser-Friedrich-Museum," in *Jahrbuch der Königlichen Preussischen Kunstsammlungen,* Bd. 37, Berlin, 1916, pp. 146 ff., p. 148.

The account of Costa's Antique Fêtes is given by Gruyer, op. cit., T. II, p. 39, and of his grisaille decorations in T. II, p. 40.

PAGE 204. In 1878 the Gulbenkian set belonged to M. Ephrussi. See Darcel, op. cit., p. 1006, where the cartoons are attributed to Jean d'Udine. The set is also discussed in Müntz, *Histoire Générale,* p. 61, and ill. Pl. 17; Müntz, *Short History,* p. 220, ill. p. 219, Fig. 52; Göbel, op. cit., II. Teil, Bd. II, Abb. 358, 359.

The set has also been attributed to the atelier of Raphael, probably Giulio Romano, by Francis Birrell, " English Tapestries at Boughton House," in the *Burlington Magazine,* Vol. XXV, London, 1914, p. 189.

Two pieces of Dossi's Metamorphoses, in good condition, however, belong to the Musée des Gobelins and were exhibited in the special exhibition of Renaissance tapestries in 1929. One is illustrated in the catalogue of the exhibition, op. p. 4. It is light, graceful, decorative, but a little thin.

The Metamorphoses also are discussed by Darcel, op. cit., p. 1007; ill. Müntz, *Histoire Générale*, Pl. 15, 16.

A tapestry with four mythological episodes including the Rape of Europa and the Rape of Proserpine, in the Kaiser Friedrich Museum, which bears a coat of arms tentatively identified as that of the Castelli of Ferrara, is presumed to be from the Ferrara looms. The cartoon has been attributed to Ercole de'Roberti (c. 1450–1496), seems clearly later than this. If Ferrarese, it is far inferior in quality to the fine productions of these looms. Cf. Schottmüller, op. cit., p. 152.

PAGE 206. The Trivulzio Months are discussed in detail in Carlo Vicenzi, " Gli Arazzi di Casa Trivulzio," in *Dedalo,* Anno X, Milan — Rome, 1929, pp. 45 ff. They are also discussed in Müntz, *Histoire Générale,* p. 44 f., ill. Pl. 2–4; Müntz, *Short History,* p. 216, ill. p. 217, Fig. 50.

An account of the Florentine shops is given in Müntz, *Histoire Générale,* pp. 62 ff., 94; Göbel, op. cit., II. Teil, Bd. I, S. 377 ff.

PAGE 207. The Bronzino Joseph series is discussed in Müntz, *Histoire Générale,* p. 35. See also Arthur McComb, *Agnolo Bronzino, His Life and Works,* Cambridge (Mass.), 1928, pp. 21 ff., 165 ff.

PAGE 208. For illustrations of Bachiacca's grotesques see Müntz, *Histoire Générale,* Pl. 3, Göbel, op. cit., II. Teil, Bd. II, Abb. 365, 366; Müntz, *Histoire Générale,* Pl. 10; Göbel, op. cit., II. Teil, Bd. II, Abb. 370, 371.

For another Florentine tapestry after Francesco Salviati (Francesco Dei Rossi, 1510–1563) see Joseph Breck, " A Florentine Tapestry," in *Art in America,* Vol. V, New York, 1916–17, pp. 135 ff.

PAGE 209. For an account of Allori see H. Geisenheimer, " Le Pitture di Alessandro Allori nel Refettorio di S. M. Novella," in *Rivista d'Arte,* Anno III, Florence, 1905, pp. 93 ff., tapestry ill. p. 98; and " Di Alcuni Arazzi nel Duomo di Como su Cartoni di Alessandro Allori," in *Rivista d'Arte,* Anno IV, Florence, 1906, pp. 108 ff.

Pierre Fèvre was director of the factory from 1630 to his death, 1669, save for three or four brief intervals during which he returned to his native country. Müntz, *Histoire Générale,* p. 71.

PAGE 210. For the portrait of Franz Stephen see Göbel, op. cit., II. Teil, Bd. II, Abb. 425.

For an account of the Naples factory see Müntz, *Histoire Générale,* pp. 81 ff., 96; Göbel, op. cit., II. Teil, Bd. I, S. 430 ff., ill. Bd. II, Abb. 470.

For an account of the Turin shop see Müntz, *Histoire Générale,* pp. 83 ff., p. 96 f.; Augusto Telluccini, " L'Arazzeria Torinese," in *Dedalo,* Anno VII, Rome-Milan, 1926–1927, pp. 101 ff., 167 ff.

PAGE 211. For illustrations of three of the Aeneas series see Giovanni Copertini, " Tre Arazzi del Museo Civico di Milano," in *Rassegna d'Arte,* Anno XV, Milan, 1915, pp. 126 ff.

For an account of the shop at Rome see Müntz, *Histoire Générale,* pp. 47 ff., p. 92 f.; Göbel, op. cit., II. Teil, Bd. I, S. 416 ff.

For the Romanelli Dido and Aeneas see Baldass, op. cit., Taf. 223–230.

PAGE 212. The portrait of Filippo Cettomai is published in Kendrick, op. cit., p. 62, No. 57A, and ill. Thomson, op. cit., p. 468.

Philip Cettomai's signature also appears on a Nativity in the Cinquantenaire Museum in Brussels.

In the eighteenth century the papal manufacturers fell to copying paintings, for example, the Creation of the Animals and Fall of Man by pupils of Raphael in the Loggia, in the Austrian Museum, dated 1733–34. See Hermann V. Trenkwald, " Zwei Wandteppiche aus der Päpstlichen Manufaktur zur San Michele in Rome," in *Kunst und Kunsthandwerk,* Jahrg. XXII, Vienna, 1919, pp. 22 et seq.

PAGE 213. For an account of the Stuttgart shop see H. Göbel, " Jacob und Moritz des Carmes," in *Monatshefte für Kunstwissenschaft,* Bd. 12, Leipzig, 1919, S. 226 ff.

For a general account of the German enterprises see Müntz, *Histoire Générale,* 2ième partie; Schmitz, op. cit., pp. 122 ff.

PAGE 214. For an account of Bombeck's work see Schmitz, op. cit., S. 137 ff.; Phyllis Ackerman, " Tapestries of Five Centuries, IV. The Weavers of Germany," in *International Studio,* Vol. LXXVI, New York, 1923, pp. 297 ff.

For a discussion of portraits in tapestry see John Böttiger, " Porträttframställning i tapisserie " (1912) , in *Konsthistoriska Uppsatser*, Stockholm, 1913, pp. 105 ff., with excellent illustrations.

The earliest recorded textile portrait is that of Alcisthenes of Sybaris, on the purple hanging which was known as the " Peplos of Alcisthenes." It was exhibited at Lacinium, but later was sold by Dionysius the Elder (c. 432–367 B.C.) . In the centre was a group of gods, above and below were borders of Persian animals, and at either end was a portrait of Alcisthenes. Cf. Louis de Ronchaud, *La Tapisserie dans l'Antiquité*, Paris, 1884, pp. 23, 38.

Dr. Marjan Morelowski attempted to identify Oriant in the Knight of the Swan series as Duke Philip the Good of Burgundy in " Der Krakauer Schwanenritter Wandteppich und sein Verhältnis zu den Französischen Wandteppichen des 15ten Jahrhunderts," in *K. K. Zentral-Kommission für Denkmalpflege, Jahrbuch Beiblatt*, Vienna, 1912. Both existing pieces of this set are illustrated in Kurth, *Gotische Bildteppiche*, Abb. 21, 22. The series is also briefly discussed in Migeon, op. cit., p. 244, ill. p. 243.

The identification of Oriant as Duke Philip is accepted by Schmitz, op. cit., S. 192, and partially accepted by Göbel, op. cit., I. Teil, Bd. I, S. 268.

Figures in scenes of daily life at this time, for example, hunting tapestries, were identified as contemporary personalities, as we know from written records, notably an item (Laborde, op. cit., T. II, p. 271, No. 4295) of the Inventory of Philip the Bold of Burgundy, describing nine large and two medium size tapestries with hawking scenes, in which were the figures of the late Duke John and of his wife, the Duchess, both ahorse and afoot. But this does not justify the assumption that the Dukes were introduced as fictional characters into illustrations of romances, nor can we say in how far such figures were really portraits. Possibly the identification was only traditional, or more probably they were indicated by some device.

How little figures representing historical personages were actually portraits even as late as c. 1510 is shown by the unidentifiable, because completely generalized, figures of the English King and Queen in the Coventry tapestry. See A. F. Kendrick, " The Coventry Tapestry," in the *Burlington Magazine*, Vol. XLIV, London, 1924, pp. 83 ff.

Another example of the attempt to identify historical personages in illustrations of romances is seen in the title " Betrothal and Marriage of Marie de Bourgogne and of Maximilian" attached to a fragment illustrating an unidentified romance, ill. Planès, op. cit., Pl. 15.

In the so-called Hunts of Maximilian (cf. pp. 149, 341) are two figures for which an identification as Charles V and Ferdinand I has been proposed by Saintenay, op. cit., p. 25.

A number of tapestries, especially of the early sixteenth-century "Marguerite" type (cf. Chap. VII) have been "identified" in the trade as representing episodes in the lives of notable contemporaries. These titles are quite without foundation. Göbel (op. cit., I. Teil, Bd. I, S. 138) also makes this point.

The "Author" is discussed by Hunter, *Practical Book*, p. 245 f.

PAGE 215. For references on Maître Philippe see notes to page 112.

The Descent signed Philip is also published in Destrée, *Tapisserie*, pp. 27 ff., No. XI, ill. (in color, poor) Pl. XIII.

The Spanish State Carrying the Cross is ill. Valencia, op. cit., Lám. 18, and Tormo Monzo y Sanchez Canton, op. cit., pp. 23 ff., Pl. VIII.

Destrée, op. cit., Nos. XXIV and XXV, believes that one of the onlookers at the Decapitation of Paul in Coeck's Saint Paul series is a self-portrait of the artist. A head in a Jacob and Esau tapestry is also supposed to be Coeck's self-portrait. Göbel, op. cit., I. Teil, Bd. I, S. 419.

Evidently donors were also sometimes used in Flemish tapestries of the early fifteenth century, for one item of the inventory of Duke Philip the Bold of Burgundy (Laborde, op. cit., T. II., p. 268, No. 4263) speaks of portraits of Duc Anthoine de Brabant and his wife and their children on a Coronation of the Virgin.

For family tree and family history tapestries see Göbel, op. cit., I. Teil, Bd. I, S. 101 f.

PAGE 216. Bombeck's Reformation Allegory is ill. Schmitz, op. cit., Abb. 74, and discussed in Göbel, op. cit., I. Teil, Bd. I, S. 130.

The account of another small factory established with Flemish weavers in the sixteenth century by the Duke of Braunschweig-Wolfenbüttel is given by H. Göbel, "Die Manufaktur der Asseburg-Teppiche," in *Berliner Museen*, Jahrg. LI, Berlin, 1930, pp. 11 ff.

PAGE 217. For information on the early shuttle weaves of Sweden, see Böttiger, op. cit., Vol. IV, pp. 2 ff.

PAGE 218. For an account of the Dutch shops see Schmitz, op. cit., S. 267 f.; and for a more complete account of the Delft shops see Göbel, op. cit., I. Teil, Bd. I, S. 538 ff.; Thomson, op. cit., pp. 231, 271 f.

PAGE 219. The Armada tapestries are published in John Pine, *The Tapestry Hangings of the House of Lords,* London, 1739; Wauters, op. cit., XVIième année, pp. 219 ff.; Guiffrey, *Tapisserie,* p. 153, ill. Fig. 79; Roxburgh Club, *Lord Howard of Effingham and the Spanish Armada,* London, 1919.

An account of the Amsterdam shops is given by Göbel, op. cit., I. Teil, Bd. I, S. 529 ff.

A good panel from the Alexander set is in Ackerman, A Catalog of . . . Collection of Frank Gair Macomber, p. 69 ff., No. 35, ill. Pl. XX.

For a general discussion of the English factories see Müntz, *Histoire Générale,* 2ième partie, pp. 19 ff.; Hunter, *Tapestries,* pp. 141 ff.; Schmitz, op. cit., S. 324 f.; Migeon, op. cit., Chap. VII, pp. 311 ff.; Thomson, op. cit., pp. 264 ff., 488 ff., ill. op. p. 26.

For a detailed account of the Sheldon looms see W. G. Thomson, *Tapestry Weaving in England from the Earliest Times to the End of the Eighteenth Century,* London, 1914; John Humphreys, *Elizabethan Sheldon Tapestries,* London, 1925; also in Society of Antiquaries, *Archaeologia,* Vol. LXXIV, pp. 881 ff.; E. A. B. Bernard and A. J. B. Wace, *The Sheldon Tapestry Weavers and Their Work,* London, 1928.

Illustrations of Sheldon tapestries are also given by W. Gordon Hunton, *English Decorative Textiles,* London, 1930, Pls. 1–23; of the Sheldon maps, Pls. 18–23.

PAGE 220. A rather more interesting map of Delft manufacture, approximately contemporary, showing Leyden, in relief, is in the Leyden City Hall. Ill. Göbel, op. cit., I. Teil, Bd. II, Abb. 490.

An interesting decorative textile map is listed in the inventory of Charles V of France (1380), made of yellow sendal, painted with castles, rivers, and people like a *mappemonde.* Jules Labarte, *Inventaire du Mobilier de Charles V,* Paris, 1879, p. 348, No. 3391.

For an account of the Mortlake Factory see Müntz, *Histoire Générale,* 2ième partie, pp. 21 ff.; Müntz, *Short History,* pp. 295 ff.; Hunter, *Tapestries,* pp. 105 ff.; Hunter, *Practical Book,* pp. 220 ff.;

Thomson, op. cit., pp. 277 ff. Mortlake tapestries are also illustrated in Hunton, op. cit., Pls. 28–35 inclusive.

Two Mortlake sets of Raphael's Apostles, two of the Playing Boys, and one of Lebrun's Four Elements are discussed by Francis Birrell, " English Tapestries at Boughton House " in the *Burlington Magazine*, Vol. XXV, London, 1914, pp. 183 ff.

PAGE 221. The Battle of Soleby is illustrated in Hunton, op. cit., pls. 26–27.

For an account of Vanderbanc's and the contemporary English shops see H. C. Marillier, *English Tapestries of the Eighteenth Century*, London, 1930. Two of the Vanderbanc Chinoiseries are published in Kendrick, op. cit., p. 18 f., Nos. 5, 6. They are also illustrated in Hunton, op. cit., Pls. 36 and 41–45.

For an account of Spanish enterprises see Müntz, *Histoire Générale*, 2ième partie, pp. 25 ff.; Thomson, op. cit., p. 413; Göbel, op. cit., II. Teil, Bd. I, S. 459 ff.; ill. Bd. II, Abb. 483, 484.

PAGE 222. The best account of the Russian factory is in A. Polovtsoff and V. Chambers, "Some Notes on the St. Petersburg Tapestry Works," in *Burlington Magazine*, Vol. XXXV, London, 1919, pp. 110 ff. There is a summary account in Schmitz, op. cit., S. 328; Hunter, *Practical Book*, p. 227; Thomson, op. cit., p. 486 f.

PAGE 223. The Montagu portrait is in Ackerman, *Macomber Catalogue*, p. 73, No. 36, ill. Pl. XXI.

For the Gobelins portraits of the Royal Family see Fenaille, op. cit., T. IV, pp. 305 ff.; Böttiger, op. cit., T. II, Pl. XLI; Baldass, op. cit., Taf. 259, 260; Göbel, op. cit., II. Teil, Bd. I, S. 192 ff., ill. Bd. II, Abb. 188–190.

One weaving of the portrait of Louis XV is published in Ackerman, *Catalogue of the Loan Exhibition*, San Francisco, p. 51, No. 64.

Other small pieces clearly of Gobelins workmanship but not listed in the otherwise very complete Gobelins archives, come to light from time to time. Some of these must have been masterpieces in the exact sense of the term, demonstrations of skill to win status or a post. Consequently they are often extraordinary *tours de force*, notably a pair copying still life subjects by Chardin, Ackerman, *Catalogue of the Loan Exhibition*, San Francisco, p. 50, Nos. 60, 61.

For Swedish eighteenth century portraits see Böttiger, op. cit., Vol. II, Pls. IX, XXXIX, XL, Vol. III; Pl. XCVI.

In the eighteenth century portraits were also made in the pile fabric usually called Savonnerie, an even less suitable medium. See, e.g., Böttiger, op. cit., T. III, Pl. XCV.

For the Dashkov portrait see A. A. Polovtsoff and V. E. Chambers, "A Tapestry Portrait of Princess Dashkoff," in *Burlington Magazine*, Vol. XXXIV, London, 1919, pp. 243 ff., ill. p. 247.

PAGE 224. The portrait of Catherine is published in Ackerman, op. cit., p. 54 f., No. 73. Mr. Milton Samuels has pointed out that the cartoon is clearly taken from the portrait by Alexandre Roslin (1718–1793) in the National Museum in Stockholm. For another tapestry portrait of Catherine see Böttiger, op. cit., Vol. III, Pl. LXXIII, and for a portrait of Peter, Pl. XCVII.

For examples of copies of paintings made at the St. Petersburg factory see Böttiger, op. cit., T. III, Pl. LXXI, LXXII, LXXIII.

Various small factories were undertaken in France also, producing, for the most part, tapestries patterned on the mannered, degenerate style of the late Italian Renaissance, distorted by the usual pseudo-primitivism of provincial work. See, for example, A. Auriol, "La Tapisserie de Saint Martial à la Cathédrale de Toulouse," in *Annales du Midi*, T. XXXI–XXXII, Toulouse, 1919–1920, pp. 339, ff.

CHAPTER XIII

PAGE 226. Aristotle discusses the silk worm in *Historia Animalorum* V, 19 (17), 11 (6).

In the later centuries some silk may have come from Khotan where seri-culture seems to have been introduced about the fourth century A.D.

PAGE 227. The Loulan tapestry is published by F. H. Andrews, *Ancient Chinese Figured Silks found by Sir Aurel Stein at Ruined Sites of Central Asia*. Reprinted with fifteen illustrations from the *Burlington Magazine*, July–September, 1920. London, 1920, p. 16 f., ill. p. 17.

The Ton Huang tapestries are published in Aurel Stein, *Serindia*, Oxford, 1921, Pl. CVI, CXII; and for a wool tapestry with conventional designs see Stein, op. cit., Vol. I, p. 435.

The other Turkestan tapestries are published in A. von le Coq,

Chotscho, Berlin, 1913, Taf. 49. The embroideries are illustrated, von le Coq, op. cit., Taf. 6, 52.

There is a brief unsatisfactory account of Asiatic tapestry in Thomson, op. cit., p. 488.

PAGE 228. A Chinese tapestry is illustrated (badly) in Hunter, *Practical Book,* Pl. II ea. A piece similar to the Metropolitan panels in the Berlin Kunstgewerbe Sammlung is ill. Schmitz, op. cit., Abb. 19.

An interesting large *K'ssu* showing the Taoist paradise, from a temple west of Pekin, presumably of the early eighteenth century, is described by Arthur Kauffmann, " Ein Chinesisches Wirkbild aus der Sammlung Sproesser," in *Cicerone,* Jahrg. 10, Leipzig, 1924, S. 813.

Some characteristic robes are published in Alan Priest and Pauline Simmons, *Chinese Textiles,* New York (Metropolitan Museum of Art) , 1931, pp. 16 ff., Figs. 2, 3, 4, 5, 6, 19. Fig. 1 is erroneously described as a fragment of Ming *K'o ssu* when actually it is a Japanese *tzuzure,* made for a bag, as Mr. Priest himself has now noted. Similarly a fragment of *tzuzure* in The Victoria and Albert Museum is labelled Chinese.

PAGE 230. Mr. Severance's piece is published in " A Chinese Tapestry " in the *Burlington Magazine,* Vol. XXV, London, 1914, p. 231, with a good color plate and it is ill. (badly) Thomson, op. cit., opposite p. 478.

PAGE 232. A brief account of Japanese tapestry on which this statement is based is given in Shojiro Nomura, *An Historical Sketch of Nishiki and Kinran Brocades,* Boston (Copley Society) , 1914, p. 18. The Kano Motonobu panel is published in the *Moslé Collection of Japanese Works of Art,* Leipzig, 1914, Portfolio I, p. 28, No. 2242, Ill. Portfolio II, Pl. CCIII; the other, loc. cit., No. 2233, Ill. Portfolio II, Pl. CCII. These references were supplied by Mr. Louis Ledoux.

PAGE 234. The Safavid tapestry is woven in silk on a cotton warp and finished on both sides to be reversible. It will be illustrated in color in the forthcoming *Survey of Persian Art,* Arthur Upham Pope, Editor.

CHAPTER XIV

PAGE 236. The chronology followed is that of Professor Philip Ainsworth Means, *A Survey of Ancient Peruvian Art*, New Haven, 1917, and " Note on the Chronology of Early Peruvian Cultures " in the Metropolitan Museum of Art, *Peruvian Textiles, Examples of the Pre-Incaic Period*, New York, 1930, pp. 9 ff.

The most important accounts of Peruvian textiles to date are:
Charles Wiener, *Péru et Bolivie*, Paris, 1880
W. Reiss and A. Stübel, *The Necropolis of Ancon in Peru*, Vol. II, Berlin, 1880–1887
Arthur Baessler, *Ancient Peruvian Art*, Leipzig, 1902–1903
Max Uhle, *Pachacamac*, Philadelphia, 1903
Ernst Fuhrmann, *Reich der Inka*, Hagen W., 1922
R. and H. d'Harcourt, *Les Tissus Indiens du Vieux Pérou*, Paris, 1924
Walter Lehmann, and Heinrich Doering, *The Art of Old Peru*, London, 1924
Gösta Montell, *Dress and Ornaments in Ancient Peru*, Gothenberg, 1929
Max Schmidt, *Kunst und Kultur von Peru*, Berlin, 1929
Heinrich Ubbelohde Doering, " Alt Peruanisches Kunstgewerbe," in H. Th. Bossert, *Geschichte des Kunstgewerbes aller Zeiten und Völker*, Bd. II, Berlin, Vienna, Zurich, 1929, S. 269 ff.
Philip Ainsworth Means, *Ancient Civilizations of the Andes*, New York, London, 1931, Chapter XI, The Art of the Loom in Ancient Peru, pp. 450 ff.

Plates of more or less interest are gathered together in
Adolphe Basler and Ernest Brummer, *L'Art Pré-colombien*, Paris, 1928
H. C. Perleberg, *Peruvian Textiles*, Jersey City, s.d.

Among the outstanding public collections of Peruvian Textiles are:
Berlin, Museum für Völkerkunde
Boston, Museum of Fine Arts
Lima Museum
Modena Museum
New York City, American Museum of Natural History

New York City, Metropolitan Museum of Art
Philadelphia, University Museum
San Francisco, Anthropological Museum of the University of
California
Washington, D. C., Textile Museum of the District of Columbia.
The list does not profess to be complete.

Herr Walther Lehmann leans to the idea that the civilizations
of Peru emanated from Mexico (*Historia del Arte de Antiquo Peru,*
Berlin and Lima, 1926), and that the original settlements were
made at Tiahuanaco, the Incaic culture being an offshoot. This
opinion is apparently considered possible by Mr. Philip Ainsworth
Means, and shared by Dr. Max Uhle. See Jean Levillier, *Paracas,*
Paris, 1928, p. 9.

It has been suggested that all the so-called Nazca textiles except
those immediately pre-Incaic really were found in Paracas; Levillier,
op. cit., p. 12.

PAGE 237. The standard Nazca-Ica stitch is analysed by M. D. C.
Crawford, "Peruvian Fabrics," in *Anthropological Papers of the
American Museum of Natural History,* Vol. XII, Part III, New
York, 1915, pp. 109 ff., p. 131.

A good Nazca embroidery with an anthropomorphic god is in
the American Museum of Natural History, No. 41.0 — 1500. There
are also several notable examples of the type in the Boston Museum of Fine Arts. The bird associated with this god is probably
the Thunder Bird. Cf. Cyril G. E. Bunt, "Symbolism in Peruvian
Art," in *Art in America,* Vol. XII, New York, 1924, pp. 165 ff.,
p. 167.

Excellent examples of embroideries with the cat motive are:
American Museum of Natural History, Numbers 410–1508, 410–
1509, 410–1515, and a fourth with no number. Three cats seem to
have figured, the jaguar, puma, and *titi* or mountain cat. Charles W.
Mead, "Conventionalized Figures in Ancient Peruvian Art," in
*Anthropological Papers of the American Museum of Natural His-
tory,* Vol. XII, Part III, New York, 1915, pp. 195 ff., p. 211. A
splendid example of a Nazca cat embroidery is published by Edward Seler, "Ein Altperuanisches besticktes Gewebe," in *Jahrbuch
der Königlich Preussischen Kunstsammlungen,* Bd. XXXVII, Berlin, 1916, S. 181 ff., with a color plate detail, Taf. II. The design
follows the scheme of six-color variation (cf. p. 246).

The protruding tongue has been interpreted to indicate: (1)

The Deity as such; (2) Knowledge or thought; or (3) Soothsaying. Levillier, op. cit.; p. 21.

PAGE 238. For Luristan bronzes with multiple masks see André Godard, *Les Bronzes du Luristan*, Paris, 1931, Pl. LII, though more elaborate and interesting examples of the type have been found.

The Incaic totemic celebration is described by Garcilasso de la Vega, *The Royal Commentaries of the Incas*, translated by Clements R. Markham. Hakluyt Society, Vols. 41–42, London, 1869, Vol. II, p. 156, cited by Montell, op. cit., p. 19. The puma mummy is described and illustrated by Baessler, op. cit., Pl. 165. The Paracas textile is published by Levillier, op. cit.

PAGE 239. The mask with symmetrical projections may be a symbol of light and life and, at least later, seems to have been associated with the sun. Bunt, op. cit., p. 168.

It is frequently difficult to distinguish with certainty between brocading, ornamentation with an extra weft or wefts inserted at the point where required on the loom, and darning, the introduction in floats parallel to the wefts of additional yarns by means of a needle on the finished web. Cf. Lila M. O'Neal and A. L. Kroeber, *Textile Periods in Ancient Peru*, Berkeley (University of California Publications in American Archaeology and Ethnology, Vol. 28, No. 2, pp. 23–56) , 1930, p. 30, N. 16; and Cyril G. E. Bunt, " Studies in Peruvian Textiles, II, Brocades and Embroideries," in *Burlington Magazine*, Vol. XXXVI, London, 1920, p. 127 f., p. 129 f.

It has been suggested that both the mountain and the coast culture were offshoots of a common root, an earlier civilization in the northern highlands, the hypothetical so-called, " Archaic Andean " culture, propounded by the Peruvian archeologist, Julio Tello, presumed to have flourished about 200 B.C.–800 A.D. Montell, op. cit., p. 15.

PAGE 240. For an excellent illustration of the winged god see Metropolitan Museum, op. cit., Pl. III. There is an interesting variant of this figure in the Boston Museum of Fine Arts, No. 16.42. This is probably the Thunder God, a beneficent deity in that he brought the rain. It is noteworthy that in the Ancient East the Creator God was closely associated with thunder, and Thor also was the Thunderer (cf. p. 53) . The staves that he carries may be thunderbolts. He is sometimes carried on a litter by two men, presumably Apocatequil and Pignero, sons of the first man, Guamansuri, cf. Bunt, *Symbolism*, p. 167. It is again interesting that the gods of the Ancient East are shown similarly carried. An excellent representation of this scene is given in Max Schmidt, " Über Altperuanische Gewebe mit Szenenhaften Darstellungen," in Baessler, *Archiv*, Bd. I, Heft I, Leipzig and Berlin, 1910, S. 1 ff., S. 30, Abb. 18.

Splendid examples of the block cat are found on two pieces in the Boston Museum of Fine Arts, Nos. 24.326, and 70, 265.

PAGE 241. Detached heads are effectively used, for example, on Boston Museum of Fine Arts No. 24.3007, a darned or brocaded cotton cloth; and Nos. 31.101, 31.003, tapestries. A more or less useful collection of typical Peruvian motives is illustrated by Charles W. Mead, *Peruvian Art, A Help for Students of Design*, New York (American Museum of Natural History Guide Leaflet Series No. 46), 1929. There are, however, no indications of dates.

Other illustrative scenes are discussed and illustrated by Schmidt, op. cit., or less fully by Max Schmidt, " Szenenhafte Darstellungen auf Alt-peruanischen Geweben," in *Zeitschrift für Ethnologie*, Jahrg. 42, Berlin, 1910, S. 154 ff.

An interesting conventional tree, probably of the next period, appears on a tapestry from Nazca in the American Museum of Natural History, No. 41.0 — 1182.

PAGE 243. It is stated that the stepped outline indicates the silhouette of mountains and so symbolizes the earth, *pacha,* two of the motives in a reciprocal relation meaning earth and sky. Bunt, op. cit., p. 166.

PAGE 244. The condors in the Boston Museum are on a brown and white double cloth No. 21-2569. Condors were associated with the Andes according to Bunt, op. cit., p. 171.

PAGE 245. A vertical stripe split by a " Greek " meander with a puma on alternate sides appears on a brown and white double cloth, American Museum of Natural History No. B. 8624.

A more complex lattice consists of a hexagonal lattice, crossed by a plain, square lattice in another color, so that the ultimate units of division are right-angled triangles with a blunt point. A very highly evolved lattice consists of a square with an equilateral triangle applied by the point to the centre of each side, alternating with a twelve-point star that is partly implicit and never complete because the units are not quite contiguous.

PAGE 246. The three men holding hands are quite common. An example is American Museum of Natural History No. B.7781.

For a discussion of the arrangement in groups of six see Charles W. Mead, "The Six-Unit Design in Ancient Peruvian Cloth," in *Boas Anniversary Volume of Anthropological Papers*, New York, 1906, pp. 193 ff.

On the Paracas piece the six colors are organized into three different groups of four, each of which is interchanged in three different sequences. The scheme could not be quite fully carried out because there are only eight rows of patterns, nor is the succession quite consistent.

The front of an Incaic *uncu* or shirt in the American Museum of Natural History (No. 14.0.1180) has a checked design composed of four types of squares. These are arranged in horizontal rows in four different sequences, but the four sequences follow each other in the vertical succession in two groups of three each, each group repeating one arrangement symmetrically on either side of a center stripe of contrasted arrangement, the whole repeat thus being in the unit of six. The scheme is as follows:

1	2	3	4	1	2	3	4	1	2	3	4
4	1	2	3	4	1	2	3	4	1	2	3
1	2	3	4	1	2	3	4	1	2	3	4
2	3	4	1	2	3	4	1	2	3	4	1
3	4	1	2	3	4	1	2	3	4	1	2
2	3	4	1	2	3	4	1	2	3	4	1
1	2	3	4	1	2	3	4	1	2	3	4
4	1	2	3	4	1	2	3	4	1	2	3

etc.

Again, another bright blue Incaic *uncu* in the same collection (No. B.1503) has, around the bottom, a band of small checks with six different types of interior design. The sequence of these is so arranged that in each successive stripe the horizontal repeat is moved one to the right, making a change of design in units of six vertically as well as horizontally, and a continuous repeat diagonally.

PAGE 247. For a discussion of Peruvian textile materials see M. D. C. Crawford, "Peruvian Textiles," in *Anthropological Papers of the*

American Museum of Natural History, Vol. XII, Part III, New York, 1915, pp. 55 ff.; and d'Harcourt, op. cit., pp. 7 ff.

" The Ancient Peruvian weavers evidently had wonderful control of the bobbins, since weft was picked at every angle; sometimes almost parallel with warps. In this way the openings between figures were closed, and in some cases by surrounding a figure with a binding weft a raised effect was produced." Crawford, op. cit., p. 91.

The lacy effect is seen in Boston Museum of Fine Arts No. 24.303. The openwork check is No. B.8540, found at Huando-Chancay. This is made by cutting out every fourth and fifth warp in a certain area of the fabric. Ten wefts in succession are then woven back and forth only across the remaining warps, in groups of three. The next four wefts, however, are then floated across the gap, and so on, in a regular repetition.

PAGE 248. The Peruvians also used dovetailing and interlocking to join a completed web to a new web in the course of weaving, a practice necessitated by the inadequate width of their looms. The dovetailing was done directly with the weft of the piece in construction, which must, however, have been inserted between the wefts of the finished piece with a needle. The interlocking was done, not directly, but by means of an additional yarn passed through a loop of weft of the completed piece at the edge and woven in a loop with the weft of the piece in construction. Interlocking was also used to make possible color changes in the warp. O'Neale and Kroeber, op. cit., p. 51.

The extra cloth weave appears in the piece in the collection of Mrs. William H. Moore, ill. Pl. 39c. This makes the piece, strictly speaking, as Miss Nancy Reath has pointed out, a kind of brocaded cloth instead of a tapestry.

Examples of Peruvian double cloth are very numerous. The American Museum of Natural History has an excellent group, Nos. B.5458-8610, B-8618, B-8624, B-8653, B-8570, B-8669, 41-0.1170, the last found at Nazca.

For a discussion of Peruvian double cloths see Cyril G. E. Bunt, "Studies in Peruvian Textiles," in *Burlington Magazine,* Vol. XXXII, London, 1918, pp. 101 ff.

It is interesting to see a conception of reversible color relations similar to that of double cloth carried out on pottery where it has, of course, no technical foundation. So on a bowl-shaped jar from

Pachacamac a conventional bird god is represented on each side, the one figure being, roughly, the color reverse of the other. Ill. Baessler, op. cit., Vol. 4, Pl. 131, Fig. 363. "With representations depicted on the same vase such interchanges of colours are frequent, although not always carried out consistently."

The double cloth idea was further elaborated in more complex evolutions of the technique, for instance, a type of girdle in which a square of double cloth in, for example, blue and white, alternates with a square which is in a sense voided, in that there are no blue wefts, but both the blue and white warps are brought to the same level alternating in pairs and cloth woven with a white weft. Boston Museum of Fine Arts, Nos. 78.91, 78.92.

The tapestry on cloth is No. 24.3051. Miss Gertrude Townsend first noted this exceptional piece. Still a different development of the same aesthetic principle is seen in another piece in the Boston Museum (No. 21.2580), with three-inch stripes of red tapestry alternating with an inch stripe brocaded on a kind of compound cloth, with a pattern of geometrical birds and flowers in dark shades (dark blue or purplish red). The pattern is woven with short floats of a single-ply weft and hence is firm and definite in texture as well as color. The ground, on the other hand, is light in tone, and it is woven with longer floats of pinkish white or yellow two-ply wefts, so that it is very loose and wavy in texture, serving aesthetically as the contrast. Rudimentary voided pile fabrics were also known, with a simple kind of looped uncut pile, and various styles of darned etamines and darned gauzes with voided spaces were common. An example of a voided pile fabric is Boston Museum of Fine Arts No. 21.2577, but these are comparatively common.

PAGE 249. The fullest description of Peruvian garments is in Montell, op. cit., *passim.*

For accounts of the finds at minor sites see Wiener, op cit., *passim.*

PAGE 251. For a readable account of the Incaic economic and political organization see Sir Clements R. Markham. *The Incas of Peru,* London, 1910. There is also a good account in Thomas A Joyce, *South American Archaeology,* New York, 1912, Chapter V, pp. 99 ff., and Chapter VI, pp. 117 ff.

PAGE 254. For a summary account of the *cumpicos* see Montell, op. cit., pp. 184 ff. For textiles as sacrifices and taxes see Montell, op. cit., pp. 179 f., 187 f.

PAGE 255. The description of Atahualpa's entry is given by Francisco de Xerez, *The Conquest of Peru,* Hakluyt Society, Vol. 47, London, 1872, p. 53, cited Montell, op. cit., p. 196.

The scene of cross worship is published by Uhle, op. cit., p. 43, Fig. 56. For Peruvian stone worship see Joyce, op. cit., p. 80.

PAGE 256. Excellent examples of the feather pattern are American Museum of Natural History No. 41.0–1109, and another piece not numbered. There is also a fine band of feathers on an *uncu,* No. B.1505. The deciduous forest was first published in Uhle, op. cit., p. 47.

PAGE 257. A very fine *uncu* from Titicaca Island is in the American Museum for Natural History, No. B.1505. Related pieces are Nos. B.1500, B.1502 (showing European influence), B.1503, and B.1506.

For a characteristic post-Conquest armorial panel see T. A. Joyce, " A Peruvian Tapestry," in *Burlington Magazine,* Vol. XXIII, London, 1918, pp. 146 ff.

PAGE 258. For an account of Maya textiles see Thomas A. Joyce, *Mexican Archaeology,* London, 1914, p. 307 f.

For a summary of the textile arts of Mexico see Friedrich Röck, " Kunstgewerbe von Mexiko, Mittelamerika und Westindien " in Bossert, op. cit., pp. 349 ff., 366 ff.; Joyce, op. cit., pp. 147 ff.; Thomas Athol Joyce, *Maya and Mexican Art,* London, 1929, op. p. 156 ff.

PAGE 259. An interesting series of designs used on Mexican ceremonial mantles (without, of course, any indication of the technique in which they were rendered) is given in a codex (known as the Magliabecchi Codex) in the Biblioteca Nazionale Centrale of Florence, a manuscript apparently of the second half of the sixteenth century, reproduced in facsimile by Zelia Nuttall, *The Book of the Life of the Ancient Mexicans,* Berkeley, 1903, pp. 1–8. The character of the designs would have required either painting or embroidery or perhaps, in part, appliqué, but if they were rendered in any kind of needlework great skill was required. Textile processes, notably weaving, are shown in a number of the Mexican Codices.

The illustrations of mantles and of weaving are especially numerous and interesting in Fr. Bernardino de Sahagún, *Historia de las Cosas de Nueva España,* Madrid, 1907.

Several European travellers of the sixteenth century have paid tribute to the weaving skill of the Mexicans, notably Henry Hawks who went there in 1572. It is interesting to note that he also states categorically that no cloth was woven in Peru. Evidently the Peruvian weavers limited themselves to more elaborate textiles. " They have much wooll and as good as the wool of Spaine. They make cloth as much as serveth the countrey, for the common people and send much cloth into Peru. I have seene cloth made in the city of Mexico, which hath beene solde for tenne pesos a vare, which is almost foure pounds English, and the vare is lesse than oure yard. They have woade growing in the country, and alum, and brasill, and divers other things to die withal, so that they make all colours. In Peru they make no cloth." " A Relation of the commodities of Nova Hispania . . . by Henry Hawks," in Richard Hakluyt, *The Principal Navigations, Voyages and Traffiques of the English Nation,* London (Everyman), 1926, Vol. 6, p. 289 f.

CHAPTER XV

PAGE 262. The basic source of all information in the Gobelins is the publication of Fenaille (see Bibliography).

For a somewhat different summary of this and the following period see Phyllis Ackerman, " Tapestries of Five Centuries, VII. The Weavers of the Louis Periods," in *International Studio,* Vol. LXXVII, New York, 1923, pp. 56 ff.

For accounts of the Comans-van den Planken shop see Wauters, op. cit., XVIième année, pp. 224 ff.; Guiffrey, *Histoire Générale,* pp. 107 ff.; Göbel, op. cit., II. Teil, Bd. I, S. 58 ff.; Migeon, op. cit., pp. 364 ff.

PAGE 263. For the account of the Pastor Fido set see Fenaille, op. cit., T. I, p. 225 f.; Göbel, op. cit., I. Teil, Bd. I, S. 193 f., ill. II. Teil, Bd. II, Abb. 40–42.

A Pastor Fido series was also made in Brussels in the middle of the eighteenth century. Ill. Göbel, op. cit., I. Teil, Bd. II, Abb. 354.

For a summary discussion of the Gobelins see Müntz, *Short History,* p. 242 f.; Guiffrey, *Histoire Générale,* pp. 117 ff.; Hunter, *Tapestries,* pp. 152 ff.; Schmitz, op. cit., S. 278 ff.; Hunter, *Practical*

Book, pp. 139 ff., 179 ff.; Göbel, op. cit., II. Teil, Bd. I, S. 113 ff.; Migeon, op. cit., Chap. XI, pp. 368 ff.; Thomson, op. cit., pp. 415 ff.

PAGE 264. The titles of the complete Gobelins Louis XIV series are:

1. The Coronation
2. The Wedding
3. The Interview of the King of France and the King of Spain
4. The Satisfaction of the Cardinal Legate
5. The Audience of the Ambassador of Spain
6. The Alliance with the Swiss
7. The Conquest of Dunkirk
8. The Conquest of Dôle
9. The Conquest of Marsal
10. The Conquest of Douai
11. The Conquest of Lille
12. The Conquest of Tournay
13. The Combat with the Comte de Marsin
14. The King at the Gobelins
15. The Entry of the Queen into Douai
16. The Academy of Sciences
17. The Governor of Cambray
18. The Passage of the Rhine
19. The King giving Thanks for his recovery at Notre Dame (by Vernonsal)
20. The Baptism of the Dauphin (by Cristophe)
21. Birth of the Duc de Bourgogne (by Dieu)
22. Marriage of the Duc de Bourgogne (by Dieu)
23. The Reception of the Doge of Genoa (by Hallé)
24. The King at the Invalides (by Dulin)
25. The King Receiving the Persian (by Dumesnil)

The first eighteen pieces are by Charles Le Brun.
Numbers 15 to 18 were never woven.
The set is discussed in Fenaille, op. cit., T. II, pp. 99 ff.; Guiffrey, *Histoire Générale,* pp. 120 ff., ill. Pl. 19–23; Müntz, *Short History,* p. 270, ill. p. 266, Fig. 69; Göbel, op. cit., II. Teil, Bd. I, S. 128 ff., ill. Abb. 85–89.

PAGE 265. The titles of the Royal Residences are:

1. The Opera at the Louvre (The Opera being given is *Psyche*)
2. A ballet in the Palais Royale

3. The King hunting at the Château de Madrid
4. The King walking at Versailles
5. The King walking with the ladies at Saint Germain
6. The King hunting at Fontainebleau
7. The King hunting at Vincennes
8. The King hunting at the Château de Marimont in Hainault
9. The King walking at Chambord
10. The King walking at the Tuileries
11. The King walking at Blois
12. The King hunting at Monceaux

The Royal Residences are ill. Guiffrey, *Histoire Générale,* Pl. 25; Göbel, op. cit., II. T., Bd. II, Abb. 90–93.

The use of Royal Residences as a decorative theme is not without precedent, for a palace or castle is the major feature of the painting at the head of each month in the calendar of the large Book of Hours of the Duc de Berri, and it has been suggested that some of these were favorite dwellings of the Duke. Jules Guiffrey, *Inventaires de Jean Duc de Berri,* p. LXXIV, LXXXV, n. 1.

Charles le Brun also designed for the Gobelins the Portière of Fame (Fenaille, op. cit., T. II, pp. 1 ff.) ; the Portière of Mars (Fenaille, op, cit., T. II, pp. 9 ff.) ; the Portière of the Triumphal Chariot (Fenaille, op. cit., T. II, pp. 16 ff.) ; the Portière of the Unicorn (Fenaille, op. cit., T. II, p. 23) ; a set of panels to fit under windows (Fenaille, op. cit., T. II, p. 24) ; a set of five Verdures (Fenaille, op. cit., T. II, pp. 25 ff.) ; three pieces illustrating the history of Constantine to supplement five adapted from Raphael's paintings in the Vatican (Fenaille, op. cit., T. II, pp. 27 ff.) ; a history of Meleager in eight pieces (Fenaille, op. cit., T. I, pp. 33 ff.) ; a history of Moses in three pieces (Fenaille, op. cit., T. II, p. 36 f.) ; the Muses in ten pieces (Fenaille, op. cit., T. II, pp. 37 ff.) ; the Elements, four pieces with several variations (Fenaille, op. cit., T. II, pp. 51 ff.) ; the Seasons, also four pieces with several variations (Fenaille, op. cit., T. II, pp. 69 ff.) ; the Children Gardening in six pieces, four representing seasons (Fenaille, op. cit., T. II, pp. 84 ff.) ; the history of Alexander in five compositions which were, however, subdivided to make eleven panels (Fenaille, op. cit., T. II, pp. 167 ff.) ; two other pieces for a history of Moses to supplement a set of eight by Poussin (Fenaille, op. cit., T. II, pp. 186 ff.; a set of entrefenêtres with Caryatides (Fenaille, op. cit., T. III, pp. 61 ff.) .

For an account of Le Brun's work in tapestry see Camilo Ródon

NOTES

y Font, *Tres Grandes Decoradores del Tejido*, Barcelona, 1922, pp. 35 ff.

PAGE 267. The most complete information on the Beauvais works is given by Badin's publication. (See Bibliography.) A summary account is given in Müntz, *Short History*, pp. 280 ff.; Guiffrey, *Histoire Générale*, pp. 135 ff.; Hunter, *Tapestries*, pp. 185 ff.; Schmitz, op. cit., S. 308 ff.; Hunter, *Practical Book*, pp. 159 ff.; Göbel, op. cit., II. Teil, Bd. I, S. 216 f.; Migeon, op. cit., Chap. XII, pp. 402 ff.; Thomson, op. cit., pp. 455 ff.

For an account of the Louis XIV Beauvais set see Badin, op. cit., pp. 1 ff., ill. Pl. op. p. 4.

The Conquest of Louis the Great is published in Ackerman, *Catalogue of Retrospective Loan Exhibition*, p. 49 f., No. 52, ill. op. p. 51; Göbel, op. cit., II. Teil, Bd. I, S. 208 ff., ill. II. Teil, Abb. 215, 216.

Behagle wove a similar set in 1699 glorifying the battles of the Swedish king Charles XI (1655–1697) after cartoons by Johann Phillip Lemke (1631–1711). See Böttiger, op. cit., T. II, Pl. XXIX, XXX, XXXI, XXXII.

PAGE 268. An account of the Aubusson factory is given in Guiffrey, *Histoire Générale*, pp. 141 ff.; Hunter, *Tapestries*, pp. 198 ff.; Hunter, *Practical Book*, pp. 193 ff.; Göbel, op. cit., II. Teil, Bd. I, S. 244 ff., and Aubusson Chinoiseries are ill. Göbel, op. cit., II. Teil, Bd. II, Abb. 275–277.

CHAPTER XVI

PAGE 270. For tapestries showing Oudry's animal drawing see Göbel, op. cit., II. Teil, Bd. II, Abb. 224; Badin, op. cit., p. 28.

For the Hunts of Louis XV see Guiffrey, *Histoire Générale*, pp. 129 ff.; Müntz, *Short History*, pp. 310, 316, ill. p. 311, Fig. 80; Fenaille, op. cit., T. III, pp. 345 ff.; Göbel, op. cit., I. Teil, Bd. I, S. 210; II. Teil, Bd. I, 175 f., ill. Bd. II, Abb. 162.

For Oudry's career at the Beauvais see Badin, op. cit., pp. 20 ff.

For the Beauvais Oudry hunt see Badin, op. cit., p. 24.

PAGE 272. For the Molière set see P. W. French and Company, *The Comedies of Molière*, New York, 1916, and Göbel, op. cit., II, Teil,

[419]

Bd. I, S. 223 f.; ill. Bd. II, Abb. 226. The fourth piece, The Doctor Despite Himself, does not exist either in tapestry or as a cartoon.

PAGE 275. A striking brief estimation of Boucher's qualities is given in Bell, op. cit., p. 117 f.
The translation is the writer's own. The original is:

> Ne cessons de craindre une belle
> Son repos même a des appas
> L'Amour fait toujours sentinelle
> Et ce Dieu ne sommeille pas.

Verses of Lepicié which were applied to Boucher's Sleeping Genius in 1735. Quoted by Paul Mantz, *François Boucher* (*Lemoyne et Natoire*), Paris, 1880.

PAGE 276. For a general account of Boucher's cartoons see Müntz, *Short History*, pp. 326 ff.; Baldass, op. cit., Taf. 255–258; Göbel, op. cit., II. Teil, Bd. I, S. 184 ff. For another account of Boucher as tapestry designer see Rodón y Font, op. cit., pp. 77 ff.

For a brief but quite complete account of the Beauvais Boucher cartoons, see Maurice Vaucaire, " Les Tapisseries de Beauvais sur les cartons de Boucher," in *Les Arts,* Année I, No. 7, Paris, August, 1902, pp. 10 ff.

For Boucher's Italian Fêtes see Badin, op. cit., p. 31, p. 60, ill. pp. 36, 40.

For the Rising and Setting Sun see Fenaille, op. cit., T. IV, pp. 173 ff.

PAGE 277. For the Boucher Loves of the Gods see Fenaille, op. cit., T. IV, pp. 189 ff. The other painters collaborating with him were J. B. Marie, Carle van Loo (1705–1765), and Joseph Marie Vien (1716–1809) ; ill. Guiffrey, *Histoire Générale,* Pl. 47; Badin, pp. 56, 60, 64, 68, 104.

For the other Boucher cartoons see Fenaille, op. cit., T. IV, pp. 225 ff.

La Musique by Boucher is ill. Badin, op. cit., Pl. VIII.

For illustrations of Boucher's Beauvais Psyche set see Böttiger, op. cit., T. II, Pl. XXXIV, XXXV, XXXVI, XXXVII, T. III, Pl. LVII.

For the Boucher Chinese set see ill. Guiffrey, *Histoire Générale,*

Pl. 48; Badin, op. cit., p. 44, 48; Göbel, op. cit., II. Teil, Bd. II, Abb. 219–222; Badin, op. cit., p. 20.

The presents sent by the King of Siam to the French Court are listed in *Mémoire des presens du Roi de Siam au Roi de France*, quoted in H. Belevitch Stankevitch, *Le Goût Chinois en France au Temps de Louis XIV*, Paris, 1910, pp. 256 ff., from *Relation du Chevalier de Chaumont à la Cour du Roi de Siam*, 1686.

Information on this and other shops where Oriental things were sold is given in Belevitch Stankevitch, op. cit., pp. 146 ff.

For the Vernansal Chinese set see Göbel, op. cit., II. Teil, Bd. II, Abb. 219–222; Badin, op. cit., p. 20.

The Oriental style was promptly imitated in Flanders. Cf. e.g. Schmitz, op. cit., Abb. 132.

PAGE 278. For Berain's tapestries see Badin, op. cit., p. 11, ill. p. 16.

PAGE 279. The Indies series is fully discussed in Fenaille, op. cit., T. II, pp. 37 ff. The eight panels of the original set were (1) The Zebra; (2) The Two Bulls; (3) The Elephant; (4) The Indian Hunter; (5) The Animal Fight; (6) The King Carried by Two Black Men; (7) The Indian Horseman; (8) The Fishermen.

The Desportes Indies are discussed in Guiffrey, *Histoire Générale*, Pl. 37; Müntz, *Short History*, ill. p. 319, Fig. 82; Fenaille, op. cit., T. IV, pp. 40 ff.; Baldass, op. cit., Taf. 251–254.

PAGE 282. The Coypel Quixote set is discussed in Guiffrey, *Histoire Générale*, ill. Pl. 42–44; Müntz, *Short History*, p. 325, Fig. 86; Böttiger, op. cit., T. III, Pl. LXIV; Fenaille, op cit., T. III, pp. 157 ff.; Göbel, op. cit., II. Teil, Bd. II, Abb. 137–149, 542.

For the Natoire Quixote see Badin, op. cit., p. 32.

For the Brussels eighteenth-century Quixote see Baldass, op. cit., Taf. 282; Göbel, op. cit., I. Teil, Bd. II, Abb. 187, 290.

For the Beauvais Don Quixote see Göbel, op. cit., II. Teil, Bd. II, Abb. 229, 547.

A piece from the Aubusson Don Quixote is published in Ackerman, *Catalogue of Loan Exhibition*, San Francisco, p. 50 f., No. 62; Göbel, op. cit., II. Teil, Bd. II, Abb. 295.

The Spanish eighteenth-century Don Quixote is in Tormo Monzo y Sanchez Canton, op. cit., pp. 139 ff., ill. Pl. XLVI.

Antoine and Charles Coypel also collaborated on the Iliad (Fenaille, op. cit., T. III, pp. 293 ff.) ; and Charles Coypel did bits of

Operas (Fenaille, op. cit., T. III, p. 323), and scenes of Opera, Tragedy, and Comedy (Fenaille, op. cit., T. IV, pp. 139 ff.).
For the Old Testament by the Coypels, see Fenaille, op. cit., T. III, pp. 81 ff.
For an illustration of the Coypel Operas see Böttiger, op. cit., T. II, Pl. XLII.

PAGE 284. For "le Costume Turc" see Fenaille, op. cit., T. IV, pp. 327 ff.
For the History of Henri IV see Fenaille, op. cit., T. IV, pp. 354 ff.

CHAPTER XVII

PAGE 285. The most complete history of the Santa Barbara looms is given by D. G. Cruzada Villaamil, *Los Tapices de Coya,* Madrid, 1870. Good accounts are also given in Tormo Monzo y Sanchez Canton, op. cit., pp. XXIII ff.; Göbel, op. cit., II. Teil, Bd. I, S. 468 ff., ill. Bd. II, Abb. 485–525. Brief accounts are given by Hunter, *Practical Book,* p. 226 f.; Schmitz, op. cit., S. 326 ff., ill. Abb. 158; Thomson, op. cit., p. 485 f.

PAGE 289. Other painters designing cartoons during the reign of Charles IV were: Mariano Salvador Maella (1739–1819); Gines de Aguirre (b. 1731); Antonio Giuseppe Barbaza (b. 1722); Antonio Gonzalez Velasquez (1723–1782), who continued Giaquinto's tradition; and his son Zacarias (1763–1834), who between 1762 and 1780 designed twenty-three cartoons.

PAGE 290. Aguirre, to be sure, had depicted scenes from Spanish life, but he had given them always a strong French cast. They were native episodes in the manner of a good quality Aubusson Fête Champêtre, and any Frenchman of mediocre talent might have painted them, given the Spanish modelo. José del Cosbello's (1737–1793) cartoons which presume to show Spanish life, on the other hand, look like pleasant theatre curtains painted by an Italian.

PAGE 291. The complete list of Goya cartoons is given in August L. Meyer, *Francisco de Goya,* London and Toronto, 1924, pp. 39 ff., following Villaamil, op. cit., pp. 110 ff. The titles are corrected here according to the Spanish originals:

1. The Picnic, 1776
2. The Ball, 1776
3. The Scuffle by the New Inn, 1777
4. A Walk in Andalusia, 1777
5. The Toper, 1777
6. The Parasol, 1777
7. The Kite, 1778
8. The Card Players, 1778
9. Children Playing with a Bladder, 1778
10. Children Picking Fruit, 1778
11. The Blind Man Playing the Guitar, 1778
12. The Rag Market, 1779
13. The Earthenware Seller, 1779
14. The Officer and the Lady, 1779
15. The *Acerolera*, 1779
16. Children Playing Soldiers, 1779
17. Children with a Cart, 1779
18. The Game of Pelota, 1779
19. The Swing, 1779
20. The Washerwomen, 1779
21. The Young Bull, 1780
22. The Dog, 1780
23. The Spring, 1780
24. The Tobacco Revenue Officers, 1780
25. The Boy and the Tree, 1780
26. The Boy and the Bird, 1780
27. The Woodcutters, 1780
28. The Singer, 1780
29. The Meeting, 1780
30. The Doctor, 1780
31. The Artificial Flower Vendor, 1786
32. The Harvest, 1786
33. The Vintage, 1786
34. The Wounded Man, 1786
35. Beggars, 1787
36. The Snowstorm, 1787
37. The Wedding, 1787
38. Water Boys, 1787
39. The Game of Giants, 1787

40. The Seesaw, 1788
41. The Stilt Dancers, 1788
42. The Jumping Jack, 1788
43. Children in a Tree, 1788
44. Blind Man's Buff, 1788
45. The Boy on a Ram, 1788

For additional illustrations of Goya tapestries, see Tormo Monzo y Sanchez Canton, op. cit., Lám. LII, which gives an excellent color illustration of Blind Man's Buff; Migeon, op. cit., p. 301; and Hispanic Society of America, *Tapestries and Carpets from the Palace of the Prado,* New York; 1917.

CHAPTER XVIII

PAGE 294. The date chosen for the realization of the steam engine is that at which James Watt patented his final major improvements. Watt's first patent dates from 1769. Prior to that there were cruder applications of the basic principle, but their utility was limited primarily to simple pumping.

The date chosen for the perfection of the power loom is again the date of the last patent which made it really practical. This patent was taken out by William Radcliffe, but the improvement was based on the work of Dr. Edmund Cartwright, who took out his first patent in 1785 and made various improvements at intervals to 1792.

Machine woven tapestry is not true tapestry, but is a version of compound cloth, usually double warp and irregular. For a diagram of a typical weaving scheme see Alan Summerly Cole, "Weaving," in *Encyclopaedia Britannica,* Eleventh Edition, New York, 1911, Vol. XXVIII, p. 442, Fig. 17.

PAGE 298. The history of the Morris's undertaking is given fully in H. C. Marillier, *History of the Merton Abbey Tapestry Works,* London, 1927. It is briefly discussed in Hunter, *Tapestry,* pp. 127 ff.; Thomson, op. cit., pp. 498 ff.

Merton Abbey tapestries are illustrated in Hunton, op. cit., Pls. 46–52; and Morris's Orchard is published in Kendrick, op. cit., p. 21, No. 8.

APPENDIX I

PAGE 303. Primitive peoples do not, however, necessarily use simple weaving techniques. The weaving of some of the California Indian baskets is quite complex, and the various Indian tribes that practised wool or cotton weaving employed a number of different techniques. Thus the Huichol, who were noteworthy weavers, made largely compound or double cloth. There are, moreover, many complicated and unexpected variations in North American Indian weaving. For a summary discussion of North American Indian textiles see H. Th. Bossert, *Geschichte des Kunstgewerbes aller Zeiten und Völker*, Bd. II, Berlin, Vienna, Zurich, 1929, pp. 210 ff., 236, 242. Bibliographies also are given.

The word " tapestry " and its derivatives, in the various languages, has been loosely used throughout the Christian centuries, to indicate many kinds of textiles. Hence the evidence of early documents must be used with great circumspection. Thomson, op. cit., Chapter III, pp. 37 ff., gives an example of erroneous implications and conclusions arrived at by insufficient caution in this respect.

For a detailed discussion of the technique see Göbel, op. cit., I. Teil, Bd. I, S. 1 ff. There is also some treatment of the question in all the standard publications: Müntz, *Short History*, Chap. XVI, pp. 356 ff.; Hunter, *Tapestries*, pp. 245 ff.; Schmitz, op. cit., S. 19 ff.; Kurth, op. cit., Bd. I, S. 3 ff.; Thomson, op. cit., p. 2 ff.

PAGE 305. For a description of early looms see H. Ling-Roth, " Ancient Egyptian and Greek Looms," *Bankfield Museum Notes*, Second Series, No. 2, London, 1913.

PAGE 307. Cf. Vasari's praise of the Raphael Act of the Apostle Tapestries made for Pope Leo X in note for page 156.

PAGE 311. There is one very limited effect, rarely used, i.e., a fancy cloth, with a design in warp or weft floats, which can be made of one warp and one weft of different colors, for example, blue and yellow, so that where the warp and weft are equally exposed in the plain cloth ground the area appears to be green, but where the yellow warp, for instance, is floated across to make the spot design, it would be in a contrast of pure yellow. This technique is feasible, however, only for small powdered designs.

APPENDIX II

PAGE 313. For the Paris regulations of 1302 see Guiffrey, *Mémoires*, p. 111 f.; Müntz, *Short History*, p. 92. For further information see Deville, *Recueil de Statuts et de Documents Relatifs à la Corporation des Tapissiers de 1258 à 1875*, Paris, 1875.

For the term *à la marche* in the regulations for the *sarrazinois* workers see Guiffrey, op. cit., p. 113 f.

Guiffrey, op. cit., p. 106, concludes that " Les tapissiers sarrazinois . . . . s'occupaient . . . . de la fabrication de ces tapis veloutés à laine qui ont pris, au XVIIe siècle, le nom de tapis de la Savonnerie, façon du Levant." But on the other hand Müntz states that: " The ' *tapissiers sarrazinois*', . . . made the shaggy and thick carpets similar to modern ' moquettes,' " and gives the following regulations: " they were only allowed to use woolen threads for their carpets and flax and hemp for the canvas borders; the use of tow was rigorously forbidden them; the dyeing of the wool, which required special care, could be done by the workers themselves." Müntz, *Short History*, p. 92, quoting Lespinasse et Bonnardot, "Le Livre des Métiers d'Étienne Boileau," 1277, Paris, 1879, p. LXVII.

Göbel, op. cit., I. Teil, Bd. I, S. 221 ff., after a somewhat detailed discussion of the term concludes that it simply means low warp tapestry.

The terms for the " *tapissiers nostrez*" were infinitely less strict: the apprenticeship was for four years instead of eight, and if they were allowed only two apprentices at a time, the number of their companions (vallés) was unlimited. In short, everything tends to prove that this corporation manufactured only ordinary stuffs that had nothing to do with the art of tapestry. Müntz, *Short History*, p. 92.

PAGE 313. For the Tournay regulations see Soil, op. cit., pp. 12 ff., 32 ff.; de la Vigne, op. cit., p. 63.

For the Ghent regulations see de la Vigne, op. cit., pp. 51 ff.

PAGE 314. For the Brussels statutes see Wauters, op. cit., T. XV, pp. 377 ff., 381 ff.; Marez, op. cit., pp. 285, 292; de la Vigne, op. cit., p. 58.

PAGE 315. For the Brussels weavers' and painters' dispute see Wauters, op. cit., T. XV, p. 391 f.

PAGE 316. Müntz, *Short History*, Appendix, pp. 367 ff., gives a good summary of monograms and marks, and even more complete illustrations are given in Göbel, op. cit., I. Teil, Bd. I, Taf. 1–24. The eighteenth-century statute specifying a tapestry weaver's qualifications is given in Müntz, *Short History*, pp. 322 ff., citing W. Chocqueel, *Essai sur l'Histoire et la Situation Actuelle de l'Industrie de Tapisserie et Tapis*, Paris, 1863, p. 46 f.

APPENDIX III

PAGE 318. For the crown and other jewels of Charles V see Jules Labarte, *Inventaire du Mobilier de Charles V*, Paris, 1879, pp. 12 ff. For the other treasures of Charles V see Labarte, op. cit., passim.

PAGE 319. For the silk hangings see Labarte, op. cit., pp. 362 ff., and for the English hangings, p. 377. For the tapestries of Charles V see Labarte, op. cit., p. 378 f.

PAGE 320. For the tapestries of Charles VI see Jules Guiffrey, *Inventaire des Tapisseries de Charles VI*, Paris, 1887, passim.

PAGE 321. For the tapestries of Louis I, Duc d'Anjou see Göbel, op. cit., I. Teil, Bd. I, S. 62, 70 quoted from G. Ledos, "Fragment de l'Inventaire des Joyaux de Louis Ier Duc d'Anjou," in *Bibliothèque de l'École des Chartes*, 1889, L.

PAGE 323. For the tapestries of Jean, Duc de Berri see J. Guiffrey, (Paris, Comité des Travaux Historiques), *Inventaires de Jean, Duc de Berri (1401–1416)*, Paris, 1894–96.

PAGE 325. The Jourdain de Blaies tapestry is illustrated in Kurth, *Gotische Bildteppiche*, Abb. 13; Migeon, op. cit., p. 213.

For the tapestry acquisitions of Philip the Bold see Bernard Prost, *Inventaires Mobiliers et Extraits des Comptes des Ducs de Bourgogne de la Maison de Valois (1363–1477)*, Paris, 1902–1904. For the inventories of Philip the Bold and Marguerite of Flanders made after their death see Pinchart, *Histoire Générale*, p. 15 f.

PAGE 326. For the books in the library of Philip and Marguerite that correspond in subject with tapestries see Georges Doutrepont, *La Littérature Française à la Cour des Ducs de Bourgogne*, Paris, 1909, pp. 9, 10, 133 f.

PAGE 331. The Musée des Arts Décoratifs romances are ill. DeMotte, op. cit., Pl. 146–151 inclusive; Migeon, op. cit., p. 215; Planès, op. cit., Pl. 25.

PAGE 332. For the tapestries acquired by Jean sans Peur see Pinchart, *Histoire Générale*, p. 19.

PAGE 333. For the inventory of Philip the Good see Léon de Laborde, *Les Ducs de Bourgogne*, T. II, Paris, 1851, pp. 268 ff.

PAGE 334. For the *Deux Pans de la Tapisserie Chrétienne* see Doutrepont, op. cit., p. 252 f.

PAGE 335. For the Hercules set at the Vow of the Pheasant see Doutrepont, op. cit., p. 107; Pinchart, op. cit., p. 29, has mistakenly assigned this series on the same evidence to Charles the Bold.

PAGE 336. For the relative place of Gideon and Jason in the Order of the Golden Fleece see Doutrepont, op. cit., pp. 147 ff., and for a discussion of the set see Göbel, op. cit., I. Teil, Bd. I, S. 66.

For the Palazzo Doria Alexander see p. 89.

For the Knight of the Swan see notes to p. 214.

PAGE 337. For the Debate in the Court Venus see Doutrepont, op. cit., p. 254 f.

For the tapestries of Charles the Bold see Pinchart, *Histoire Générale*, p. 29, and Göbel, op. cit., I. Teil, Bd. I, S. 68, 478, 508.

PAGE 339. For the tapestries of the Emperor Maximilian and his wife, Marie of Burgundy, see Pinchart, *Histoire Générale*, p. 61; Göbel, op. cit., I. Teil, Bd. I, S. 302, 309; Soil, op. cit., p. 41.

For the tapestries of Philip the Fair see Soil, op. cit., pp. 35 f.,
246 f., 248, 249 f.; Göbel, op. cit., I. Teil, Bd. I, S. 302, 303, 468;
Valencia, op. cit., Vol. I, pp. 1, 3, 5, 7.

PAGE 340. For the tapestries of Marguerite of Austria see Comte de
Laborde, *Inventaire des Tableaux, Livres, Joyaux et Meubles de
Marguerite d'Autriche,* Paris, 1850; Soil, op. cit., p. 258; Göbel, op.
cit., I. Teil, Bd. I, S. 308; Valencia, op. cit., Vol. I, pp. 13, 17, 21 f.

PAGE 341. For the tapestries of Marie of Hungary see Pinchart, *Histoire Générale,* p. 88; Göbel, op. cit., I. Teil, Bd. I, S. 144 f., 311, 420.
For the tapestries of Charles V see Göbel, op. cit., I. Teil, Bd. I,
S. 307, 308, 326; Valencia, op. cit., Vol. I, pp. 4, 17, 23 f.

PAGE 342. For the tapestries of Philip II see Valencia, op. cit., Vol. I,
pp. 15, 17.

The two other notable state collections are those belonging to
Austria, published by Baldass, op. cit., and to Sweden, published by
Böttiger, op. cit. The Italian Government has a good collection of
Italian tapestries, most of them exhibited in the Uffizzi and the
Pitti Palace, but no adequate publication of them has ever been
made.

There are notable church collections in Spain, at Saragossa, and at
Zamorra, and in France, especially at Angers and Le Mans. The best
museum collections are to be seen in Paris, in the Musée Cluny, the
Musée des Arts Décoratifs, and the Louvre. The Victoria and Albert
Museum and the Metropolitan Museum of Art both have good
collections.

BIBLIOGRAPHY

The bibliography does not presume to be complete but represents only a selection of the most useful publications. Additional publications on specific problems are referred to in the notes. The bibliography is arranged alphabetically for convenience of reference, but the notes are in each instance arranged chronologically.

Ackerman, Phyllis,
  Catalogue of the Retrospective Loan Exhibition of European Tapestries: San Francisco, 1922
Badin, Jules,
  La Manufacture de Tapisseries de Beauvais, Depuis Ses Origines Jusqu'à Nos Jours, Paris, 1909
Baldass, Ludwig,
  Die Wiener Gobelinssammlung, Vienna, 1920
Böttiger, John Frederik,
  Svenska Statens Samling af Väfda tapeter, Stockholm, 1895; and Volume IV, *La Collection des Tapisseries de l'État Suédois; Résumé de l'Édition Suédoise,* Stockholm, 1898
DeMotte, G. J.,
  La Tapisserie Gothique, Paris, 1921–24
Destrée, Joseph,
  Tapisseries et Sculptures Bruxelloises, Brussels, 1906
Drival, E. van,
  Les Tapisseries d'Arras, Arras, 1864
Fenaille, Maurice,
  État Général des Tapisseries de la Manufacture des Gobelins Depuis Son Origine Jusqu'à Nos Jours, 1600–1900
  Volume I, Paris, 1923; Volume II, 1903; Volume III, 1904; Volume IV, 1907
Göbel, Heinrich,
  Wandteppiche: I *Die Niederlande,* Leipzig, 1923
              II *Die Romanischen Länder,* Leipzig, 1928

Guiffrey, Jules; Müntz, Eugène; et Pinchart, Alexandre,
Histoire Générale de la Tapisserie, Paris, 1878–85
Volume I Guiffrey, Jules, *Histoire de la Tapisserie en France,* Paris, 1878–85
Volume II Müntz, Eugène, *Histoire de la Tapisserie en Italie, en Allemagne, en Angleterre, en Espagne, en Danemark, en Hongrie, en Pologne, en Russie, et en Turquie,* Paris, 1878–84
Volume III Pinchart, Alexandre, *Histoire de la Tapisserie dans les Flandres,* Paris, 1879
Guiffrey, Jules,
"Les Origines de la Tapisserie de Haute et Basse-Lice à Paris," in *Mémoires de la Société de l'Histoire de Paris et de l'Île-de-France,* Volume VIII, Paris, 1882, pp. 107 ff.
"Les Tapisseries du XIIe à la Fin du XVIe Siècle," in E. Molinier, *Histoire Générale des Arts Appliqués à l'Industrie,* Volume VI, Paris, 1911
Hunter, George Leland,
Tapestries, Their Origin, History and Renaissance, New York, 1912
The Practical Book of Tapestries, Philadelphia, and London, 1925
Jubinal, Achille,
Les Anciennes Tapisseries Historiées, Paris, 1838
Kendrick, Albert Frank,
Catalogue of Tapestries (Victoria and Albert Museum, Department of Textiles) , London, 1924
Kurth, Betty,
Gotische Bildteppiche aus Frankreich und Flandern, Munich, 1923
Migeon, Gaston,
Les Arts du Tissu (Manuels d'Histoire de l'Art) , 2nd edition, Paris, 1929. Troisième Partie, pp. 180–411
Müntz, Eugène,
A Short History of Tapestry From the Earliest Time to the End of the 18th Century, London, 1885
Planès, E.,
La Tapisserie Gothique, Paris, s.d. (1929)
Rubinstein-Bloch, Stella,
Catalogue of the Collection of George and Florence Blumenthal, New York, Volume IV, *Tapestries and Furniture,* Paris, 1927

BIBLIOGRAPHY

Schmitz, Hermann,
Bildteppiche, Berlin, 1919
Thomson, Walter G.,
*A History of Tapestry from the Earliest Times until the Present
Day,* 2nd edition, London, 1930
Tormo y Monzó, Elias, and Cantón, J. Sanchez,
Los Tapices de la Casa del Rey N. S., Madrid, 1919
Valencia de Don Juan, Conde Viudo de,
Tapices de la Corona de España, Madrid, 1903
Wauters, Alphonse,
" Essai Historique sur les Tapisseries et les Tapissiers de Haute
et de Basse-Lice de Bruxelles " in *Bulletin des Commissions
Royales d'Art et d'Archéologie,* XVième année, Brussels, 1876,
pp. 349 ff.; XVIième année, 1877, pp. 194 ff.; XVIIième année,
1878, pp. 149 ff.

INDEX

Aaron's rod, 57
Abel, 48
Abelard, 64
Abraham, 30, 128, 129, 189, 342, 379
Absalom, 339
Abstinence, 128
Achab, 199
Achilles, 123, 189, 264
Achmin, 21, 22
Acts of the Apostles, 112, 156, 157, 158, 165, 405
Adam and Eve, 48, 58, 338
Adolphe, Comte de Clèves et de la Marche, 332
Adonis, 144, 147
Adoration of the Magi, 44, 54, 115, 155, 301, 338, 339, 342, 379
Adrastus, 123
Adrian, 125
Aelst, Peter van, 111, 157, 164 f., 365, 384
Aeneas, 123, 211
Aesop, 47
Africa, African, 139, 140
Age, 337
Agincourt, 330
Agnes, Abbess of Quedlinburg, 29, 30, 32
Agnes of Blois, 43
Agnus Dei, 318
Aguirre, Gines de, 422
Alba, Duke of, 165, 342, 378, 381
Alberino, Cardinal, 285, 288
Alcisthenes of Sybaris, 402
Alençon, Duc d', 178
Alexander, 10, 88, 89, 90, 100, 108, 123, 124, 210, 219, 336, 337, 341, 342
Alexandria, Alexandrian, 10, 11, 13, 14, 15, 17, 18, 20, 21, 189, 204
Allemagna, Rigo da, 398
Allori, Alessandro, 209
Alsace, 56
Altenburg Museum, 216
Ambition, 124
Amedée VI, 66
Amenothes II, 12

America, American, 135, 221, 236, 259, 279
American Museum of Natural History, 238, 247, 409, 411, 412, 415
Amigoni, Jacopo, 289
Amis and Amile, 319, 320, 326
Amsterdam, 219, 223
Ancon, 241
Andrea, Piero d', 199
Andromeda, 117, 121
Anet, Château d', 146
Angers, 66, 67, 72, 102, 106, 322, 330
Angoulême, Charles d', 174
Angoulême, Jean d', 174
Anguish, 324
Anne, 129, 155, 335
Anne de Beaujeu, 67, 122
Annunciation, 56, 87, 92, 93, 153, 201, 202, 322, 331, 340
Anthoine, Bastard of Burgundy, 116
Anthony, 124
Antoine de Brabant, 333
Antoninus Pius, 129
Antwerp, 96, 115, 153, 154, 159, 164, 196, 218, 341
Aonis, 126
Apocalypse, Apocalyptic, 63, 64, 66, 69, 71, 74, 75, 102, 106, 107, 173, 178, 322, 324, 328, 330, 342
Apollinarus, Sidonius, 26
Apollo, 20, 170
Apostles, 31, 68, 74, 202, 205, 319, 333. See also Acts of the Apostles
Appius Claudius, 122
Apprentices, Apprenticeship, 102, 113, 134, 135, 313
April, 40, 41, 143, 150
Aquitaine, Duke of, 319
Arachne, 9
Architecture, 164
Ardsteene, Jean, 340
Argentine, 240, 250
Arion, 121, 123
Aristotle, 123
Armada, 219